Akame Ga KILL! ZERO VIII

TAKAHIRO × KEI TORU

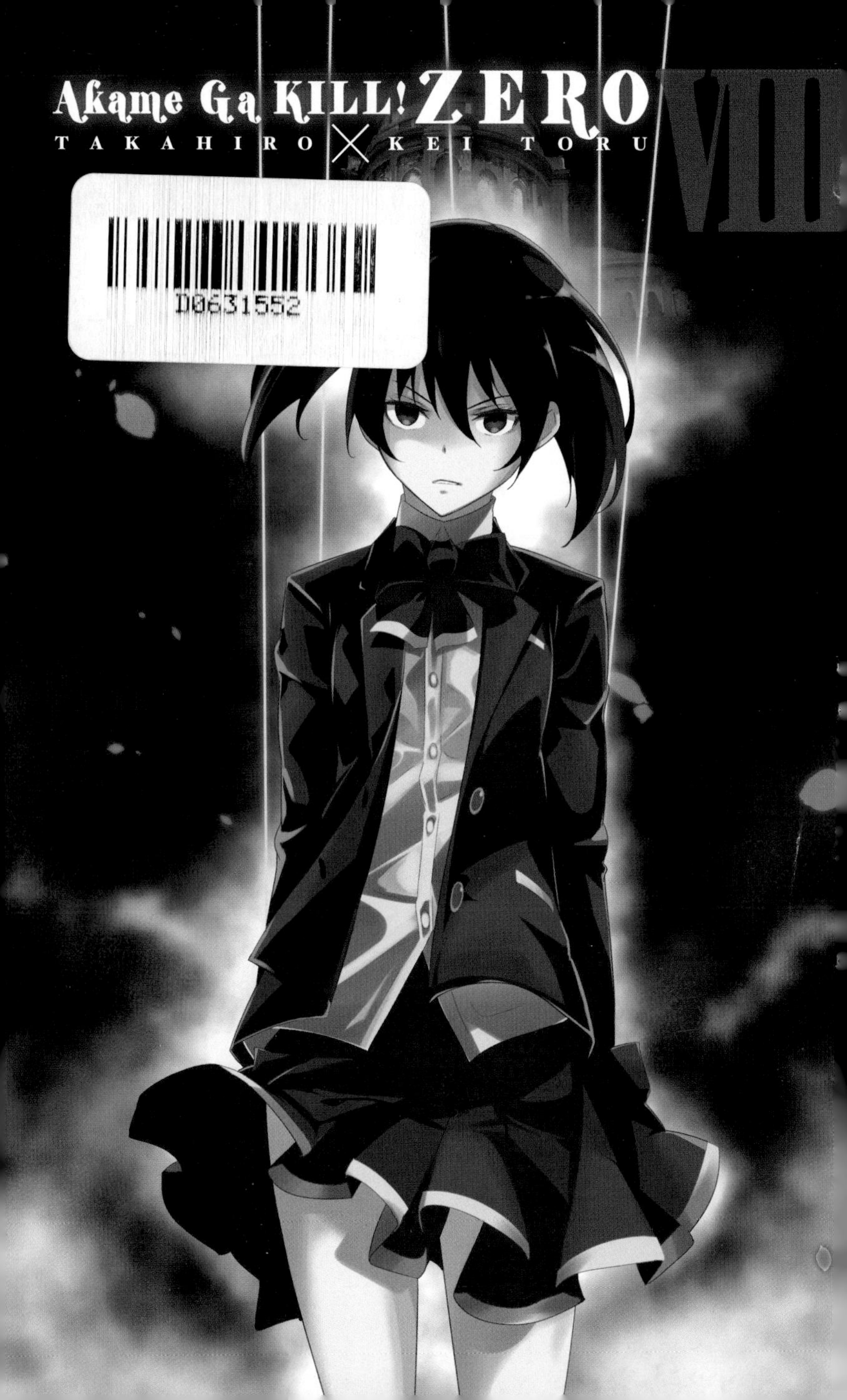

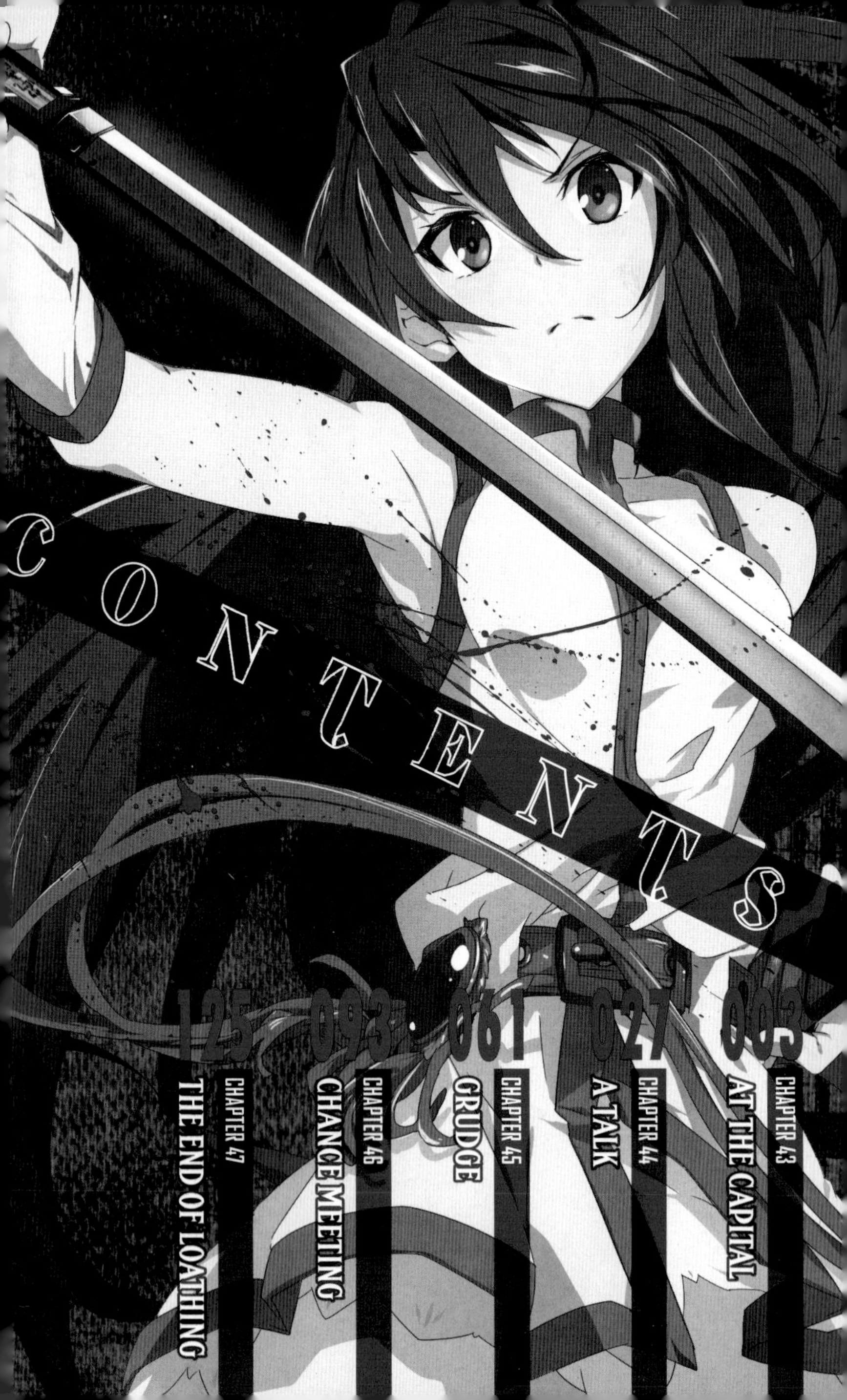

CONTENTS

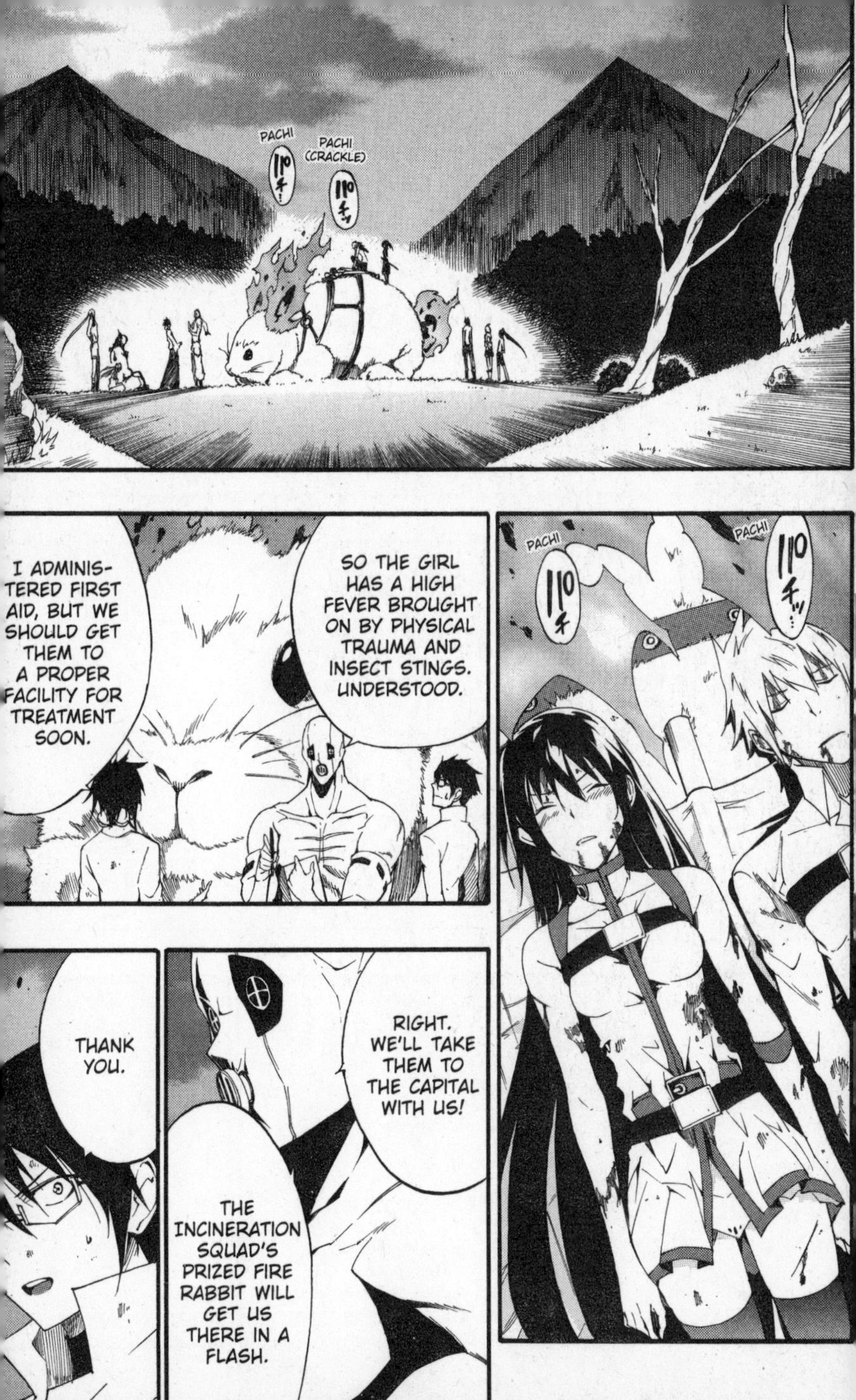
PACHI (CRACKLE)
PACHI
PACHI
PACHI
SO THE GIRL HAS A HIGH FEVER BROUGHT ON BY PHYSICAL TRAUMA AND INSECT STINGS. UNDERSTOOD.
I ADMINIS-TERED FIRST AID, BUT WE SHOULD GET THEM TO A PROPER FACILITY FOR TREATMENT SOON.
RIGHT. WE'LL TAKE THEM TO THE CAPITAL WITH US!
THE INCINERATION SQUAD'S PRIZED FIRE RABBIT WILL GET US THERE IN A FLASH.
THANK YOU.

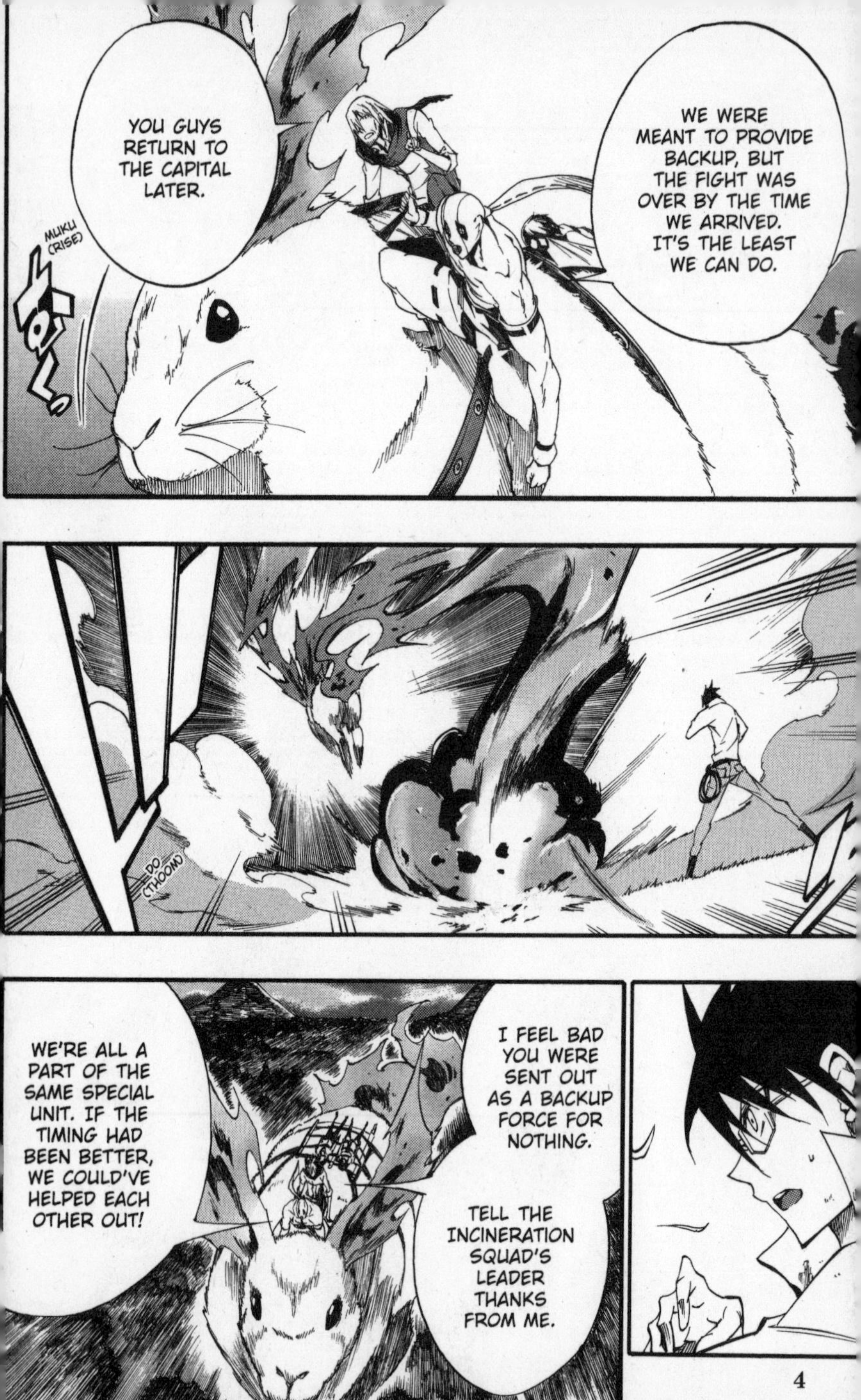
WE WERE MEANT TO PROVIDE BACKUP, BUT THE FIGHT WAS OVER BY THE TIME WE ARRIVED. IT'S THE LEAST WE CAN DO.
YOU GUYS RETURN TO THE CAPITAL LATER.
MUKU (RISE)
DO (THOOM)
I FEEL BAD YOU WERE SENT OUT AS A BACKUP FORCE FOR NOTHING.
TELL THE INCINERATION SQUAD'S LEADER THANKS FROM ME.
WE'RE ALL A PART OF THE SAME SPECIAL UNIT. IF THE TIMING HAD BEEN BETTER, WE COULD'VE HELPED EACH OTHER OUT!

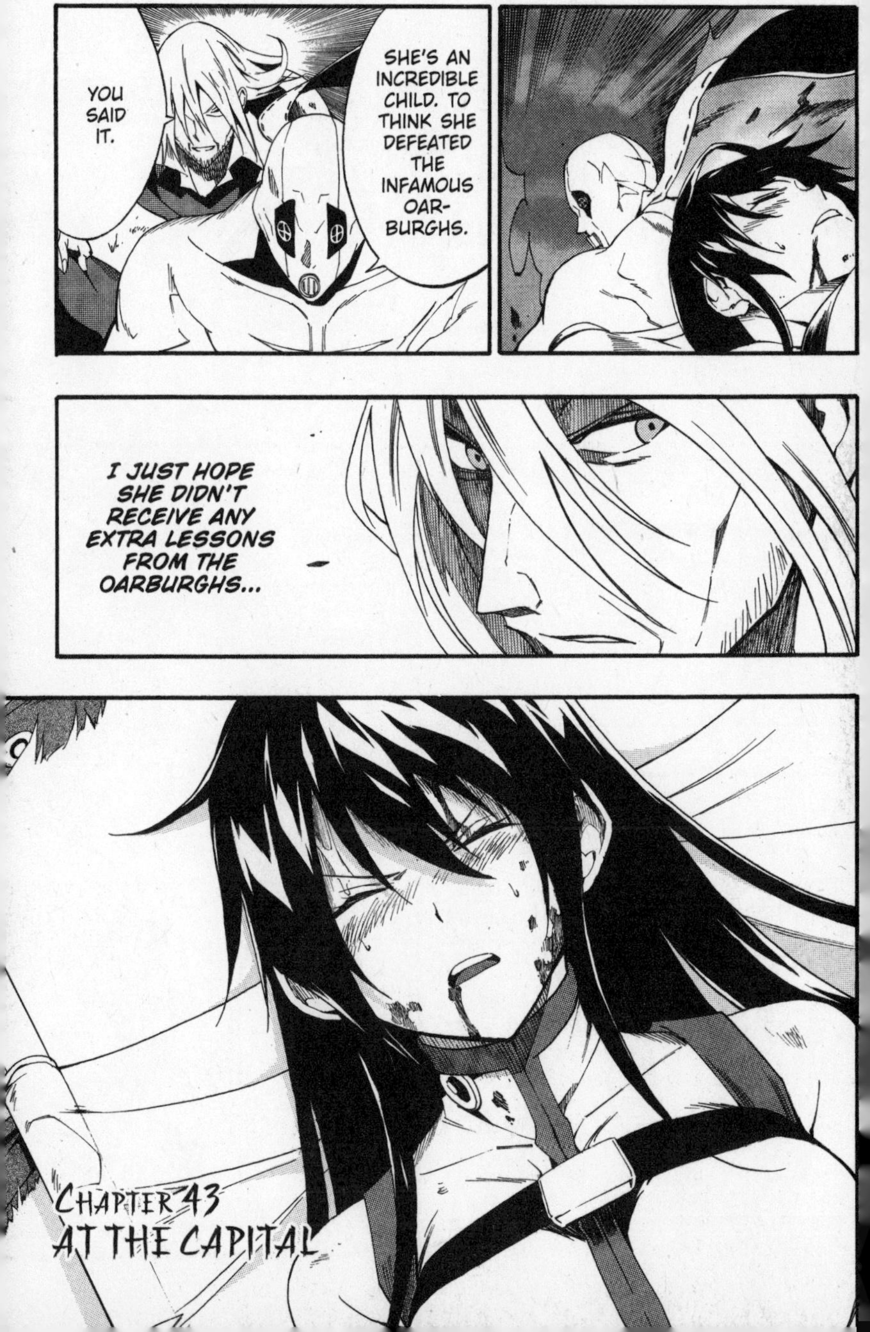
SHE'S AN INCREDIBLE CHILD. TO THINK SHE DEFEATED THE INFAMOUS OAR-BURGHS.
YOU SAID IT.
I JUST HOPE SHE DIDN'T RECEIVE ANY EXTRA LESSONS FROM THE OARBURGHS...
CHAPTER 43
AT THE CAPITAL

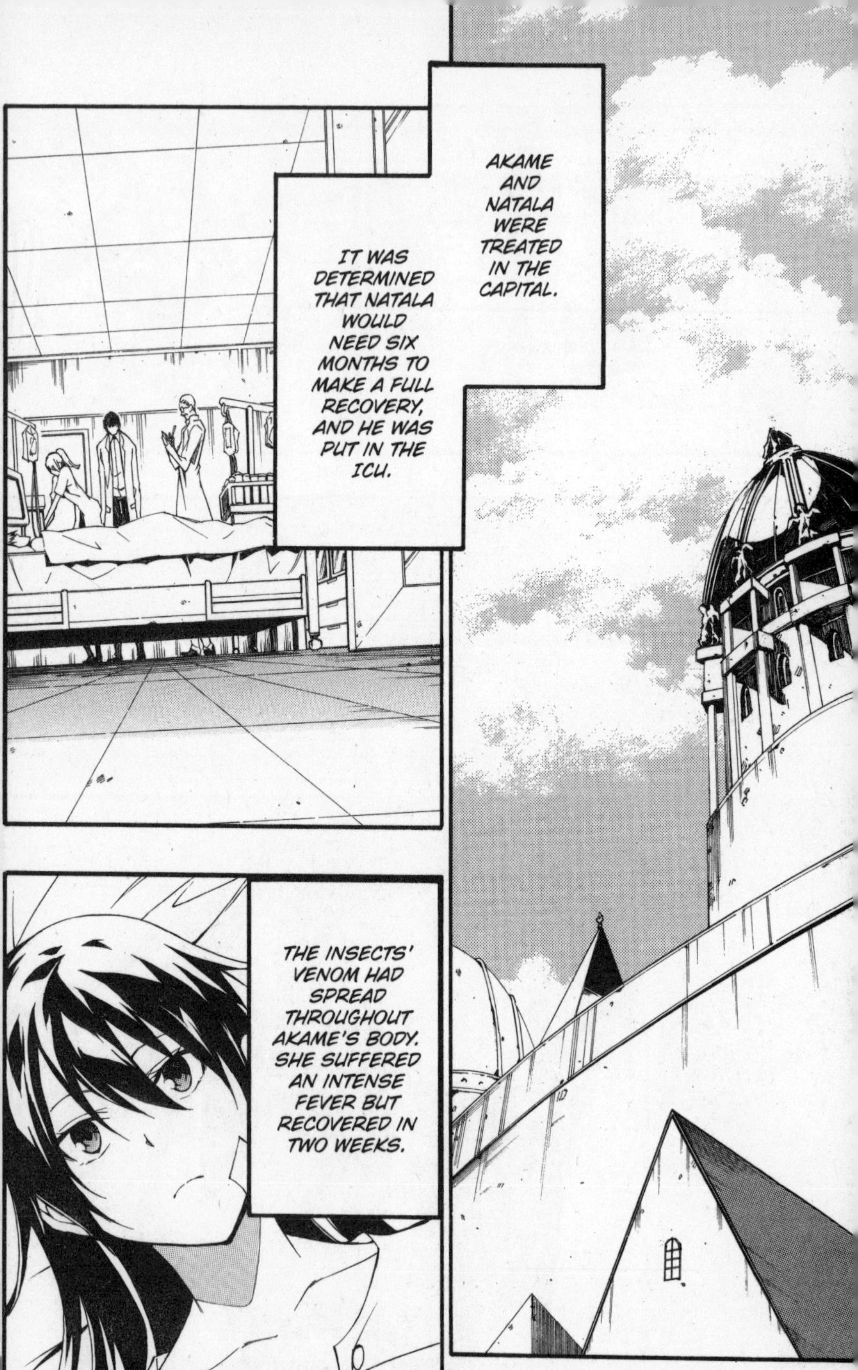
AKAME AND NATALA WERE TREATED IN THE CAPITAL.
IT WAS DETERMINED THAT NATALA WOULD NEED SIX MONTHS TO MAKE A FULL RECOVERY, AND HE WAS PUT IN THE ICU.
THE INSECTS' VENOM HAD SPREAD THROUGHOUT AKAME'S BODY. SHE SUFFERED AN INTENSE FEVER BUT RECOVERED IN TWO WEEKS.

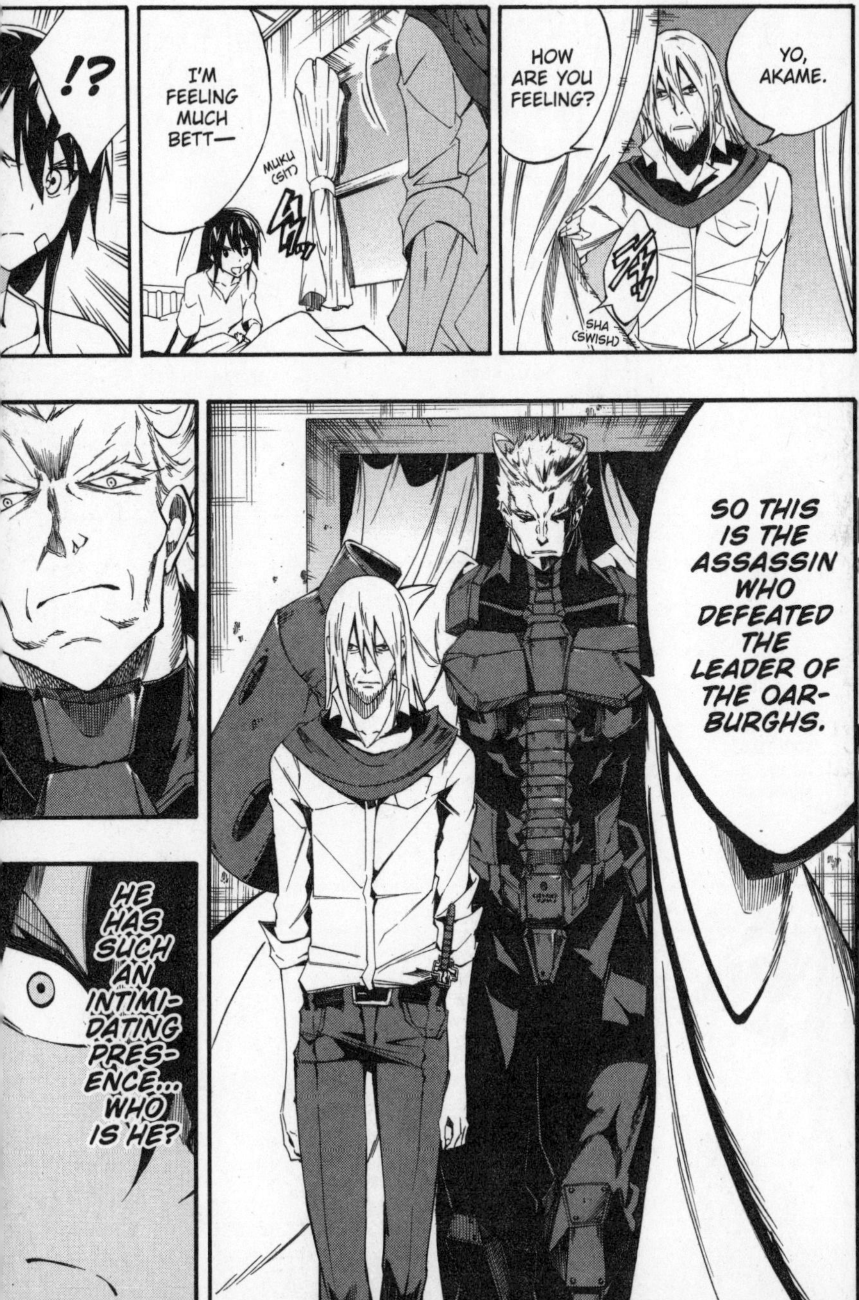
YO, AKAME.
HOW ARE YOU FEELING?
SHA (SWISH)
I'M FEELING MUCH BETT—
MUKU (SIT)
!?
SO THIS IS THE ASSASSIN WHO DEFEATED THE LEADER OF THE OAR-BURGHS.
HE HAS SUCH AN INTIMI-DATING PRES-ENCE... WHO IS HE?

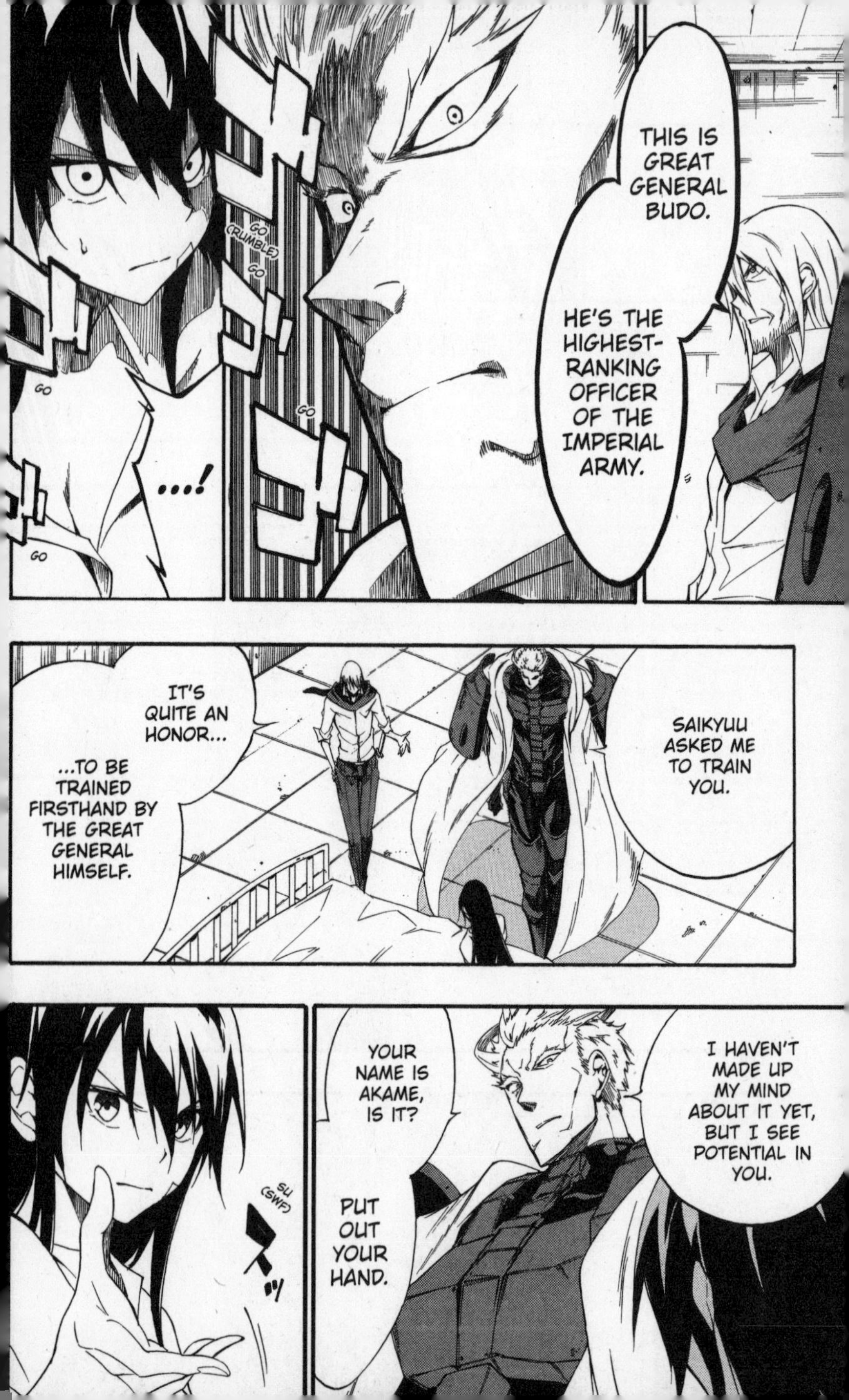
THIS IS GREAT GENERAL BUDO.
HE'S THE HIGHEST-RANKING OFFICER OF THE IMPERIAL ARMY.
GO (RUMBLE) GO
GO
...!
GO
GO
SAIKYUU ASKED ME TO TRAIN YOU.
IT'S QUITE AN HONOR...
...TO BE TRAINED FIRSTHAND BY THE GREAT GENERAL HIMSELF.
I HAVEN'T MADE UP MY MIND ABOUT IT YET, BUT I SEE POTENTIAL IN YOU.
YOUR NAME IS AKAME, IS IT?
PUT OUT YOUR HAND.
SU (SWF)

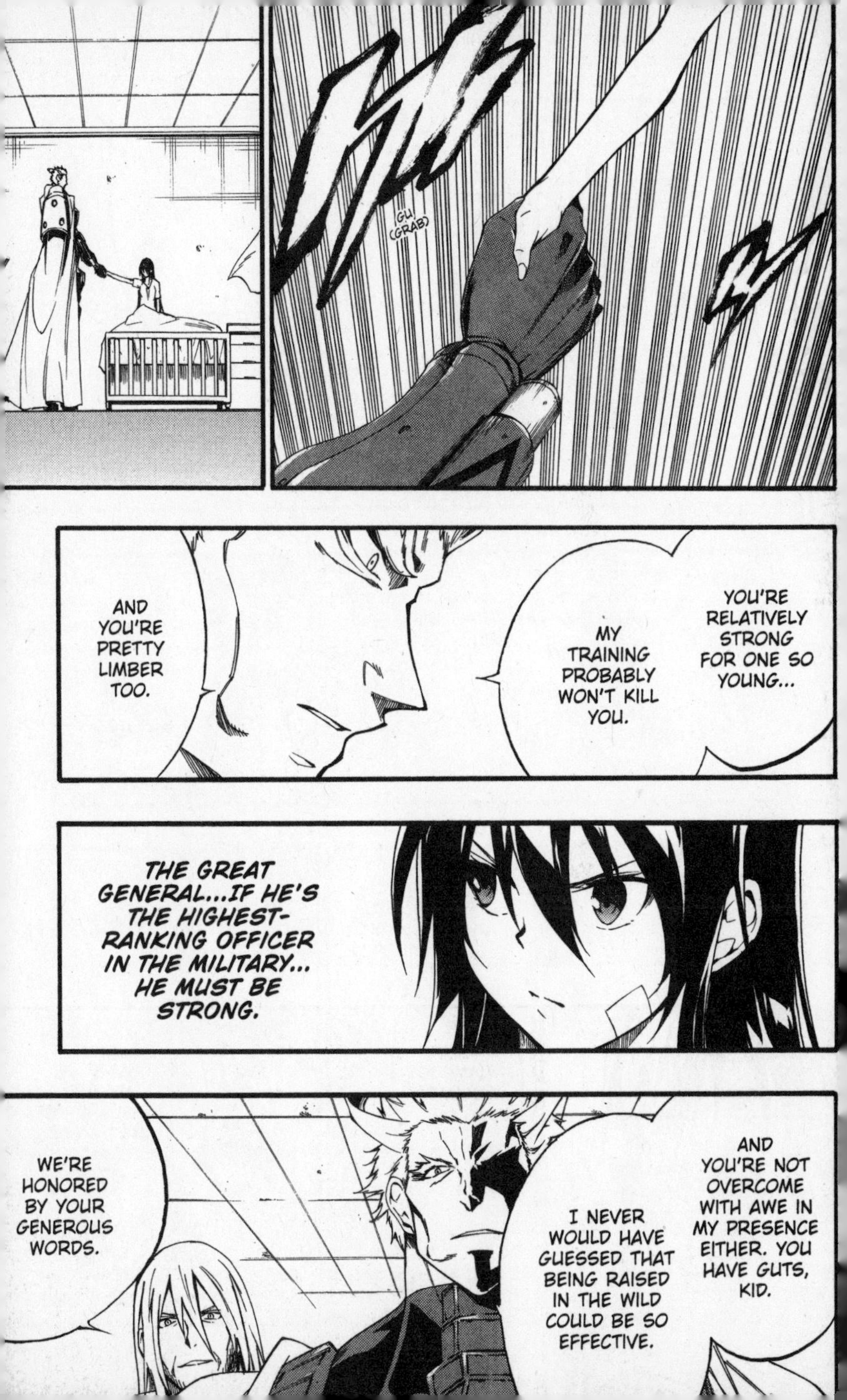
GU (GRAB)
YOU'RE RELATIVELY STRONG FOR ONE SO YOUNG...
MY TRAINING PROBABLY WON'T KILL YOU.
AND YOU'RE PRETTY LIMBER TOO.
THE GREAT GENERAL...IF HE'S THE HIGHEST-RANKING OFFICER IN THE MILITARY... HE MUST BE STRONG.
AND YOU'RE NOT OVERCOME WITH AWE IN MY PRESENCE EITHER. YOU HAVE GUTS, KID.
I NEVER WOULD HAVE GUESSED THAT BEING RAISED IN THE WILD COULD BE SO EFFECTIVE.
WE'RE HONORED BY YOUR GENEROUS WORDS.

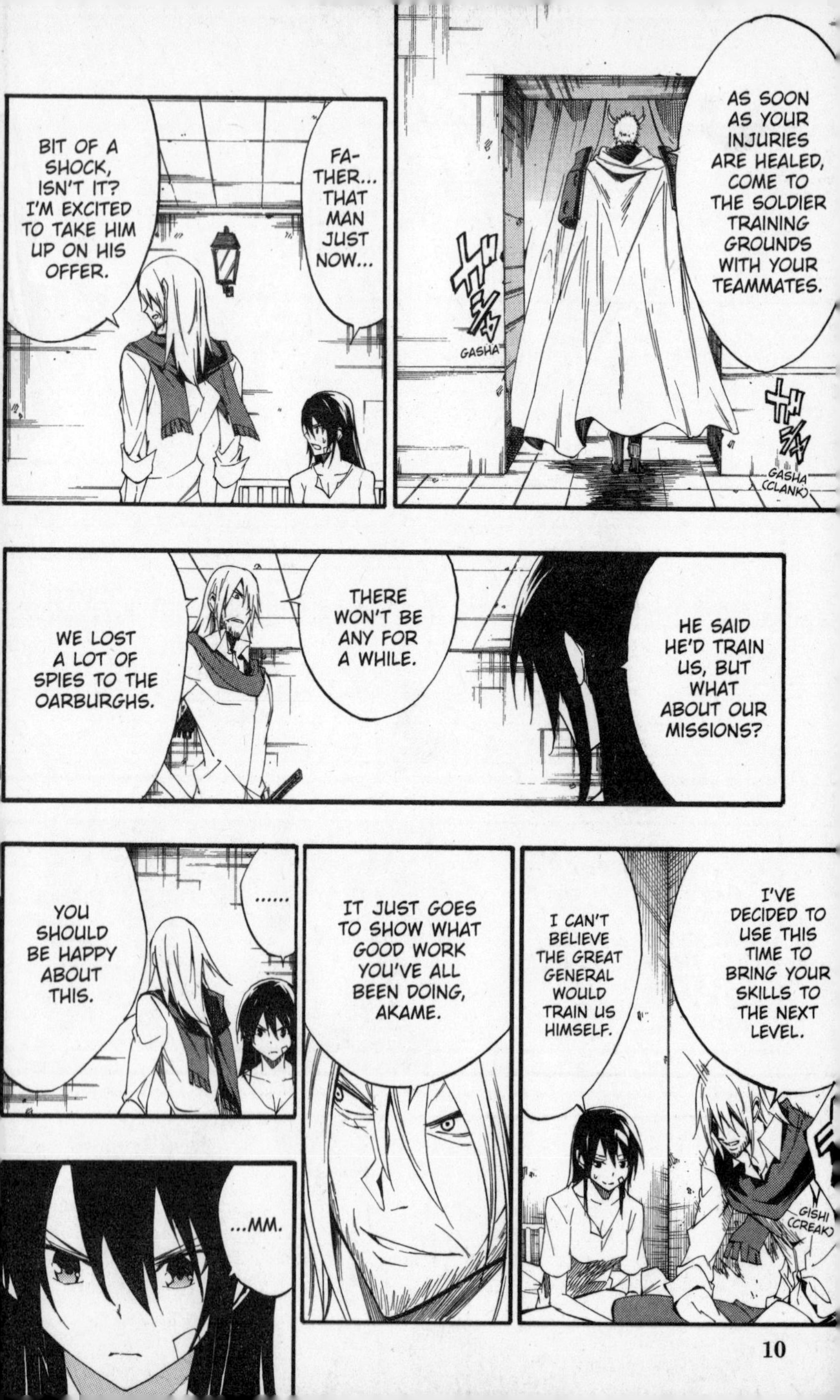
AS SOON AS YOUR INJURIES ARE HEALED, COME TO THE SOLDIER TRAINING GROUNDS WITH YOUR TEAMMATES.
GASHA (CLANK)
GASHA
FA-THER... THAT MAN JUST NOW...
BIT OF A SHOCK, ISN'T IT? I'M EXCITED TO TAKE HIM UP ON HIS OFFER.
HE SAID HE'D TRAIN US, BUT WHAT ABOUT OUR MISSIONS?
THERE WON'T BE ANY FOR A WHILE.
WE LOST A LOT OF SPIES TO THE OARBURGHS.
I'VE DECIDED TO USE THIS TIME TO BRING YOUR SKILLS TO THE NEXT LEVEL.
I CAN'T BELIEVE THE GREAT GENERAL WOULD TRAIN US HIMSELF.
GISHI (CREAK)
IT JUST GOES TO SHOW WHAT GOOD WORK YOU'VE ALL BEEN DOING, AKAME.
......
YOU SHOULD BE HAPPY ABOUT THIS.
...MM.

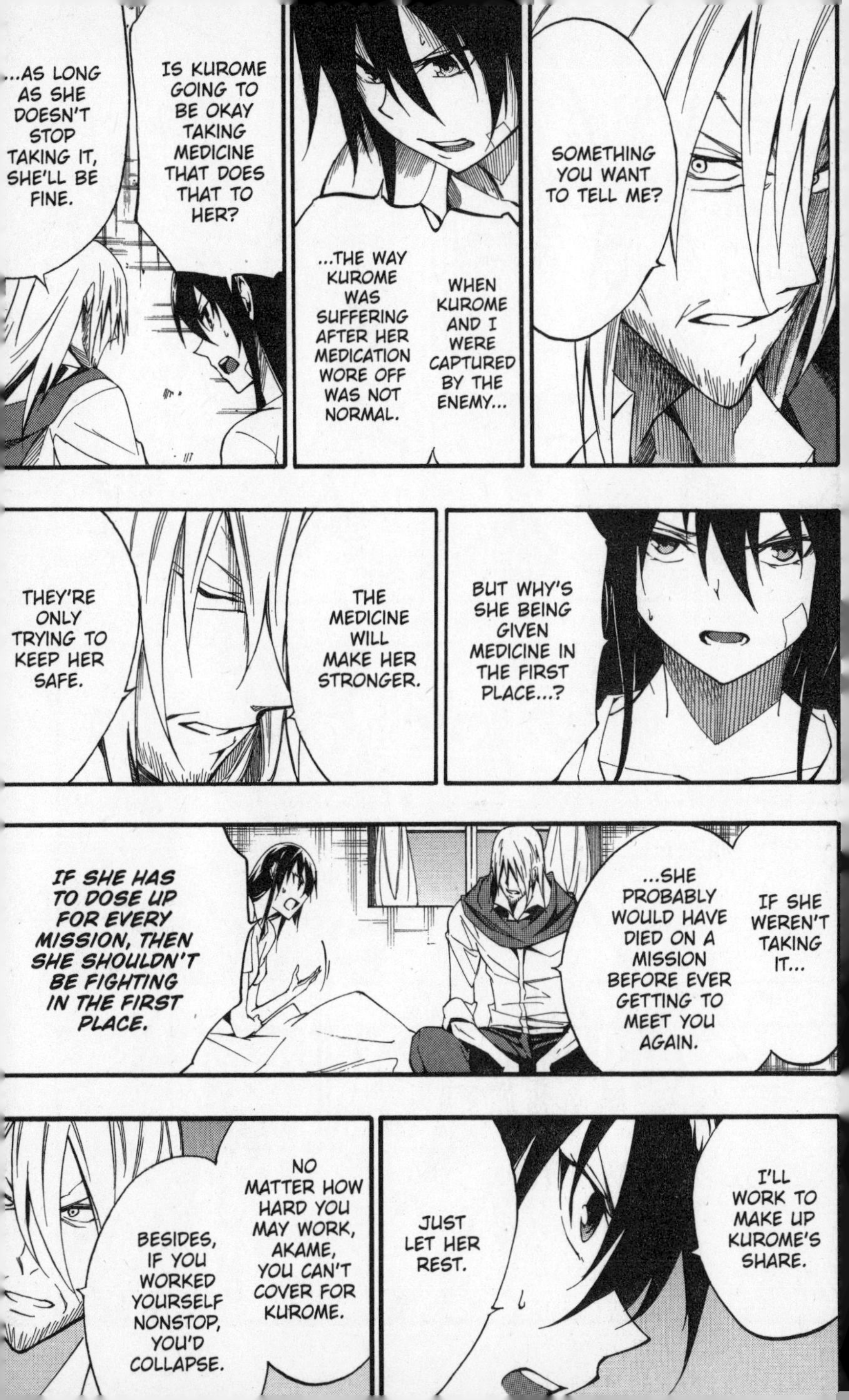
SOMETHING YOU WANT TO TELL ME?
WHEN KUROME AND I WERE CAPTURED BY THE ENEMY...
...THE WAY KUROME WAS SUFFERING AFTER HER MEDICATION WORE OFF WAS NOT NORMAL.
IS KUROME GOING TO BE OKAY TAKING MEDICINE THAT DOES THAT TO HER?
...AS LONG AS SHE DOESN'T STOP TAKING IT, SHE'LL BE FINE.
BUT WHY'S SHE BEING GIVEN MEDICINE IN THE FIRST PLACE...?
THE MEDICINE WILL MAKE HER STRONGER.
THEY'RE ONLY TRYING TO KEEP HER SAFE.
IF SHE WEREN'T TAKING IT...
...SHE PROBABLY WOULD HAVE DIED ON A MISSION BEFORE EVER GETTING TO MEET YOU AGAIN.
IF SHE HAS TO DOSE UP FOR EVERY MISSION, THEN SHE SHOULDN'T BE FIGHTING IN THE FIRST PLACE.
I'LL WORK TO MAKE UP KUROME'S SHARE.
JUST LET HER REST.
NO MATTER HOW HARD YOU MAY WORK, AKAME, YOU CAN'T COVER FOR KUROME.
BESIDES, IF YOU WORKED YOURSELF NONSTOP, YOU'D COLLAPSE.

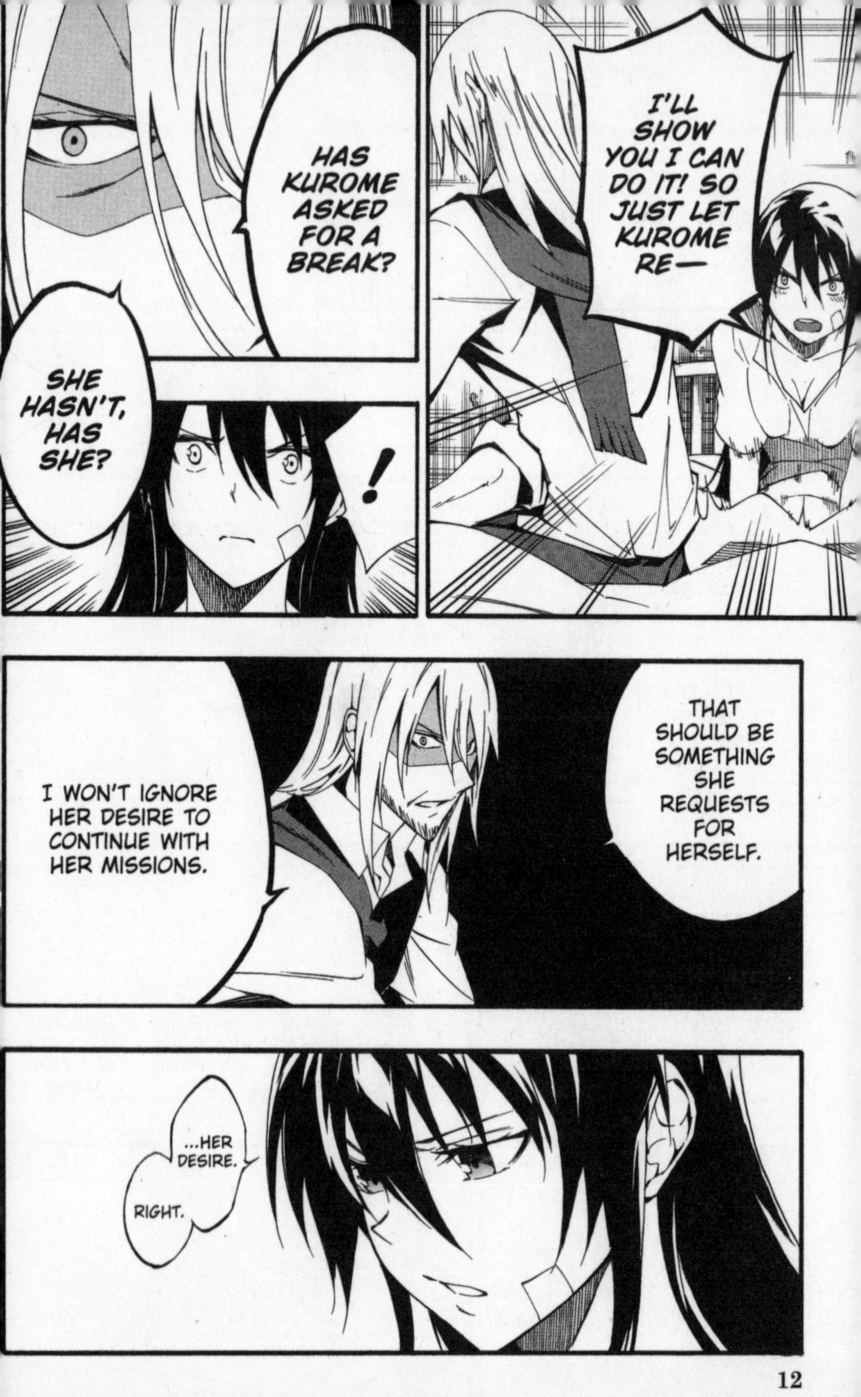
I'LL SHOW YOU I CAN DO IT! SO JUST LET KUROME RE—
HAS KUROME ASKED FOR A BREAK?
SHE HASN'T, HAS SHE?
!
THAT SHOULD BE SOMETHING SHE REQUESTS FOR HERSELF.
I WON'T IGNORE HER DESIRE TO CONTINUE WITH HER MISSIONS.
...HER DESIRE.
RIGHT.

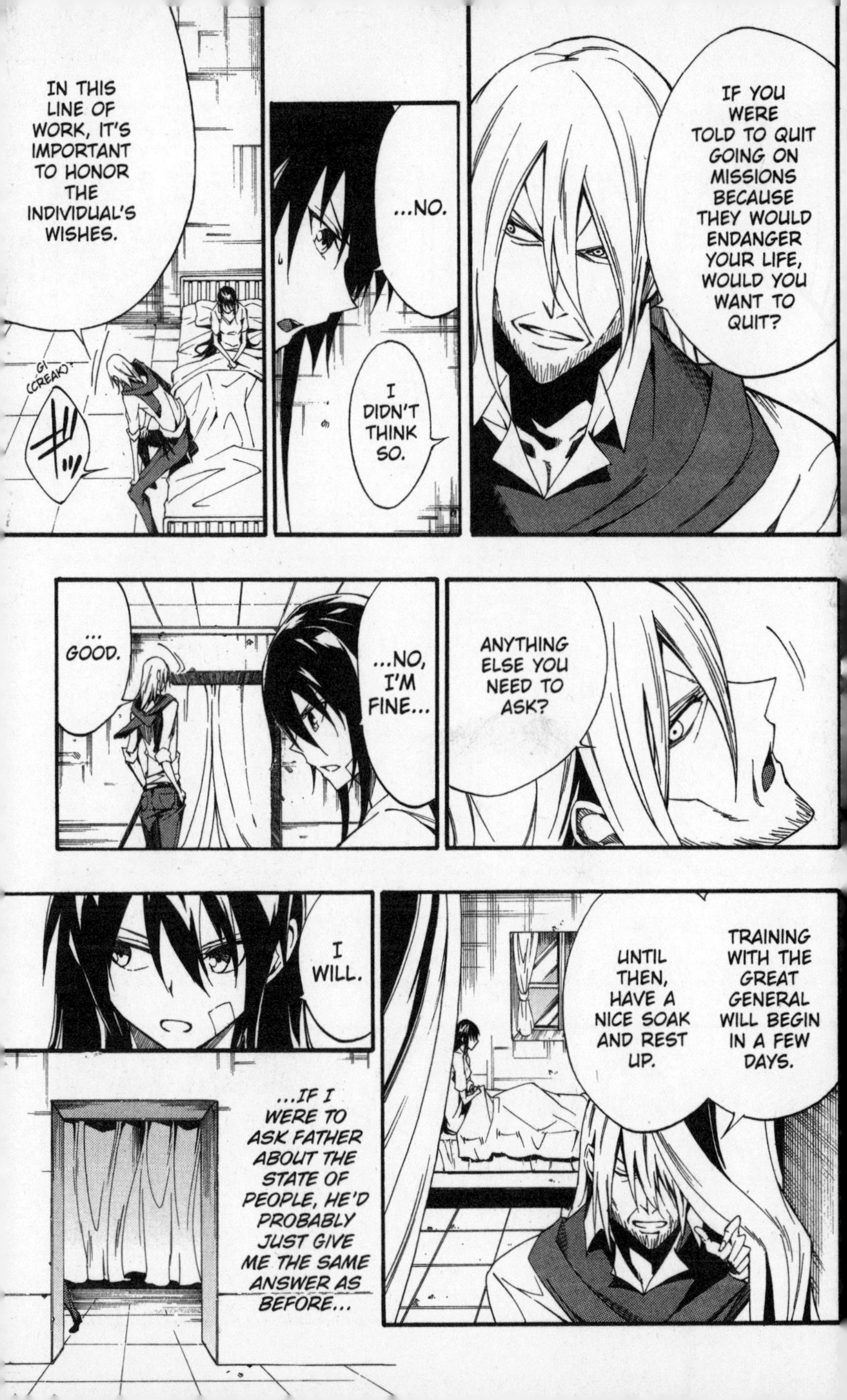
IF YOU WERE TOLD TO QUIT GOING ON MISSIONS BECAUSE THEY WOULD ENDANGER YOUR LIFE, WOULD YOU WANT TO QUIT?
...NO.
I DIDN'T THINK SO.
IN THIS LINE OF WORK, IT'S IMPORTANT TO HONOR THE INDIVIDUAL'S WISHES.
GI (CREAK)
ANYTHING ELSE YOU NEED TO ASK?
...NO, I'M FINE...
... GOOD.
TRAINING WITH THE GREAT GENERAL WILL BEGIN IN A FEW DAYS.
UNTIL THEN, HAVE A NICE SOAK AND REST UP.
I WILL.
...IF I WERE TO ASK FATHER ABOUT THE STATE OF PEOPLE, HE'D PROBABLY JUST GIVE ME THE SAME ANSWER AS BEFORE...

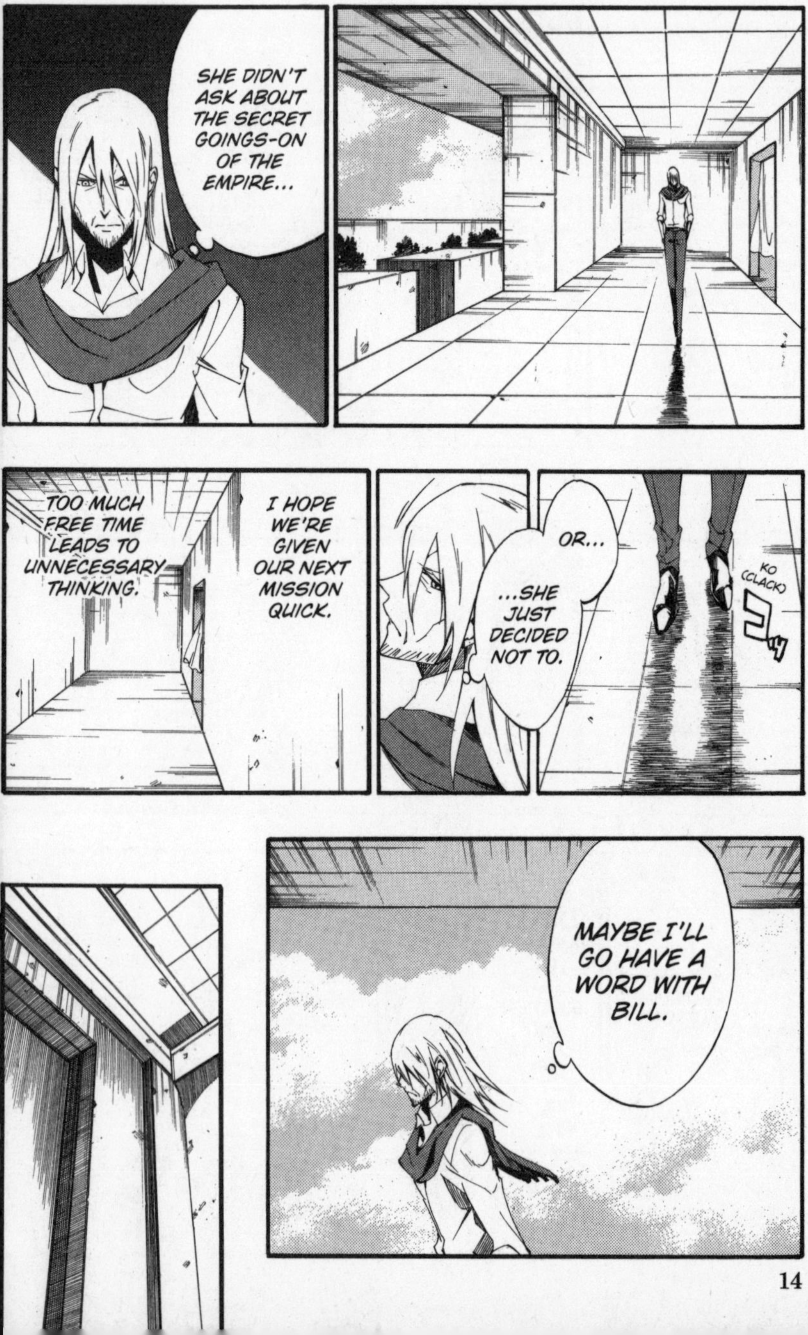
SHE DIDN'T ASK ABOUT THE SECRET GOINGS-ON OF THE EMPIRE...
TOO MUCH FREE TIME LEADS TO UNNECESSARY THINKING.
I HOPE WE'RE GIVEN OUR NEXT MISSION QUICK.
OR...
...SHE JUST DECIDED NOT TO.
KO (CLACK)
MAYBE I'LL GO HAVE A WORD WITH BILL.

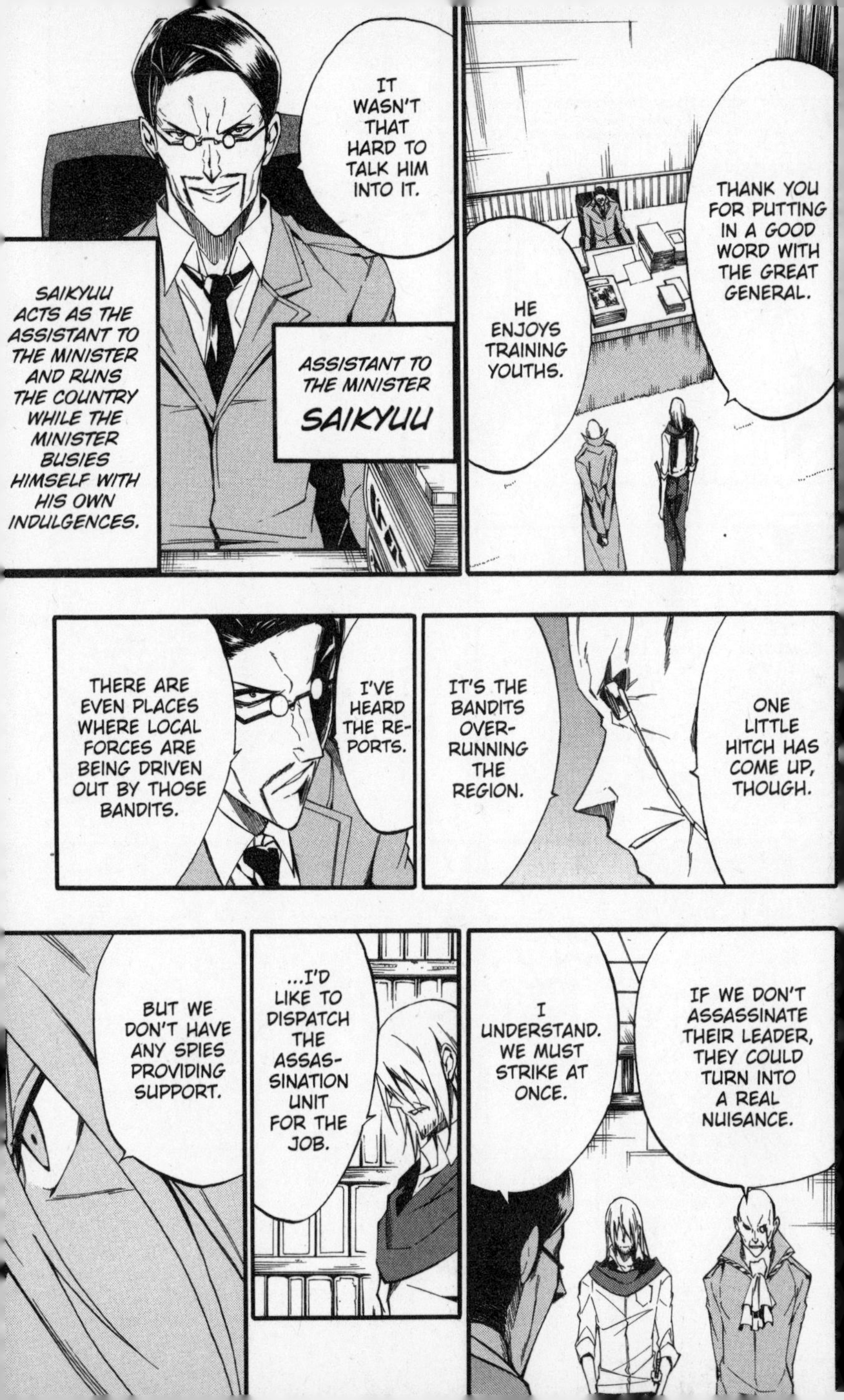
THANK YOU FOR PUTTING IN A GOOD WORD WITH THE GREAT GENERAL.
HE ENJOYS TRAINING YOUTHS.
IT WASN'T THAT HARD TO TALK HIM INTO IT.
ASSISTANT TO THE MINISTER SAIKYUU
SAIKYUU ACTS AS THE ASSISTANT TO THE MINISTER AND RUNS THE COUNTRY WHILE THE MINISTER BUSIES HIMSELF WITH HIS OWN INDULGENCES.
ONE LITTLE HITCH HAS COME UP, THOUGH.
IT'S THE BANDITS OVER-RUNNING THE REGION.
I'VE HEARD THE RE-PORTS.
THERE ARE EVEN PLACES WHERE LOCAL FORCES ARE BEING DRIVEN OUT BY THOSE BANDITS.
IF WE DON'T ASSASSINATE THEIR LEADER, THEY COULD TURN INTO A REAL NUISANCE.
I UNDERSTAND. WE MUST STRIKE AT ONCE.
...I'D LIKE TO DISPATCH THE ASSAS-SINATION UNIT FOR THE JOB.
BUT WE DON'T HAVE ANY SPIES PROVIDING SUPPORT.

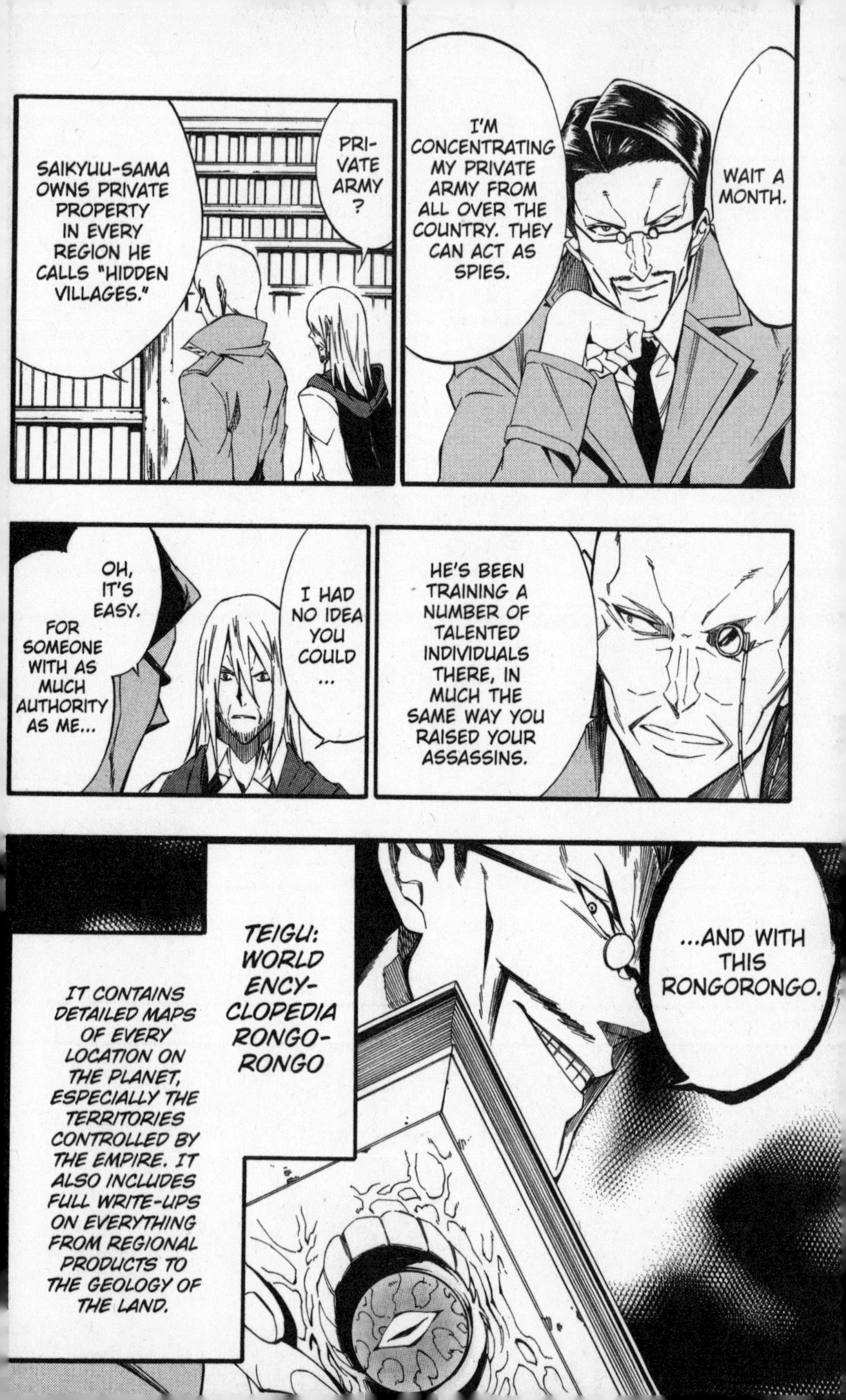
WAIT A MONTH.
I'M CONCENTRATING MY PRIVATE ARMY FROM ALL OVER THE COUNTRY. THEY CAN ACT AS SPIES.
PRI-VATE ARMY?
SAIKYUU-SAMA OWNS PRIVATE PROPERTY IN EVERY REGION HE CALLS "HIDDEN VILLAGES."
HE'S BEEN TRAINING A NUMBER OF TALENTED INDIVIDUALS THERE, IN MUCH THE SAME WAY YOU RAISED YOUR ASSASSINS.
I HAD NO IDEA YOU COULD...
OH, IT'S EASY.
FOR SOMEONE WITH AS MUCH AUTHORITY AS ME...
...AND WITH THIS RONGORONGO.
TEIGU: WORLD ENCY-CLOPEDIA RONGO-RONGO
IT CONTAINS DETAILED MAPS OF EVERY LOCATION ON THE PLANET, ESPECIALLY THE TERRITORIES CONTROLLED BY THE EMPIRE. IT ALSO INCLUDES FULL WRITE-UPS ON EVERYTHING FROM REGIONAL PRODUCTS TO THE GEOLOGY OF THE LAND.

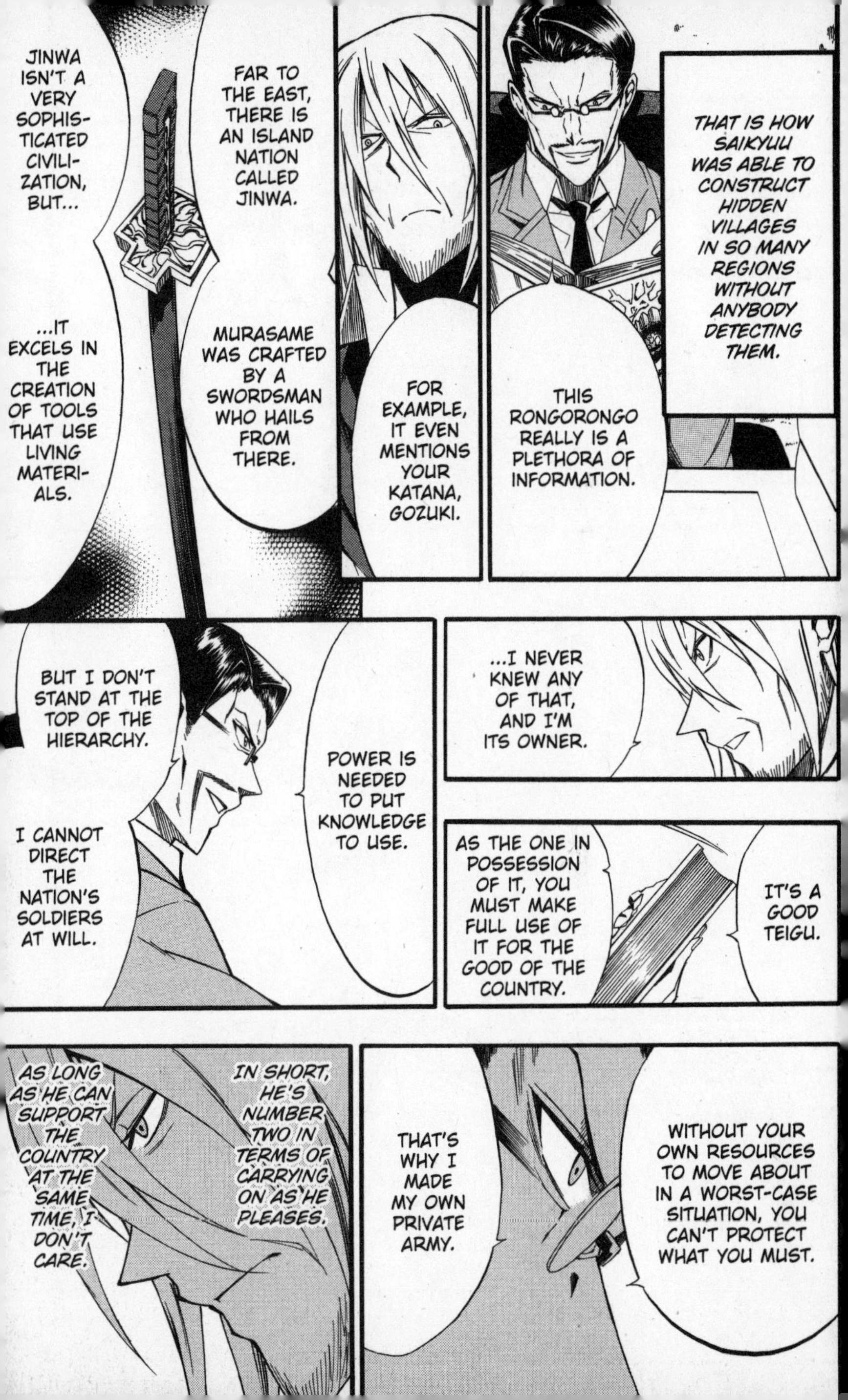
THAT IS HOW SAIKYUU WAS ABLE TO CONSTRUCT HIDDEN VILLAGES IN SO MANY REGIONS WITHOUT ANYBODY DETECTING THEM.
THIS RONGORONGO REALLY IS A PLETHORA OF INFORMATION.
FOR EXAMPLE, IT EVEN MENTIONS YOUR KATANA, GOZUKI.
FAR TO THE EAST, THERE IS AN ISLAND NATION CALLED JINWA.
MURASAME WAS CRAFTED BY A SWORDSMAN WHO HAILS FROM THERE.
JINWA ISN'T A VERY SOPHISTICATED CIVILIZATION, BUT...
...IT EXCELS IN THE CREATION OF TOOLS THAT USE LIVING MATERIALS.
...I NEVER KNEW ANY OF THAT, AND I'M ITS OWNER.
IT'S A GOOD TEIGU.
AS THE ONE IN POSSESSION OF IT, YOU MUST MAKE FULL USE OF IT FOR THE GOOD OF THE COUNTRY.
POWER IS NEEDED TO PUT KNOWLEDGE TO USE.
BUT I DON'T STAND AT THE TOP OF THE HIERARCHY.
I CANNOT DIRECT THE NATION'S SOLDIERS AT WILL.
WITHOUT YOUR OWN RESOURCES TO MOVE ABOUT IN A WORST-CASE SITUATION, YOU CAN'T PROTECT WHAT YOU MUST.
THAT'S WHY I MADE MY OWN PRIVATE ARMY.
IN SHORT, HE'S NUMBER TWO IN TERMS OF CARRYING ON AS HE PLEASES.
AS LONG AS HE CAN SUPPORT THE COUNTRY AT THE SAME TIME, I DON'T CARE.

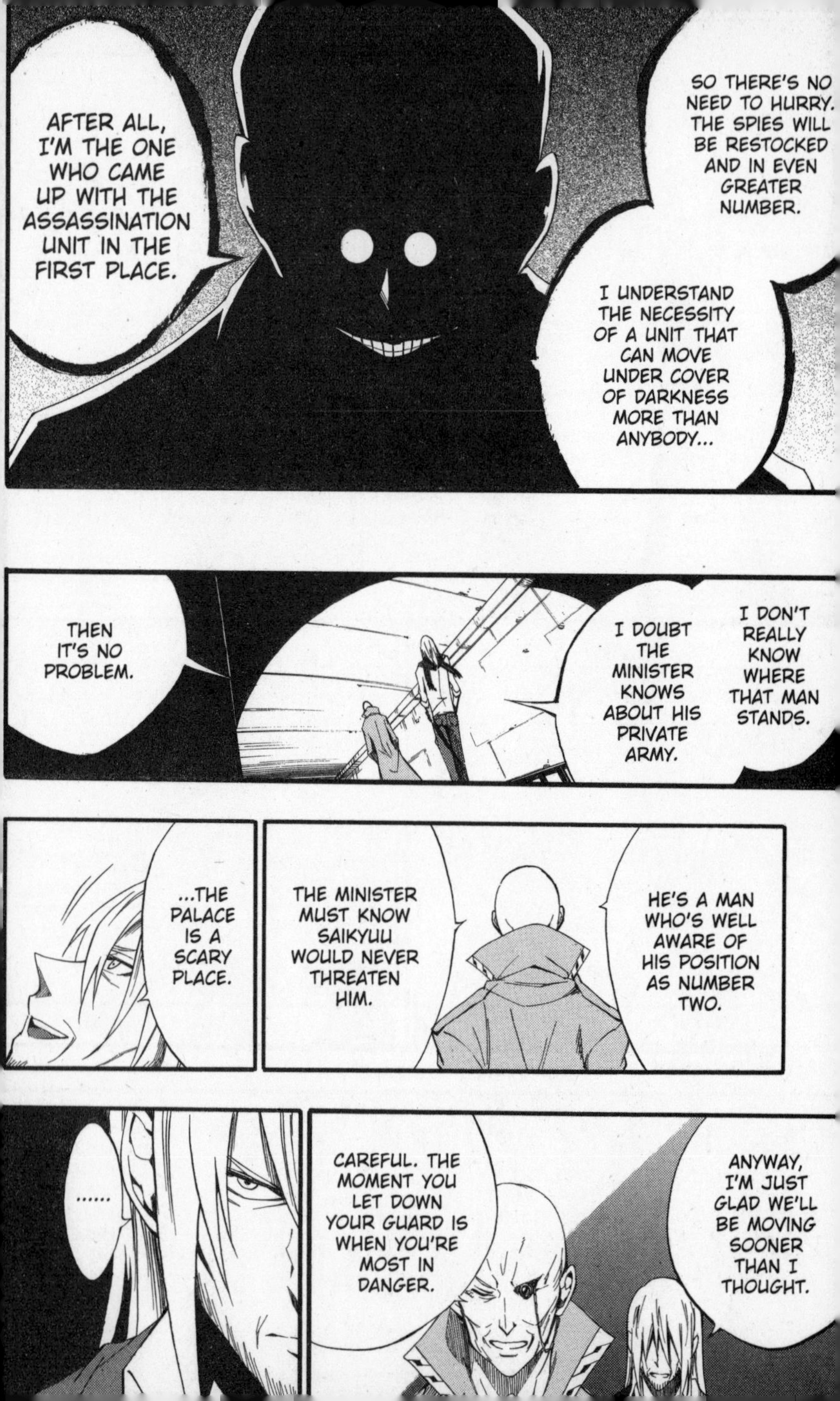
SO THERE'S NO NEED TO HURRY. THE SPIES WILL BE RESTOCKED AND IN EVEN GREATER NUMBER.
I UNDERSTAND THE NECESSITY OF A UNIT THAT CAN MOVE UNDER COVER OF DARKNESS MORE THAN ANYBODY...
AFTER ALL, I'M THE ONE WHO CAME UP WITH THE ASSASSINATION UNIT IN THE FIRST PLACE.
I DON'T REALLY KNOW WHERE THAT MAN STANDS.
I DOUBT THE MINISTER KNOWS ABOUT HIS PRIVATE ARMY.
THEN IT'S NO PROBLEM.
HE'S A MAN WHO'S WELL AWARE OF HIS POSITION AS NUMBER TWO.
THE MINISTER MUST KNOW SAIKYUU WOULD NEVER THREATEN HIM.
...THE PALACE IS A SCARY PLACE.
ANYWAY, I'M JUST GLAD WE'LL BE MOVING SOONER THAN I THOUGHT.
CAREFUL. THE MOMENT YOU LET DOWN YOUR GUARD IS WHEN YOU'RE MOST IN DANGER.
......

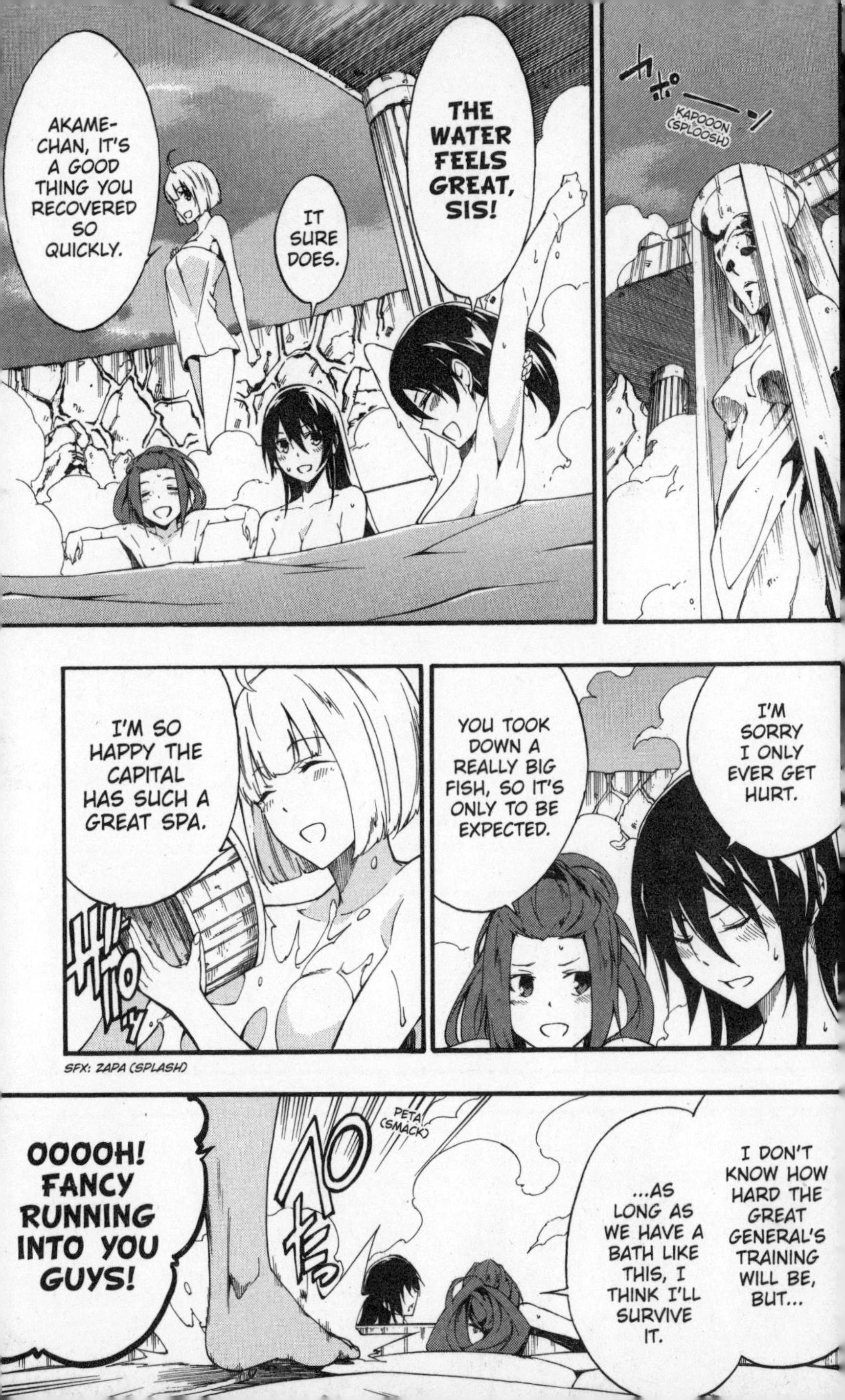
KAPOOON (SPLOOSH)
THE WATER FEELS GREAT, SIS!
IT SURE DOES.
AKAME-CHAN, IT'S A GOOD THING YOU RECOVERED SO QUICKLY.
I'M SORRY I ONLY EVER GET HURT.
YOU TOOK DOWN A REALLY BIG FISH, SO IT'S ONLY TO BE EXPECTED.
I'M SO HAPPY THE CAPITAL HAS SUCH A GREAT SPA.
SFX: ZAPA (SPLASH)
I DON'T KNOW HOW HARD THE GREAT GENERAL'S TRAINING WILL BE, BUT...
...AS LONG AS WE HAVE A BATH LIKE THIS, I THINK I'LL SURVIVE IT.
PETA (SMACK)
OOOOH! FANCY RUNNING INTO YOU GUYS!

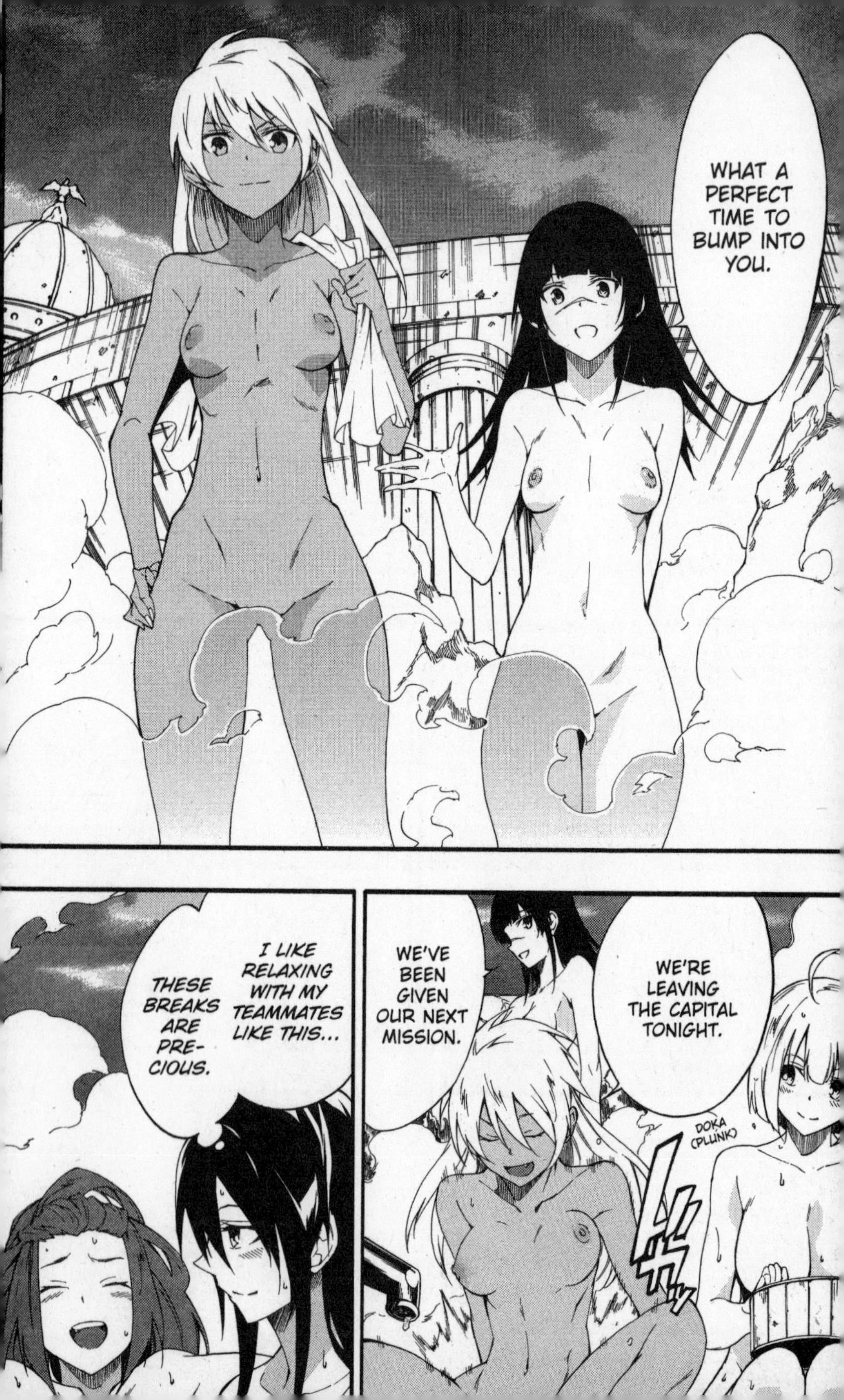
WHAT A PERFECT TIME TO BUMP INTO YOU.
WE'RE LEAVING THE CAPITAL TONIGHT.
WE'VE BEEN GIVEN OUR NEXT MISSION.
DOKA (PLUNK)
I LIKE RELAXING WITH MY TEAMMATES LIKE THIS...
THESE BREAKS ARE PRE-CIOUS.

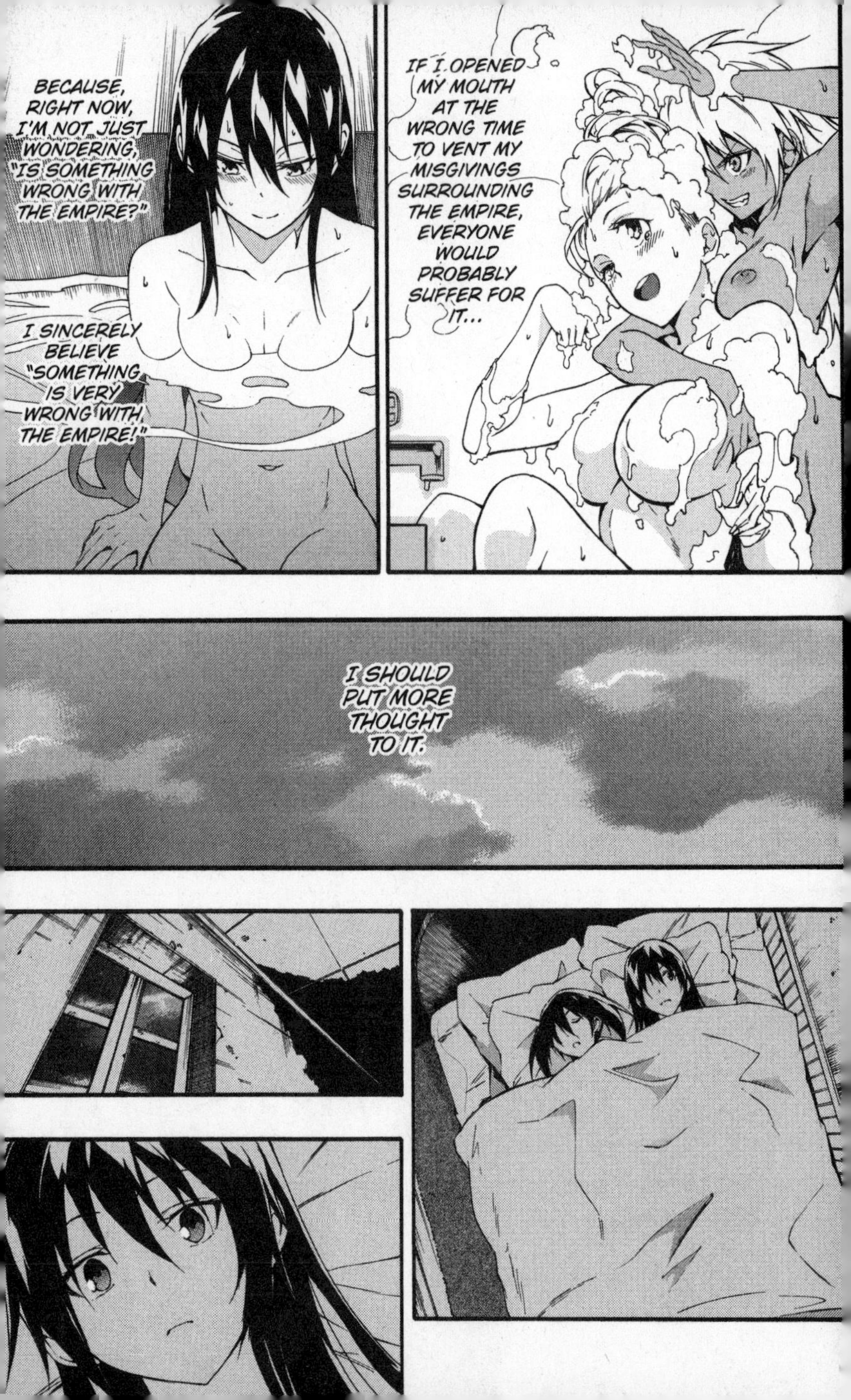
IF I OPENED MY MOUTH AT THE WRONG TIME TO VENT MY MISGIVINGS SURROUNDING THE EMPIRE, EVERYONE WOULD PROBABLY SUFFER FOR IT...
BECAUSE, RIGHT NOW, I'M NOT JUST WONDERING, "IS SOMETHING WRONG WITH THE EMPIRE?"
I SINCERELY BELIEVE "SOMETHING IS VERY WRONG WITH THE EMPIRE!"
I SHOULD PUT MORE THOUGHT TO IT.

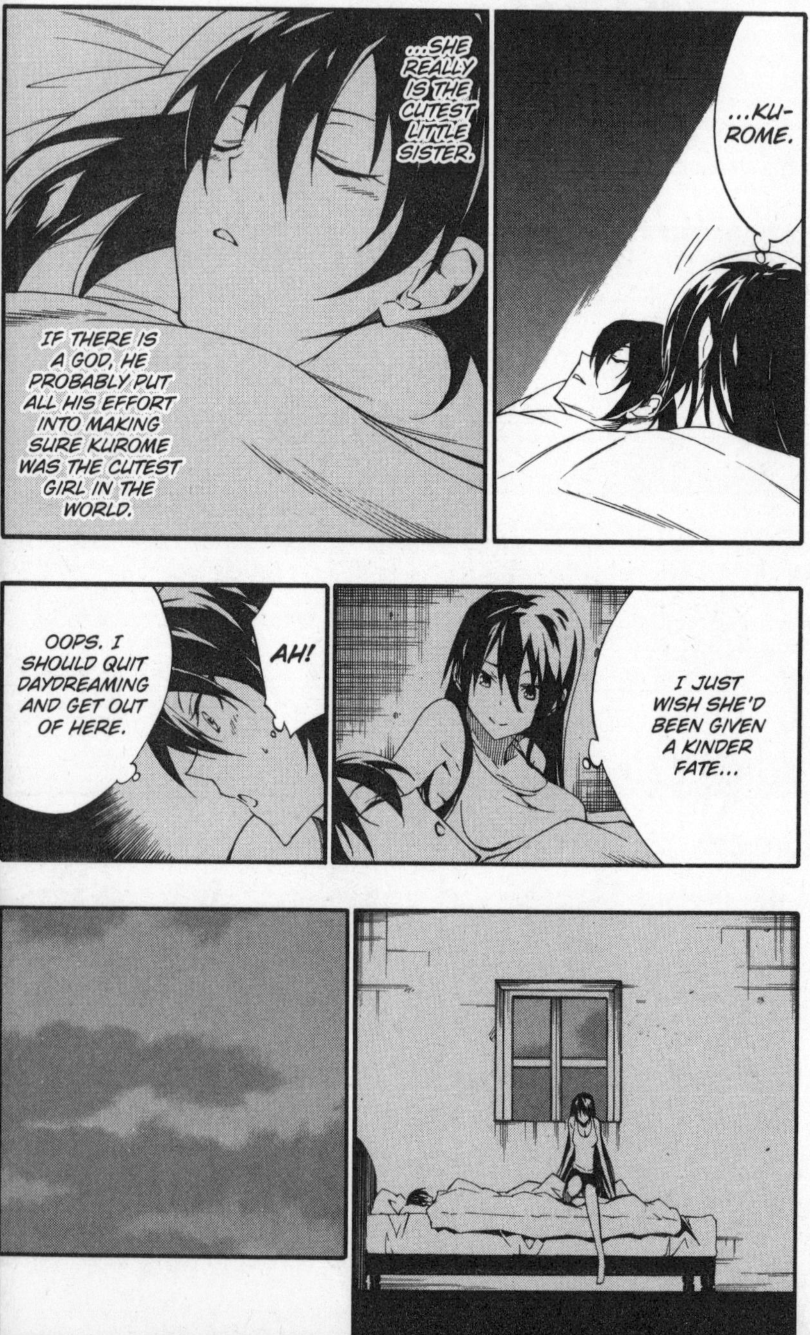
...KU-ROME.
...SHE REALLY IS THE CUTEST LITTLE SISTER.
IF THERE IS A GOD, HE PROBABLY PUT ALL HIS EFFORT INTO MAKING SURE KUROME WAS THE CUTEST GIRL IN THE WORLD.
I JUST WISH SHE'D BEEN GIVEN A KINDER FATE...
AH!
OOPS. I SHOULD QUIT DAYDREAMING AND GET OUT OF HERE.

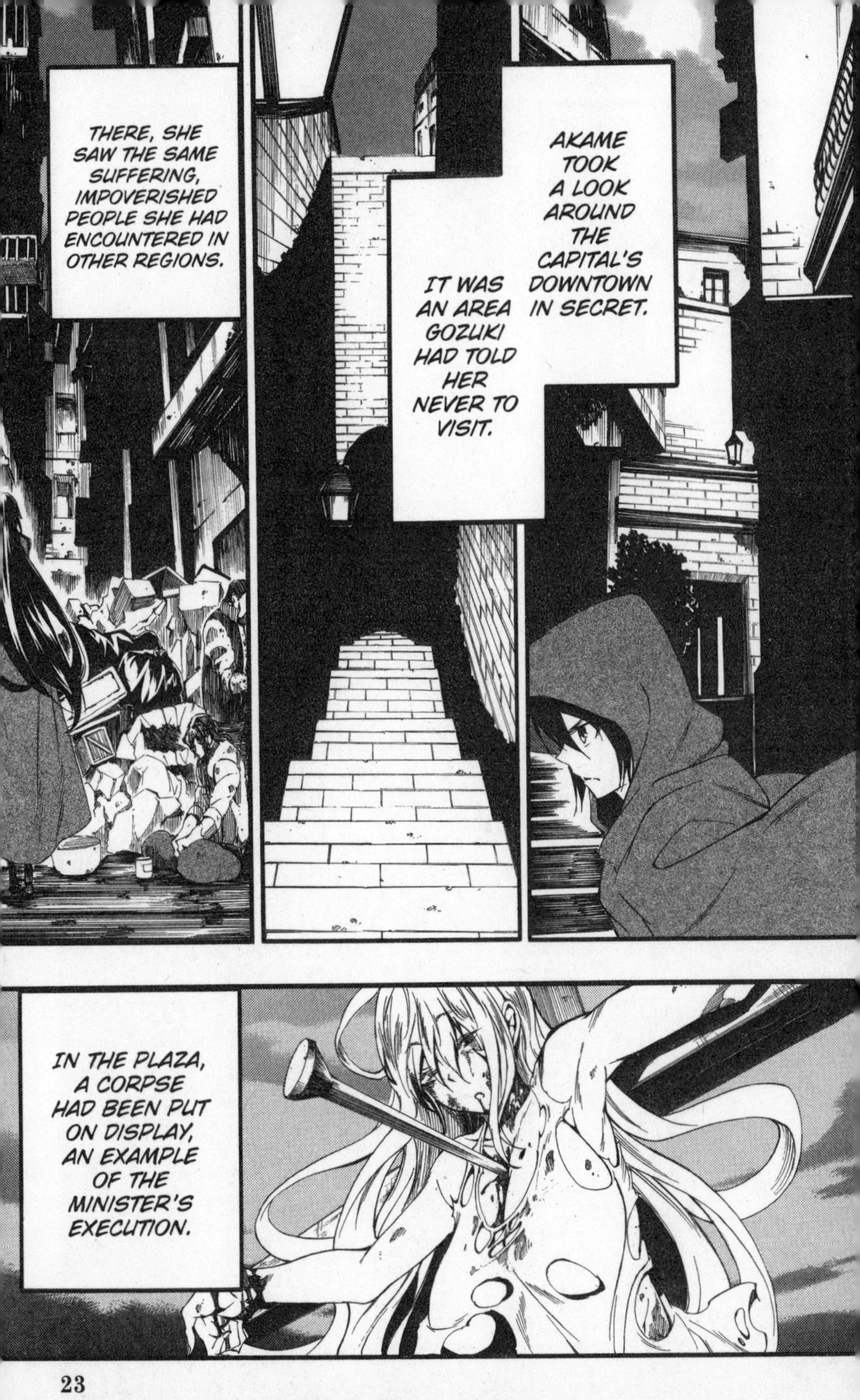
AKAME TOOK A LOOK AROUND THE CAPITAL'S DOWNTOWN IN SECRET.
IT WAS AN AREA GOZUKI HAD TOLD HER NEVER TO VISIT.
THERE, SHE SAW THE SAME SUFFERING, IMPOVERISHED PEOPLE SHE HAD ENCOUNTERED IN OTHER REGIONS.
IN THE PLAZA, A CORPSE HAD BEEN PUT ON DISPLAY, AN EXAMPLE OF THE MINISTER'S EXECUTION.

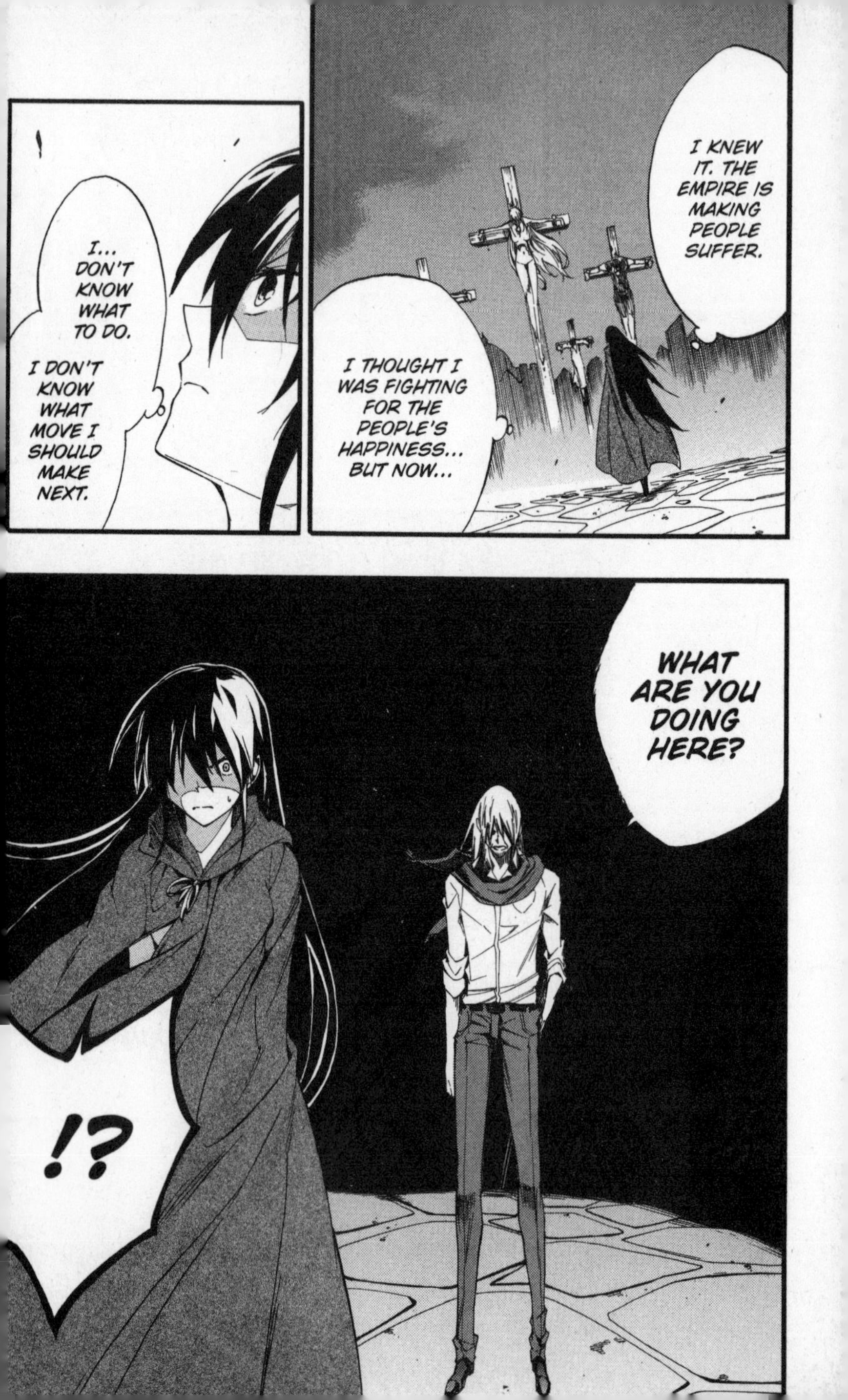
I KNEW IT. THE EMPIRE IS MAKING PEOPLE SUFFER.
I THOUGHT I WAS FIGHTING FOR THE PEOPLE'S HAPPINESS... BUT NOW...
I... DON'T KNOW WHAT TO DO.
I DON'T KNOW WHAT MOVE I SHOULD MAKE NEXT.
WHAT ARE YOU DOING HERE?
!?

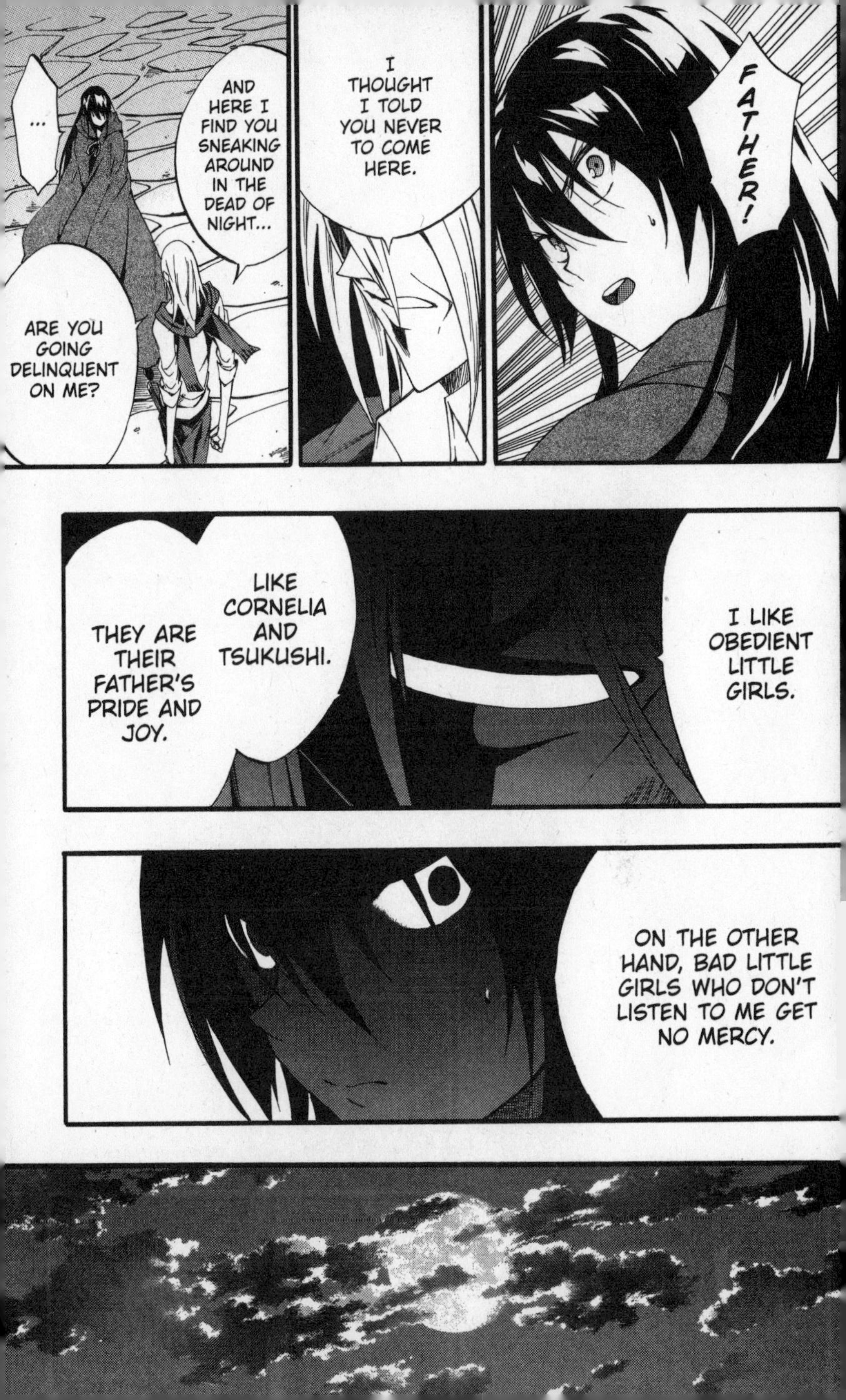
...
AND HERE I FIND YOU SNEAKING AROUND IN THE DEAD OF NIGHT...
ARE YOU GOING DELINQUENT ON ME?
I THOUGHT I TOLD YOU NEVER TO COME HERE.
FATHER!
I LIKE OBEDIENT LITTLE GIRLS.
LIKE CORNELIA AND TSUKUSHI.
THEY ARE THEIR FATHER'S PRIDE AND JOY.
ON THE OTHER HAND, BAD LITTLE GIRLS WHO DON'T LISTEN TO ME GET NO MERCY.

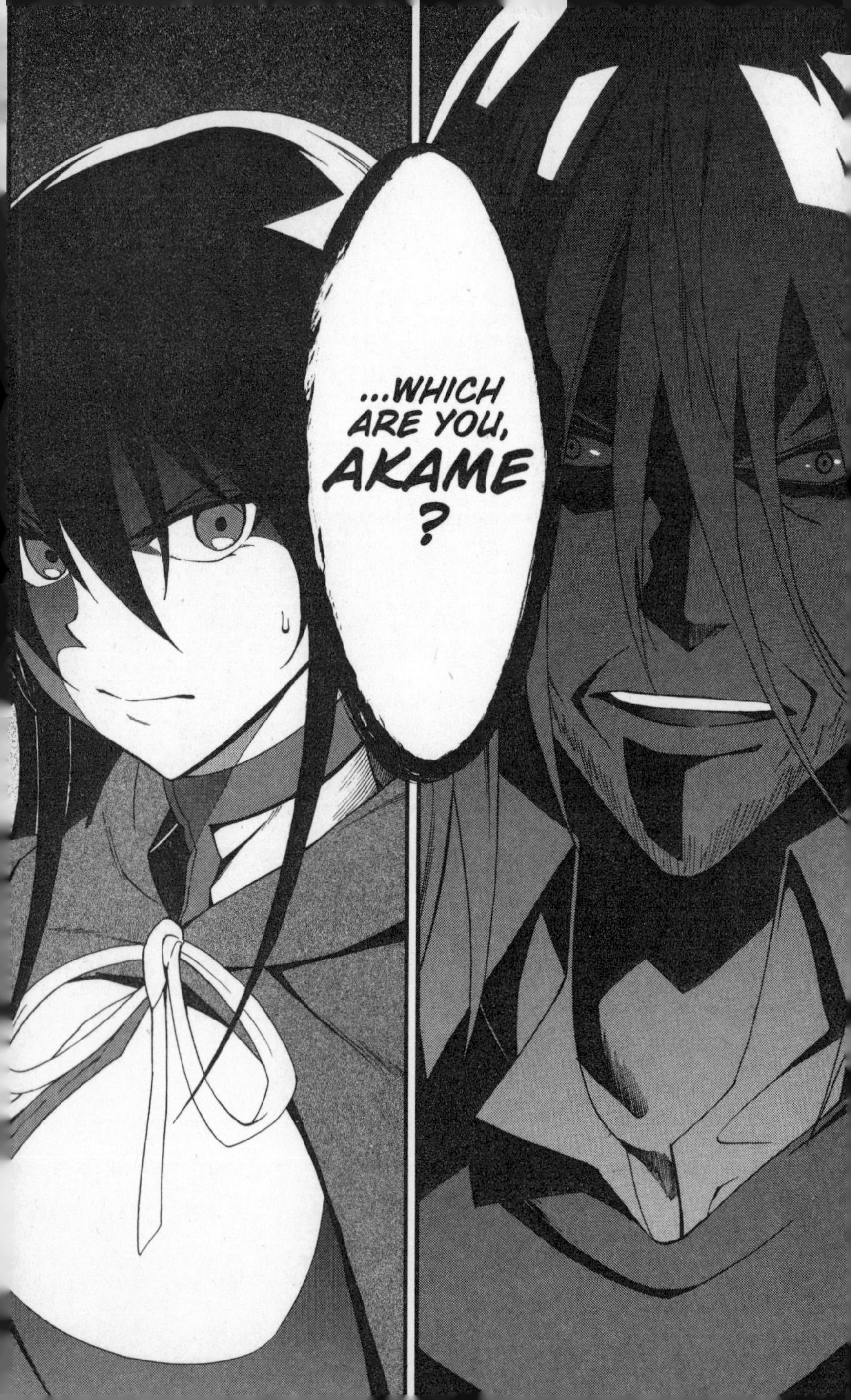
...WHICH ARE YOU, AKAME ?

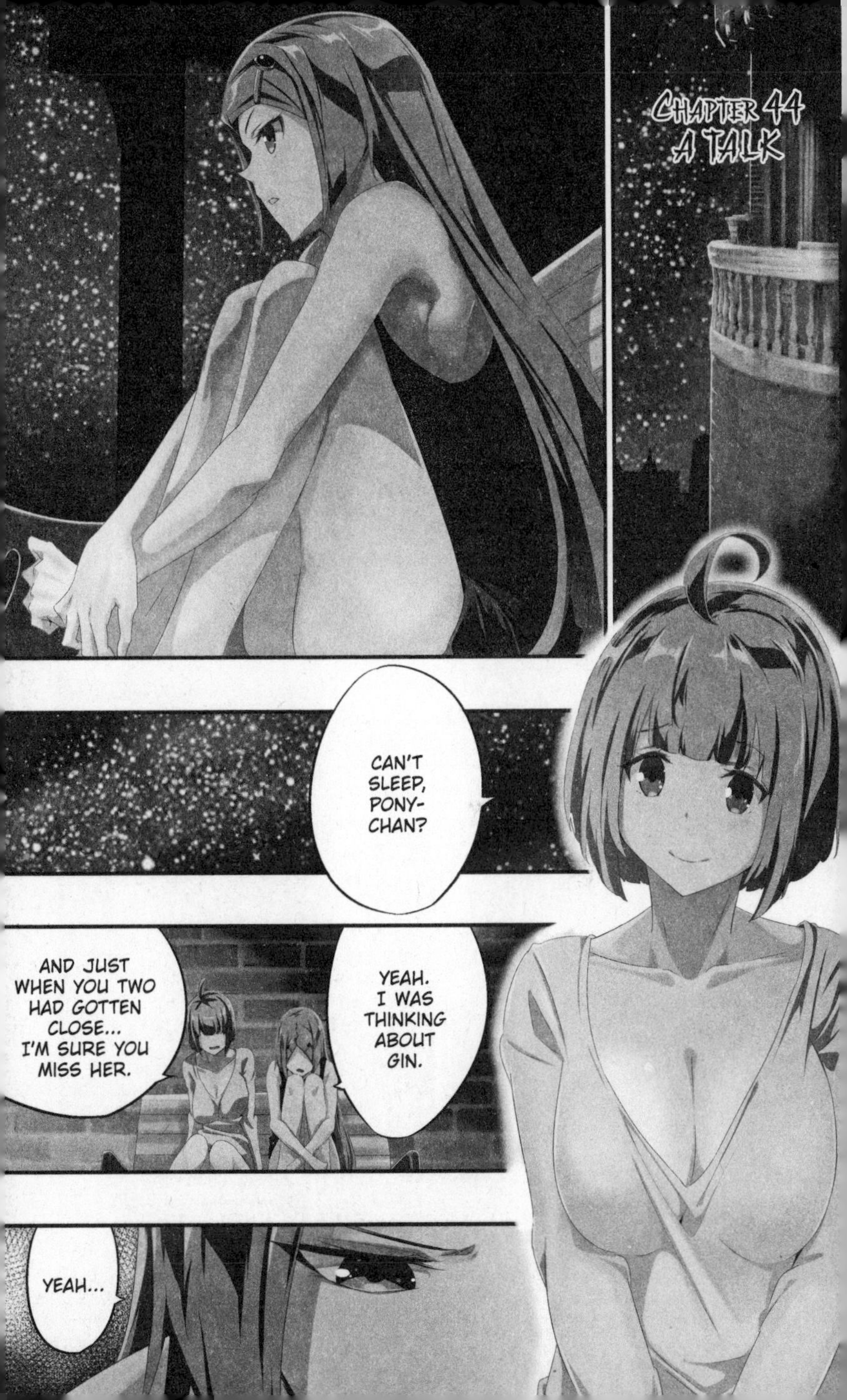
CHAPTER 44
A TALK
CAN'T SLEEP, PONY-CHAN?
YEAH. I WAS THINKING ABOUT GIN.
AND JUST WHEN YOU TWO HAD GOTTEN CLOSE... I'M SURE YOU MISS HER.
YEAH...

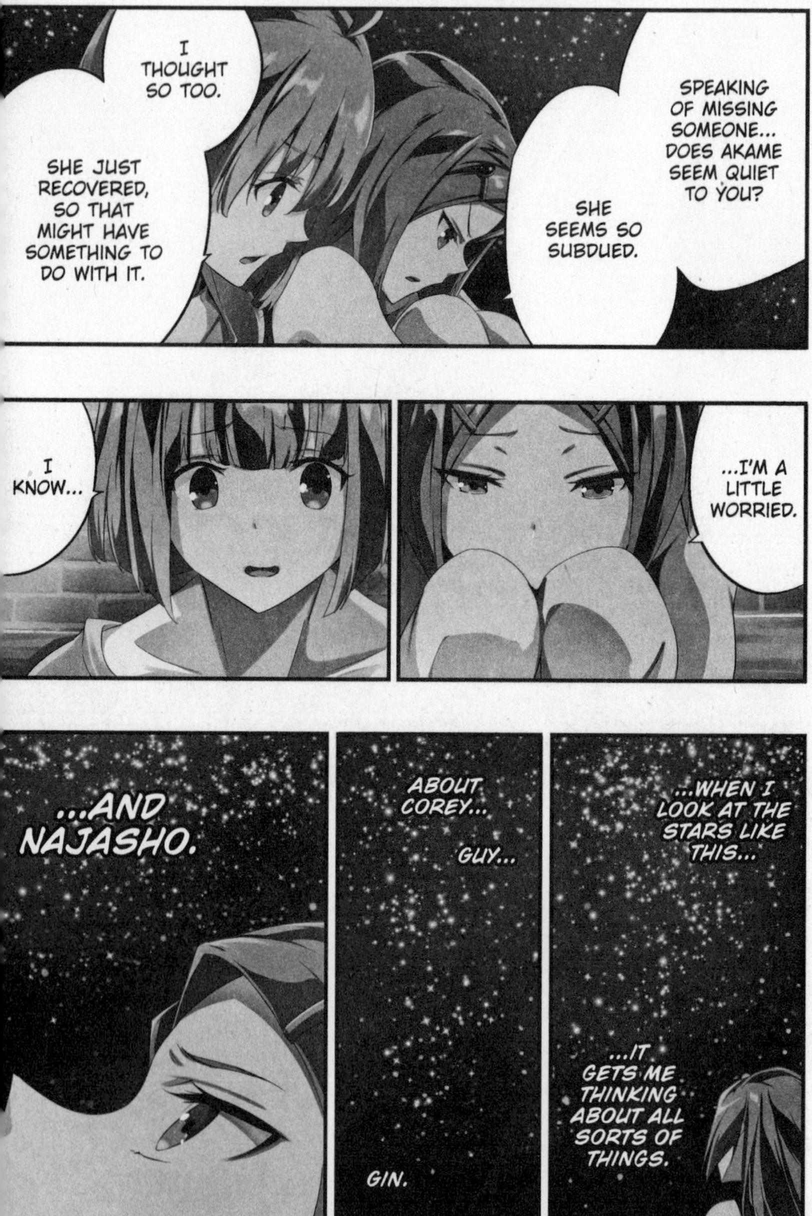
SPEAKING OF MISSING SOMEONE... DOES AKAME SEEM QUIET TO YOU?
SHE SEEMS SO SUBDUED.
I THOUGHT SO TOO.
SHE JUST RECOVERED, SO THAT MIGHT HAVE SOMETHING TO DO WITH IT.
...I'M A LITTLE WORRIED.
I KNOW...
...WHEN I LOOK AT THE STARS LIKE THIS...
...IT GETS ME THINKING ABOUT ALL SORTS OF THINGS.
ABOUT COREY...
GUY...
GIN.
...AND NAJASHO.

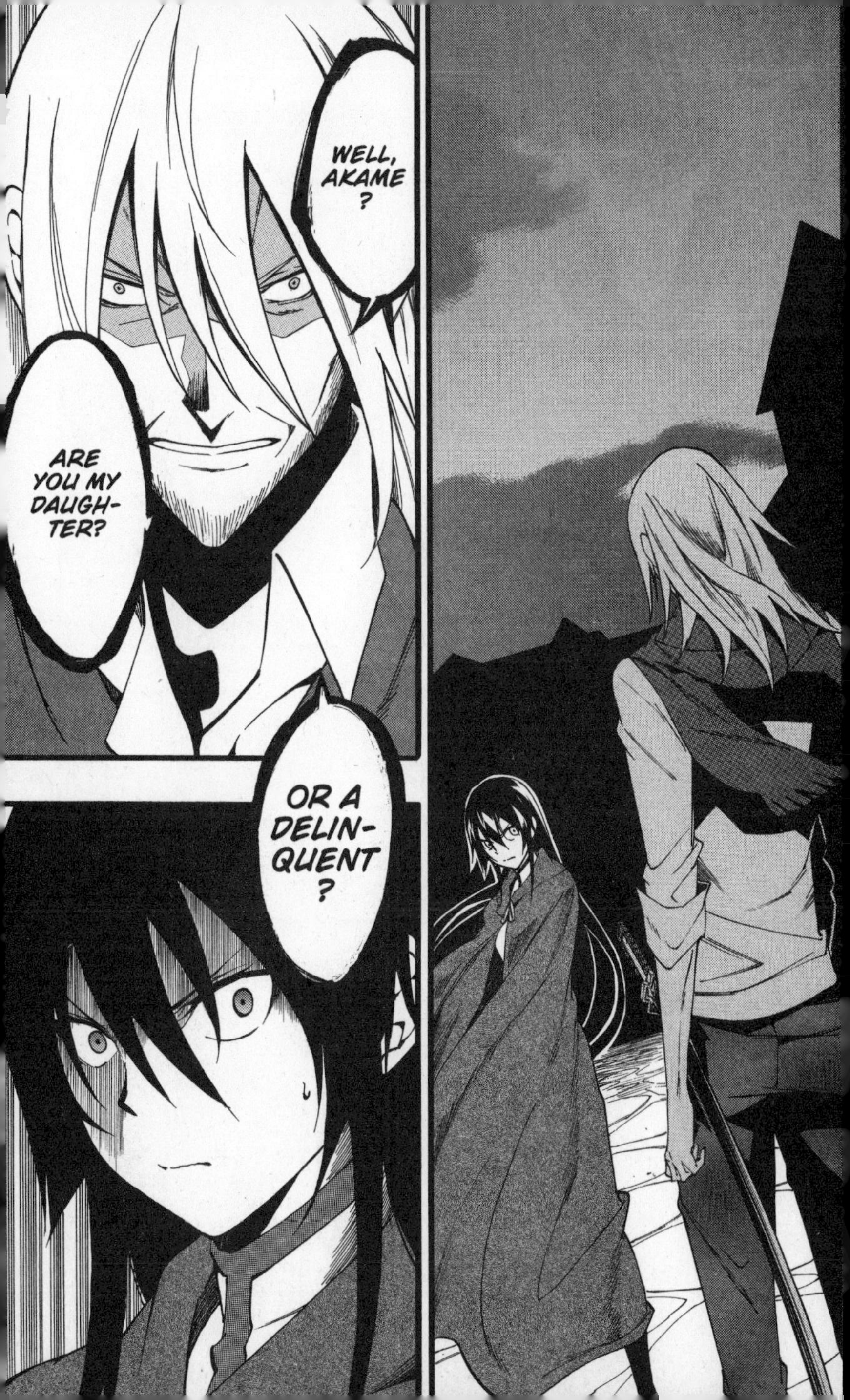
WELL, AKAME?
ARE YOU MY DAUGH-TER?
OR A DELIN-QUENT?

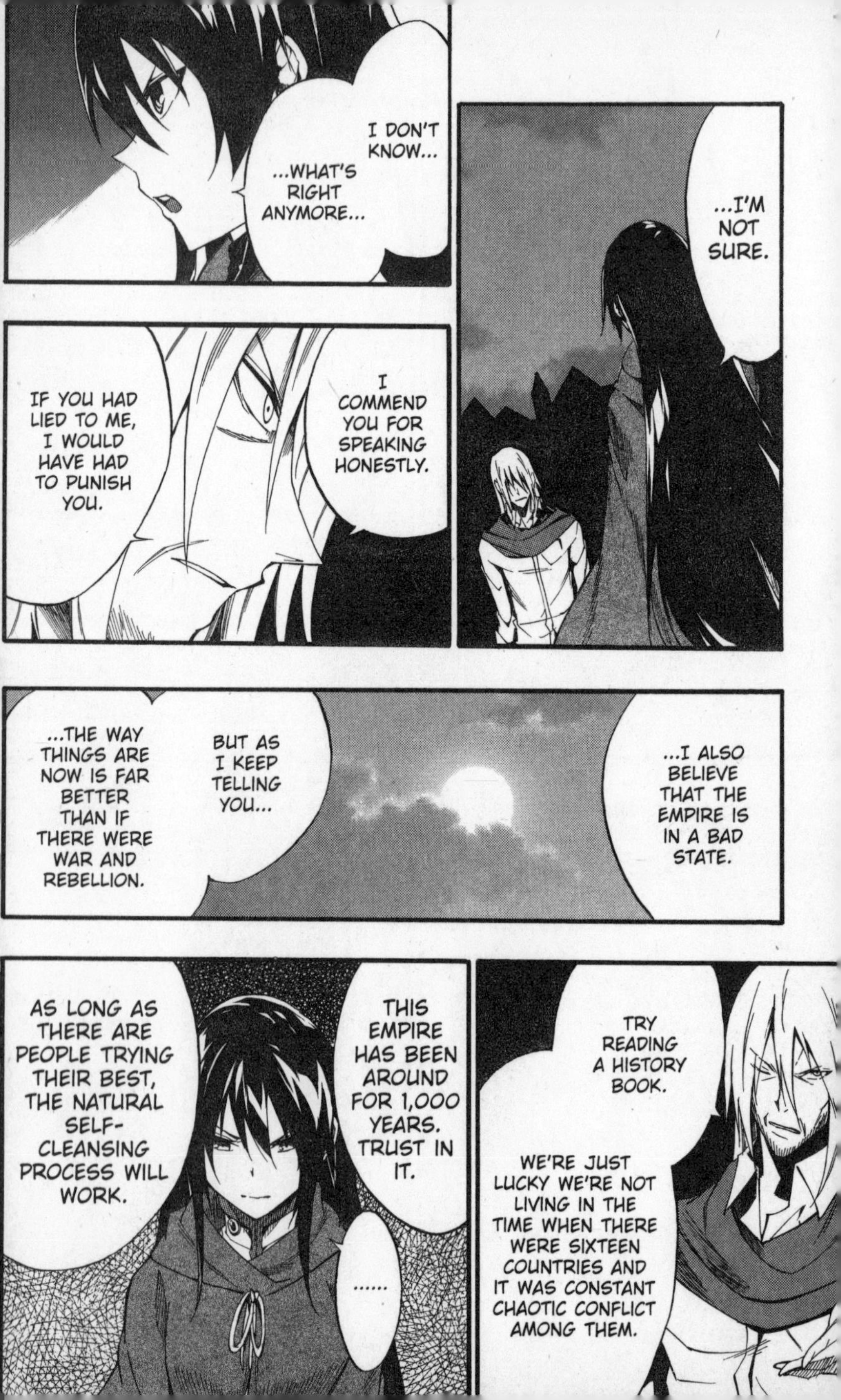
...I'M NOT SURE.
I DON'T KNOW...
...WHAT'S RIGHT ANYMORE...
I COMMEND YOU FOR SPEAKING HONESTLY.
IF YOU HAD LIED TO ME, I WOULD HAVE HAD TO PUNISH YOU.
...I ALSO BELIEVE THAT THE EMPIRE IS IN A BAD STATE.
BUT AS I KEEP TELLING YOU...
...THE WAY THINGS ARE NOW IS FAR BETTER THAN IF THERE WERE WAR AND REBELLION.
TRY READING A HISTORY BOOK.
WE'RE JUST LUCKY WE'RE NOT LIVING IN THE TIME WHEN THERE WERE SIXTEEN COUNTRIES AND IT WAS CONSTANT CHAOTIC CONFLICT AMONG THEM.
THIS EMPIRE HAS BEEN AROUND FOR 1,000 YEARS. TRUST IN IT.
AS LONG AS THERE ARE PEOPLE TRYING THEIR BEST, THE NATURAL SELF-CLEANSING PROCESS WILL WORK.
......

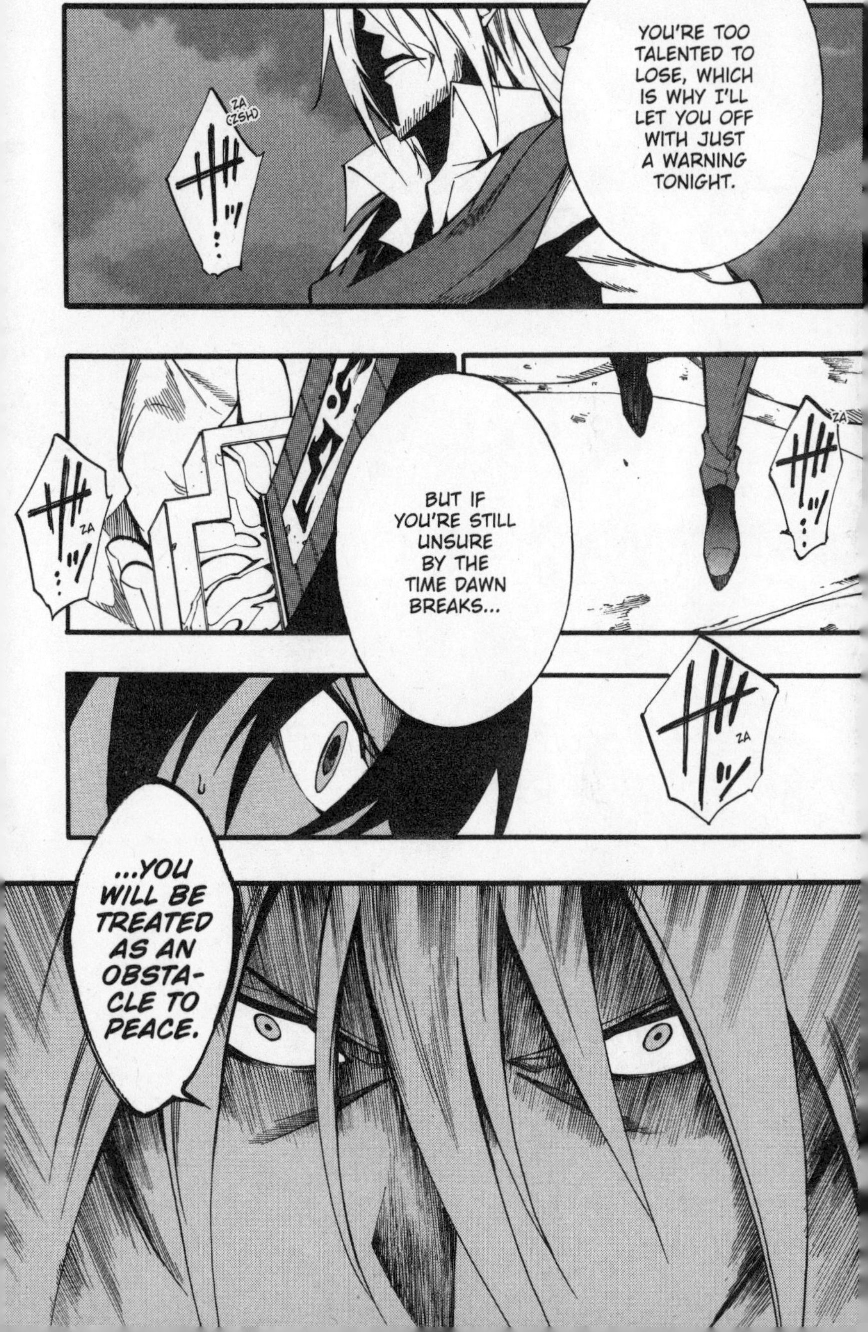
YOU'RE TOO TALENTED TO LOSE, WHICH IS WHY I'LL LET YOU OFF WITH JUST A WARNING TONIGHT.
ZA
ZA
BUT IF YOU'RE STILL UNSURE BY THE TIME DAWN BREAKS...
ZA
ZA
...YOU WILL BE TREATED AS AN OBSTA-CLE TO PEACE.

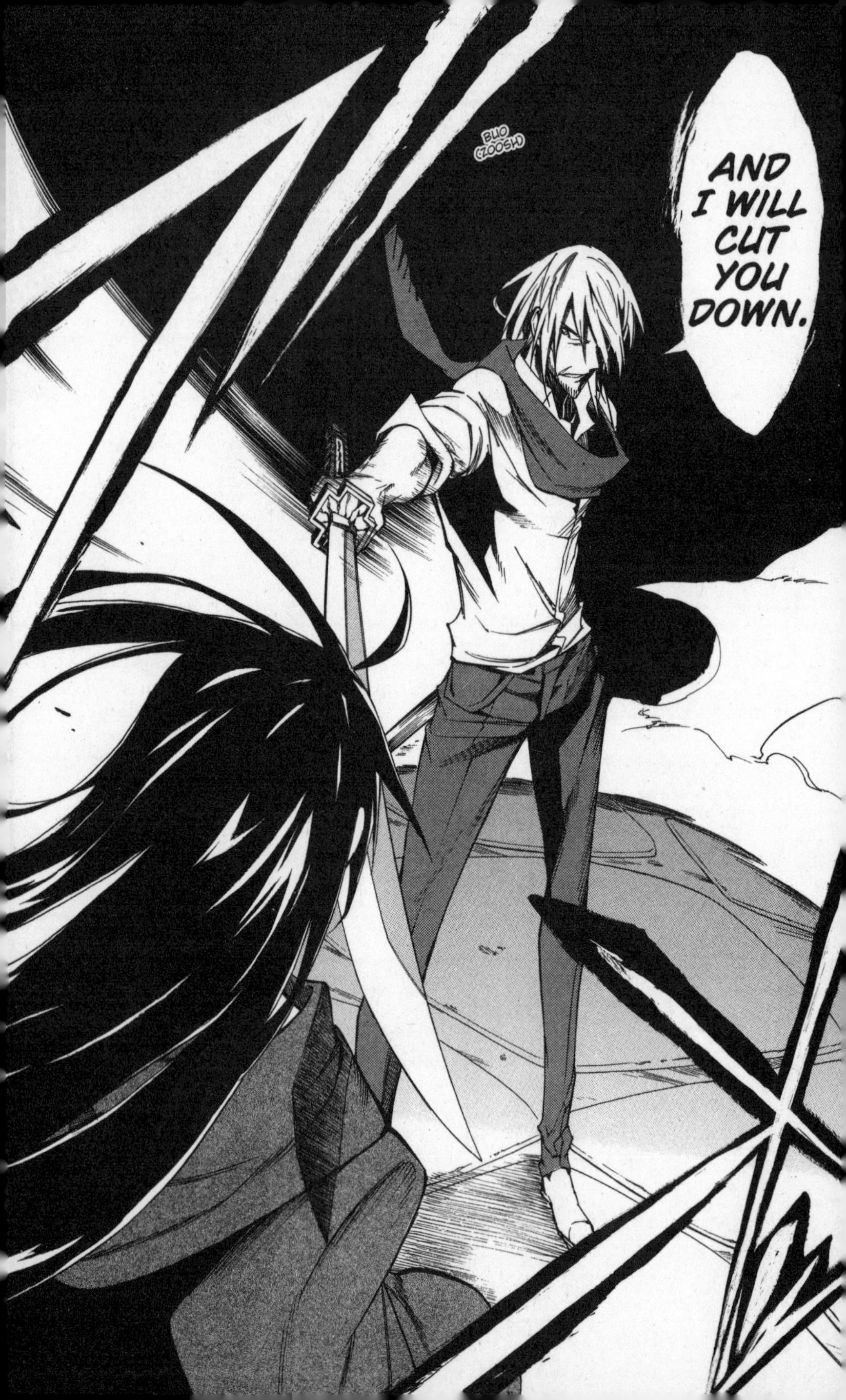
BUO (ZOOSH)
AND I WILL CUT YOU DOWN.

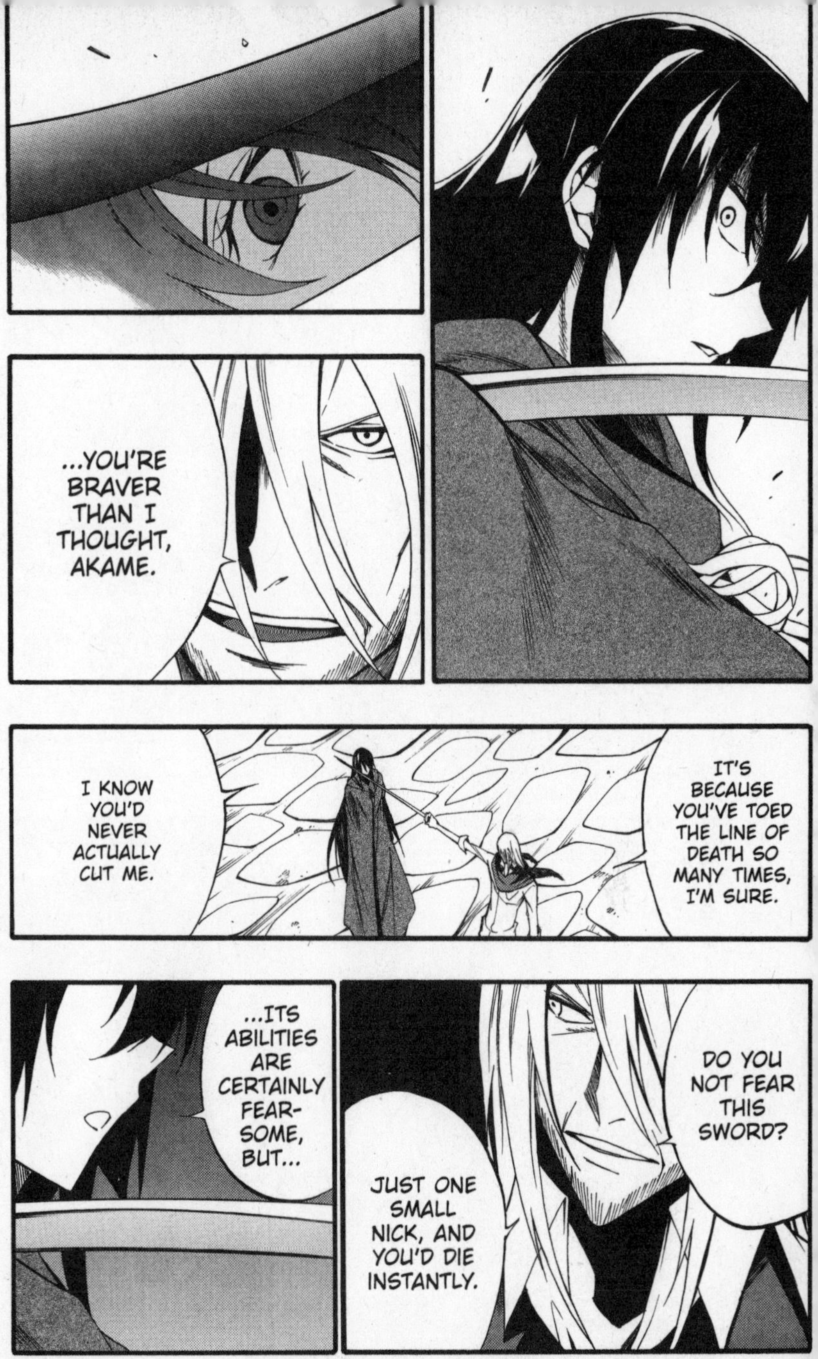
...YOU'RE BRAVER THAN I THOUGHT, AKAME.
IT'S BECAUSE YOU'VE TOED THE LINE OF DEATH SO MANY TIMES, I'M SURE.
I KNOW YOU'D NEVER ACTUALLY CUT ME.
DO YOU NOT FEAR THIS SWORD?
JUST ONE SMALL NICK, AND YOU'D DIE INSTANTLY.
...ITS ABILITIES ARE CERTAINLY FEAR-SOME, BUT...

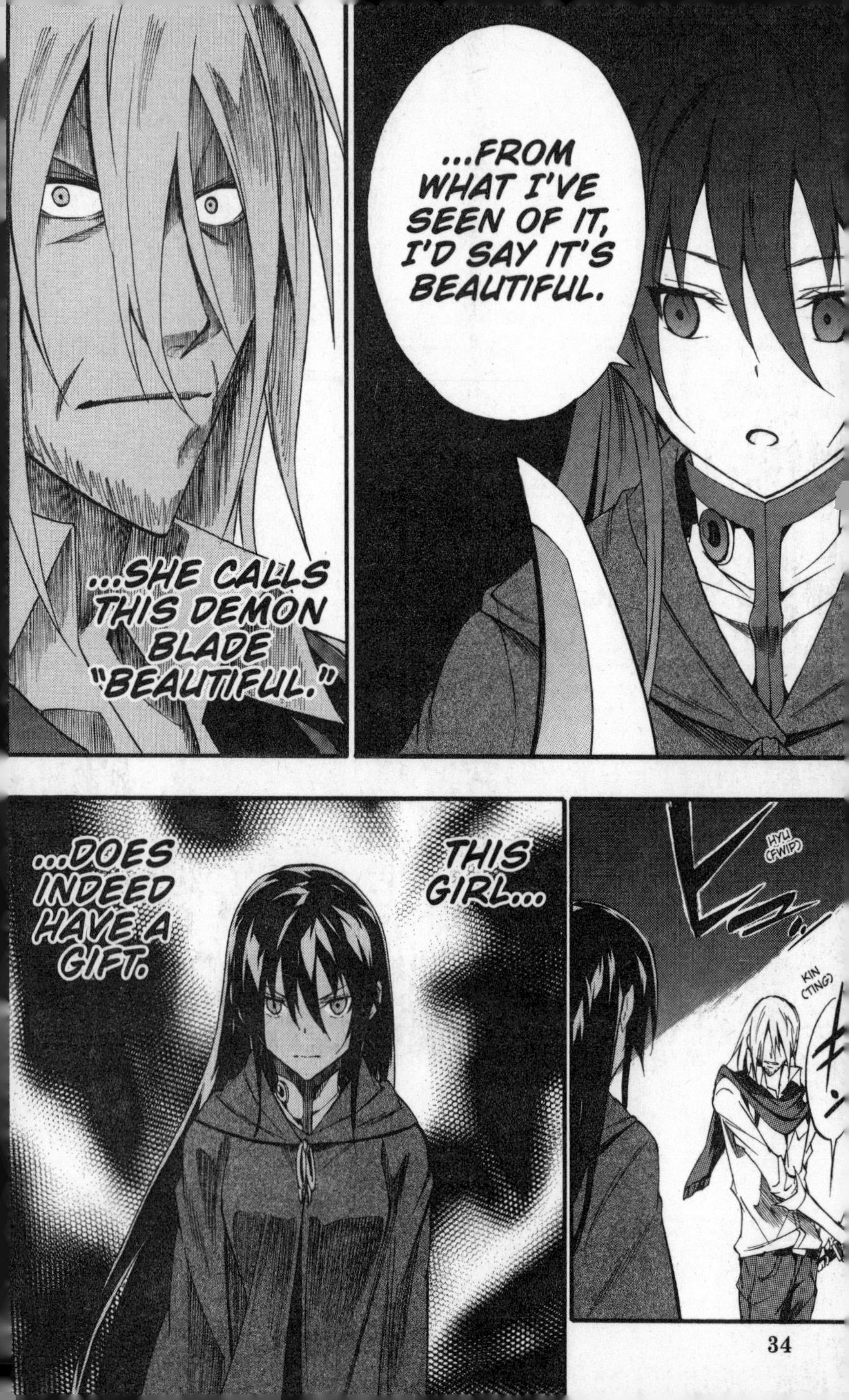
...FROM WHAT I'VE SEEN OF IT, I'D SAY IT'S BEAUTIFUL.
...SHE CALLS THIS DEMON BLADE "BEAUTIFUL."
HYU (FWIP)
KIN (TING)
THIS GIRL...
...DOES INDEED HAVE A GIFT.

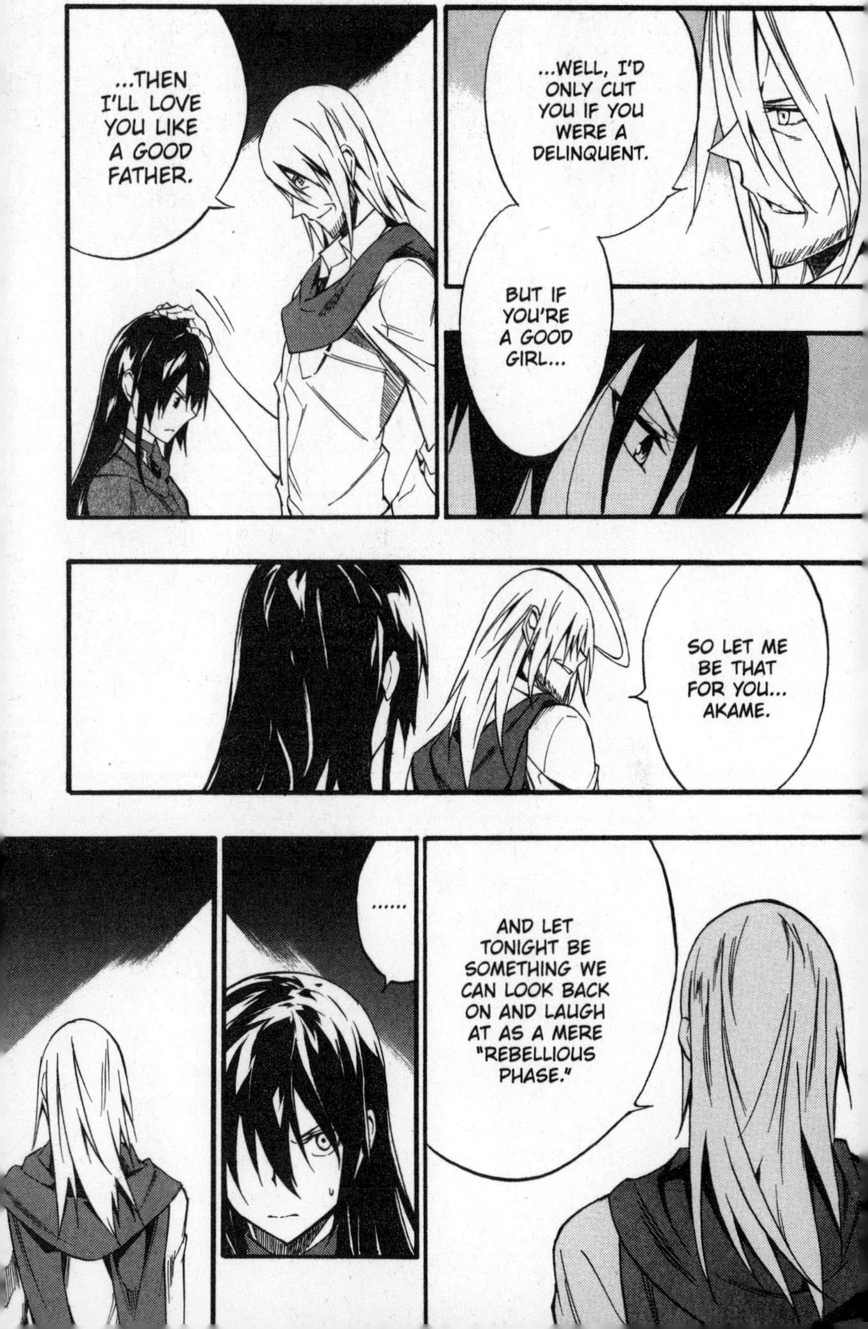
...WELL, I'D ONLY CUT YOU IF YOU WERE A DELINQUENT.
BUT IF YOU'RE A GOOD GIRL...
...THEN I'LL LOVE YOU LIKE A GOOD FATHER.
SO LET ME BE THAT FOR YOU... AKAME.
AND LET TONIGHT BE SOMETHING WE CAN LOOK BACK ON AND LAUGH AT AS A MERE "REBELLIOUS PHASE."
......

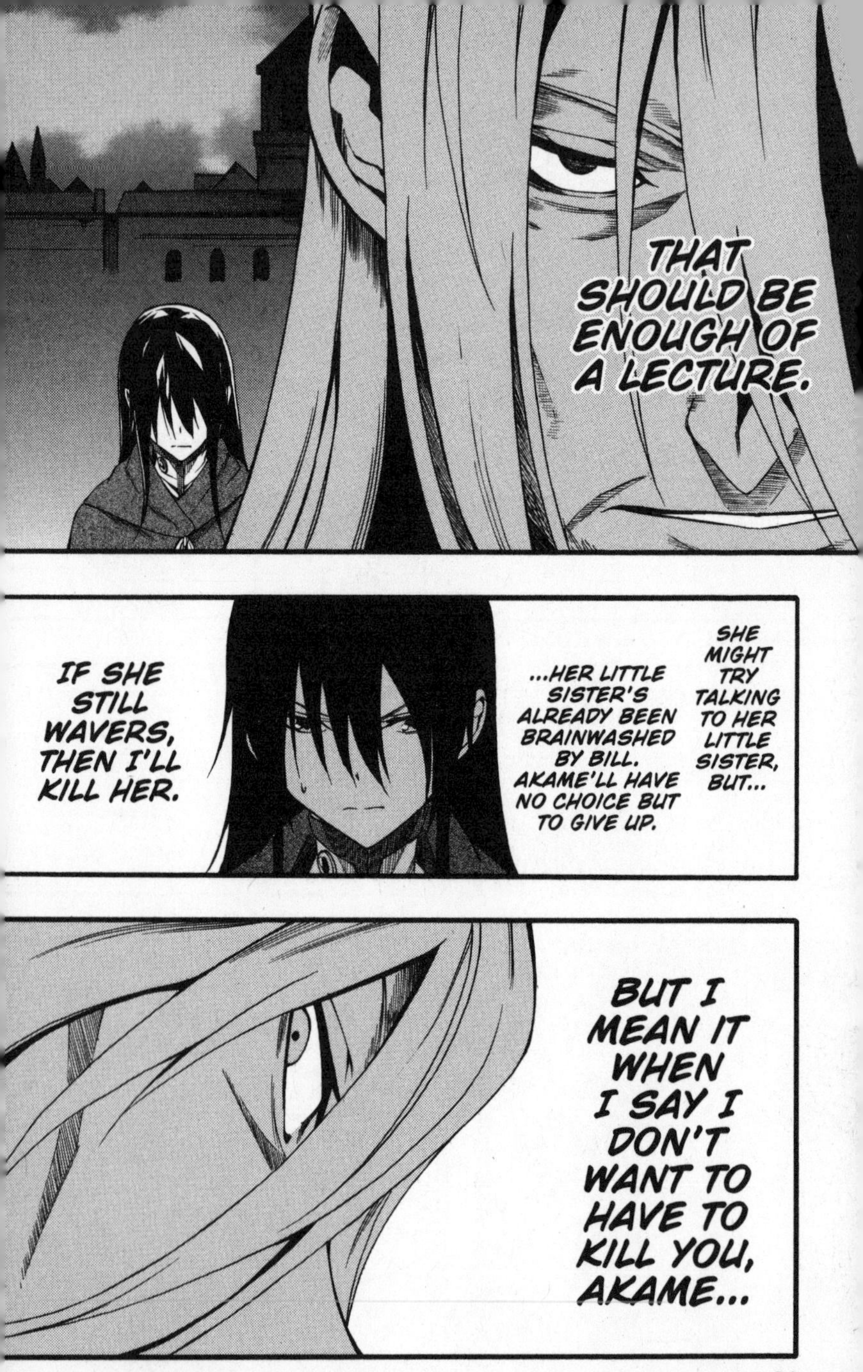
THAT SHOULD BE ENOUGH OF A LECTURE.
SHE MIGHT TRY TALKING TO HER LITTLE SISTER, BUT...
...HER LITTLE SISTER'S ALREADY BEEN BRAINWASHED BY BILL. AKAME'LL HAVE NO CHOICE BUT TO GIVE UP.
IF SHE STILL WAVERS, THEN I'LL KILL HER.
BUT I MEAN IT WHEN I SAY I DON'T WANT TO HAVE TO KILL YOU, AKAME...

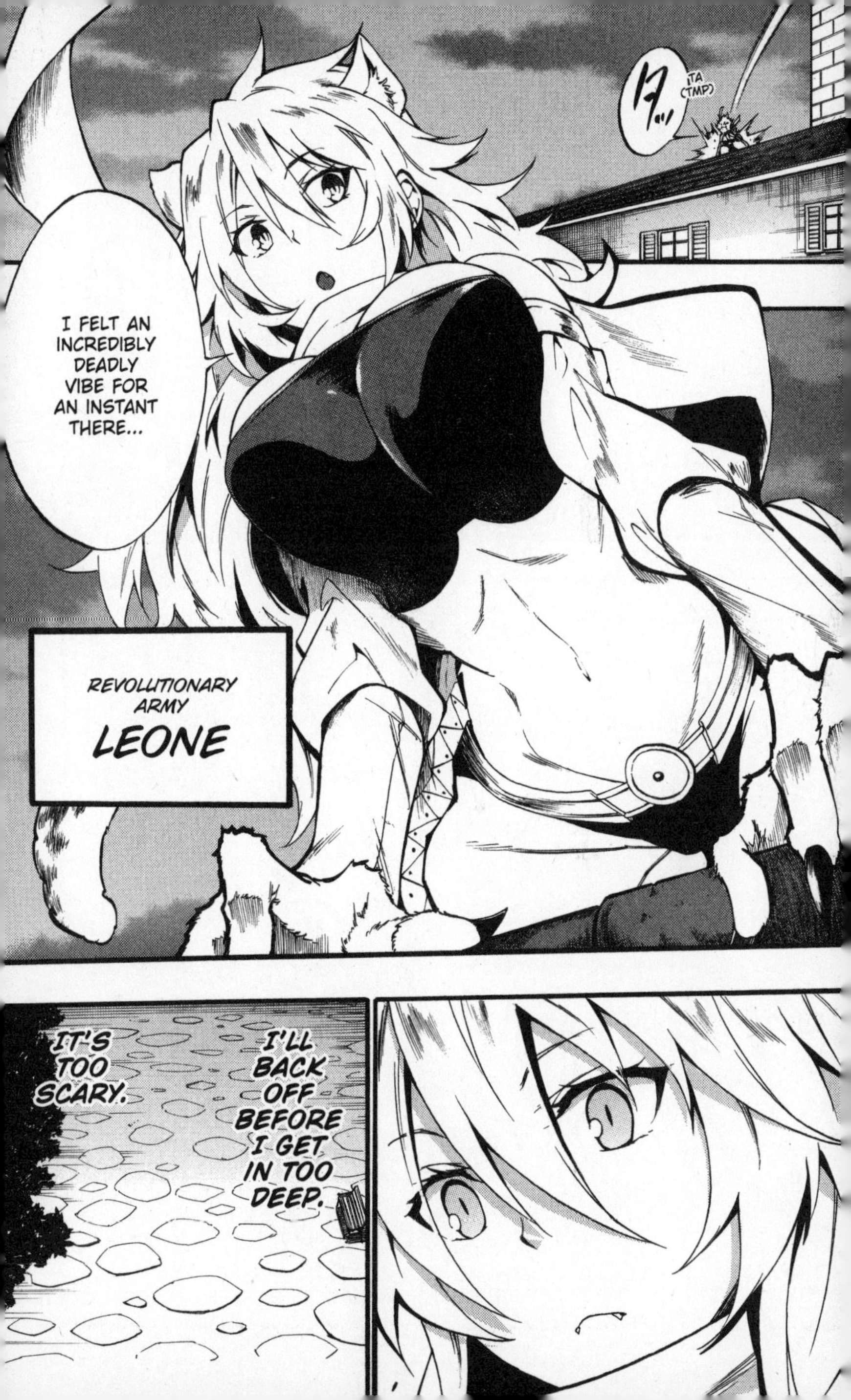
TA (TMP)
I FELT AN INCREDIBLY DEADLY VIBE FOR AN INSTANT THERE...
REVOLUTIONARY ARMY
LEONE
IT'S TOO SCARY.
I'LL BACK OFF BEFORE I GET IN TOO DEEP.

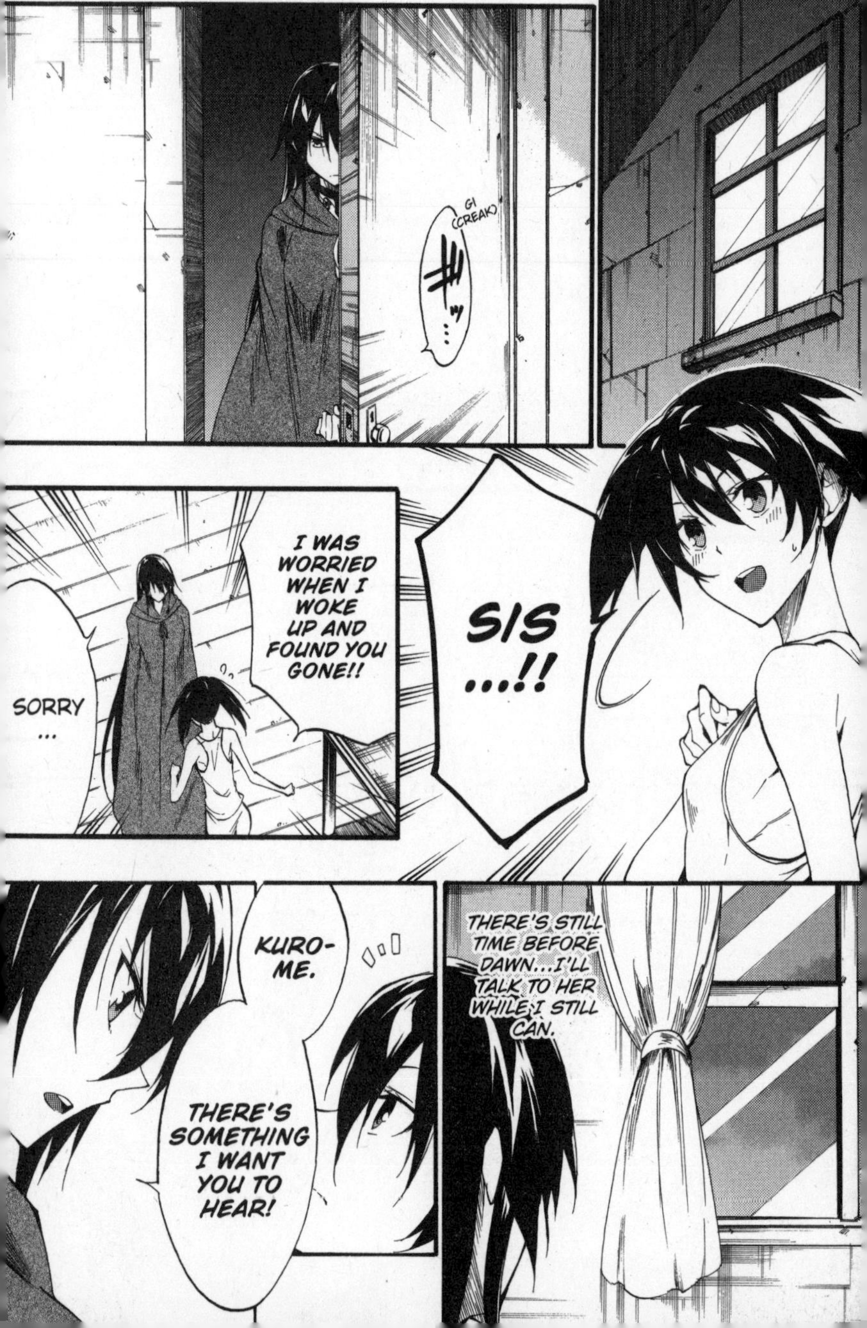
GI (CREAK)
ギッ…
SIS ...!!
I WAS WORRIED WHEN I WOKE UP AND FOUND YOU GONE!!
SORRY ...
THERE'S STILL TIME BEFORE DAWN...I'LL TALK TO HER WHILE I STILL CAN.
KURO-ME.
THERE'S SOMETHING I WANT YOU TO HEAR!

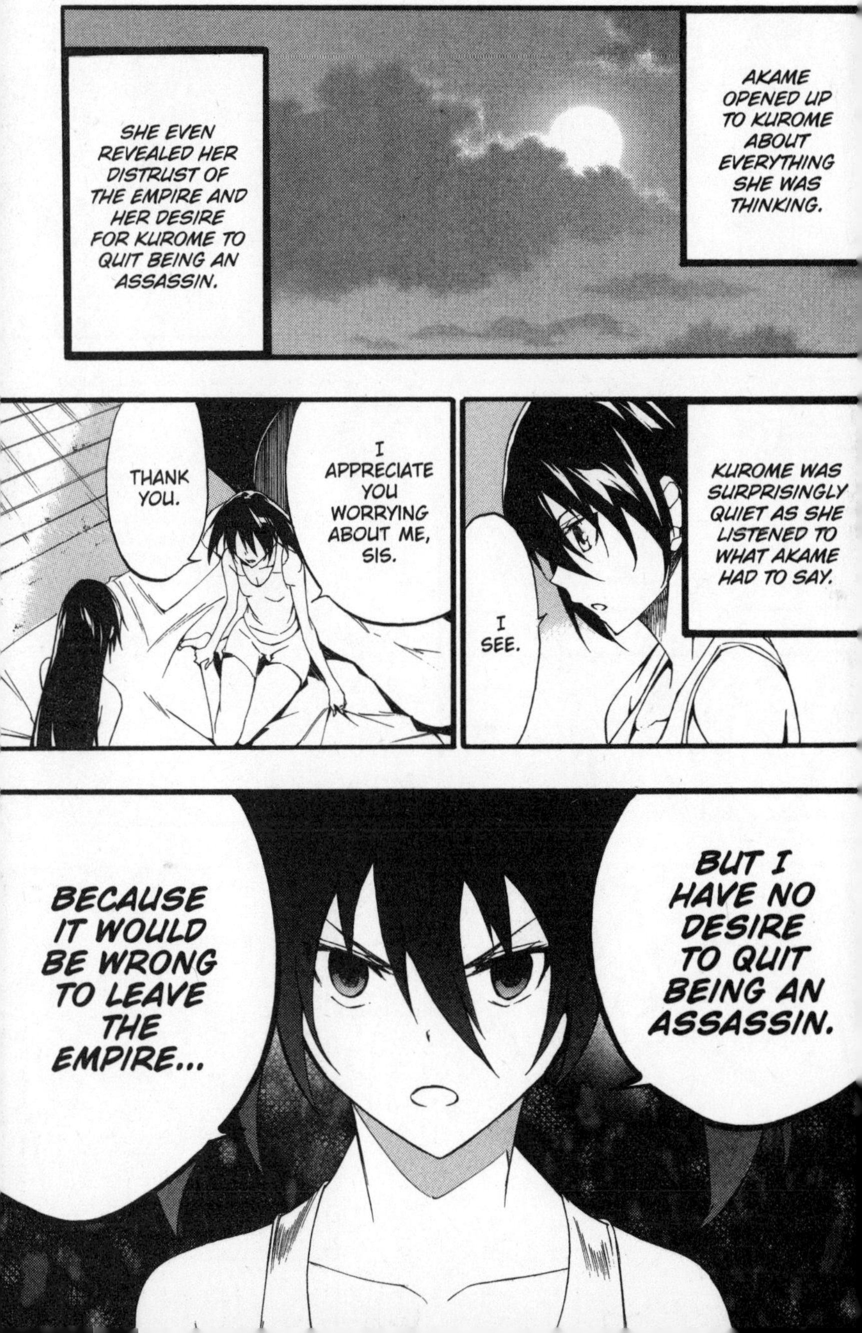
AKAME OPENED UP TO KUROME ABOUT EVERYTHING SHE WAS THINKING.
SHE EVEN REVEALED HER DISTRUST OF THE EMPIRE AND HER DESIRE FOR KUROME TO QUIT BEING AN ASSASSIN.
KUROME WAS SURPRISINGLY QUIET AS SHE LISTENED TO WHAT AKAME HAD TO SAY.
I SEE.
I APPRECIATE YOU WORRYING ABOUT ME, SIS.
THANK YOU.
BUT I HAVE NO DESIRE TO QUIT BEING AN ASSASSIN.
BECAUSE IT WOULD BE WRONG TO LEAVE THE EMPIRE...

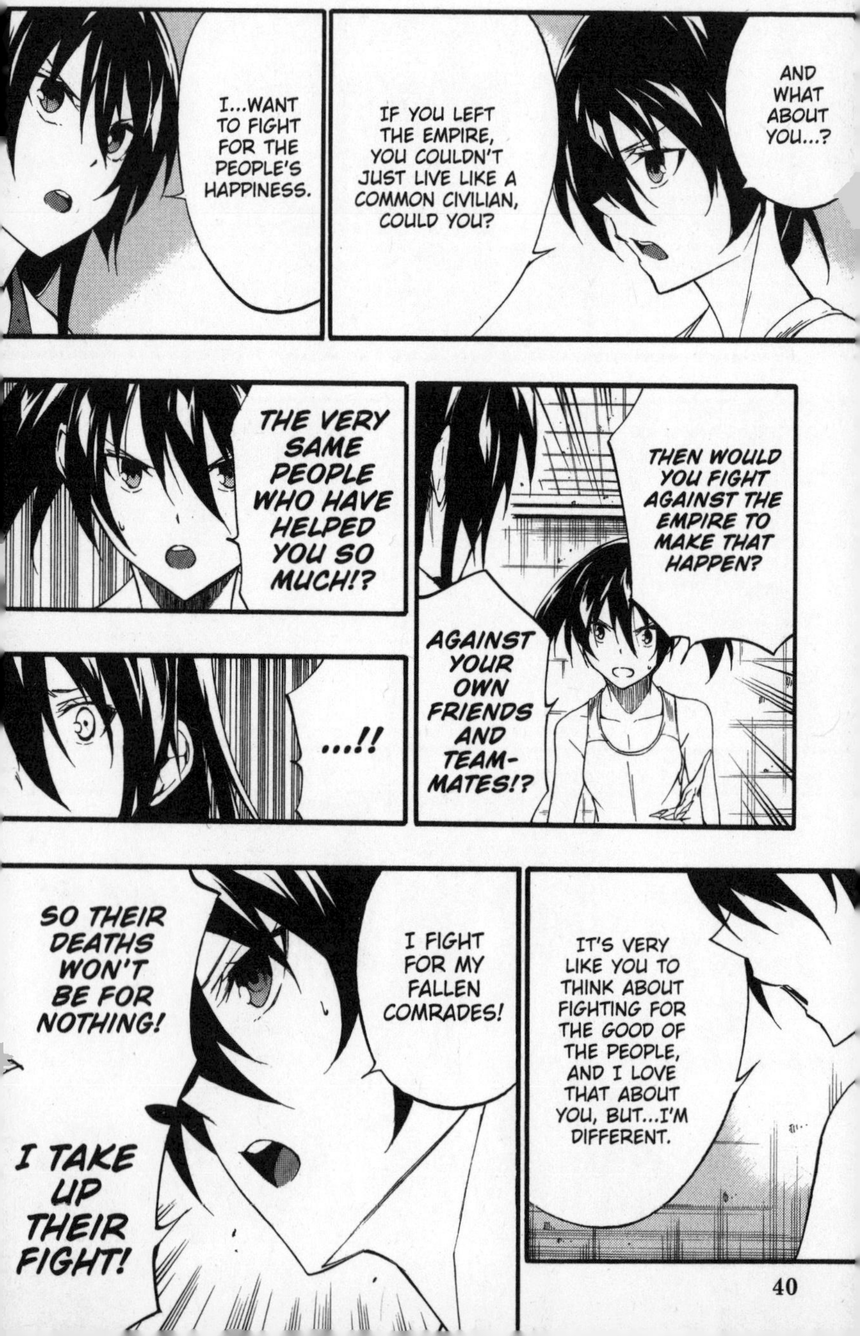
AND WHAT ABOUT YOU...?
IF YOU LEFT THE EMPIRE, YOU COULDN'T JUST LIVE LIKE A COMMON CIVILIAN, COULD YOU?
I...WANT TO FIGHT FOR THE PEOPLE'S HAPPINESS.
THEN WOULD YOU FIGHT AGAINST THE EMPIRE TO MAKE THAT HAPPEN?
AGAINST YOUR OWN FRIENDS AND TEAM-MATES!?
THE VERY SAME PEOPLE WHO HAVE HELPED YOU SO MUCH!?
...!!
IT'S VERY LIKE YOU TO THINK ABOUT FIGHTING FOR THE GOOD OF THE PEOPLE, AND I LOVE THAT ABOUT YOU, BUT...I'M DIFFERENT.
I FIGHT FOR MY FALLEN COMRADES!
SO THEIR DEATHS WON'T BE FOR NOTHING!
I TAKE UP THEIR FIGHT!

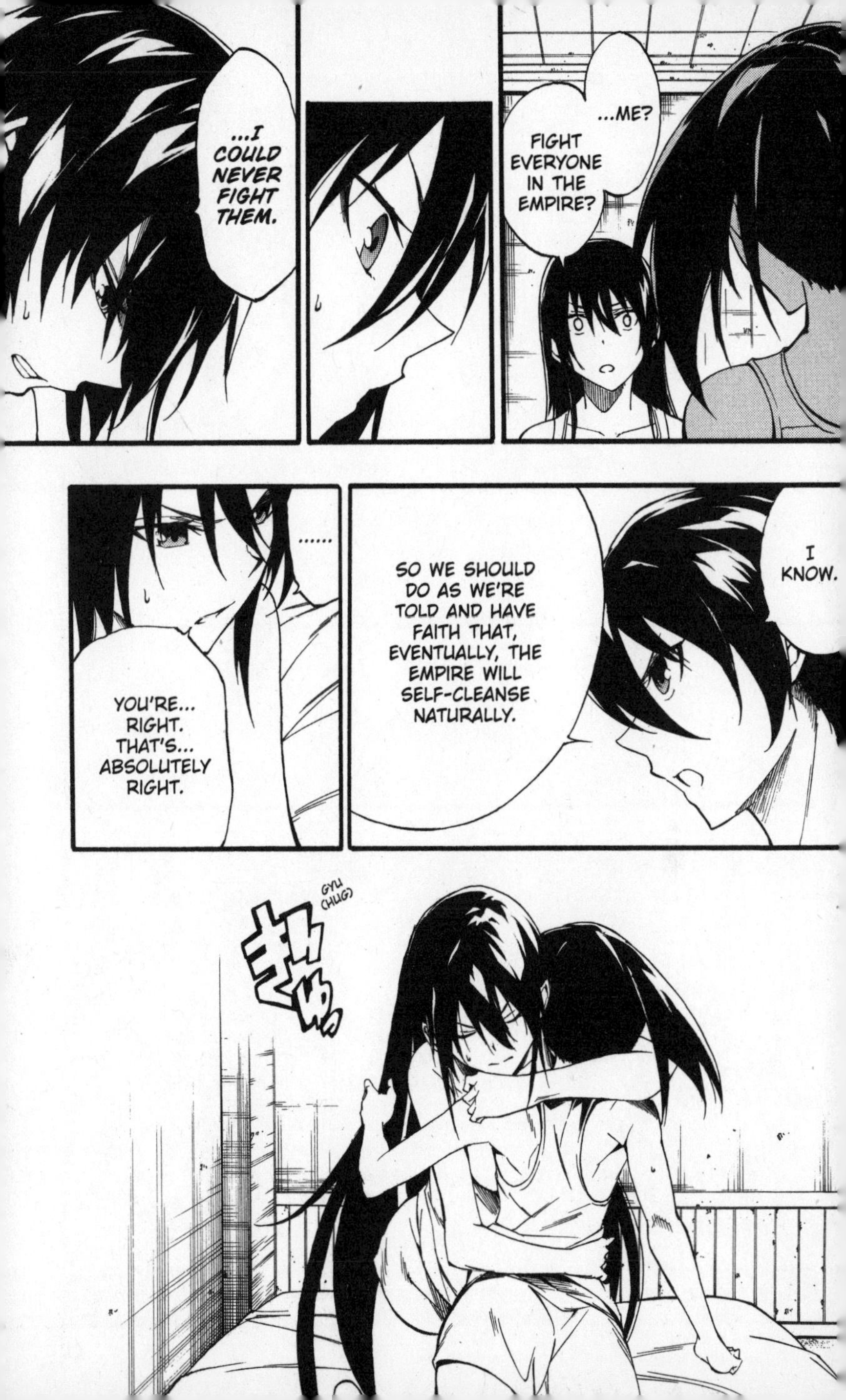
...ME?
FIGHT EVERYONE IN THE EMPIRE?
...I COULD NEVER FIGHT THEM.
I KNOW.
SO WE SHOULD DO AS WE'RE TOLD AND HAVE FAITH THAT, EVENTUALLY, THE EMPIRE WILL SELF-CLEANSE NATURALLY.
......
YOU'RE... RIGHT. THAT'S... ABSOLUTELY RIGHT.
GYU (HUG)

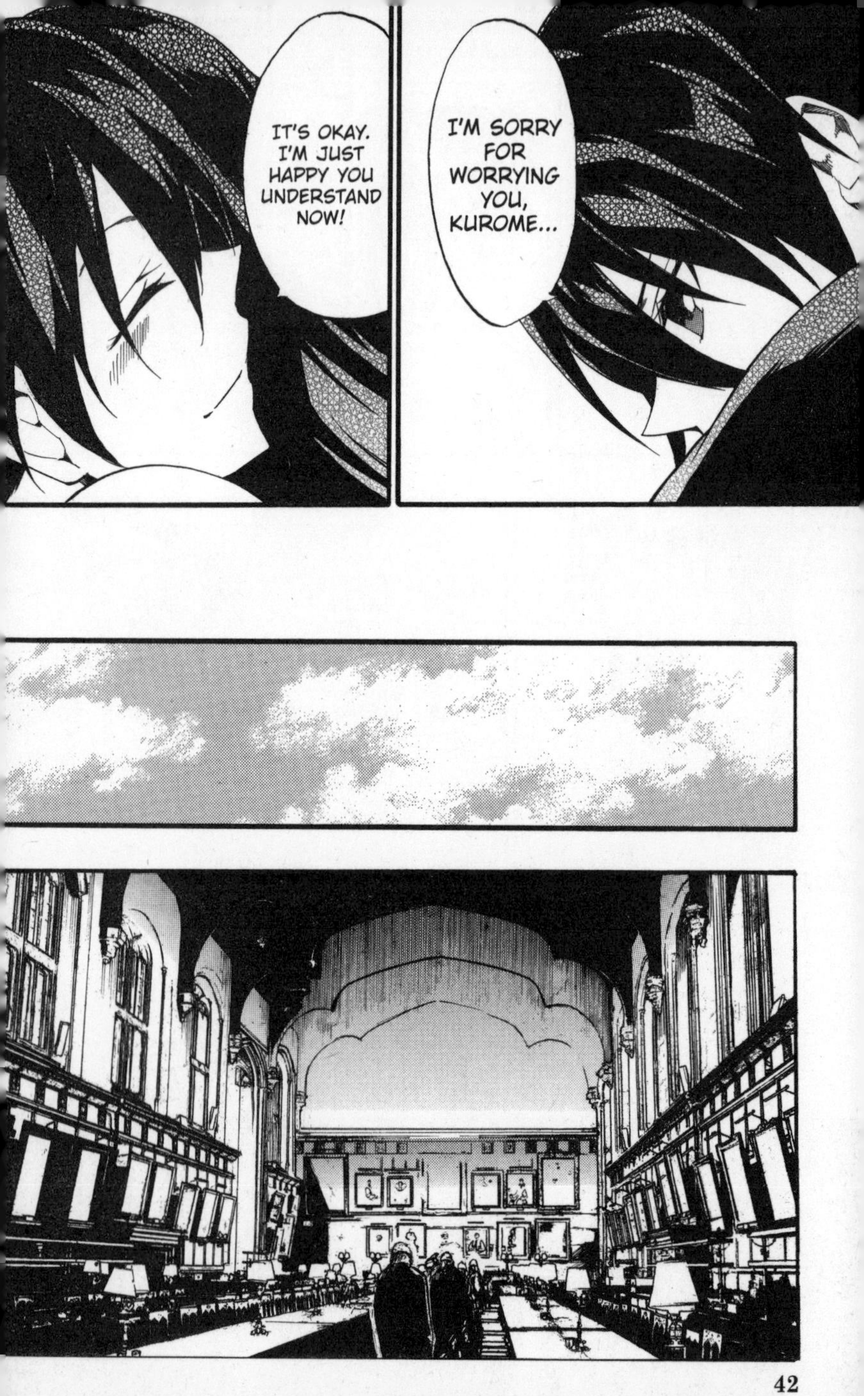
I'M SORRY FOR WORRYING YOU, KUROME...
IT'S OKAY. I'M JUST HAPPY YOU UNDERSTAND NOW!

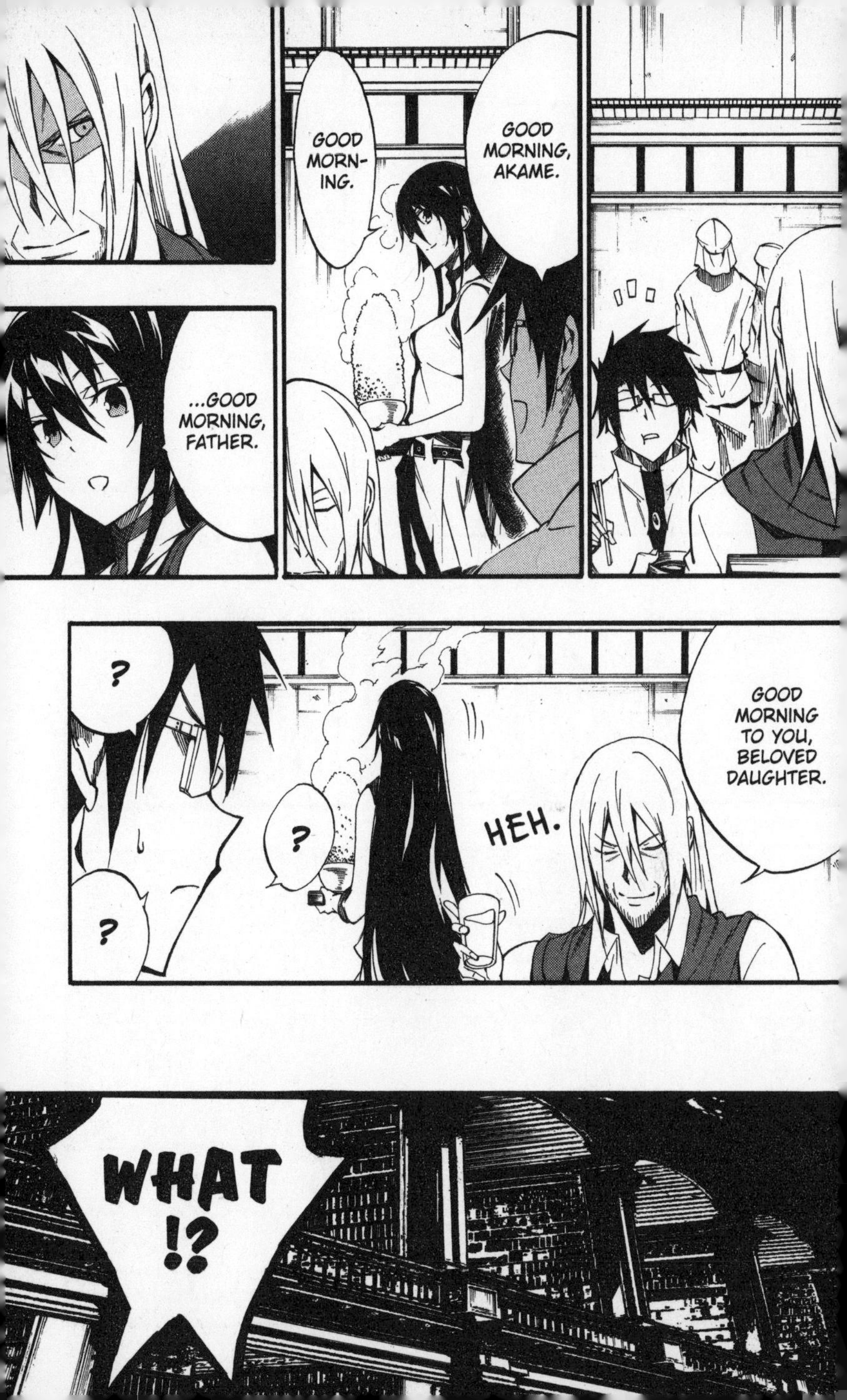
GOOD MORNING, AKAME.
GOOD MORN-ING.
...GOOD MORNING, FATHER.
GOOD MORNING TO YOU, BELOVED DAUGHTER.
HEH.
?
?
?
WHAT!?

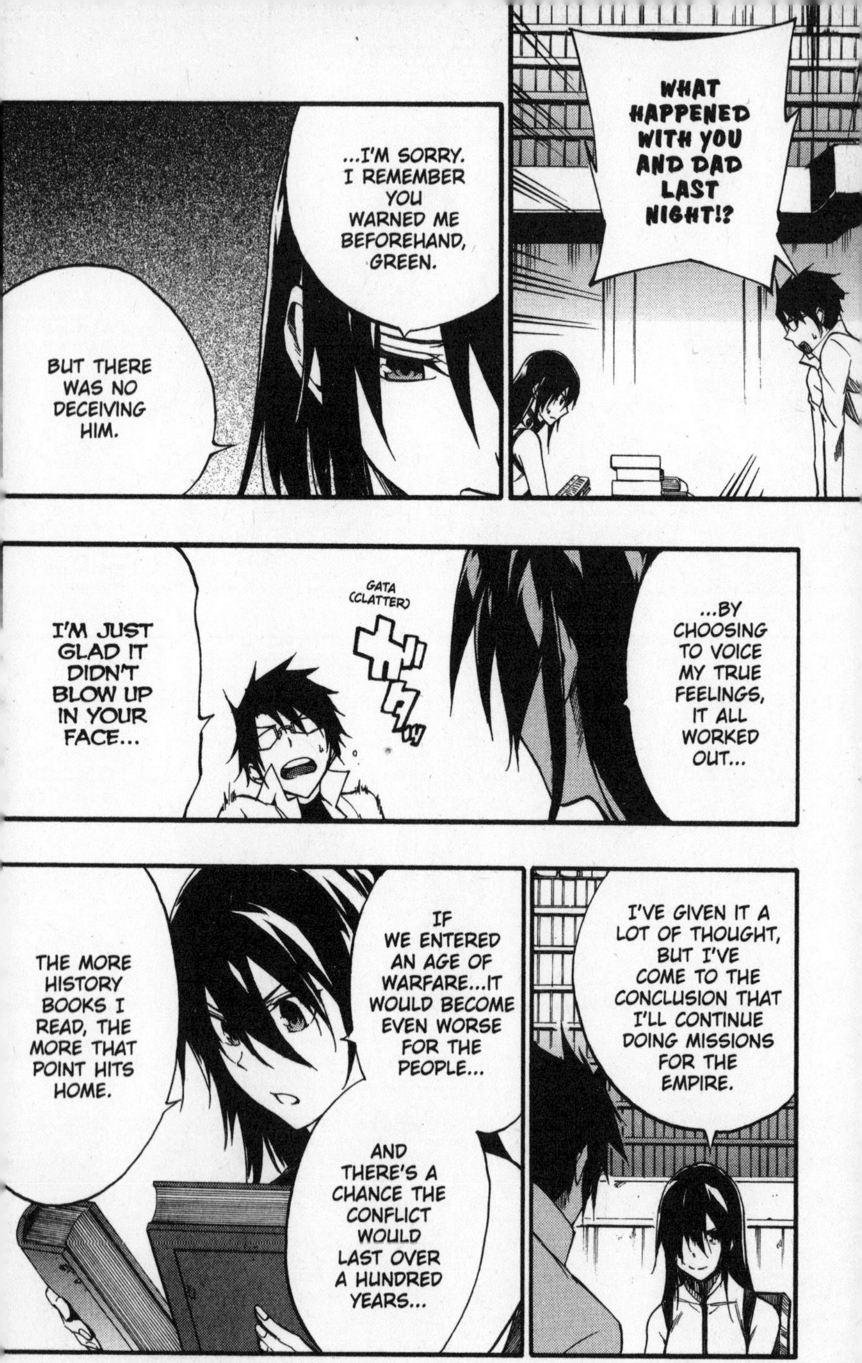
WHAT HAPPENED WITH YOU AND DAD LAST NIGHT!?
...I'M SORRY. I REMEMBER YOU WARNED ME BEFOREHAND, GREEN.
BUT THERE WAS NO DECEIVING HIM.
...BY CHOOSING TO VOICE MY TRUE FEELINGS, IT ALL WORKED OUT...
GATA (CLATTER)
I'M JUST GLAD IT DIDN'T BLOW UP IN YOUR FACE...
I'VE GIVEN IT A LOT OF THOUGHT, BUT I'VE COME TO THE CONCLUSION THAT I'LL CONTINUE DOING MISSIONS FOR THE EMPIRE.
IF WE ENTERED AN AGE OF WARFARE...IT WOULD BECOME EVEN WORSE FOR THE PEOPLE...
AND THERE'S A CHANCE THE CONFLICT WOULD LAST OVER A HUNDRED YEARS...
THE MORE HISTORY BOOKS I READ, THE MORE THAT POINT HITS HOME.

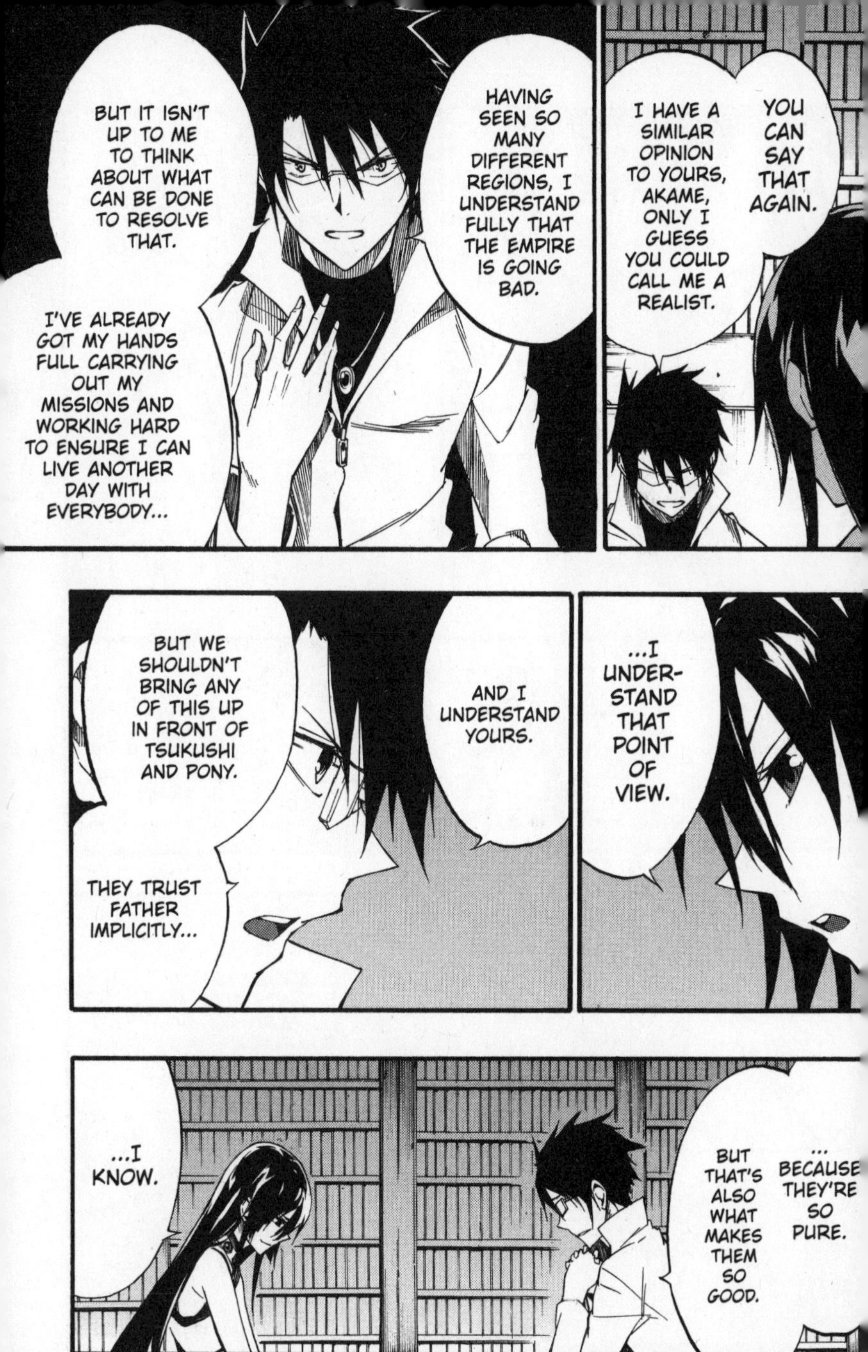
YOU CAN SAY THAT AGAIN.
I HAVE A SIMILAR OPINION TO YOURS, AKAME, ONLY I GUESS YOU COULD CALL ME A REALIST.
HAVING SEEN SO MANY DIFFERENT REGIONS, I UNDERSTAND FULLY THAT THE EMPIRE IS GOING BAD.
BUT IT ISN'T UP TO ME TO THINK ABOUT WHAT CAN BE DONE TO RESOLVE THAT.
I'VE ALREADY GOT MY HANDS FULL CARRYING OUT MY MISSIONS AND WORKING HARD TO ENSURE I CAN LIVE ANOTHER DAY WITH EVERYBODY...
...I UNDER-STAND THAT POINT OF VIEW.
AND I UNDERSTAND YOURS.
BUT WE SHOULDN'T BRING ANY OF THIS UP IN FRONT OF TSUKUSHI AND PONY.
THEY TRUST FATHER IMPLICITLY...
...BECAUSE THEY'RE SO PURE.
BUT THAT'S ALSO WHAT MAKES THEM SO GOOD.
...I KNOW.

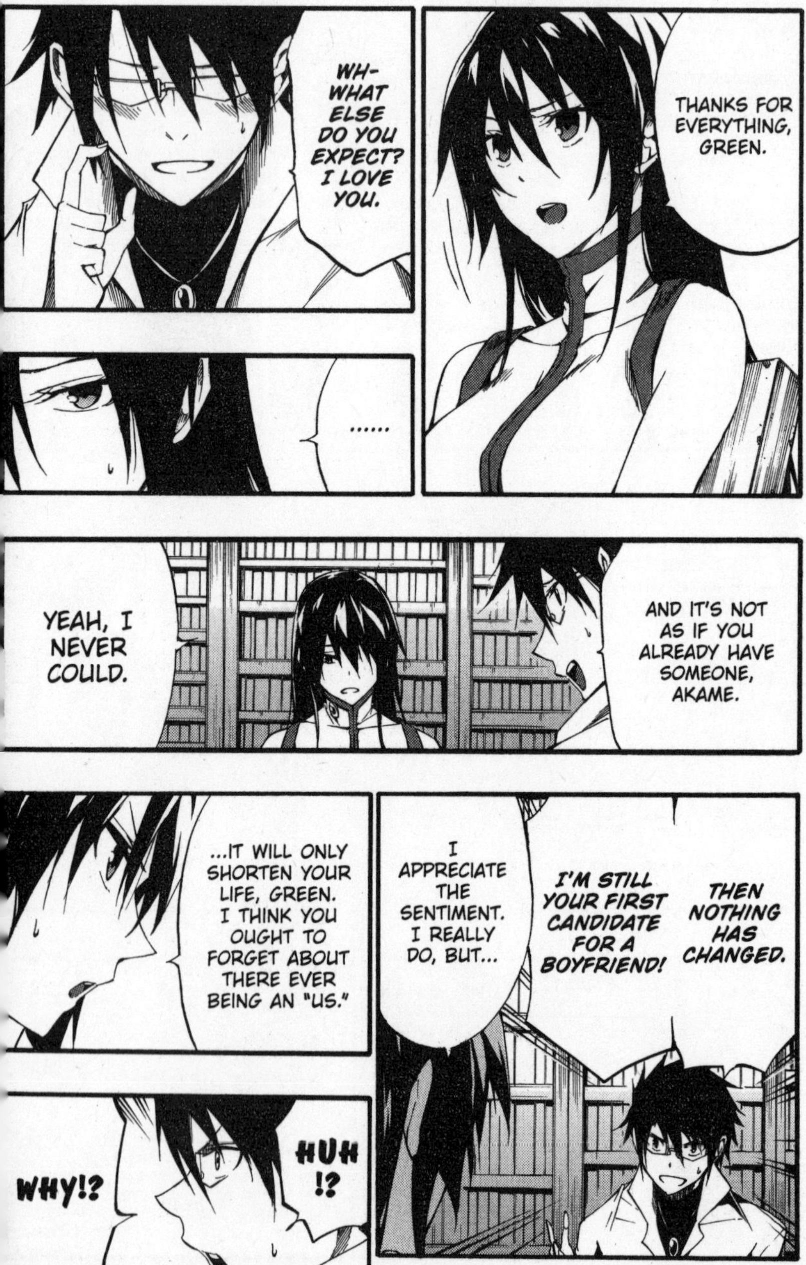
THANKS FOR EVERYTHING, GREEN.
WH- WHAT ELSE DO YOU EXPECT? I LOVE YOU.
......
AND IT'S NOT AS IF YOU ALREADY HAVE SOMEONE, AKAME.
YEAH, I NEVER COULD.
THEN NOTHING HAS CHANGED.
I'M STILL YOUR FIRST CANDIDATE FOR A BOYFRIEND!
I APPRECIATE THE SENTIMENT. I REALLY DO, BUT...
...IT WILL ONLY SHORTEN YOUR LIFE, GREEN. I THINK YOU OUGHT TO FORGET ABOUT THERE EVER BEING AN "US."
HUH!?
WHY!?

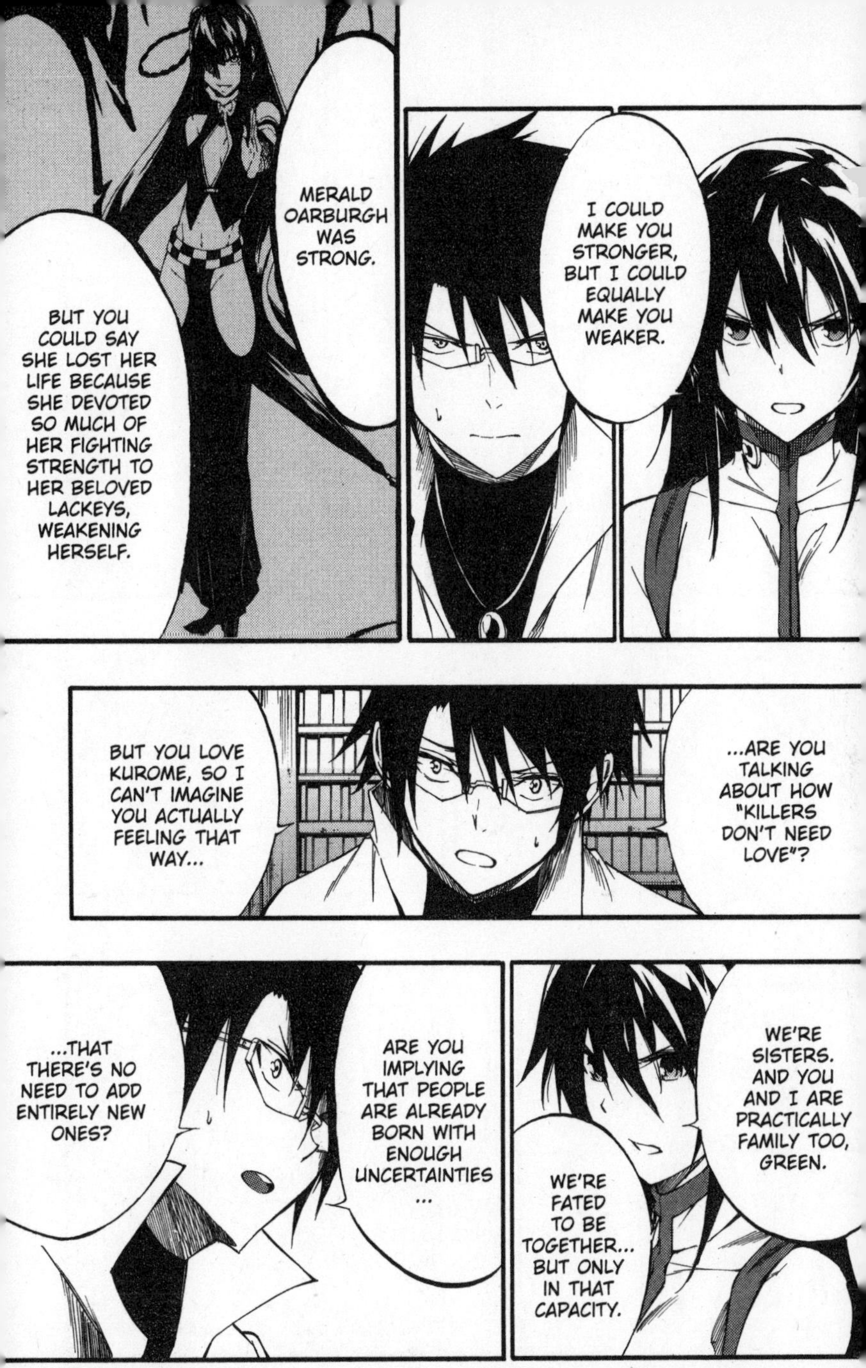
MERALD OARBURGH WAS STRONG.
BUT YOU COULD SAY SHE LOST HER LIFE BECAUSE SHE DEVOTED SO MUCH OF HER FIGHTING STRENGTH TO HER BELOVED LACKEYS, WEAKENING HERSELF.
I COULD MAKE YOU STRONGER, BUT I COULD EQUALLY MAKE YOU WEAKER.
...ARE YOU TALKING ABOUT HOW "KILLERS DON'T NEED LOVE"?
BUT YOU LOVE KUROME, SO I CAN'T IMAGINE YOU ACTUALLY FEELING THAT WAY...
WE'RE SISTERS. AND YOU AND I ARE PRACTICALLY FAMILY TOO, GREEN.
WE'RE FATED TO BE TOGETHER... BUT ONLY IN THAT CAPACITY.
ARE YOU IMPLYING THAT PEOPLE ARE ALREADY BORN WITH ENOUGH UNCERTAINTIES ...
...THAT THERE'S NO NEED TO ADD ENTIRELY NEW ONES?

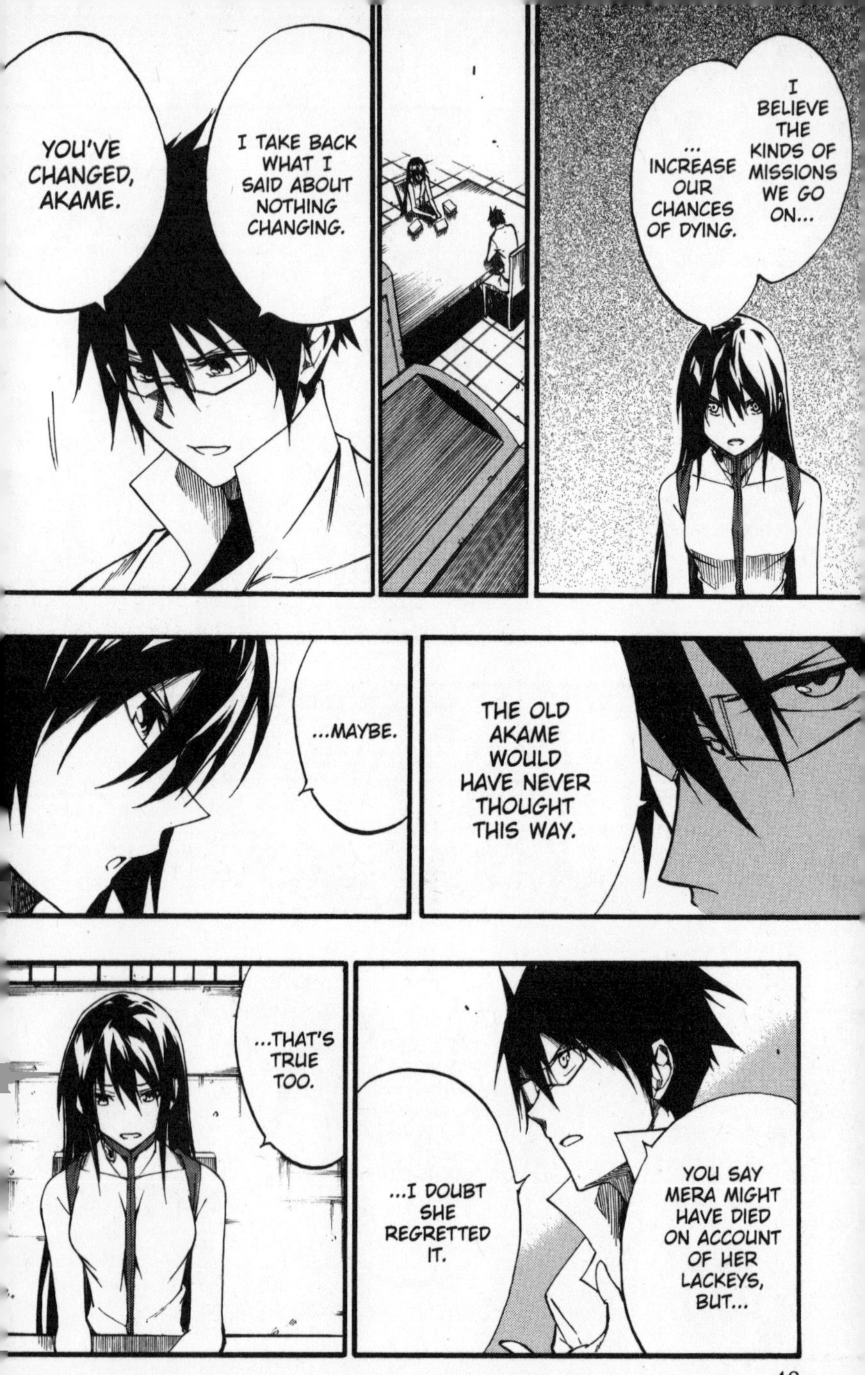
I BELIEVE THE KINDS OF MISSIONS WE GO ON...
...INCREASE OUR CHANCES OF DYING.
I TAKE BACK WHAT I SAID ABOUT NOTHING CHANGING.
YOU'VE CHANGED, AKAME.
THE OLD AKAME WOULD HAVE NEVER THOUGHT THIS WAY.
...MAYBE.
YOU SAY MERA MIGHT HAVE DIED ON ACCOUNT OF HER LACKEYS, BUT...
...I DOUBT SHE REGRETTED IT.
...THAT'S TRUE TOO.

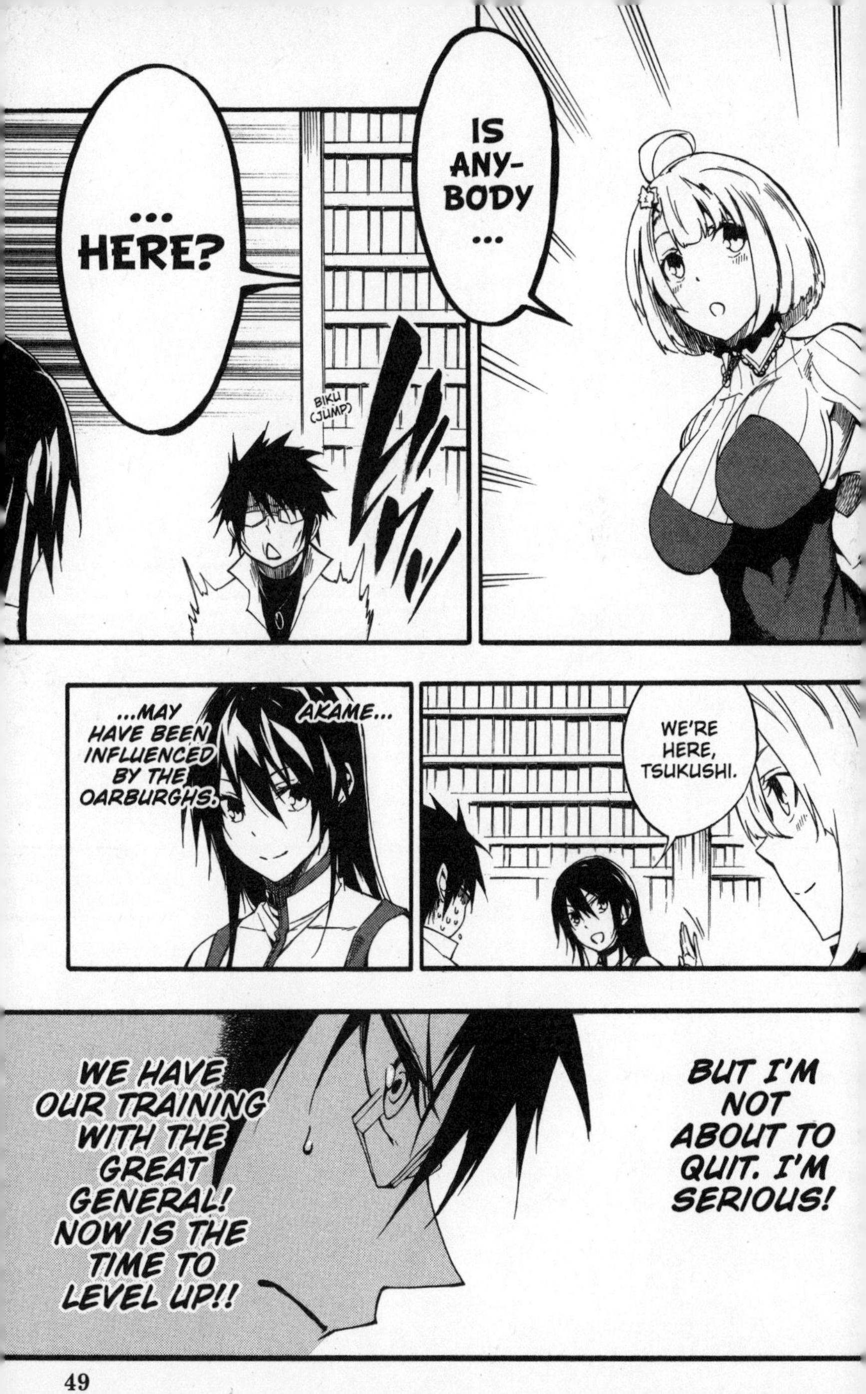
IS ANY-BODY ...
... HERE?
BIKU (JUMP)
WE'RE HERE, TSUKUSHI.
AKAME...
...MAY HAVE BEEN INFLUENCED BY THE OARBURGHS.
BUT I'M NOT ABOUT TO QUIT. I'M SERIOUS!
WE HAVE OUR TRAINING WITH THE GREAT GENERAL! NOW IS THE TIME TO LEVEL UP!!

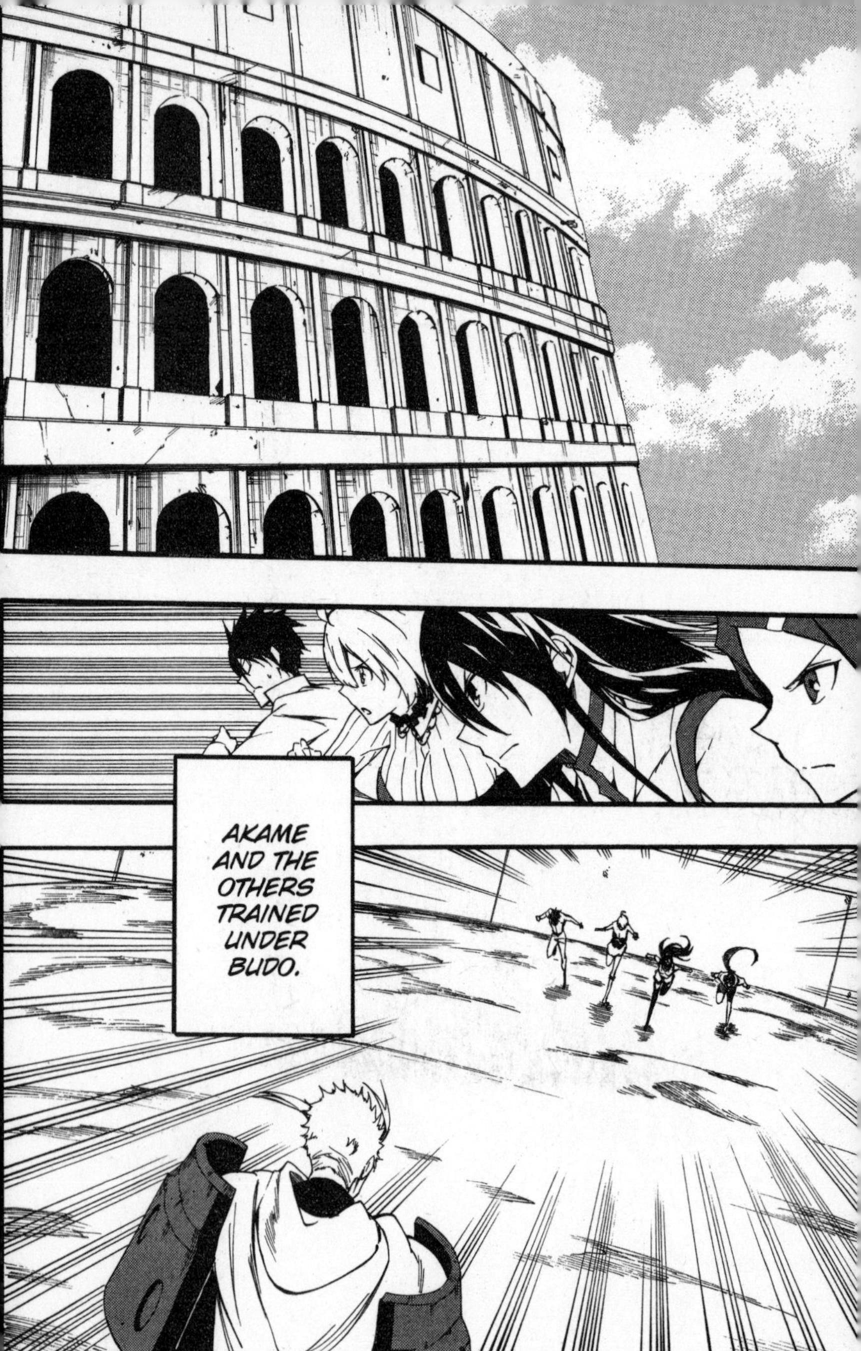
AKAME AND THE OTHERS TRAINED UNDER BUDO.

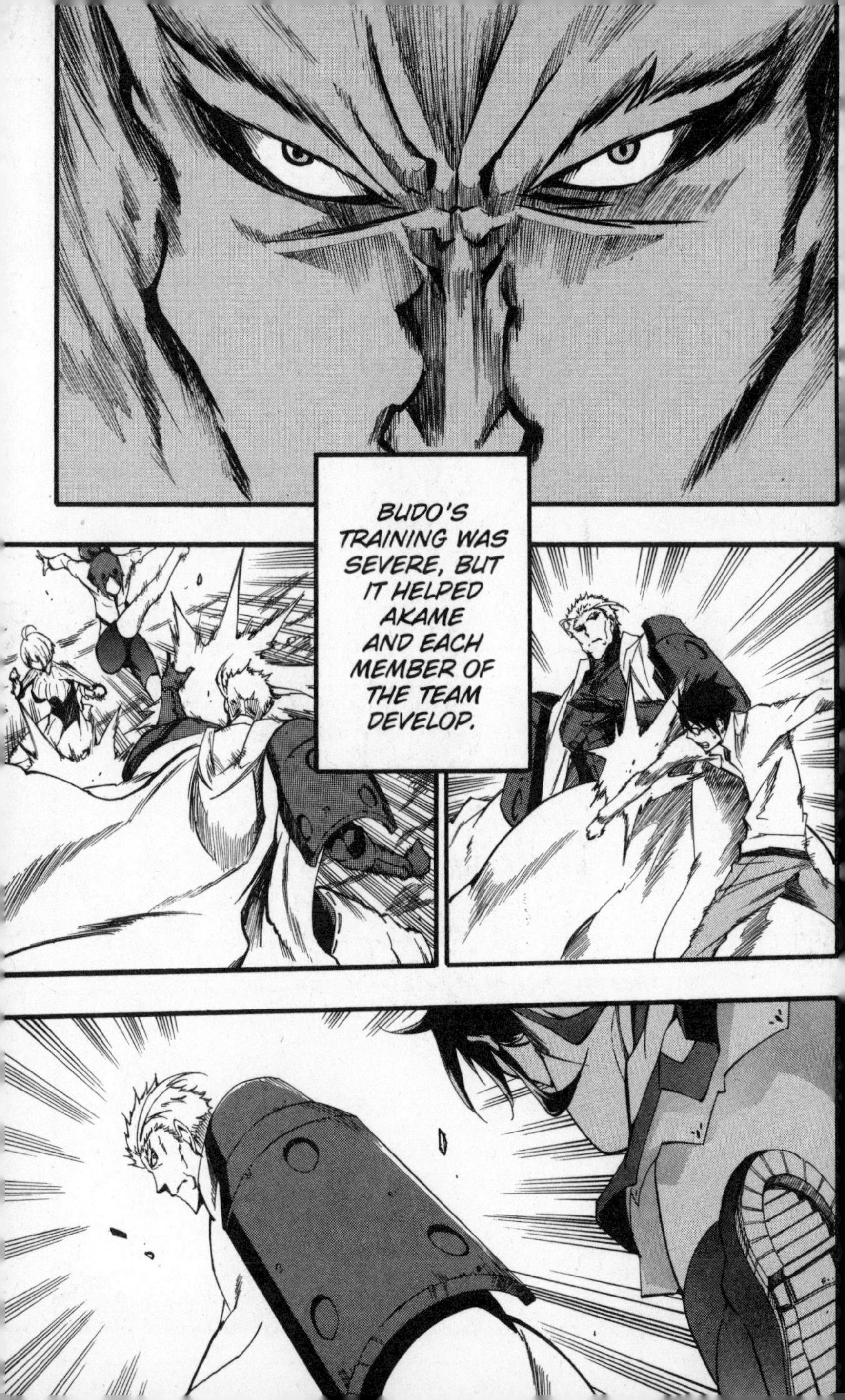
BUDO'S TRAINING WAS SEVERE, BUT IT HELPED AKAME AND EACH MEMBER OF THE TEAM DEVELOP.

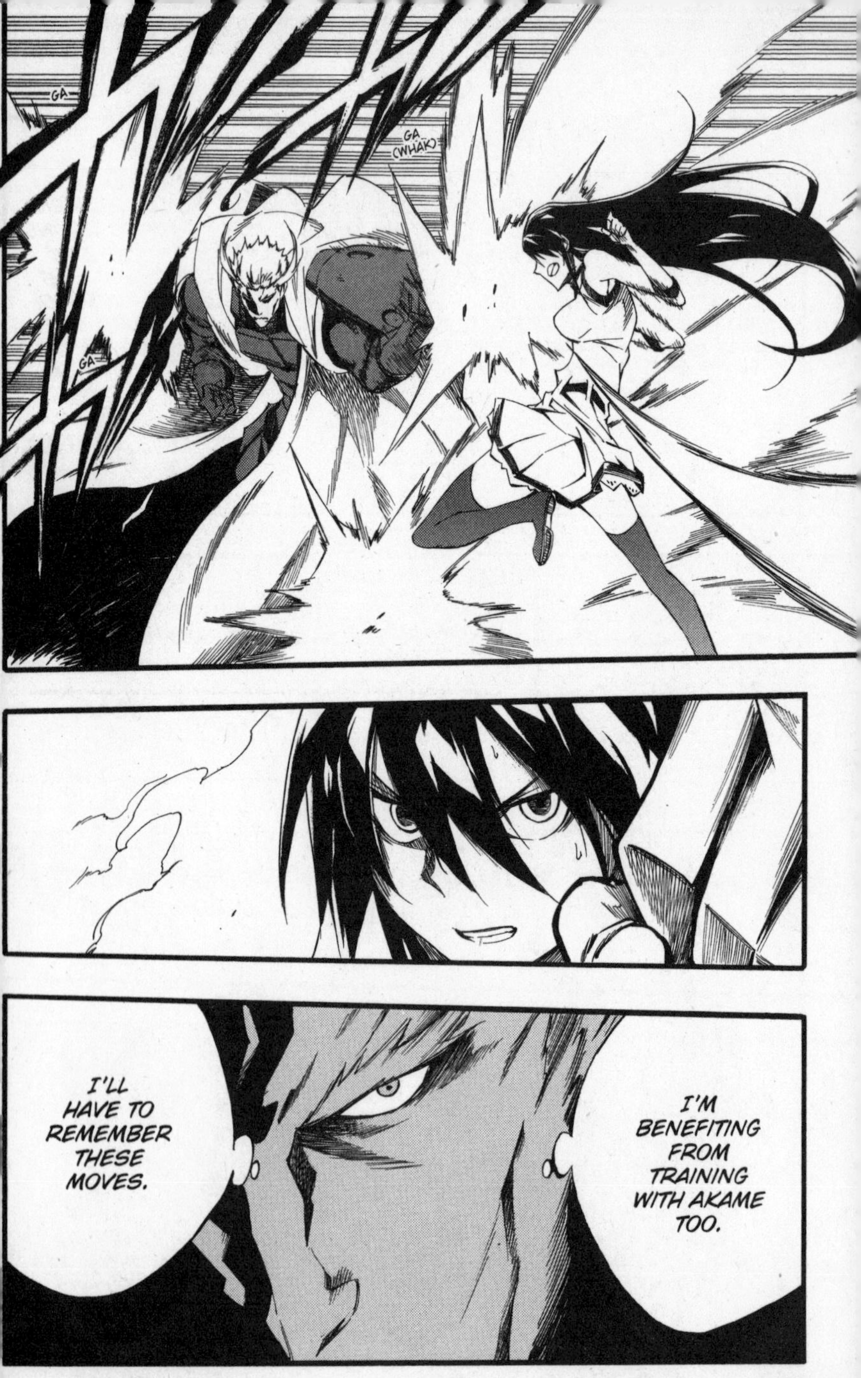
GA
(WHAK)
GA
GA
I'M BENEFITING FROM TRAINING WITH AKAME TOO.
I'LL HAVE TO REMEMBER THESE MOVES.

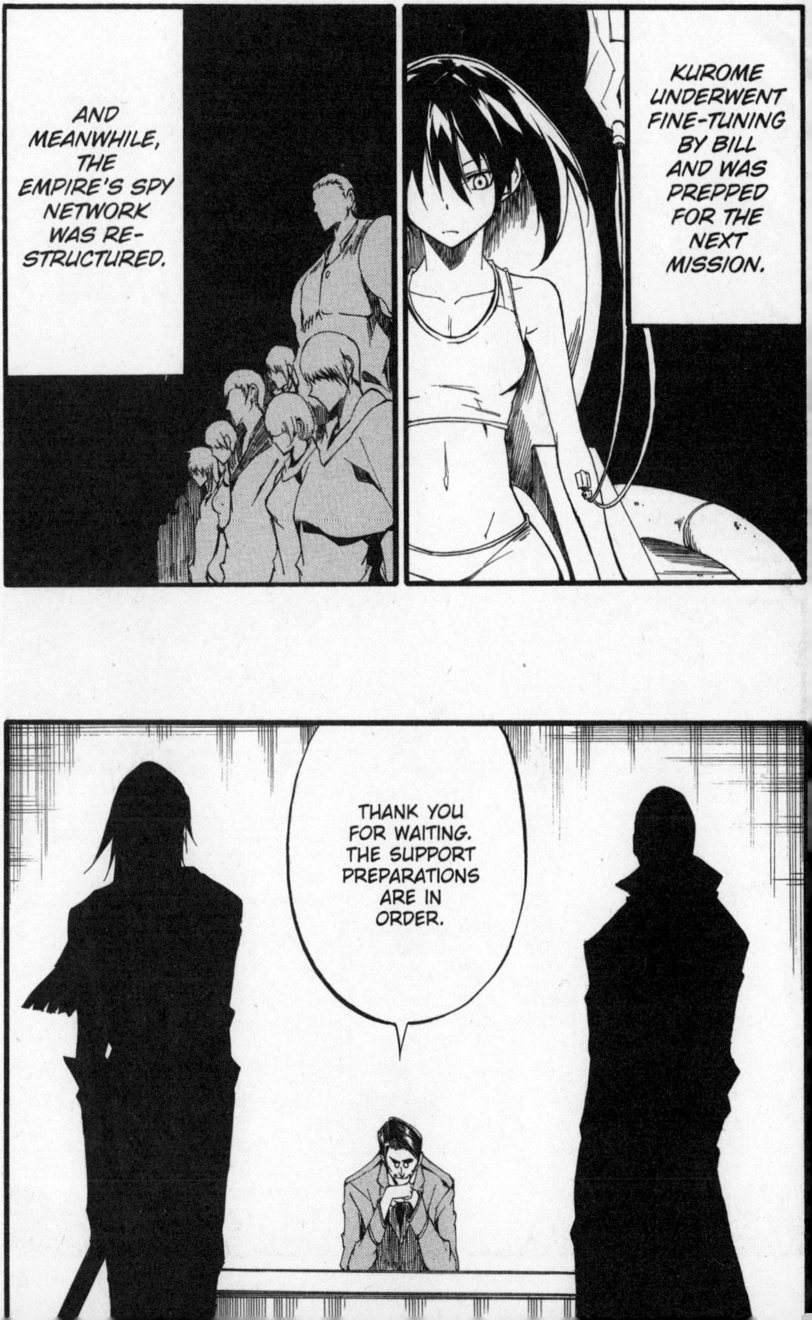
KUROME UNDERWENT FINE-TUNING BY BILL AND WAS PREPPED FOR THE NEXT MISSION.
AND MEANWHILE, THE EMPIRE'S SPY NETWORK WAS RE-STRUCTURED.
THANK YOU FOR WAITING. THE SUPPORT PREPARATIONS ARE IN ORDER.

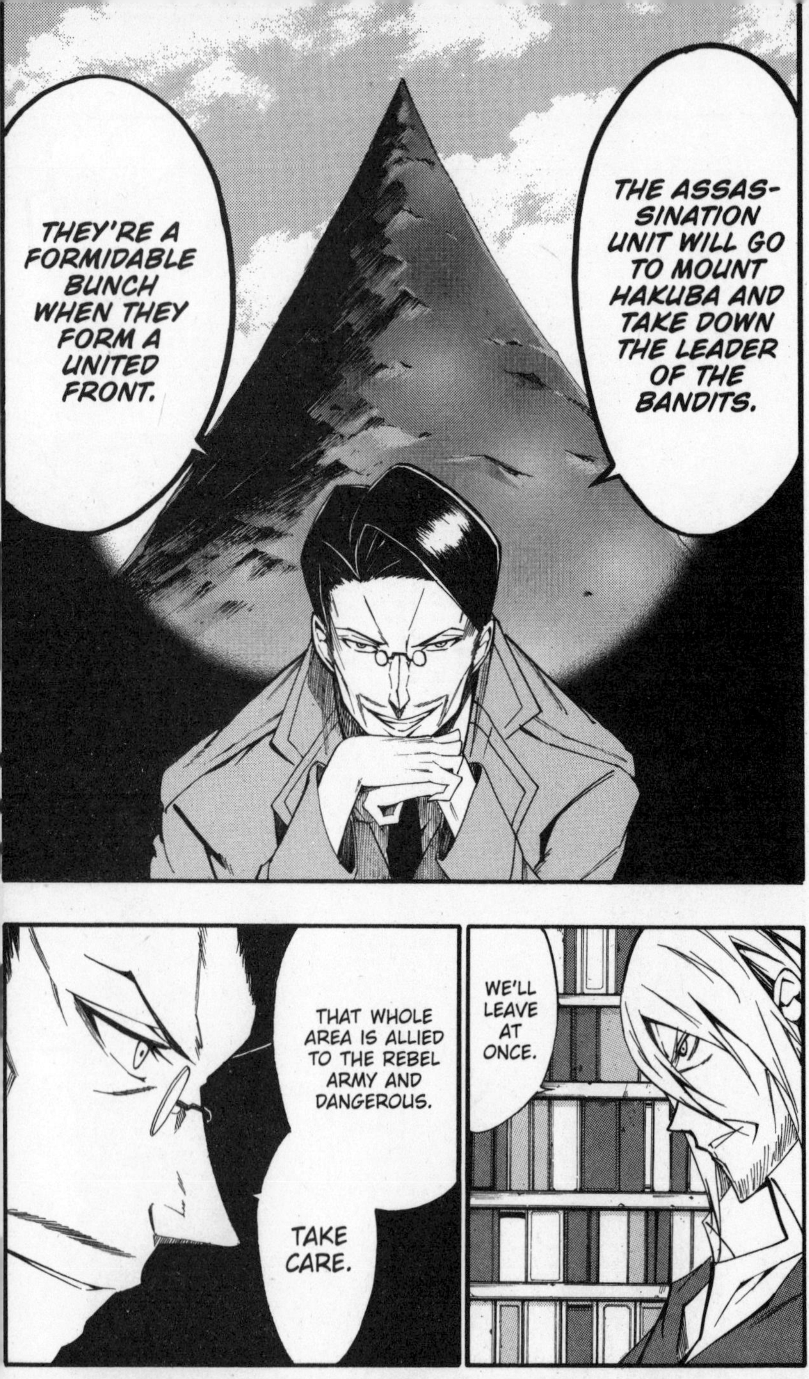
THE ASSASSINATION UNIT WILL GO TO MOUNT HAKUBA AND TAKE DOWN THE LEADER OF THE BANDITS.
THEY'RE A FORMIDABLE BUNCH WHEN THEY FORM A UNITED FRONT.
WE'LL LEAVE AT ONCE.
THAT WHOLE AREA IS ALLIED TO THE REBEL ARMY AND DANGEROUS.
TAKE CARE.

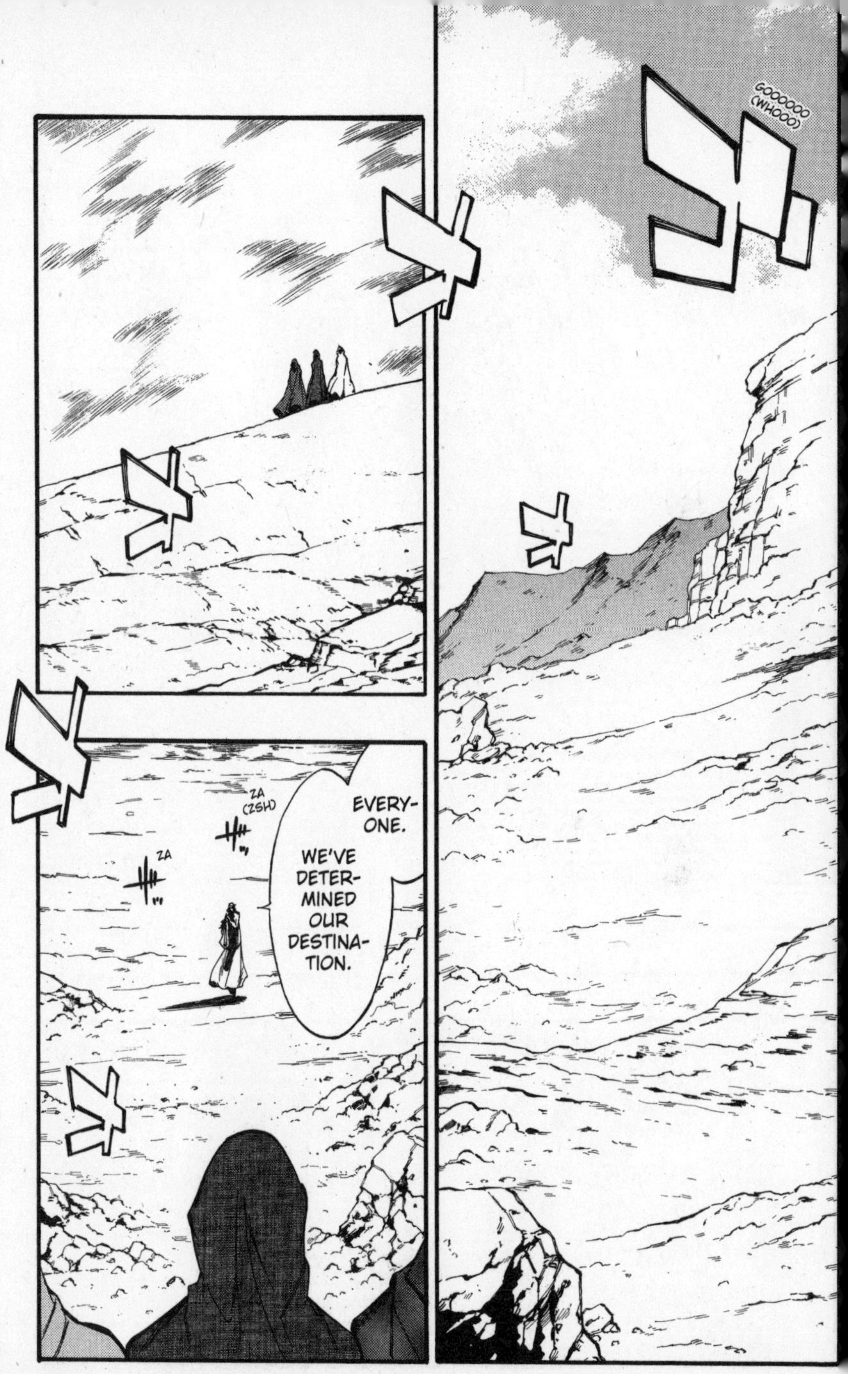
GOOOOOO
(WHOOO)
ZA
(ZSH)
ZA
EVERY-ONE.
WE'VE DETER-MINED OUR DESTINA-TION.

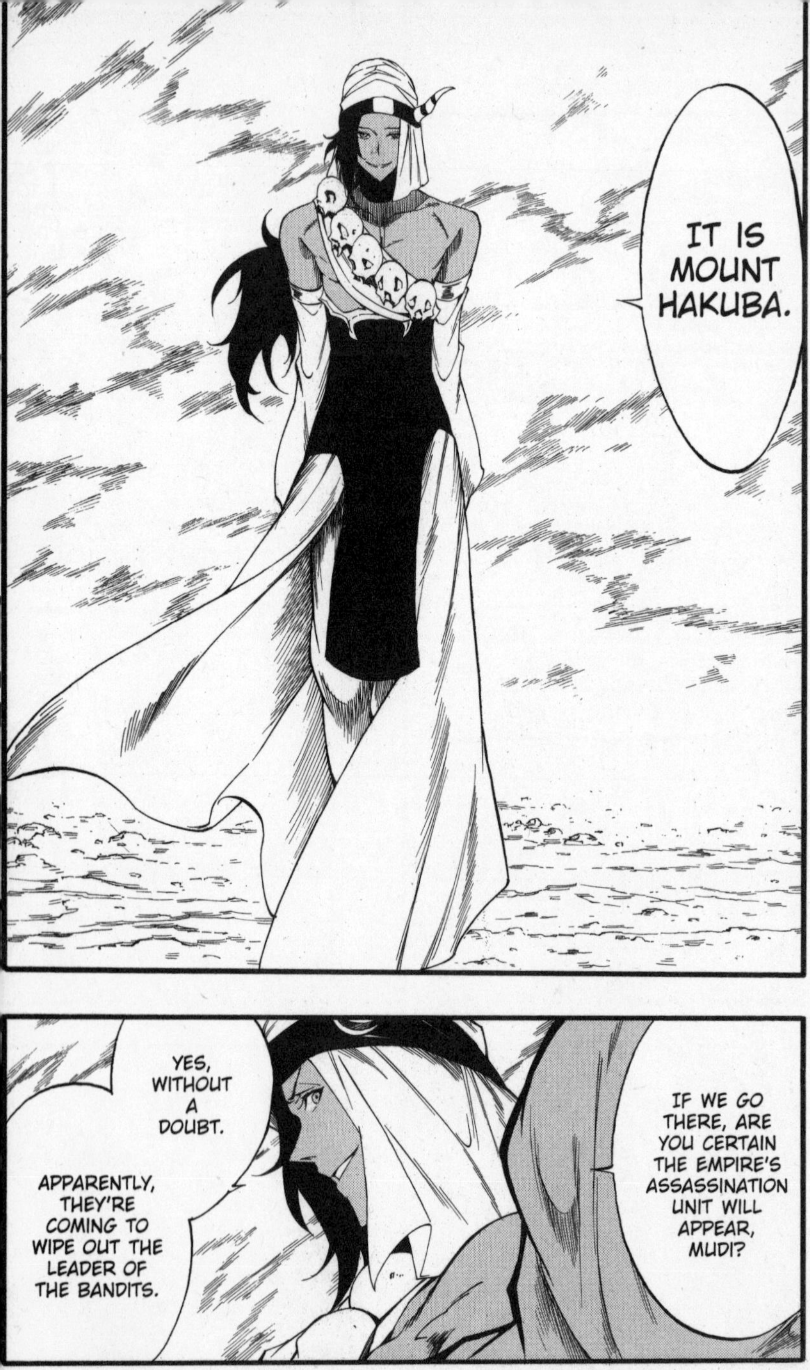
IT IS MOUNT HAKUBA.
IF WE GO THERE, ARE YOU CERTAIN THE EMPIRE'S ASSASSINATION UNIT WILL APPEAR, MUDI?
YES, WITHOUT A DOUBT.
APPARENTLY, THEY'RE COMING TO WIPE OUT THE LEADER OF THE BANDITS.

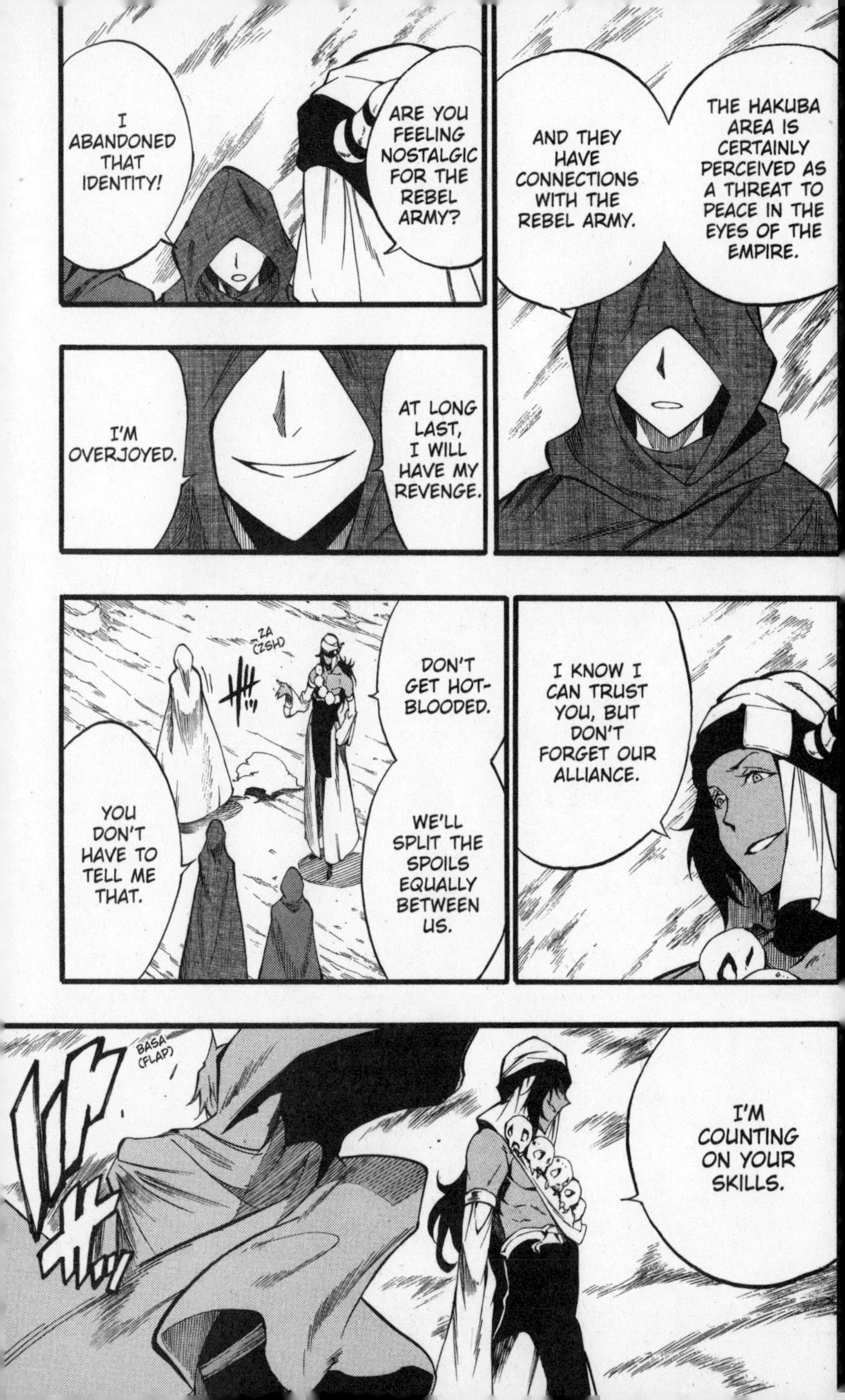
THE HAKUBA AREA IS CERTAINLY PERCEIVED AS A THREAT TO PEACE IN THE EYES OF THE EMPIRE.
AND THEY HAVE CONNECTIONS WITH THE REBEL ARMY.
ARE YOU FEELING NOSTALGIC FOR THE REBEL ARMY?
I ABANDONED THAT IDENTITY!
AT LONG LAST, I WILL HAVE MY REVENGE.
I'M OVERJOYED.
I KNOW I CAN TRUST YOU, BUT DON'T FORGET OUR ALLIANCE.
ZA (ZSH)
DON'T GET HOT-BLOODED.
WE'LL SPLIT THE SPOILS EQUALLY BETWEEN US.
YOU DON'T HAVE TO TELL ME THAT.
I'M COUNTING ON YOUR SKILLS.
BASA (FLAP)

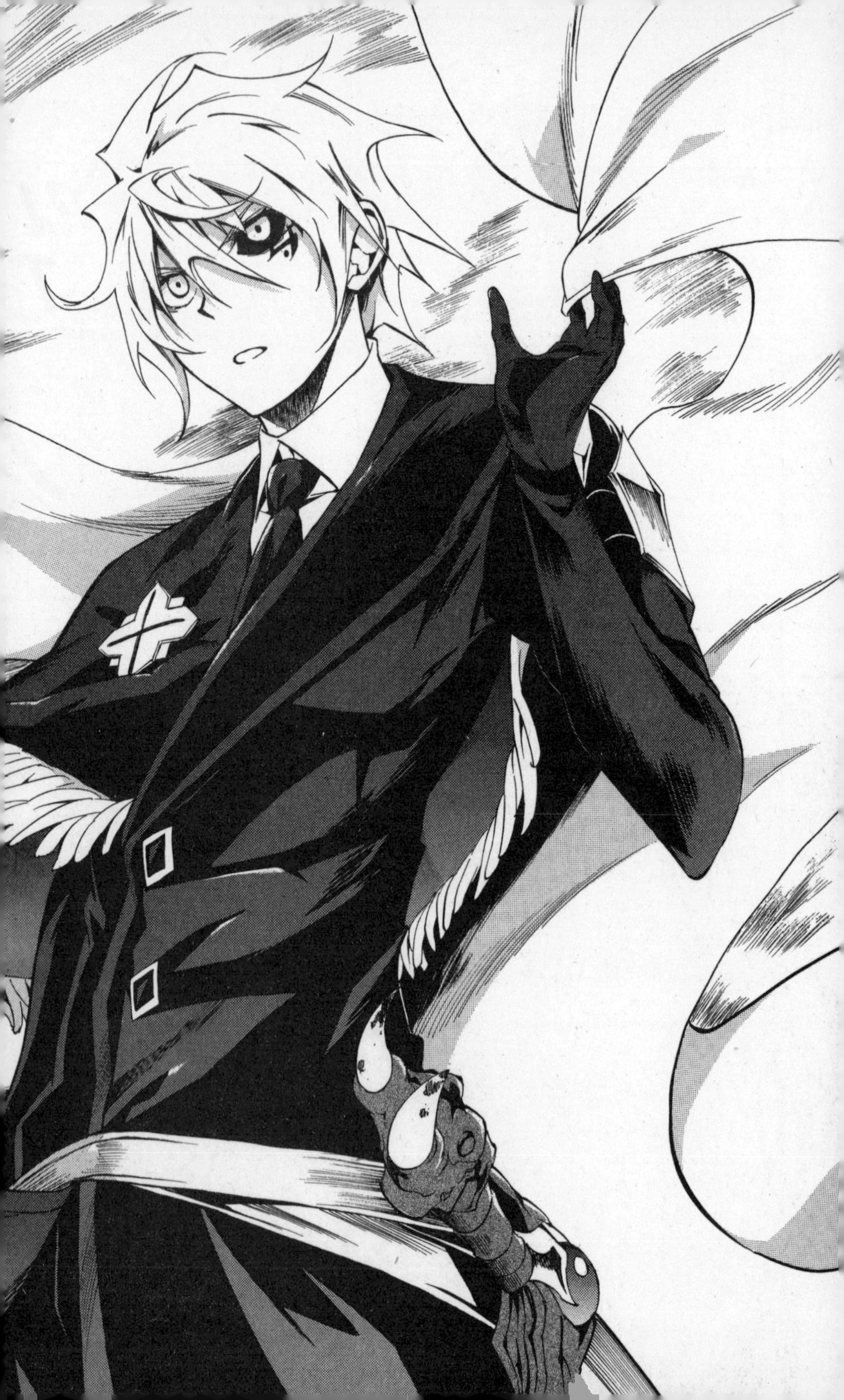

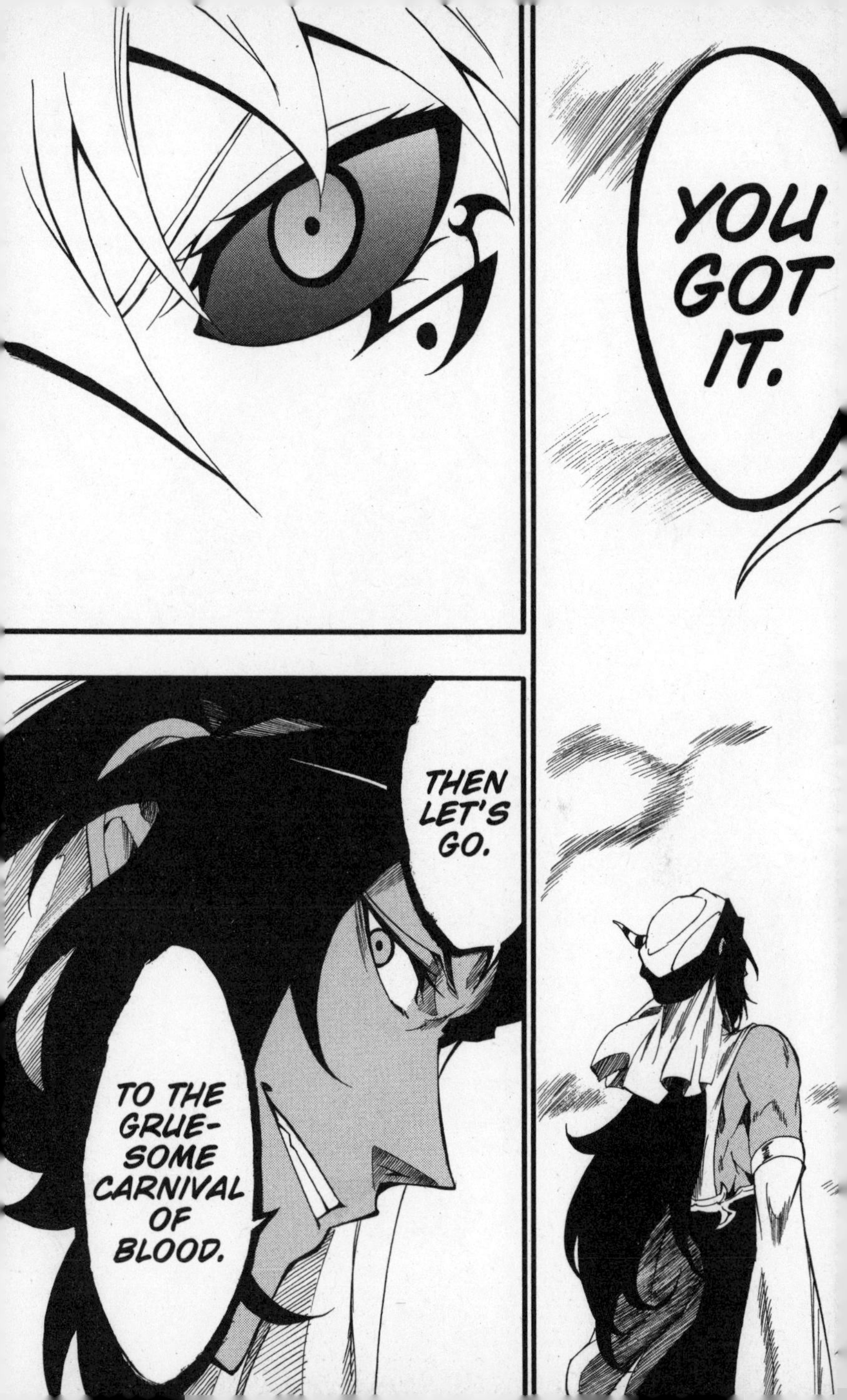
YOU GOT IT.
THEN LET'S GO.
TO THE GRUE-SOME CARNIVAL OF BLOOD.

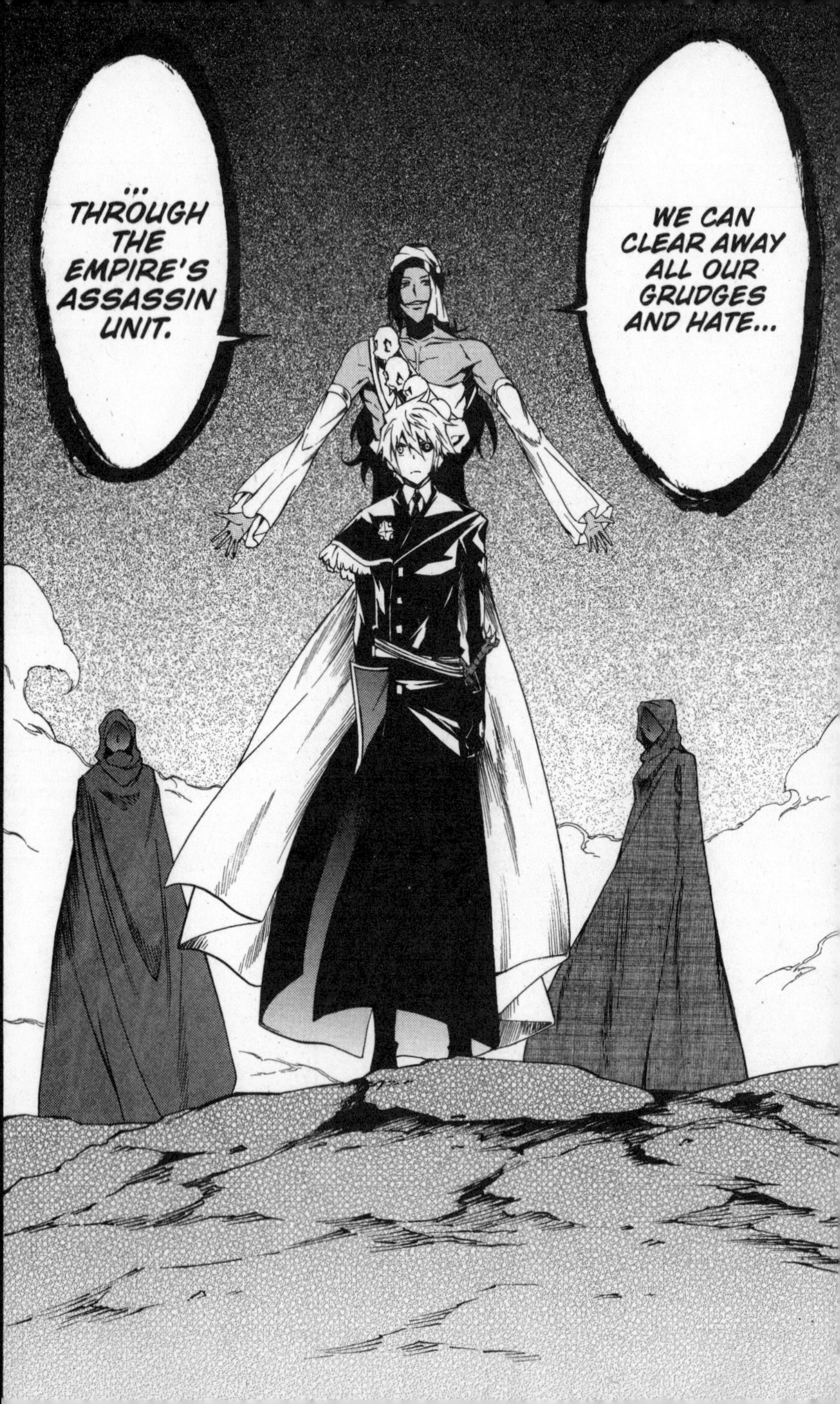
WE CAN CLEAR AWAY ALL OUR GRUDGES AND HATE...
...THROUGH THE EMPIRE'S ASSASSIN UNIT.

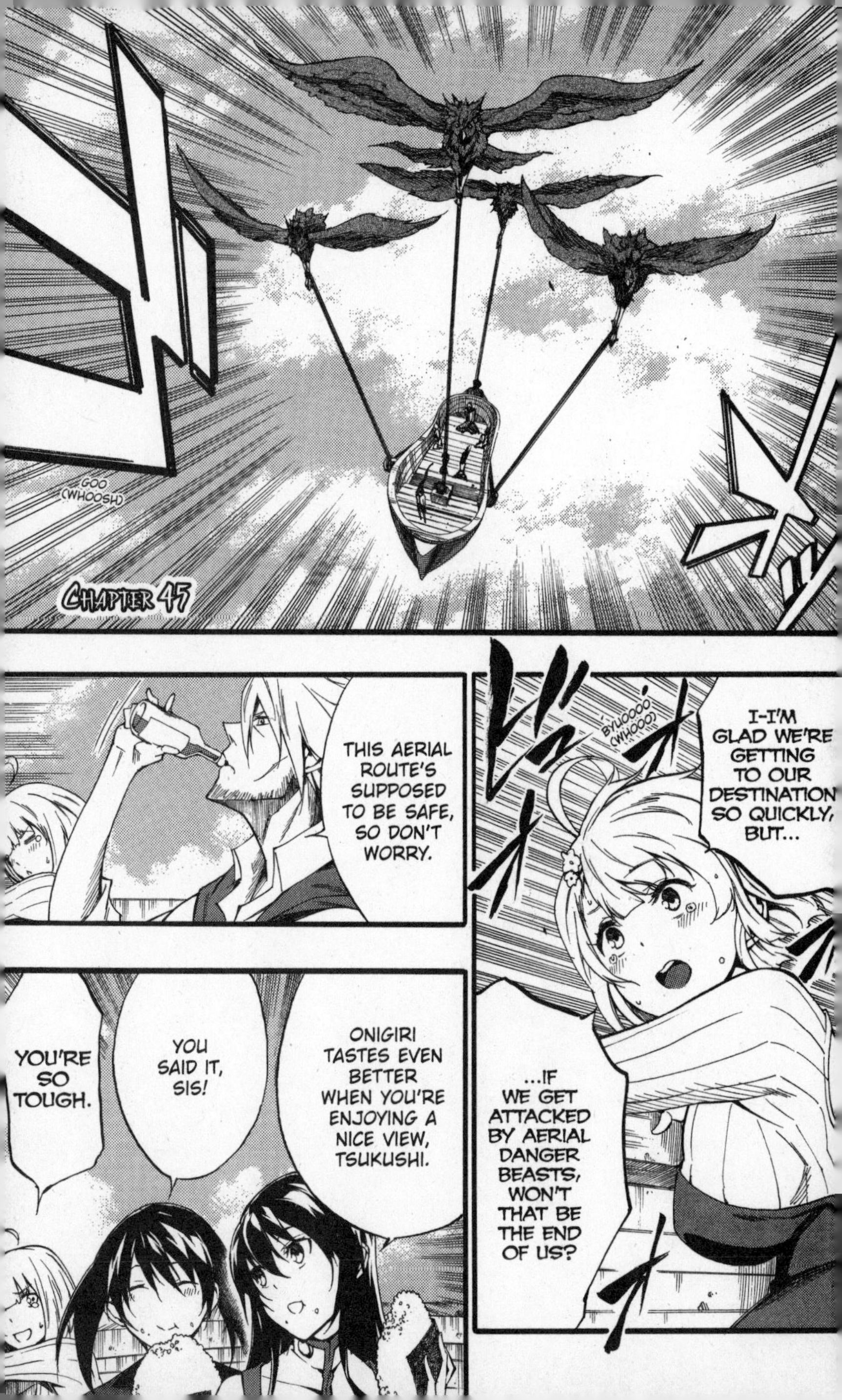
GOO (WHOOSH)
CHAPTER 45
I-I'M GLAD WE'RE GETTING TO OUR DESTINATION SO QUICKLY, BUT...
BYUOOOO (WHOOO)
THIS AERIAL ROUTE'S SUPPOSED TO BE SAFE, SO DON'T WORRY.
...IF WE GET ATTACKED BY AERIAL DANGER BEASTS, WON'T THAT BE THE END OF US?
ONIGIRI TASTES EVEN BETTER WHEN YOU'RE ENJOYING A NICE VIEW, TSUKUSHI.
YOU SAID IT, SIS!
YOU'RE SO TOUGH.

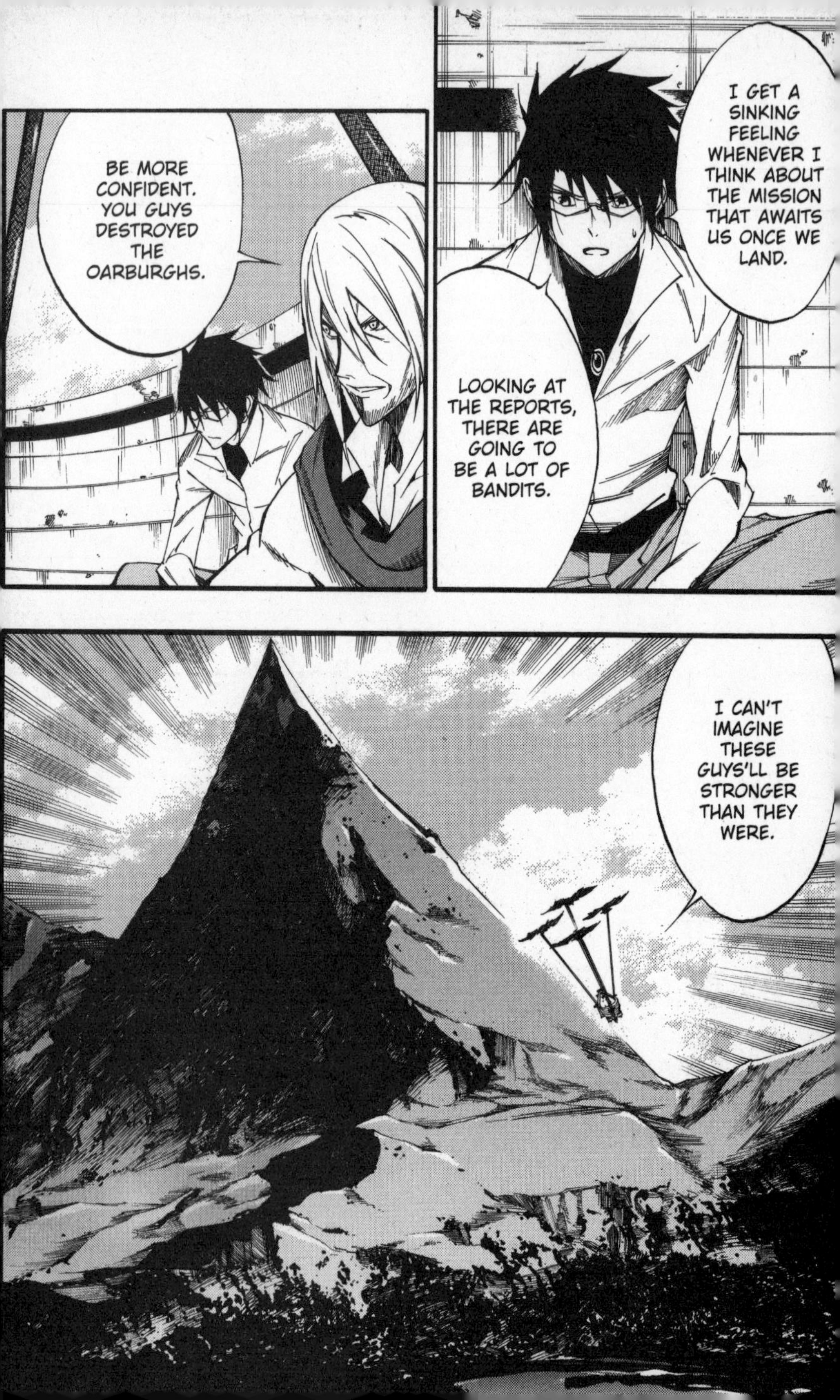
I GET A SINKING FEELING WHENEVER I THINK ABOUT THE MISSION THAT AWAITS US ONCE WE LAND.
LOOKING AT THE REPORTS, THERE ARE GOING TO BE A LOT OF BANDITS.
BE MORE CONFIDENT. YOU GUYS DESTROYED THE OARBURGHS.
I CAN'T IMAGINE THESE GUYS'LL BE STRONGER THAN THEY WERE.

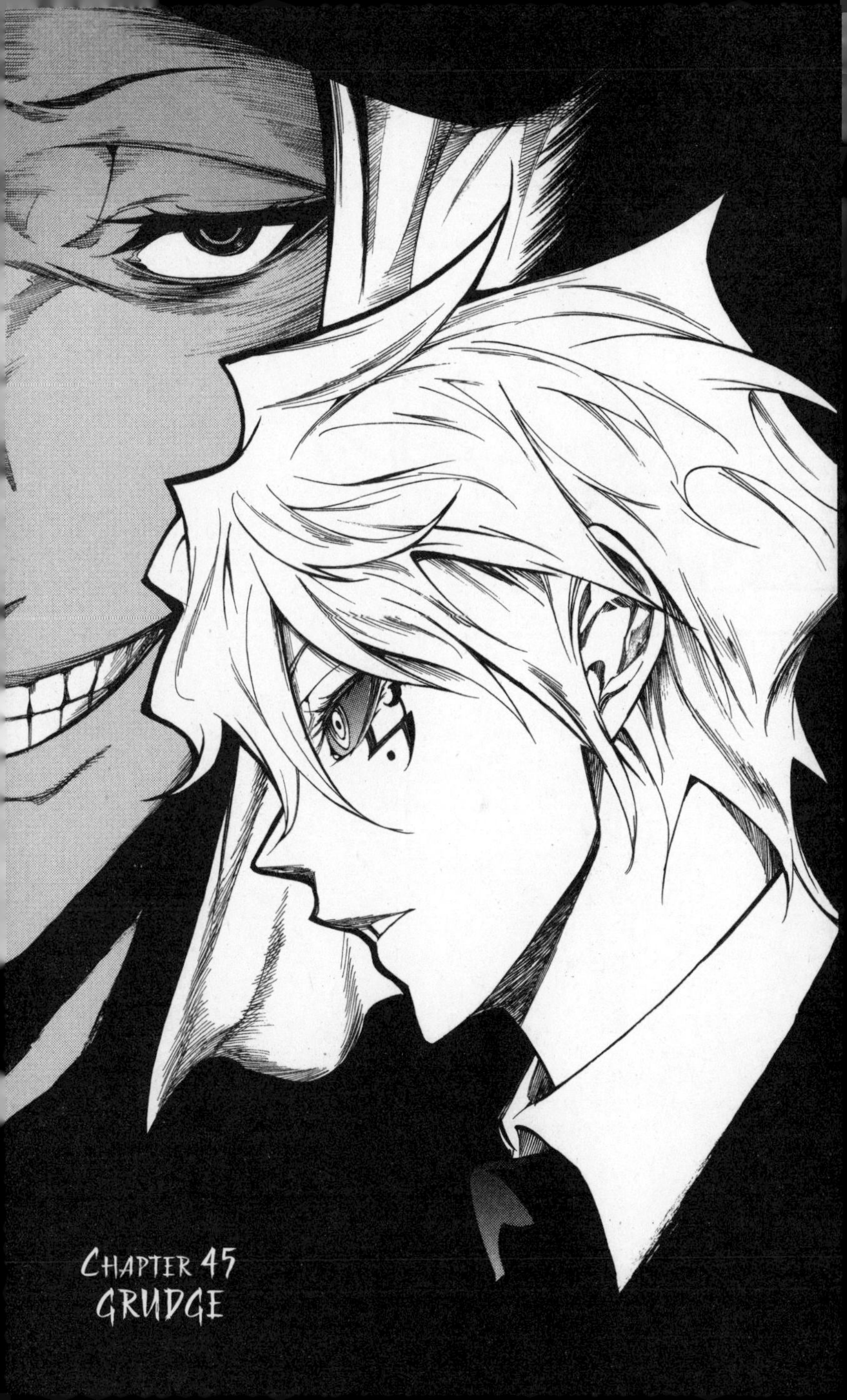
Chapter 45
GRUDGE

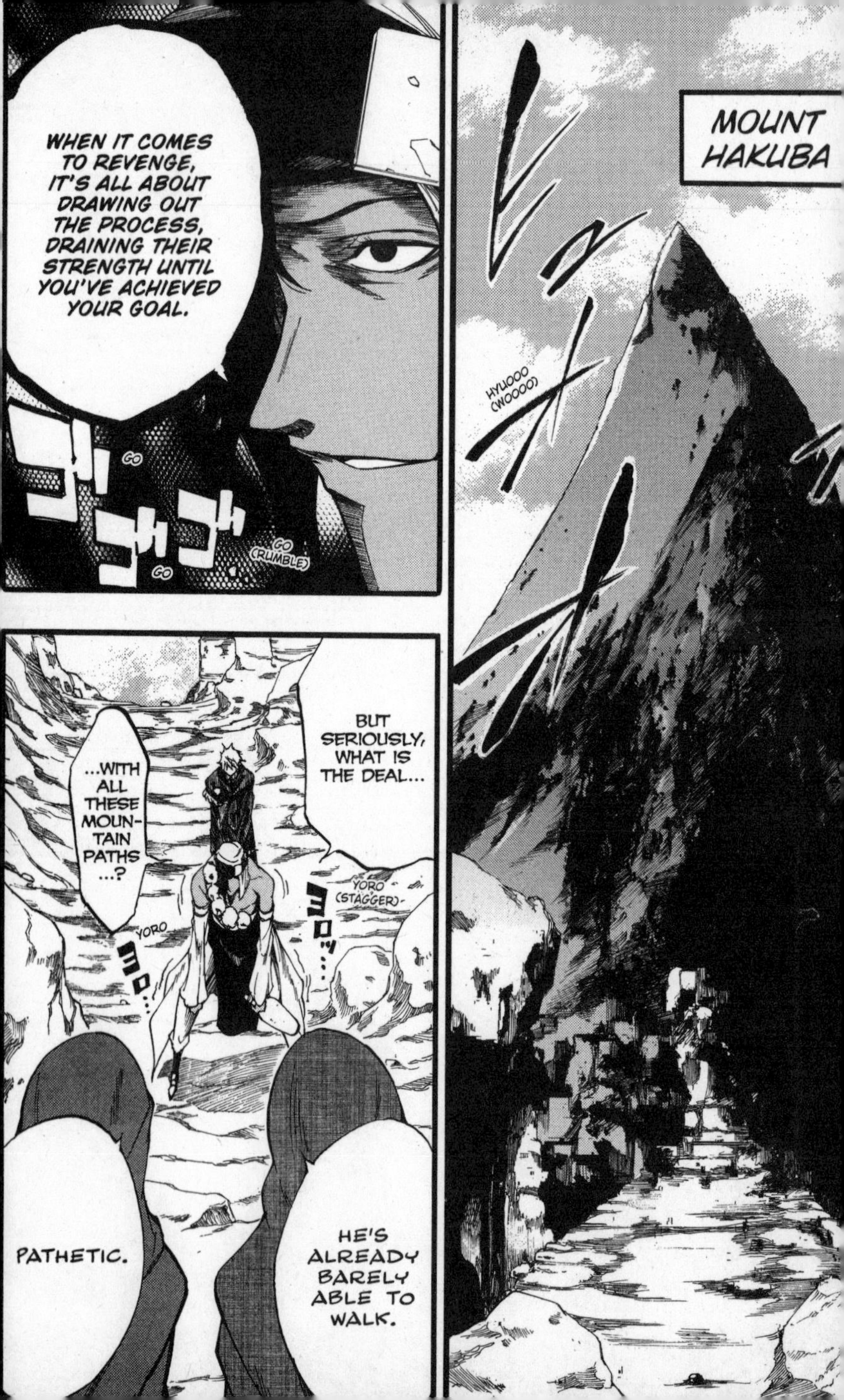
MOUNT HAKUBA
HYUOOO (WOOOO)
WHEN IT COMES TO REVENGE, IT'S ALL ABOUT DRAWING OUT THE PROCESS, DRAINING THEIR STRENGTH UNTIL YOU'VE ACHIEVED YOUR GOAL.
GO GO GO (RUMBLE)
BUT SERIOUSLY, WHAT IS THE DEAL...
...WITH ALL THESE MOUNTAIN PATHS ...?
YORO (STAGGER)
YORO
HE'S ALREADY BARELY ABLE TO WALK.
PATHETIC.

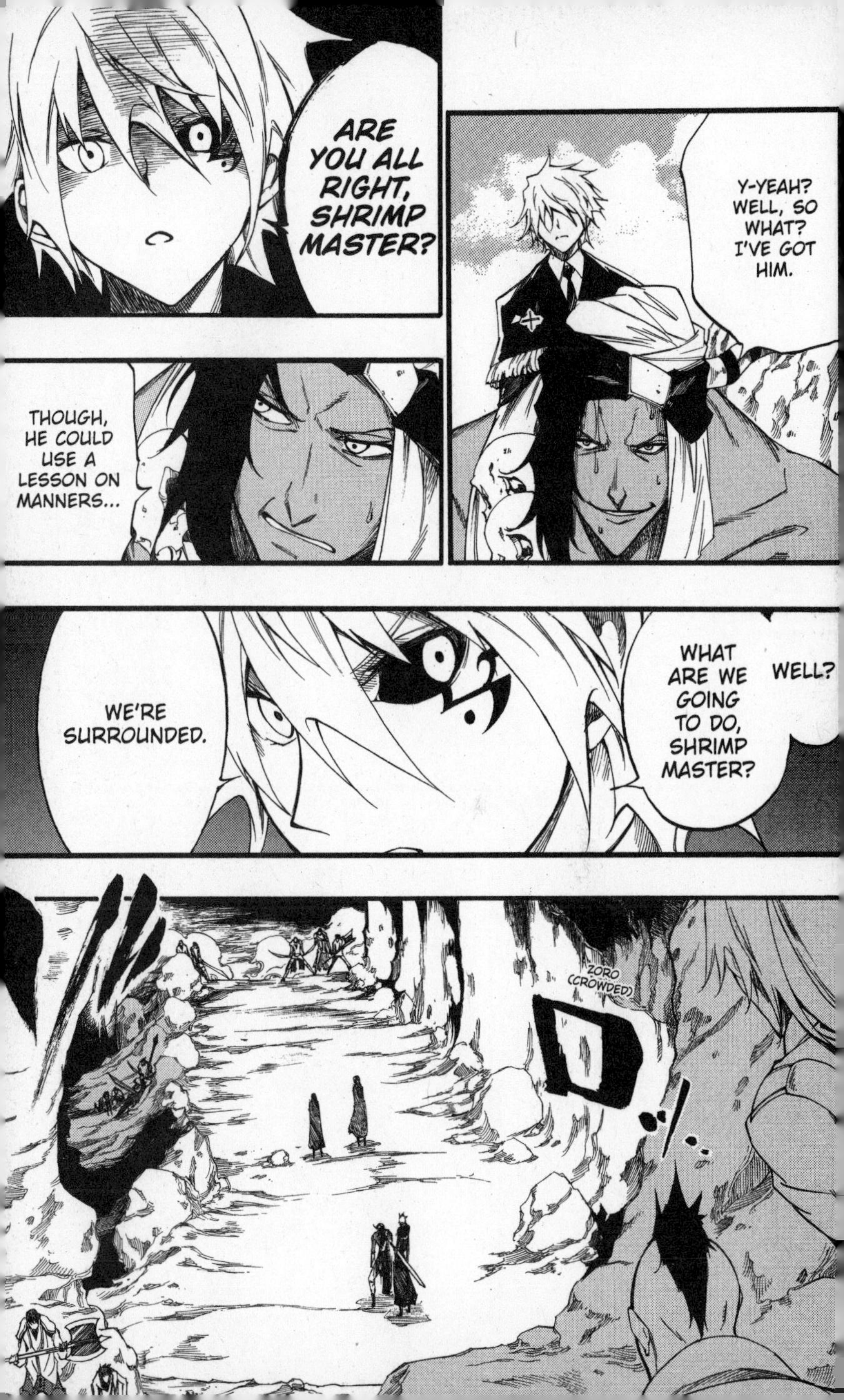
ARE YOU ALL RIGHT, SHRIMP MASTER?
Y-YEAH? WELL, SO WHAT? I'VE GOT HIM.
THOUGH, HE COULD USE A LESSON ON MANNERS...
WELL?
WHAT ARE WE GOING TO DO, SHRIMP MASTER?
WE'RE SURROUNDED.
ZORO (CROWDED)

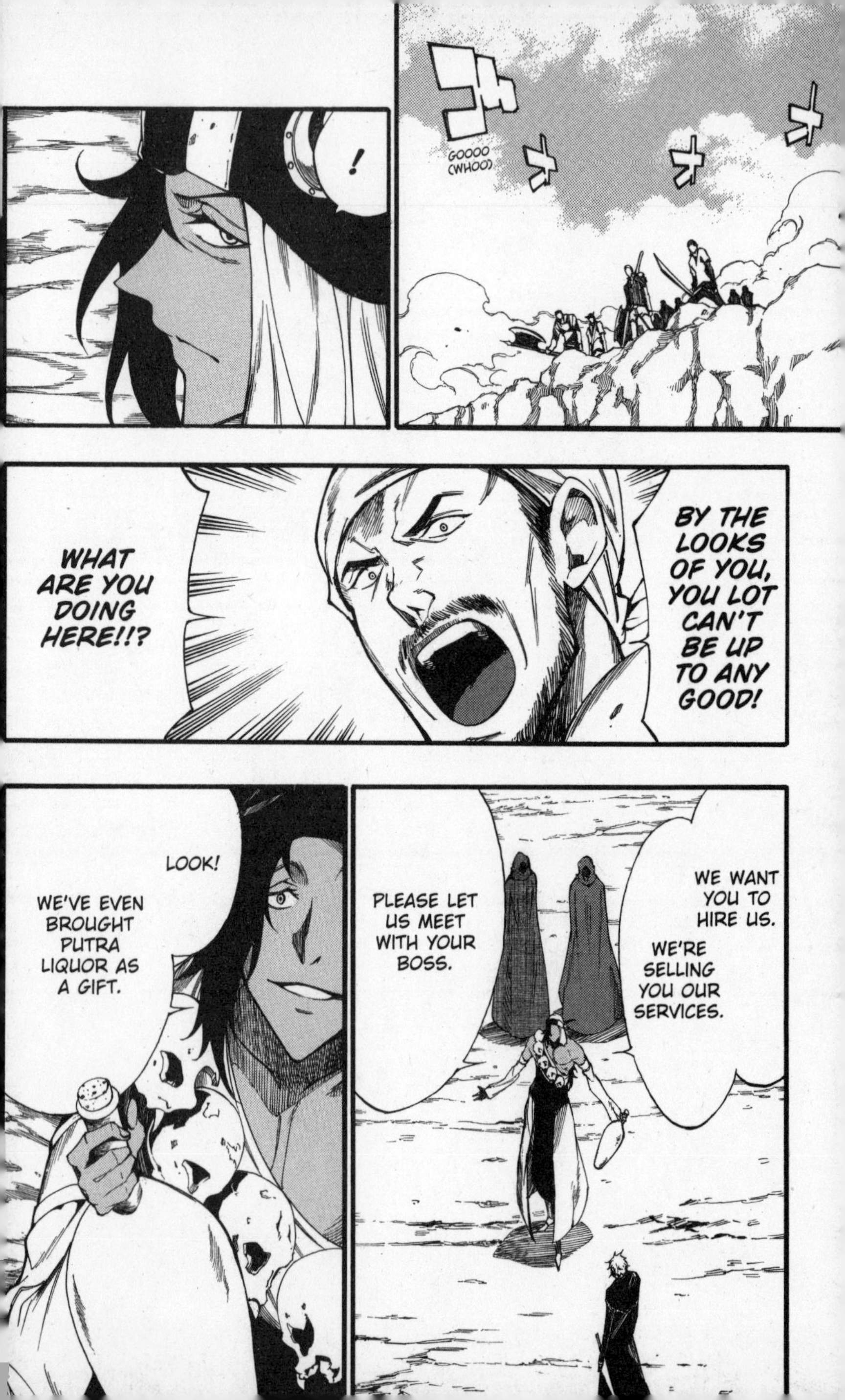
ゴォォォ
GOOOO (WHOO)
!
BY THE LOOKS OF YOU, YOU LOT CAN'T BE UP TO ANY GOOD!
WHAT ARE YOU DOING HERE!!?
WE WANT YOU TO HIRE US.
WE'RE SELLING YOU OUR SERVICES.
PLEASE LET US MEET WITH YOUR BOSS.
LOOK!
WE'VE EVEN BROUGHT PUTRA LIQUOR AS A GIFT.

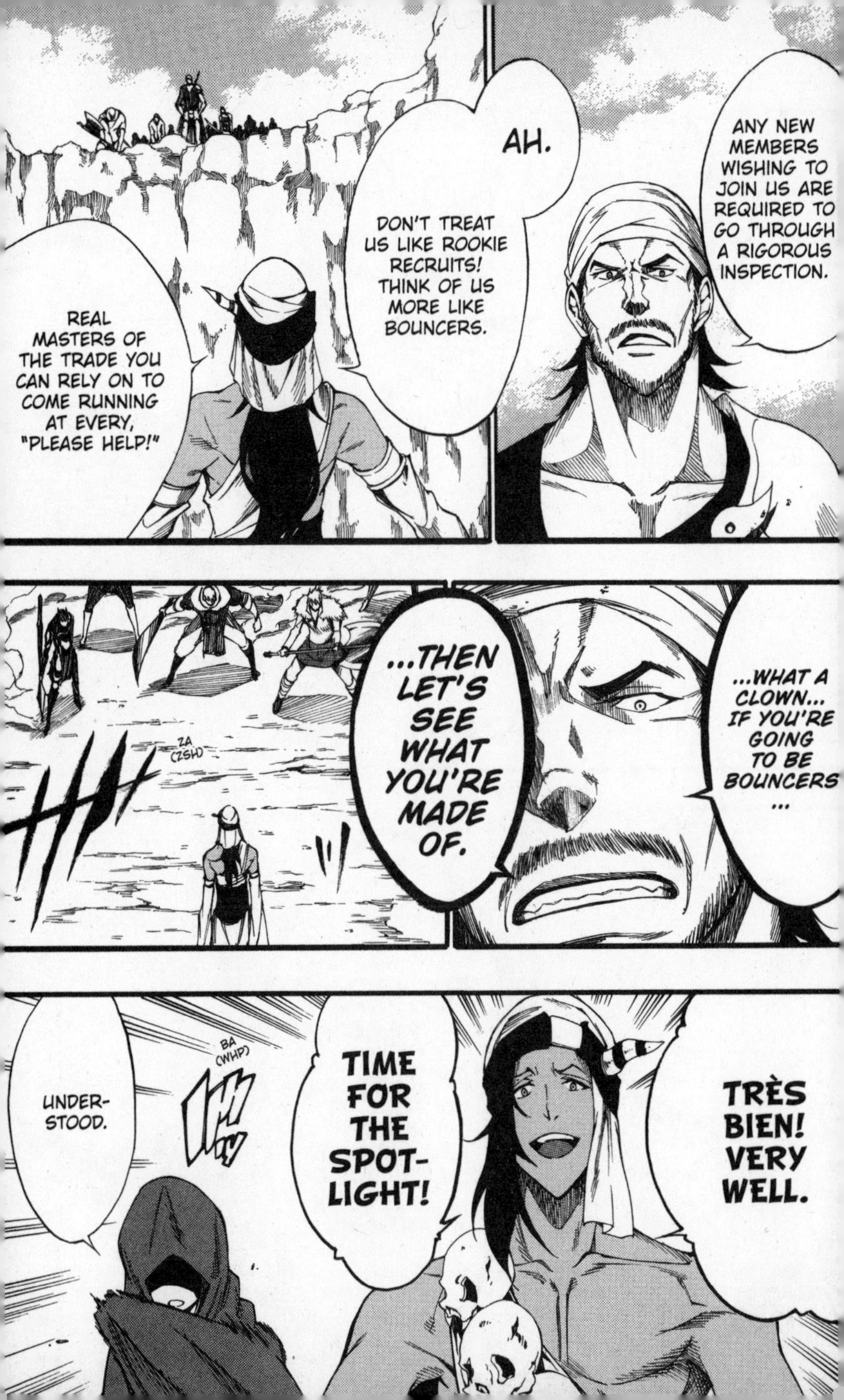
REAL MASTERS OF THE TRADE YOU CAN RELY ON TO COME RUNNING AT EVERY, "PLEASE HELP!"
DON'T TREAT US LIKE ROOKIE RECRUITS! THINK OF US MORE LIKE BOUNCERS.
AH.
ANY NEW MEMBERS WISHING TO JOIN US ARE REQUIRED TO GO THROUGH A RIGOROUS INSPECTION.
ZA (ZSH)
...THEN LET'S SEE WHAT YOU'RE MADE OF.
...WHAT A CLOWN... IF YOU'RE GOING TO BE BOUNCERS ...
UNDER-STOOD.
BA (WHP)
TIME FOR THE SPOT-LIGHT!
TRÈS BIEN! VERY WELL.

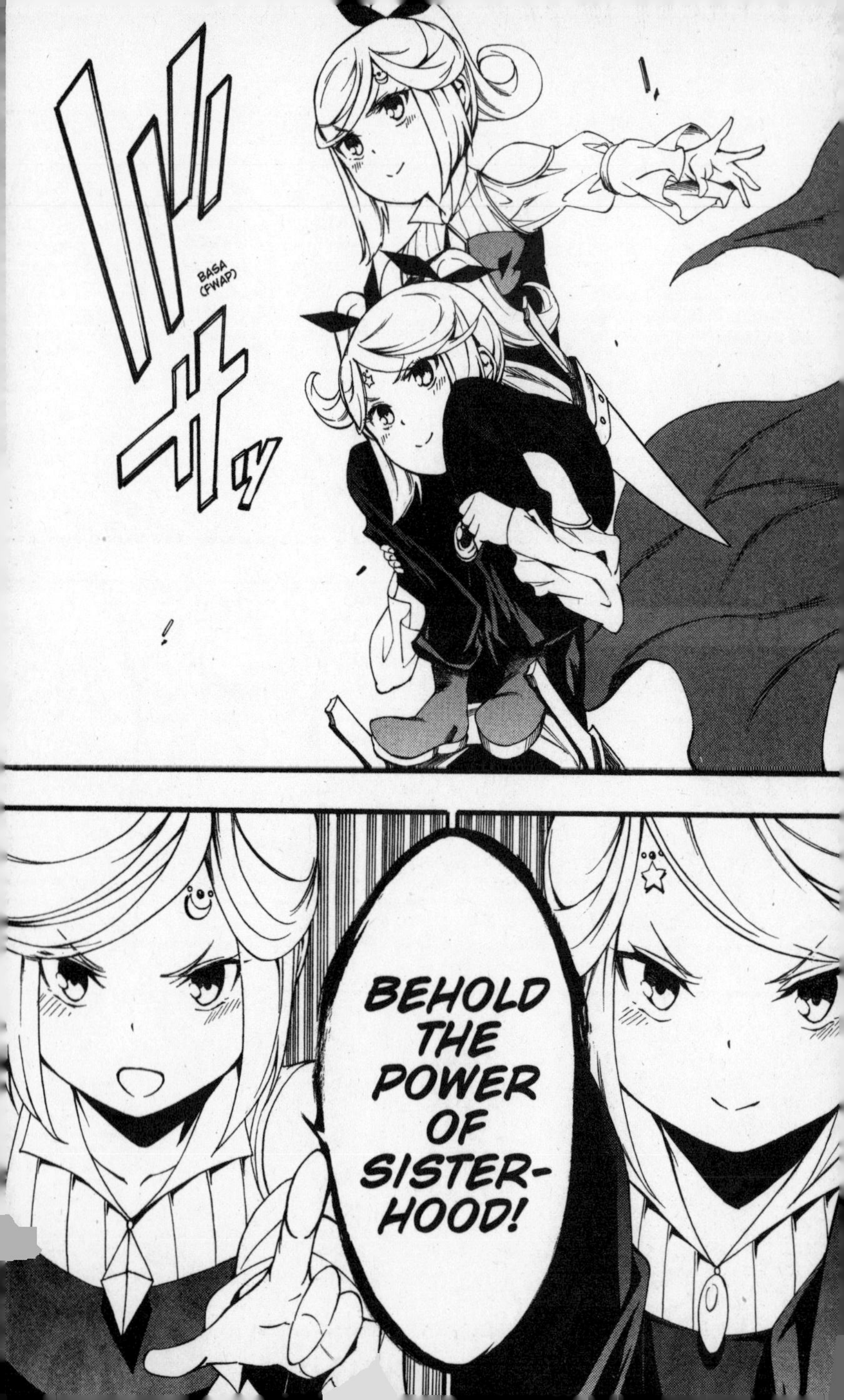
BASA
(FWAP)
BEHOLD THE POWER OF SISTER-HOOD!

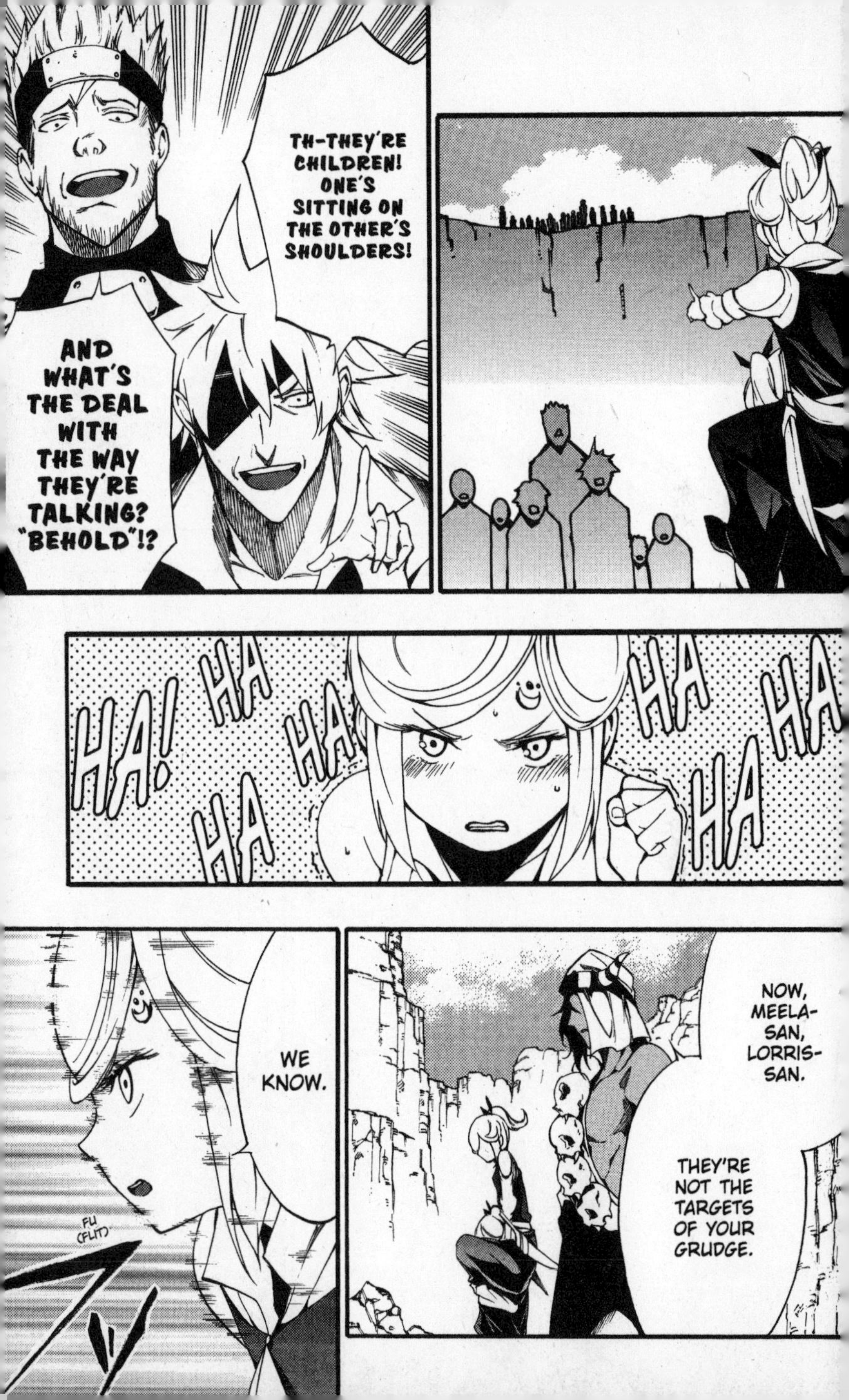
TH-THEY'RE CHILDREN! ONE'S SITTING ON THE OTHER'S SHOULDERS!
AND WHAT'S THE DEAL WITH THE WAY THEY'RE TALKING? "BEHOLD"!?
HA HA HA HA HA HA
HA! HA HA HA HA HA
NOW, MEELA-SAN, LORRIS-SAN.
THEY'RE NOT THE TARGETS OF YOUR GRUDGE.
WE KNOW.
FU (FLIT)

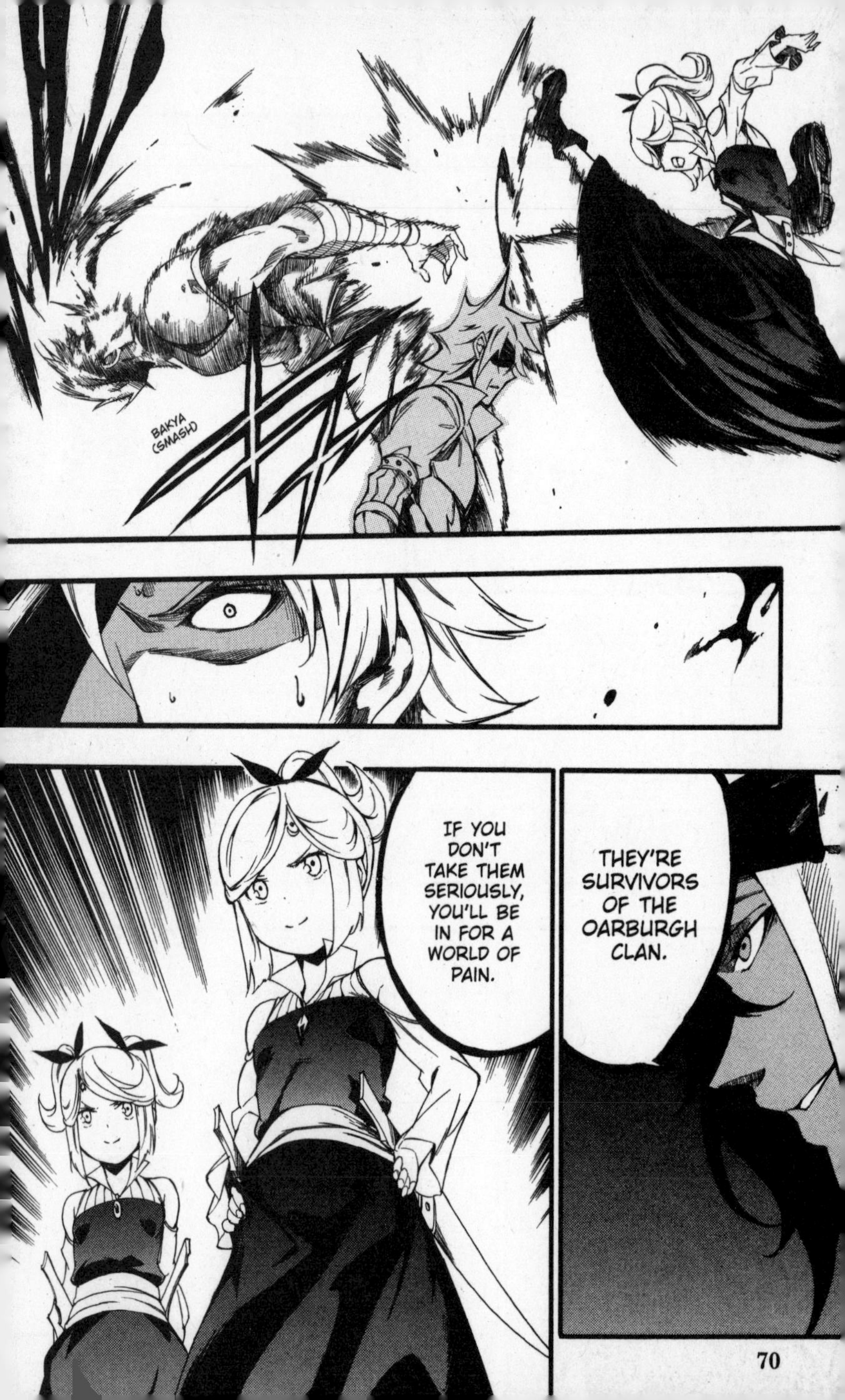
BAKYA (SMASH)
THEY'RE SURVIVORS OF THE OARBURGH CLAN.
IF YOU DON'T TAKE THEM SERIOUSLY, YOU'LL BE IN FOR A WORLD OF PAIN.

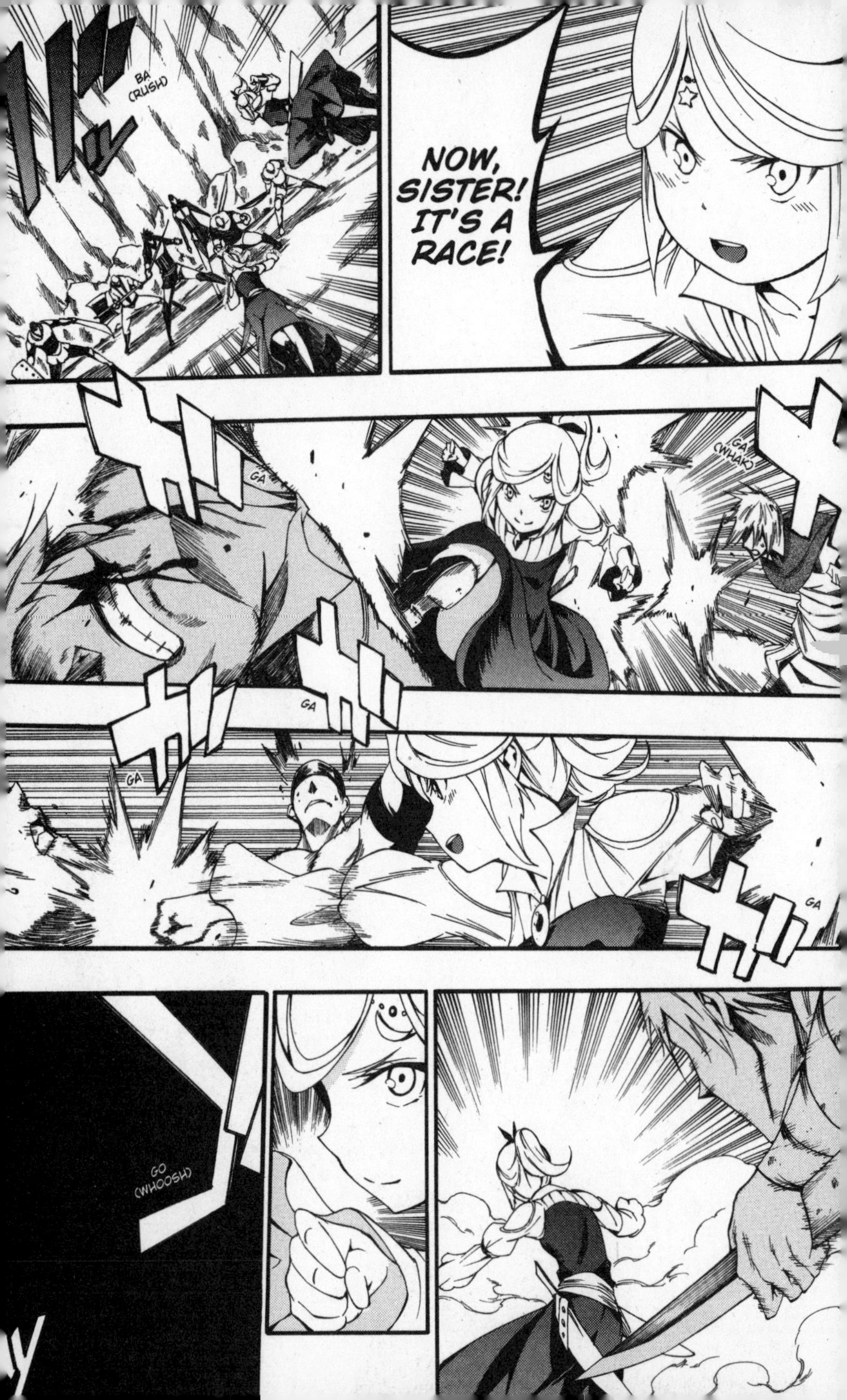
NOW, SISTER! IT'S A RACE!
BA (RUSH)
GA (WHAK)
GA
GA
GA
GA
GO (WHOOSH)

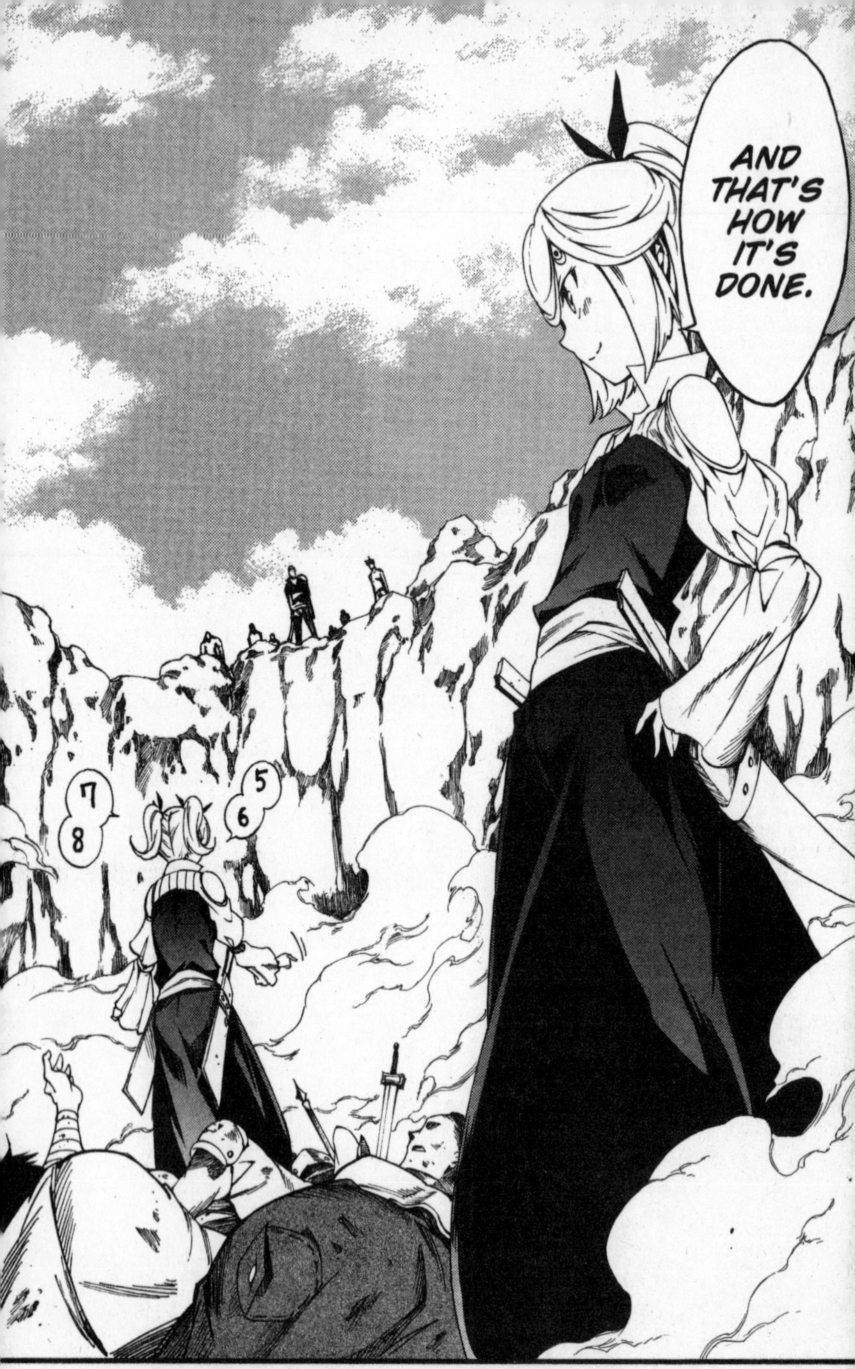
AND THAT'S HOW IT'S DONE.
5 6
7 8

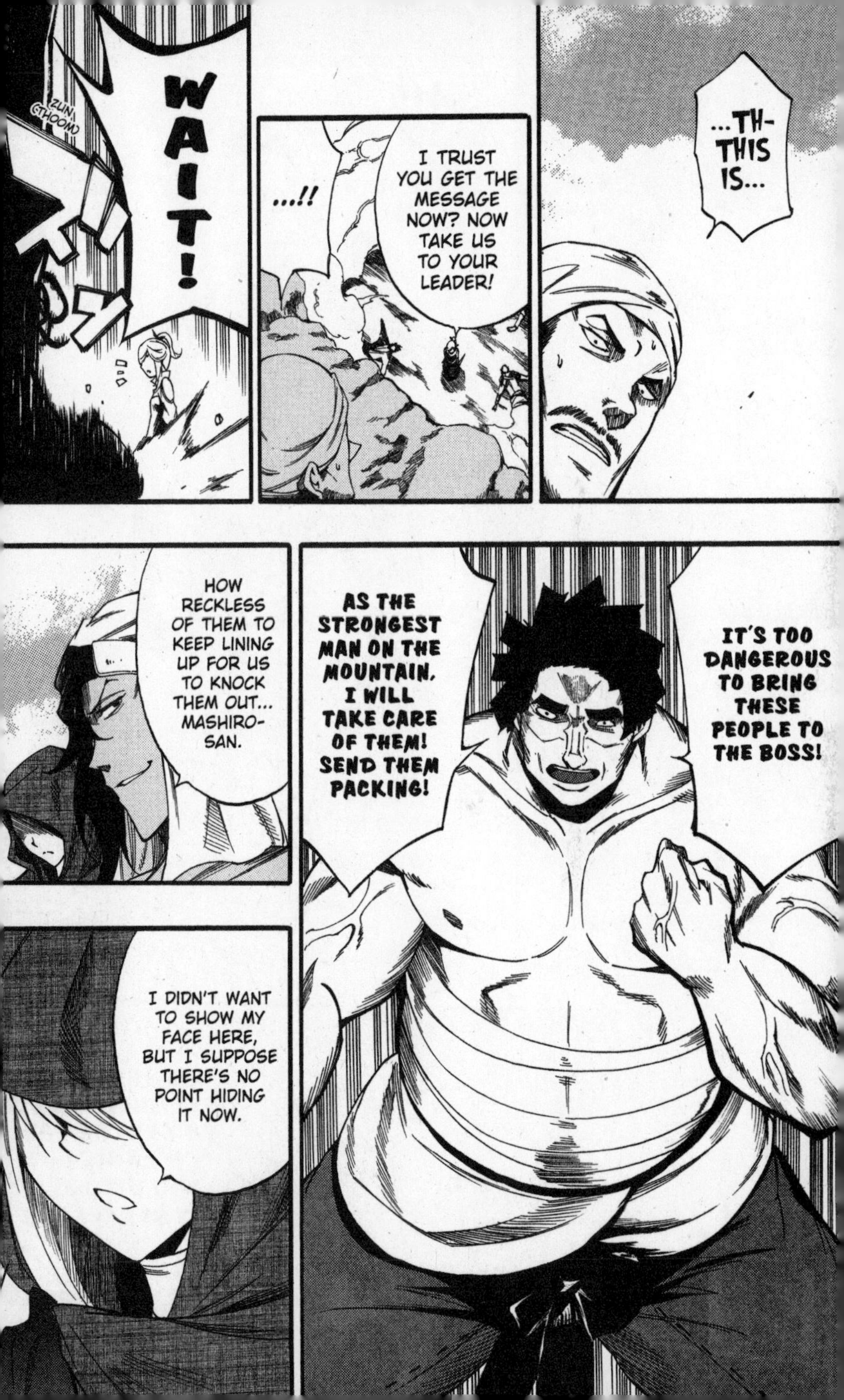
...TH- THIS IS...
I TRUST YOU GET THE MESSAGE NOW? NOW TAKE US TO YOUR LEADER!
...!!
WAIT!
ZUN (THOOM)
IT'S TOO DANGEROUS TO BRING THESE PEOPLE TO THE BOSS!
AS THE STRONGEST MAN ON THE MOUNTAIN, I WILL TAKE CARE OF THEM! SEND THEM PACKING!
HOW RECKLESS OF THEM TO KEEP LINING UP FOR US TO KNOCK THEM OUT... MASHIRO-SAN.
I DIDN'T WANT TO SHOW MY FACE HERE, BUT I SUPPOSE THERE'S NO POINT HIDING IT NOW.

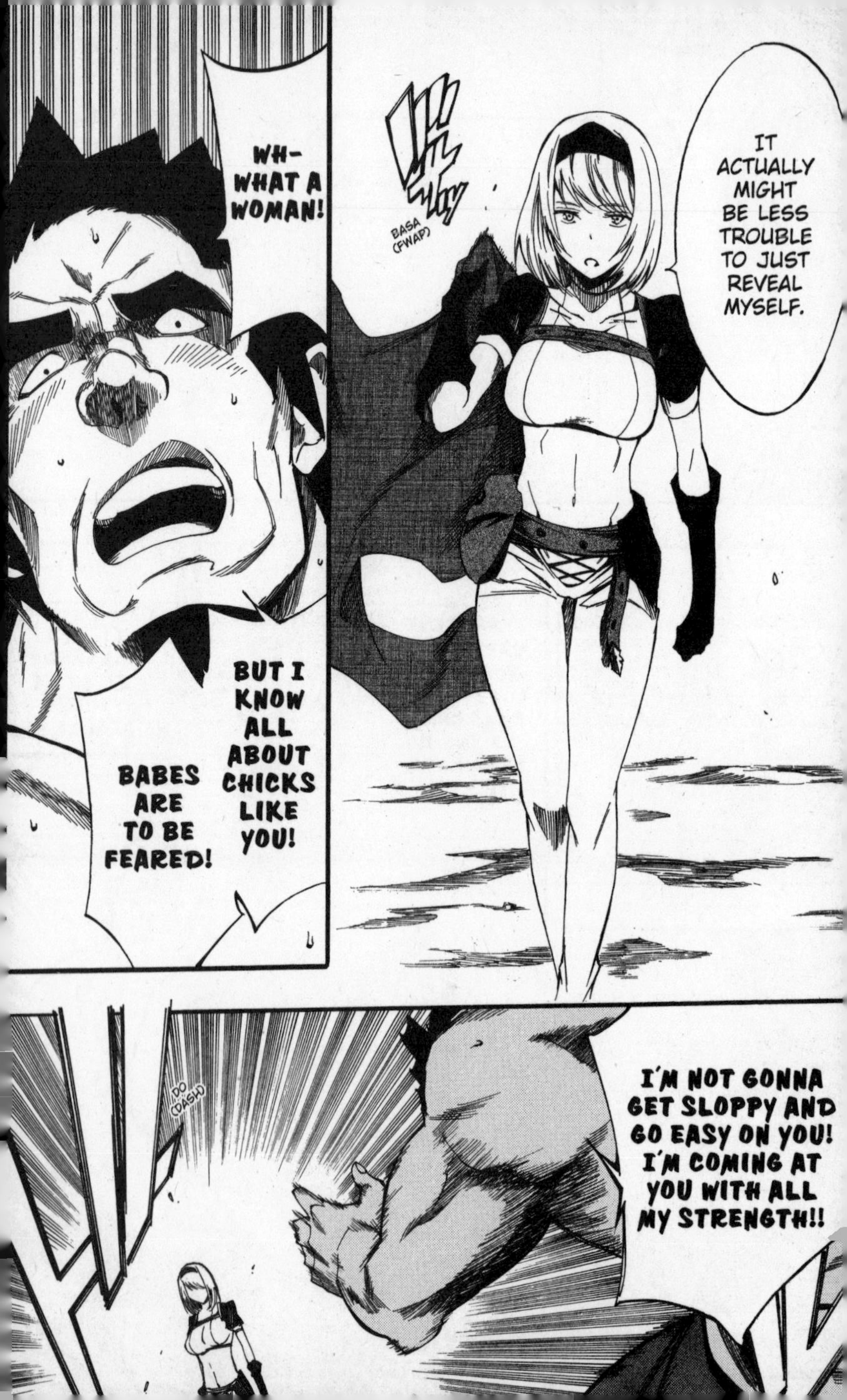
IT ACTUALLY MIGHT BE LESS TROUBLE TO JUST REVEAL MYSELF.
BASA (FWAP)
WH- WHAT A WOMAN!
BUT I KNOW ALL ABOUT CHICKS LIKE YOU!
BABES ARE TO BE FEARED!
I'M NOT GONNA GET SLOPPY AND GO EASY ON YOU! I'M COMING AT YOU WITH ALL MY STRENGTH!!
DO (DASH)

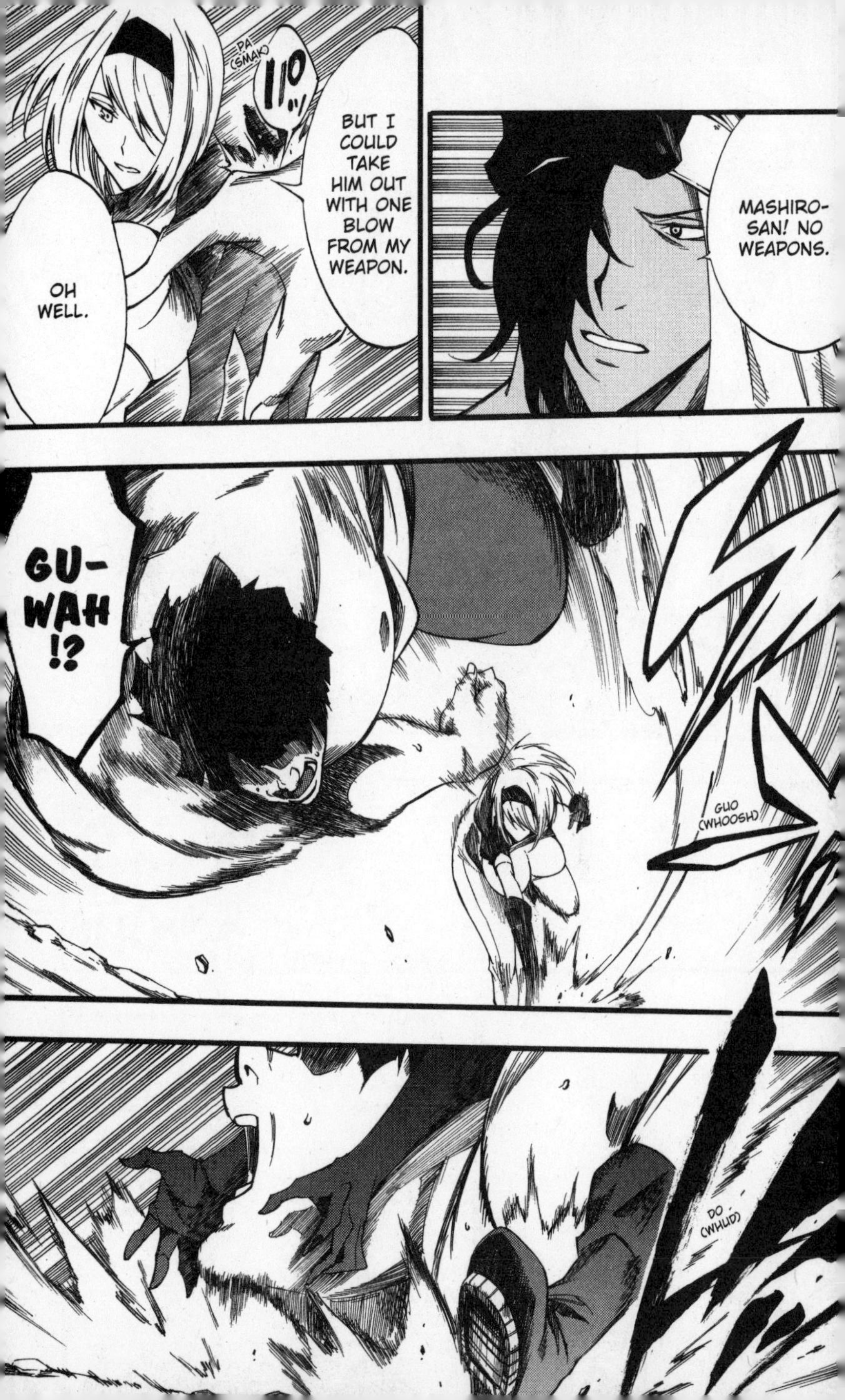

MASHIRO-SAN! NO WEAPONS.
PA (SMAK)
BUT I COULD TAKE HIM OUT WITH ONE BLOW FROM MY WEAPON.
OH WELL.
GU-WAH!?
GUO (WHOOSH)
DO (WHUD)

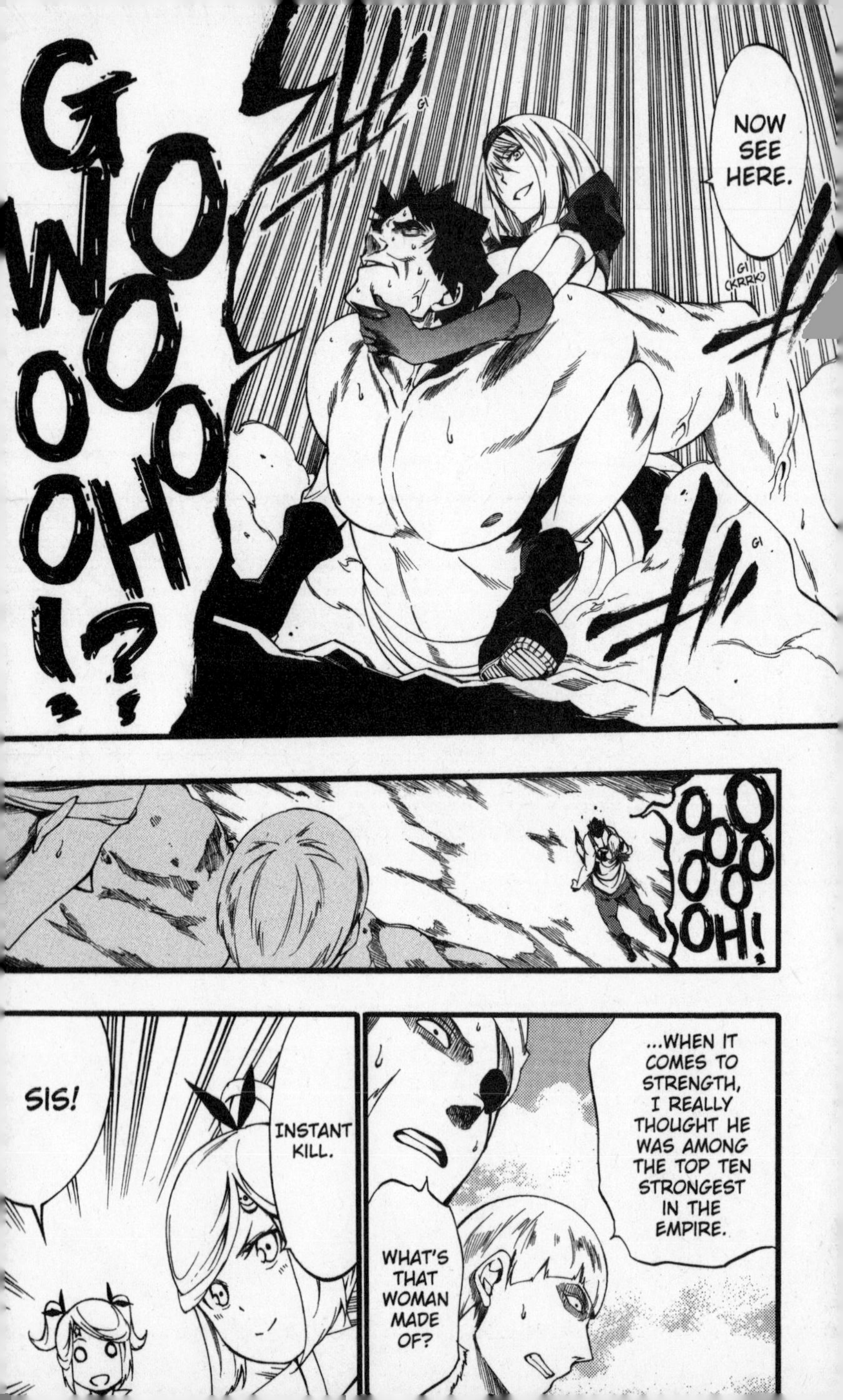
NOW SEE HERE.
GI
GI (KRRK)
GI
GWOOOOOOH!?
OOOOOOOOOH!
...WHEN IT COMES TO STRENGTH, I REALLY THOUGHT HE WAS AMONG THE TOP TEN STRONGEST IN THE EMPIRE.
WHAT'S THAT WOMAN MADE OF?
INSTANT KILL.
SIS!

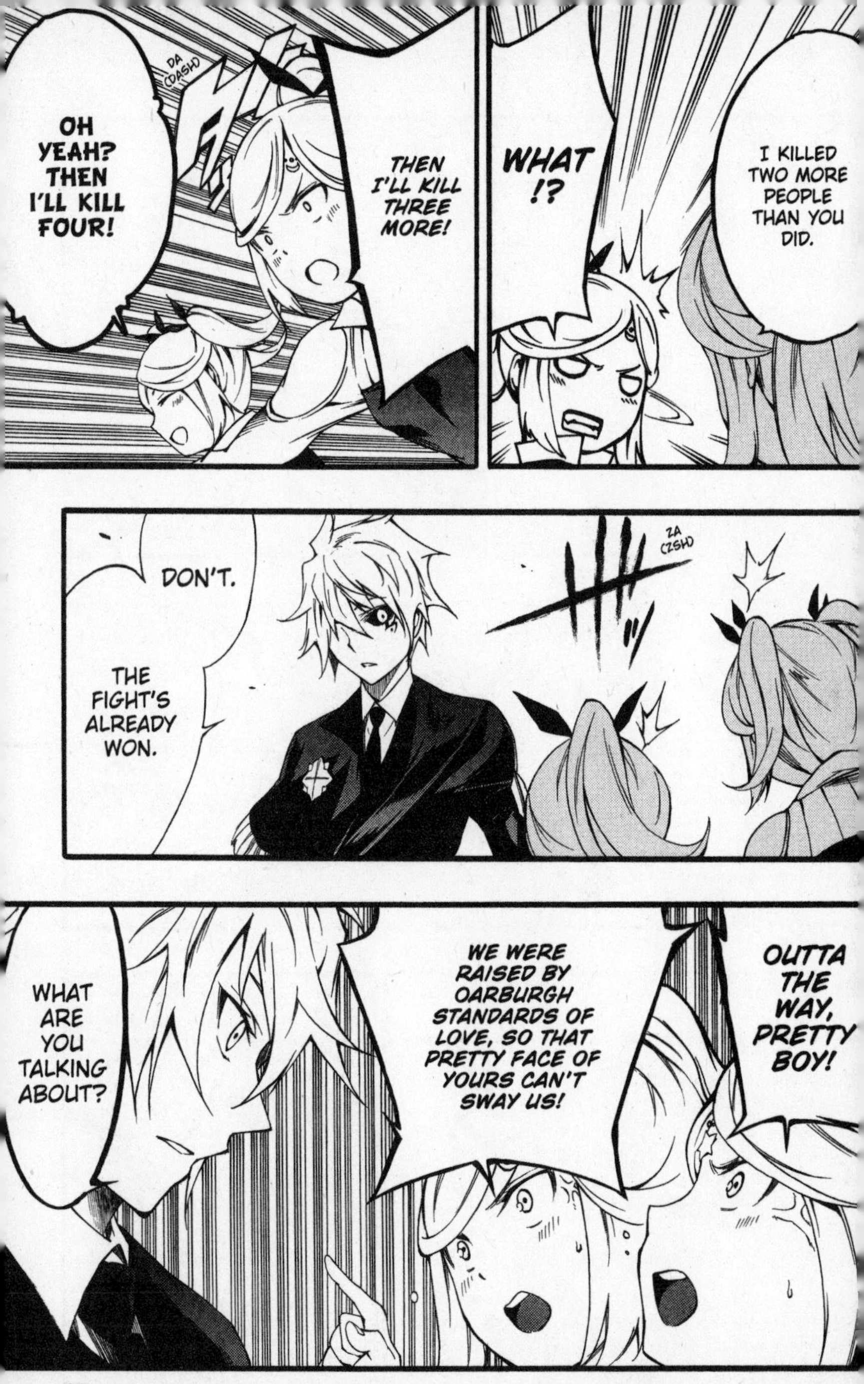
I KILLED TWO MORE PEOPLE THAN YOU DID.
WHAT !?
THEN I'LL KILL THREE MORE!
DA (DASH)
OH YEAH? THEN I'LL KILL FOUR!
ZA (ZSH)
DON'T.
THE FIGHT'S ALREADY WON.
OUTTA THE WAY, PRETTY BOY!
WE WERE RAISED BY OARBURGH STANDARDS OF LOVE, SO THAT PRETTY FACE OF YOURS CAN'T SWAY US!
WHAT ARE YOU TALKING ABOUT?

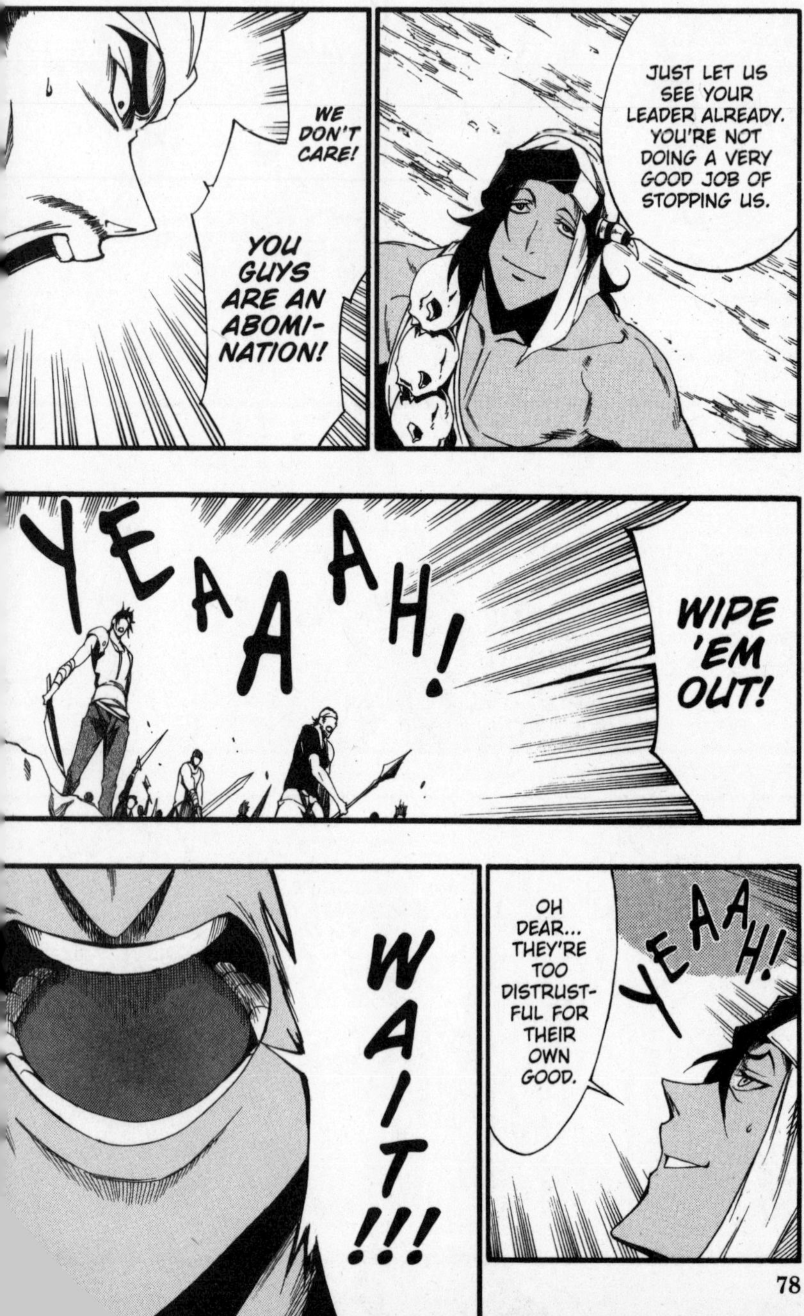
JUST LET US SEE YOUR LEADER ALREADY. YOU'RE NOT DOING A VERY GOOD JOB OF STOPPING US.
WE DON'T CARE!
YOU GUYS ARE AN ABOMI-NATION!
WIPE 'EM OUT!
YEAAAH!
OH DEAR... THEY'RE TOO DISTRUST-FUL FOR THEIR OWN GOOD.
YEAAH!
WAIT!!!

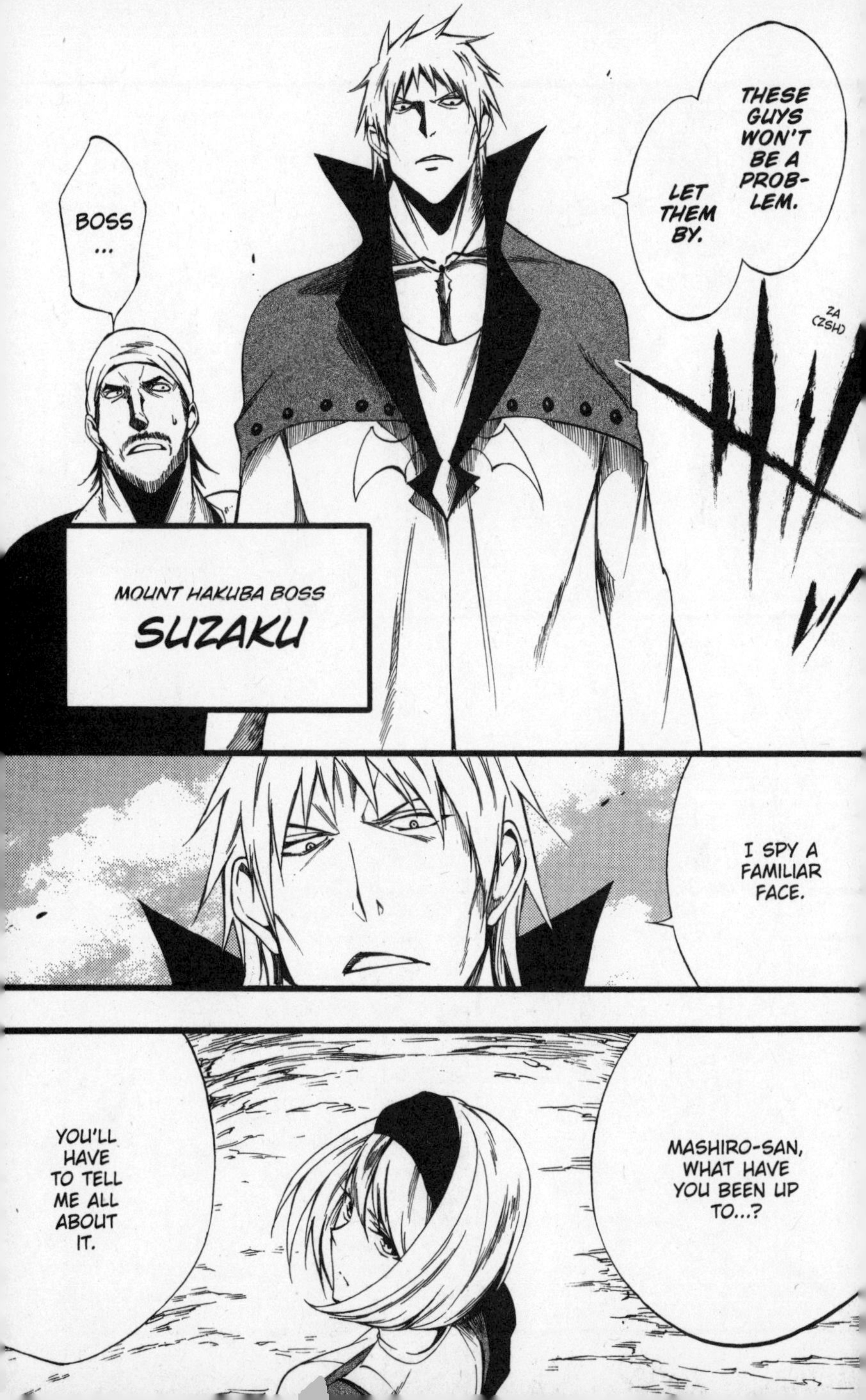
THESE GUYS WON'T BE A PROBLEM.
LET THEM BY.
ZA (ZSH)
BOSS ...
MOUNT HAKUBA BOSS
SUZAKU
I SPY A FAMILIAR FACE.
MASHIRO-SAN, WHAT HAVE YOU BEEN UP TO...?
YOU'LL HAVE TO TELL ME ALL ABOUT IT.

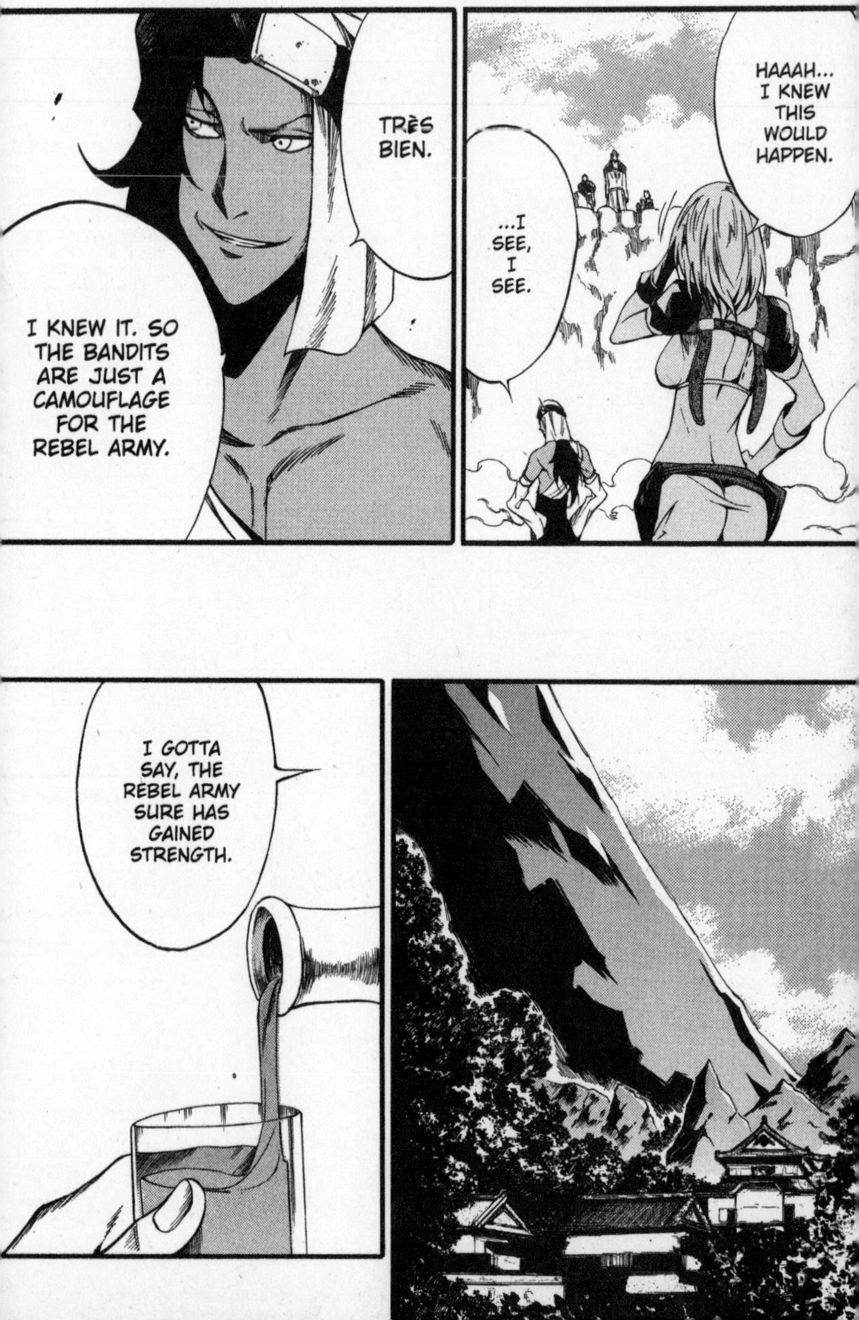
HAAAH... I KNEW THIS WOULD HAPPEN.
...I SEE, I SEE.
TRÈS BIEN.
I KNEW IT. SO THE BANDITS ARE JUST A CAMOUFLAGE FOR THE REBEL ARMY.
I GOTTA SAY, THE REBEL ARMY SURE HAS GAINED STRENGTH.

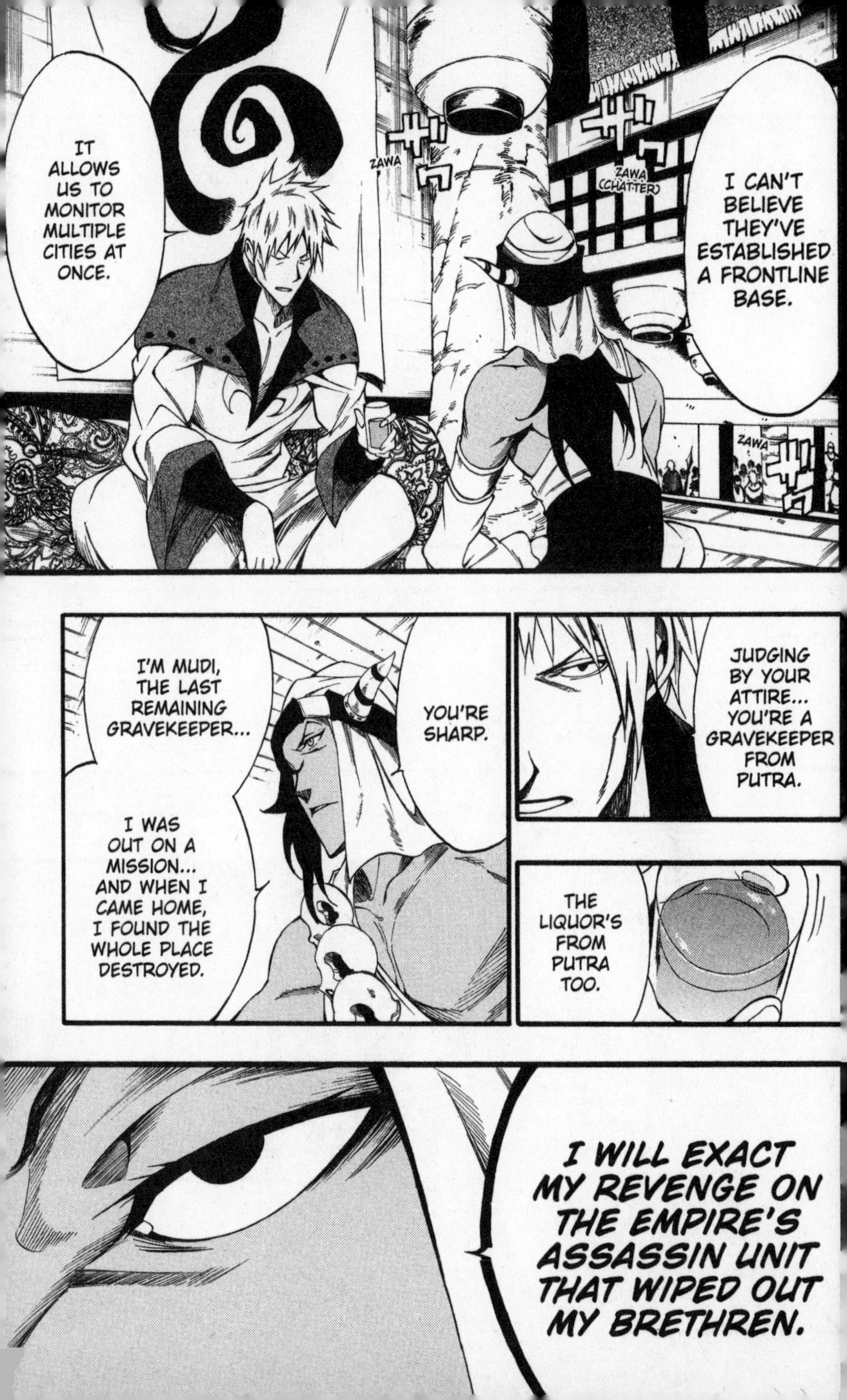
ZAWA
ZAWA (CHATTER)
I CAN'T BELIEVE THEY'VE ESTABLISHED A FRONTLINE BASE.
IT ALLOWS US TO MONITOR MULTIPLE CITIES AT ONCE.
ZAWA
JUDGING BY YOUR ATTIRE... YOU'RE A GRAVEKEEPER FROM PUTRA.
THE LIQUOR'S FROM PUTRA TOO.
YOU'RE SHARP.
I'M MUDI, THE LAST REMAINING GRAVEKEEPER...
I WAS OUT ON A MISSION... AND WHEN I CAME HOME, I FOUND THE WHOLE PLACE DESTROYED.
I WILL EXACT MY REVENGE ON THE EMPIRE'S ASSASSIN UNIT THAT WIPED OUT MY BRETHREN.

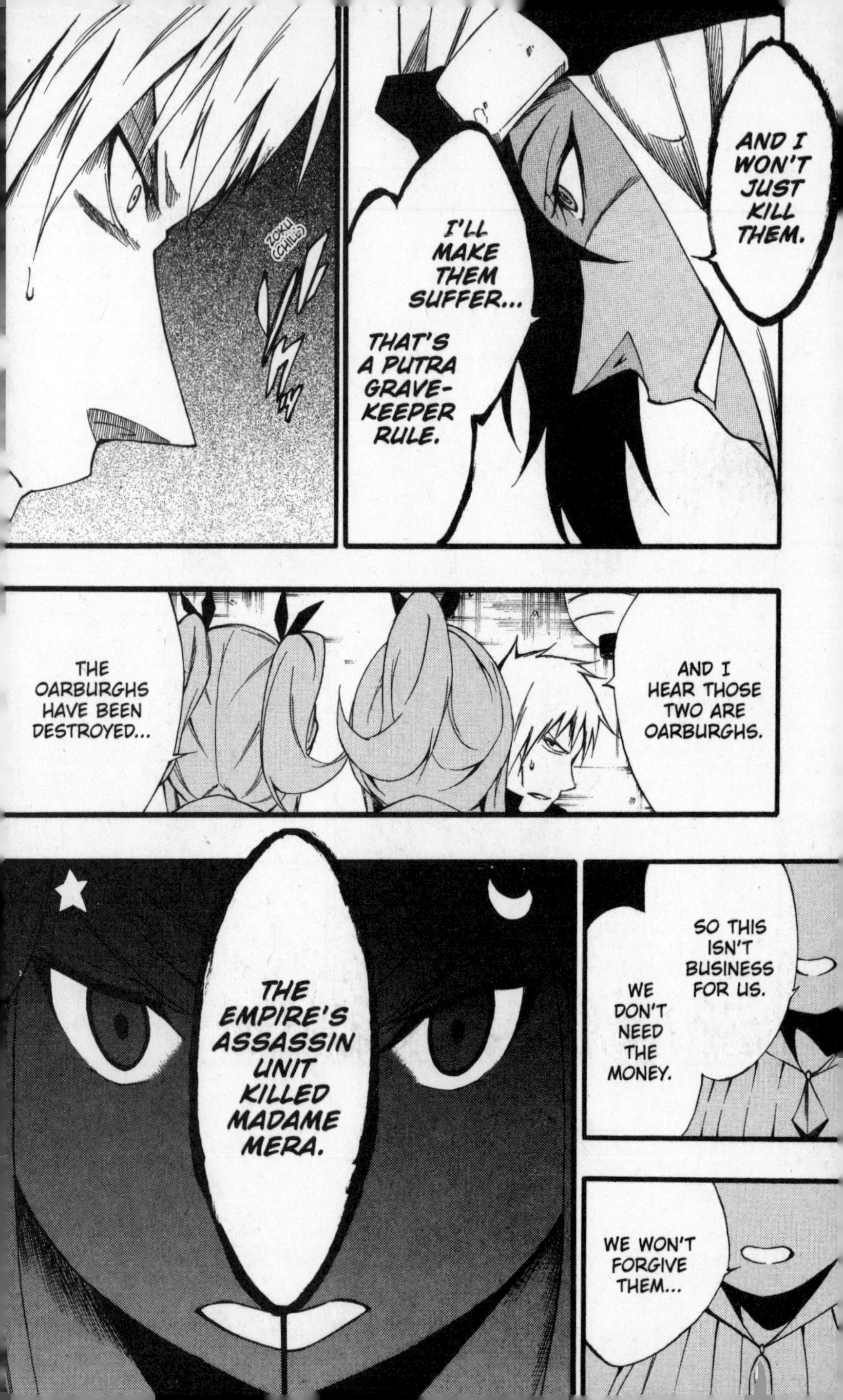
AND I WON'T JUST KILL THEM.
I'LL MAKE THEM SUFFER...
THAT'S A PUTRA GRAVE-KEEPER RULE.
ZOKU (CHILL)
AND I HEAR THOSE TWO ARE OARBURGHS.
THE OARBURGHS HAVE BEEN DESTROYED...
SO THIS ISN'T BUSINESS FOR US.
WE DON'T NEED THE MONEY.
THE EMPIRE'S ASSASSIN UNIT KILLED MADAME MERA.
WE WON'T FORGIVE THEM...

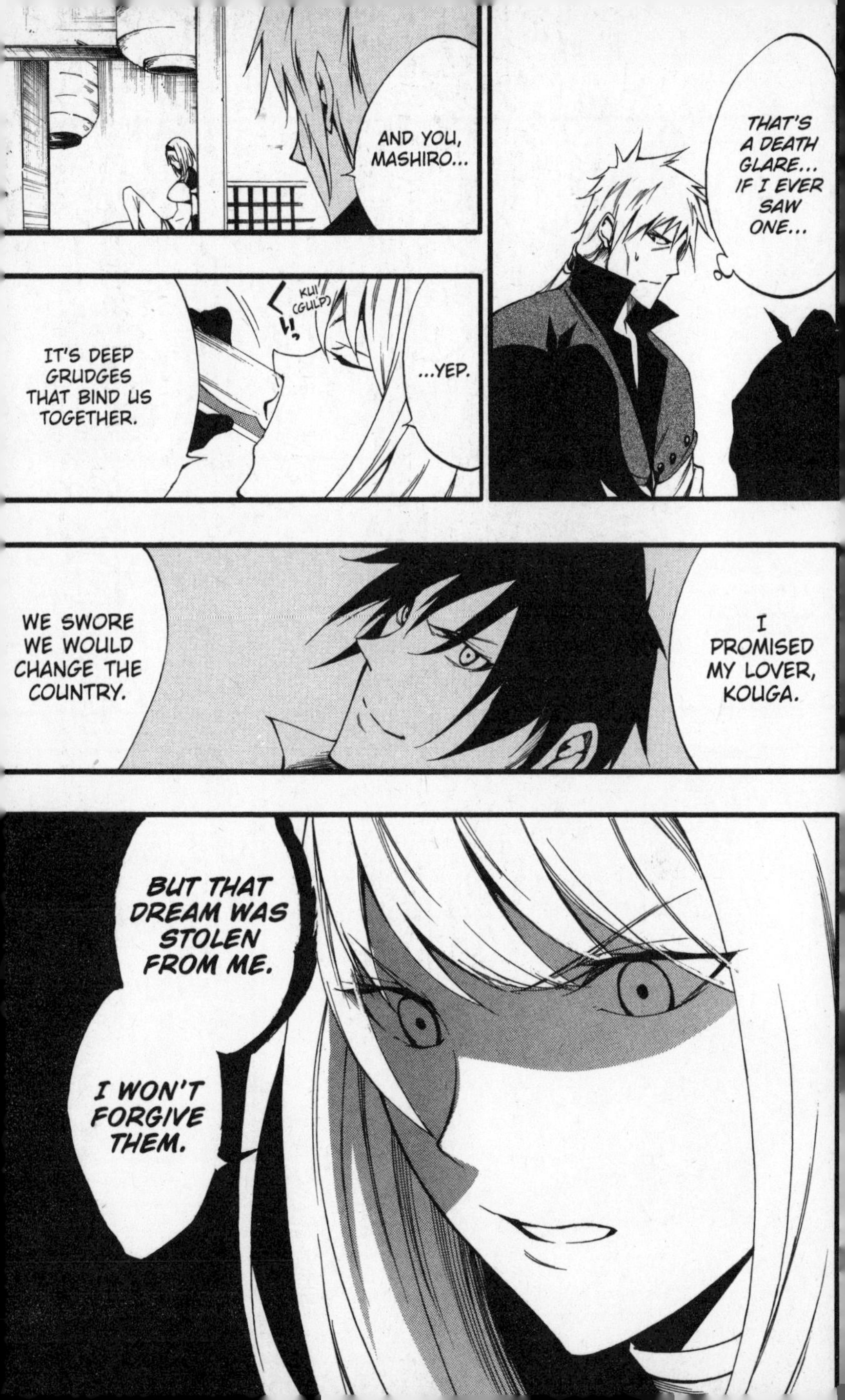
THAT'S A DEATH GLARE... IF I EVER SAW ONE...
AND YOU, MASHIRO...
...YEP.
KU! (GULP)
IT'S DEEP GRUDGES THAT BIND US TOGETHER.
I PROMISED MY LOVER, KOUGA.
WE SWORE WE WOULD CHANGE THE COUNTRY.
BUT THAT DREAM WAS STOLEN FROM ME.
I WON'T FORGIVE THEM.

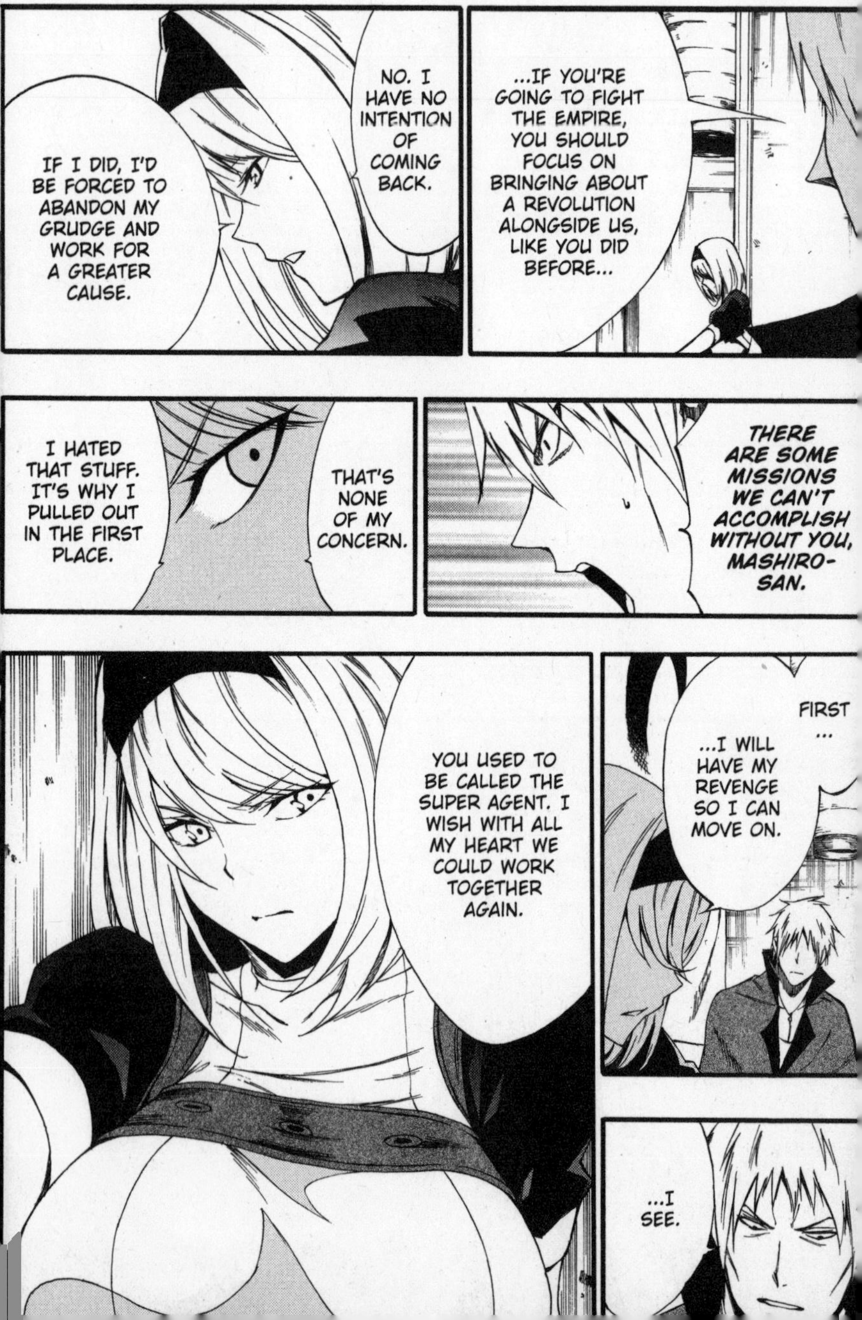
...IF YOU'RE GOING TO FIGHT THE EMPIRE, YOU SHOULD FOCUS ON BRINGING ABOUT A REVOLUTION ALONGSIDE US, LIKE YOU DID BEFORE...
NO. I HAVE NO INTENTION OF COMING BACK.
IF I DID, I'D BE FORCED TO ABANDON MY GRUDGE AND WORK FOR A GREATER CAUSE.
THERE ARE SOME MISSIONS WE CAN'T ACCOMPLISH WITHOUT YOU, MASHIRO-SAN.
THAT'S NONE OF MY CONCERN.
I HATED THAT STUFF. IT'S WHY I PULLED OUT IN THE FIRST PLACE.
YOU USED TO BE CALLED THE SUPER AGENT. I WISH WITH ALL MY HEART WE COULD WORK TOGETHER AGAIN.
FIRST...
...I WILL HAVE MY REVENGE SO I CAN MOVE ON.
...I SEE.

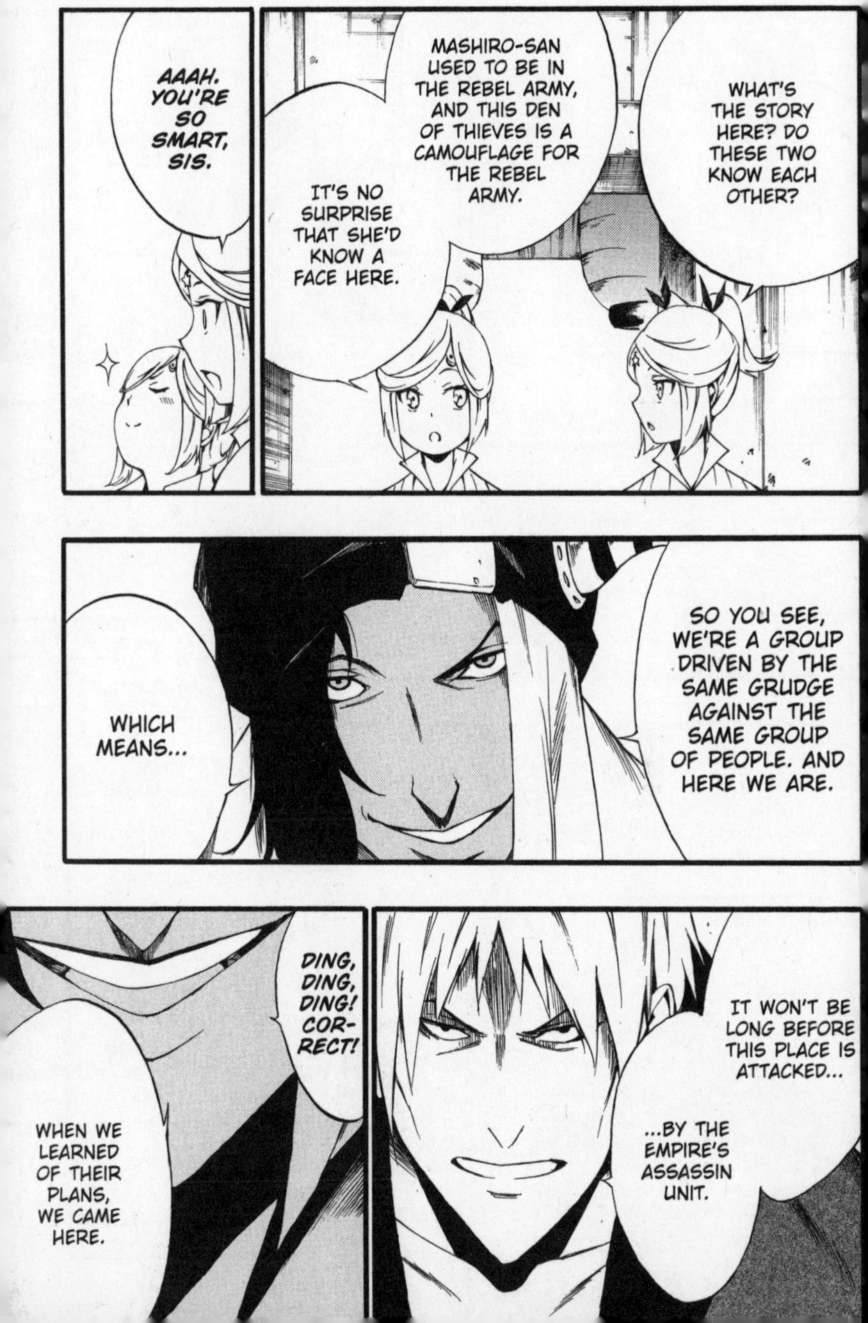
WHAT'S THE STORY HERE? DO THESE TWO KNOW EACH OTHER?
MASHIRO-SAN USED TO BE IN THE REBEL ARMY, AND THIS DEN OF THIEVES IS A CAMOUFLAGE FOR THE REBEL ARMY.
IT'S NO SURPRISE THAT SHE'D KNOW A FACE HERE.
AAAH. YOU'RE SO SMART, SIS.
SO YOU SEE, WE'RE A GROUP DRIVEN BY THE SAME GRUDGE AGAINST THE SAME GROUP OF PEOPLE. AND HERE WE ARE.
WHICH MEANS...
IT WON'T BE LONG BEFORE THIS PLACE IS ATTACKED...
...BY THE EMPIRE'S ASSASSIN UNIT.
DING, DING, DING! COR-RECT!
WHEN WE LEARNED OF THEIR PLANS, WE CAME HERE.

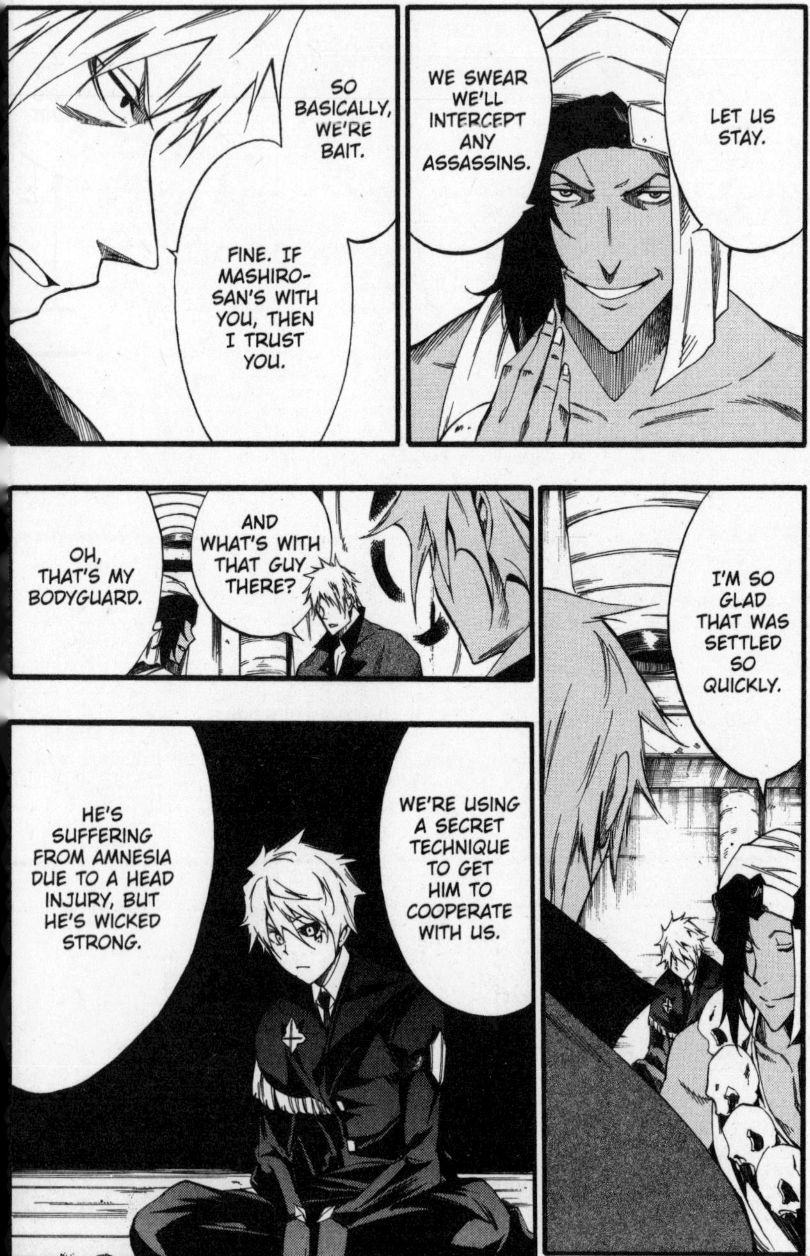
LET US STAY.
WE SWEAR WE'LL INTERCEPT ANY ASSASSINS.
SO BASICALLY, WE'RE BAIT.
FINE. IF MASHIRO-SAN'S WITH YOU, THEN I TRUST YOU.
I'M SO GLAD THAT WAS SETTLED SO QUICKLY.
AND WHAT'S WITH THAT GUY THERE?
OH, THAT'S MY BODYGUARD.
HE'S SUFFERING FROM AMNESIA DUE TO A HEAD INJURY, BUT HE'S WICKED STRONG.
WE'RE USING A SECRET TECHNIQUE TO GET HIM TO COOPERATE WITH US.

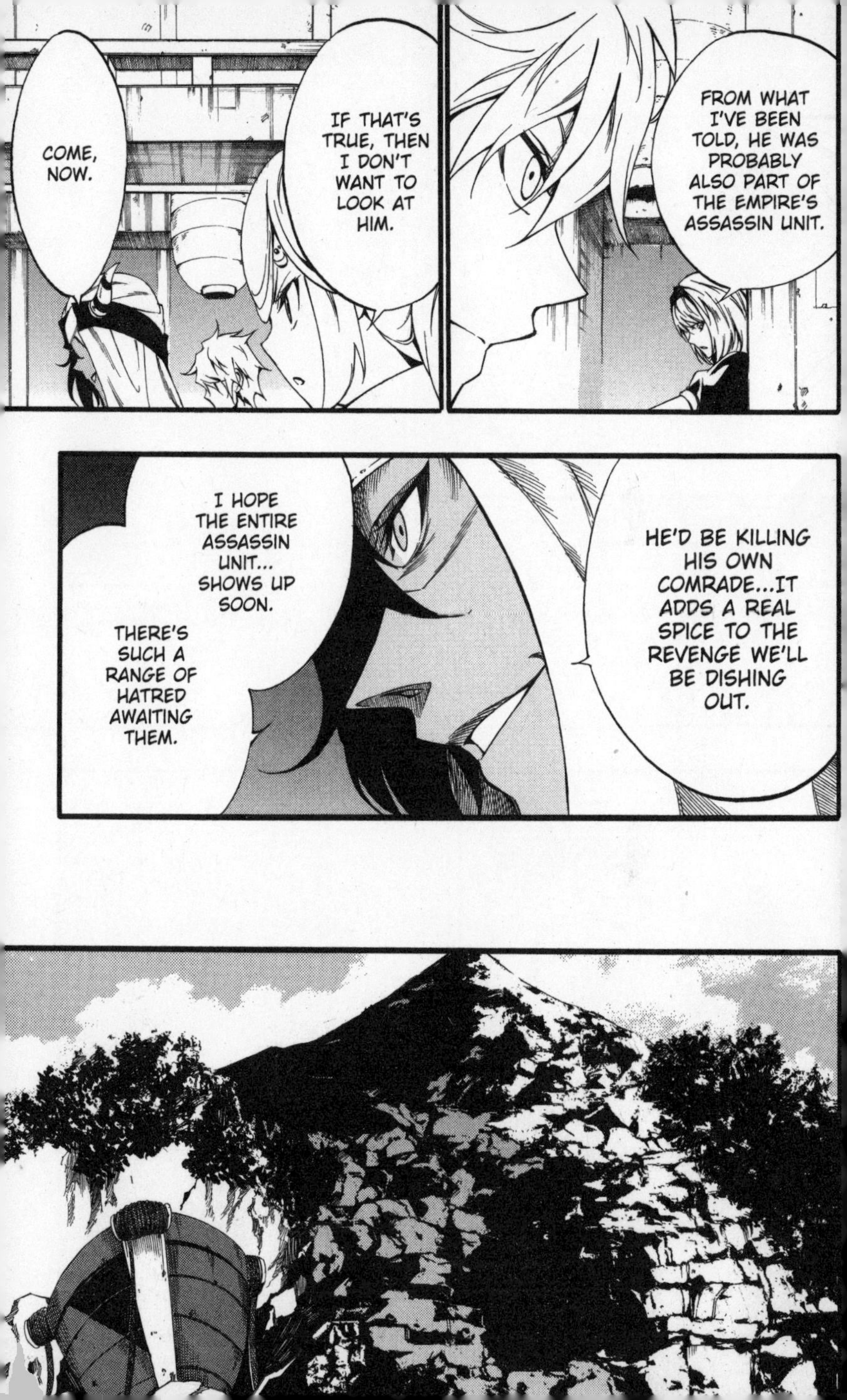
FROM WHAT I'VE BEEN TOLD, HE WAS PROBABLY ALSO PART OF THE EMPIRE'S ASSASSIN UNIT.
IF THAT'S TRUE, THEN I DON'T WANT TO LOOK AT HIM.
COME, NOW.
HE'D BE KILLING HIS OWN COMRADE...IT ADDS A REAL SPICE TO THE REVENGE WE'LL BE DISHING OUT.
I HOPE THE ENTIRE ASSASSIN UNIT... SHOWS UP SOON.
THERE'S SUCH A RANGE OF HATRED AWAITING THEM.

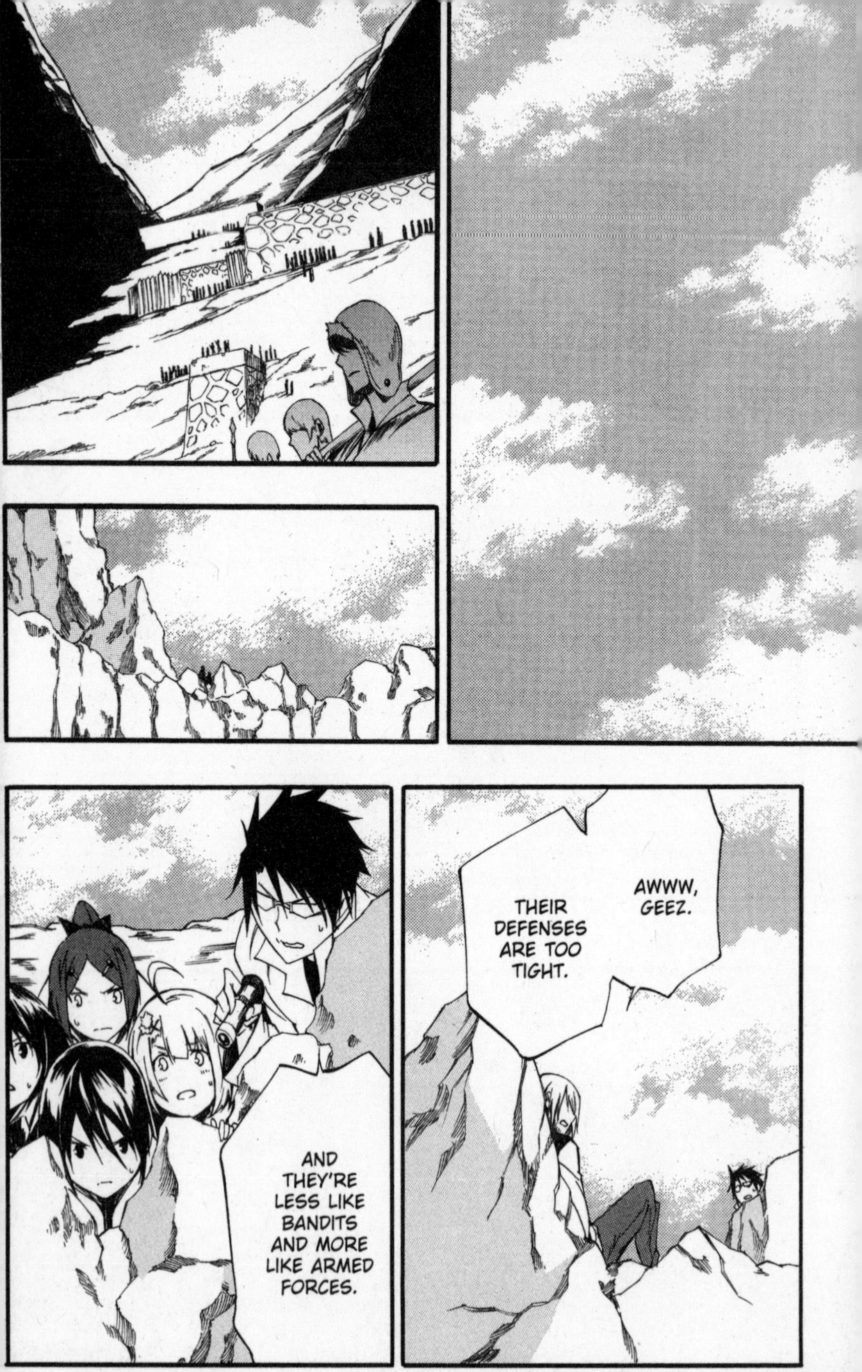
AWWW, GEEZ.
THEIR DEFENSES ARE TOO TIGHT.
AND THEY'RE LESS LIKE BANDITS AND MORE LIKE ARMED FORCES.

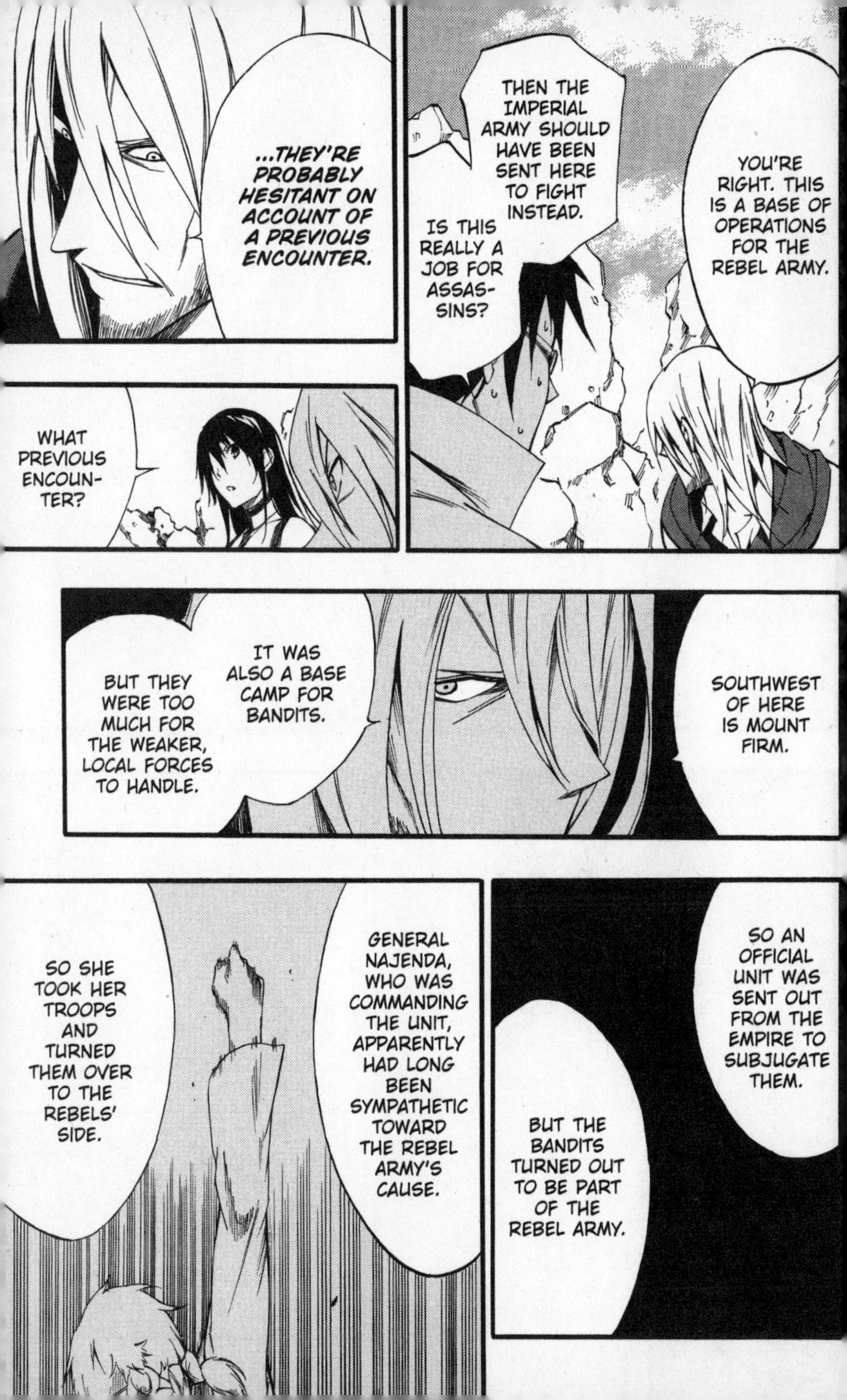

YOU'RE RIGHT. THIS IS A BASE OF OPERATIONS FOR THE REBEL ARMY.
THEN THE IMPERIAL ARMY SHOULD HAVE BEEN SENT HERE TO FIGHT INSTEAD.
IS THIS REALLY A JOB FOR ASSAS-SINS?
...THEY'RE PROBABLY HESITANT ON ACCOUNT OF A PREVIOUS ENCOUNTER.
WHAT PREVIOUS ENCOUN-TER?
SOUTHWEST OF HERE IS MOUNT FIRM.
IT WAS ALSO A BASE CAMP FOR BANDITS.
BUT THEY WERE TOO MUCH FOR THE WEAKER, LOCAL FORCES TO HANDLE.
SO AN OFFICIAL UNIT WAS SENT OUT FROM THE EMPIRE TO SUBJUGATE THEM.
BUT THE BANDITS TURNED OUT TO BE PART OF THE REBEL ARMY.
GENERAL NAJENDA, WHO WAS COMMANDING THE UNIT, APPARENTLY HAD LONG BEEN SYMPATHETIC TOWARD THE REBEL ARMY'S CAUSE.
SO SHE TOOK HER TROOPS AND TURNED THEM OVER TO THE REBELS' SIDE.

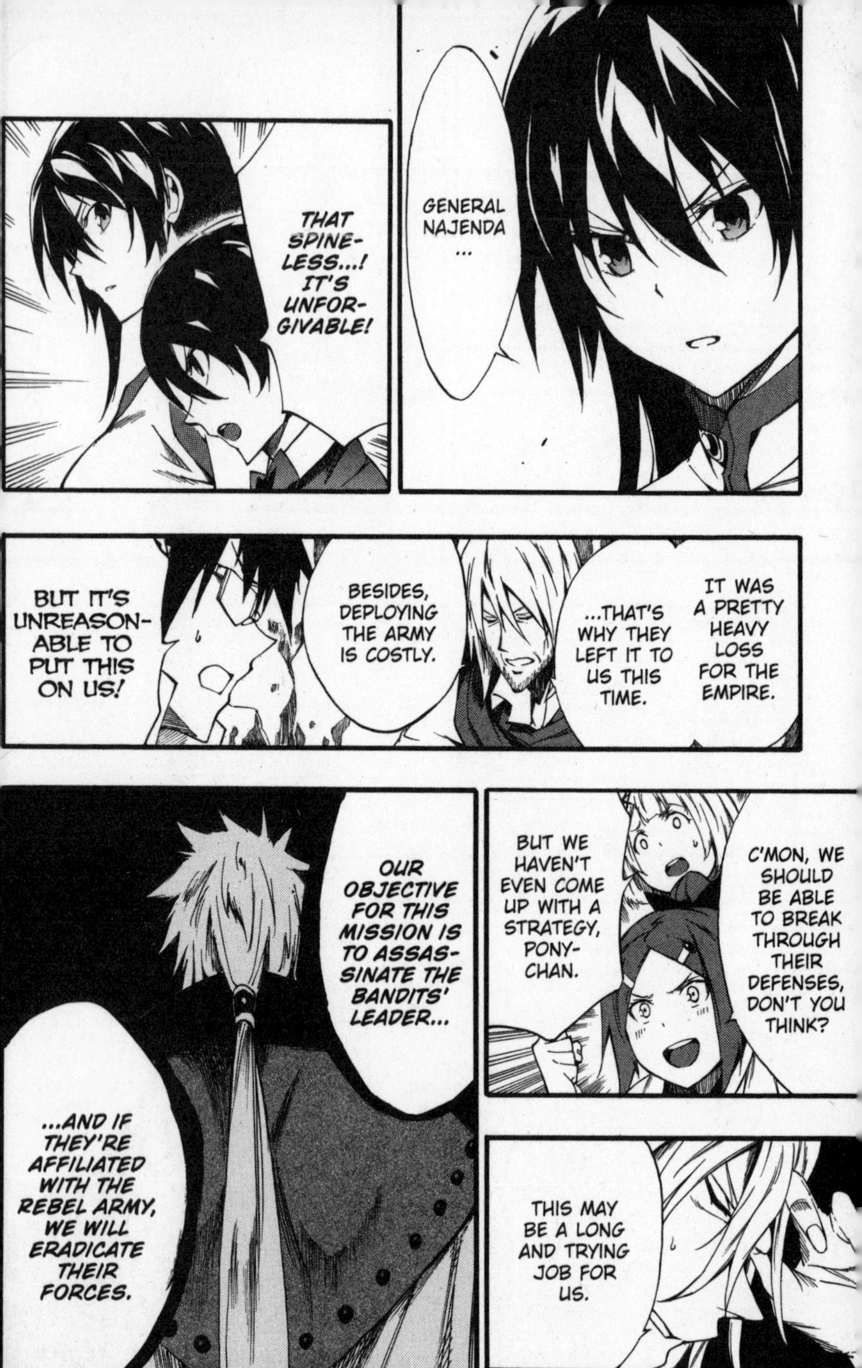
GENERAL NAJENDA ...
THAT SPINELESS...! IT'S UNFORGIVABLE!
IT WAS A PRETTY HEAVY LOSS FOR THE EMPIRE.
...THAT'S WHY THEY LEFT IT TO US THIS TIME.
BESIDES, DEPLOYING THE ARMY IS COSTLY.
BUT IT'S UNREASONABLE TO PUT THIS ON US!
C'MON, WE SHOULD BE ABLE TO BREAK THROUGH THEIR DEFENSES, DON'T YOU THINK?
BUT WE HAVEN'T EVEN COME UP WITH A STRATEGY, PONY-CHAN.
THIS MAY BE A LONG AND TRYING JOB FOR US.
OUR OBJECTIVE FOR THIS MISSION IS TO ASSASSINATE THE BANDITS' LEADER...
...AND IF THEY'RE AFFILIATED WITH THE REBEL ARMY, WE WILL ERADICATE THEIR FORCES.

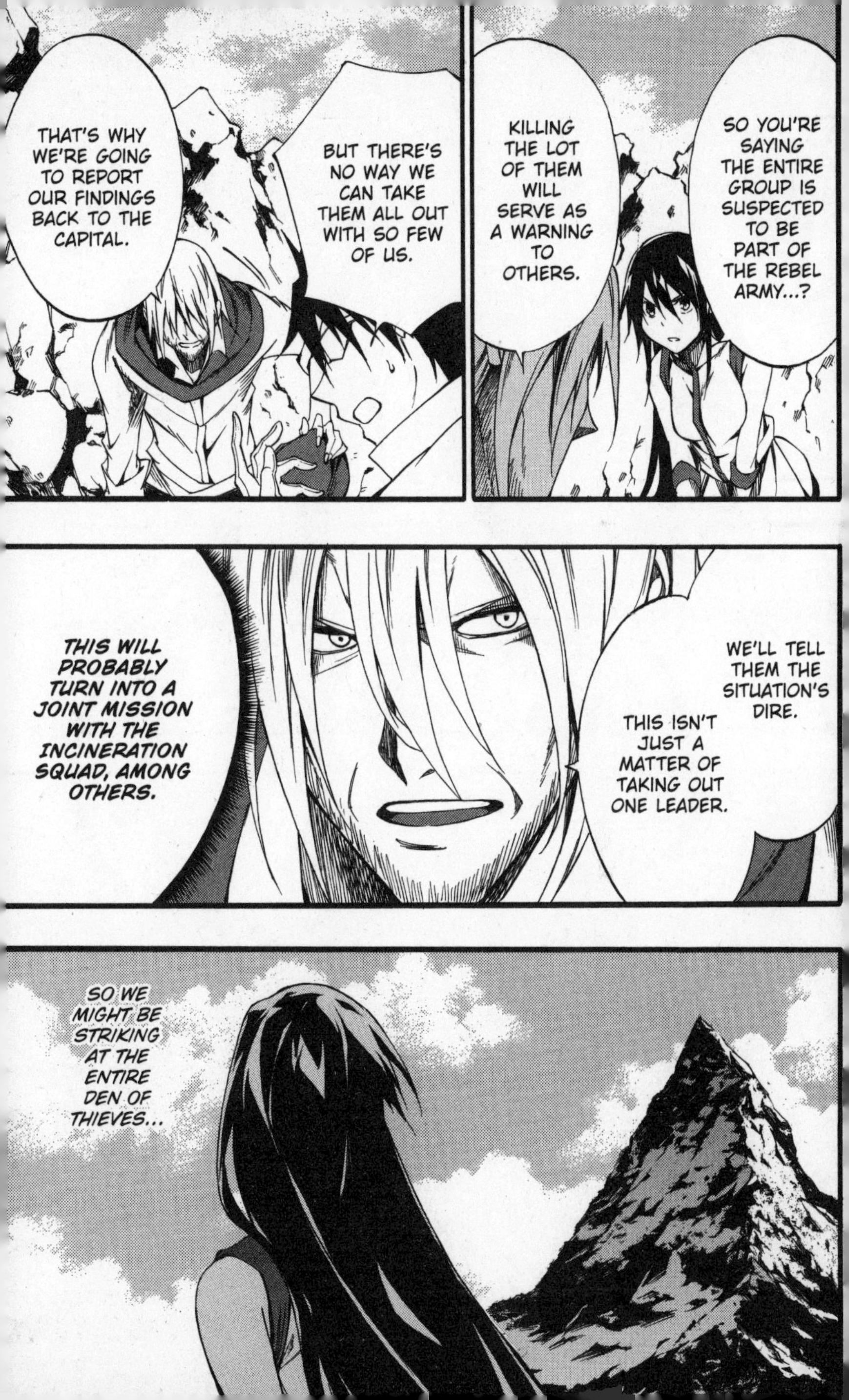
SO YOU'RE SAYING THE ENTIRE GROUP IS SUSPECTED TO BE PART OF THE REBEL ARMY...?
KILLING THE LOT OF THEM WILL SERVE AS A WARNING TO OTHERS.
BUT THERE'S NO WAY WE CAN TAKE THEM ALL OUT WITH SO FEW OF US.
THAT'S WHY WE'RE GOING TO REPORT OUR FINDINGS BACK TO THE CAPITAL.
WE'LL TELL THEM THE SITUATION'S DIRE.
THIS ISN'T JUST A MATTER OF TAKING OUT ONE LEADER.
THIS WILL PROBABLY TURN INTO A JOINT MISSION WITH THE INCINERATION SQUAD, AMONG OTHERS.
SO WE MIGHT BE STRIKING AT THE ENTIRE DEN OF THIEVES...

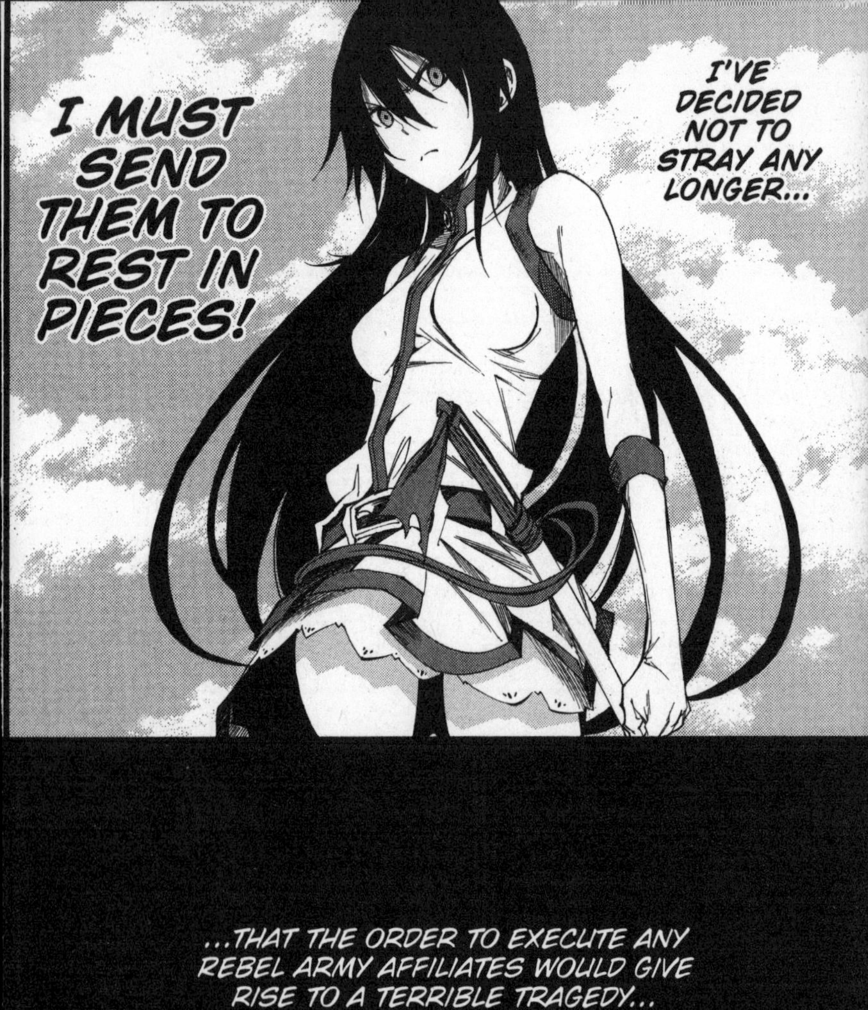
I'VE DECIDED NOT TO STRAY ANY LONGER...
I MUST SEND THEM TO REST IN PIECES!
...THAT THE ORDER TO EXECUTE ANY REBEL ARMY AFFILIATES WOULD GIVE RISE TO A TERRIBLE TRAGEDY...

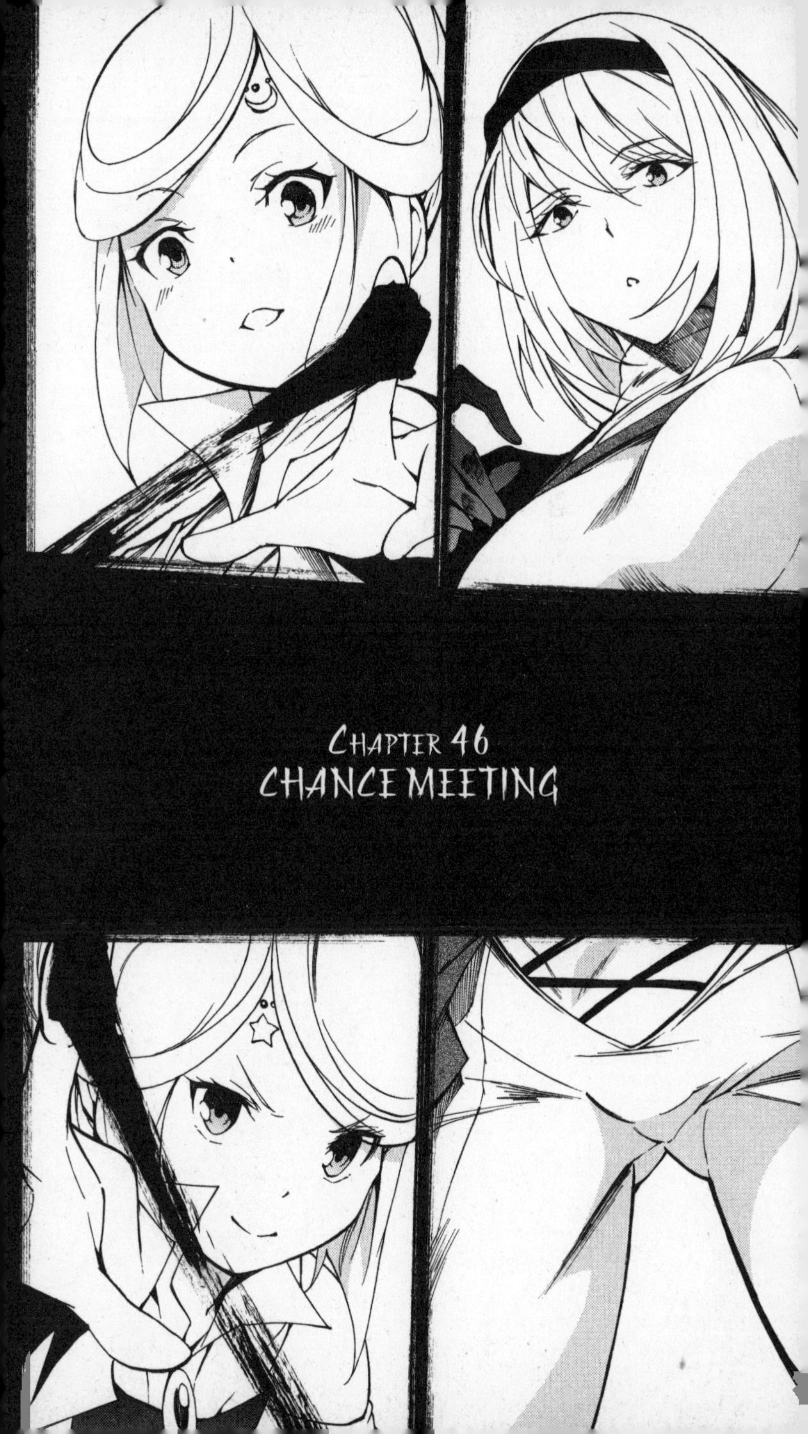
Chapter 46
Chance Meeting

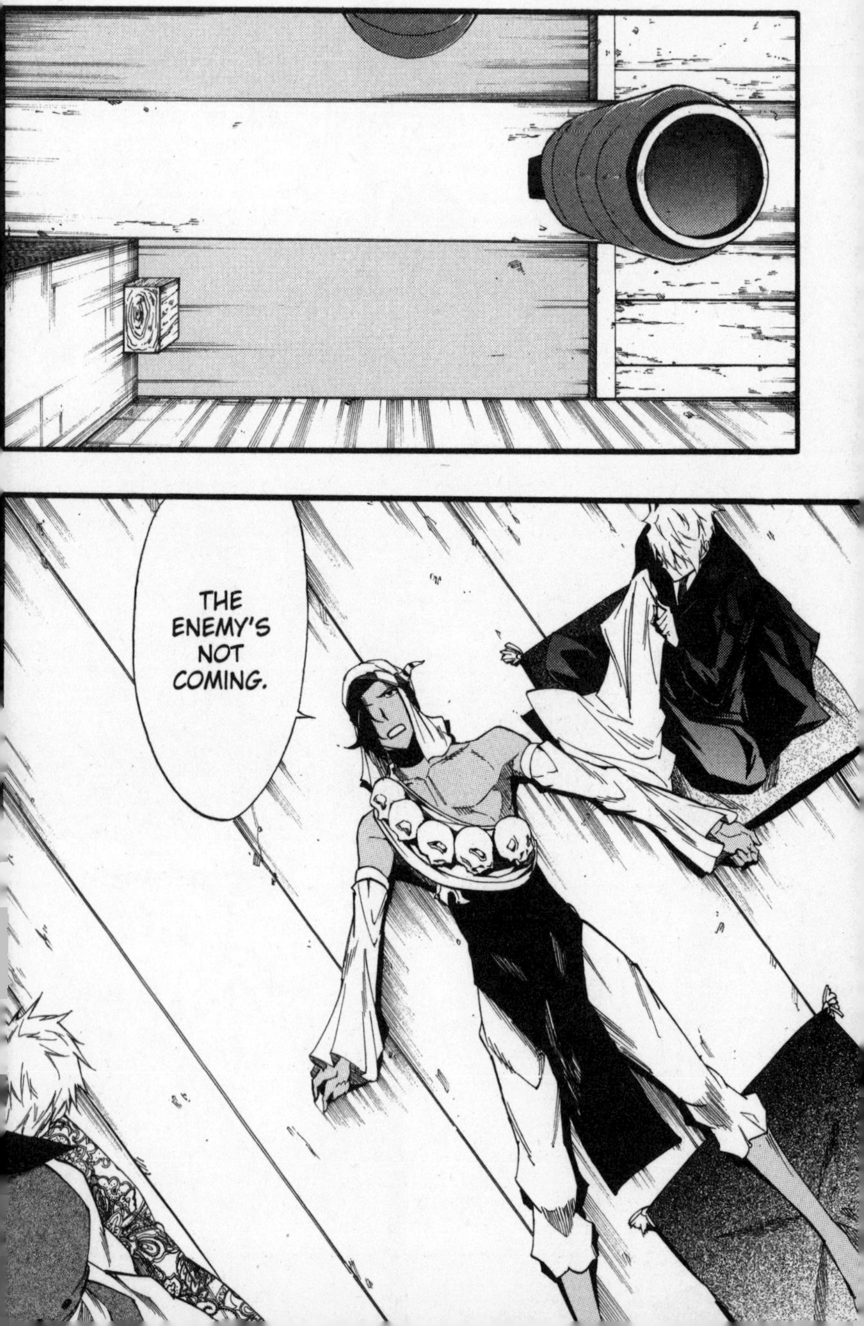
THE ENEMY'S NOT COMING.

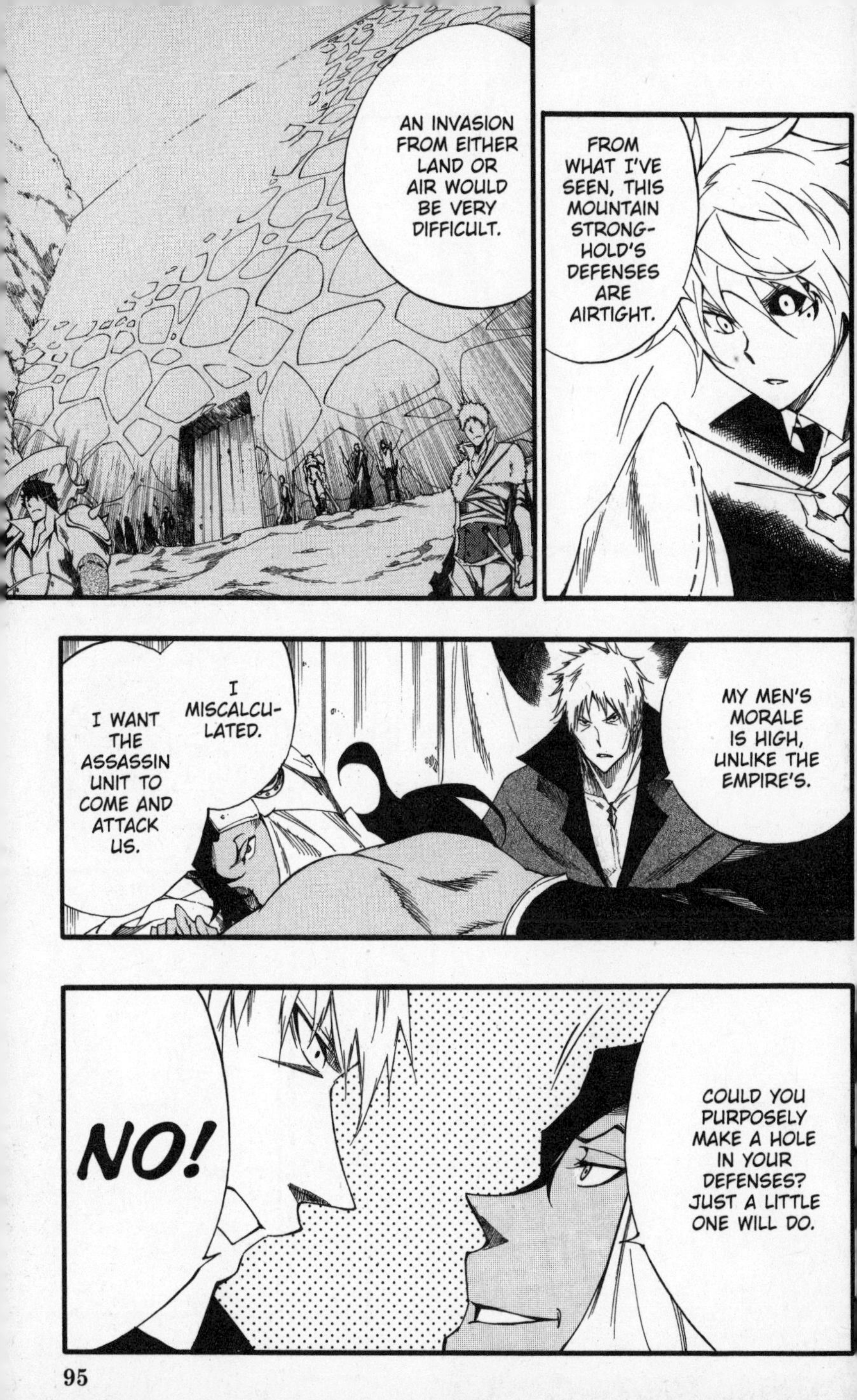
FROM WHAT I'VE SEEN, THIS MOUNTAIN STRONG-HOLD'S DEFENSES ARE AIRTIGHT.
AN INVASION FROM EITHER LAND OR AIR WOULD BE VERY DIFFICULT.
MY MEN'S MORALE IS HIGH, UNLIKE THE EMPIRE'S.
I MISCALCU-LATED.
I WANT THE ASSASSIN UNIT TO COME AND ATTACK US.
COULD YOU PURPOSELY MAKE A HOLE IN YOUR DEFENSES? JUST A LITTLE ONE WILL DO.
NO!

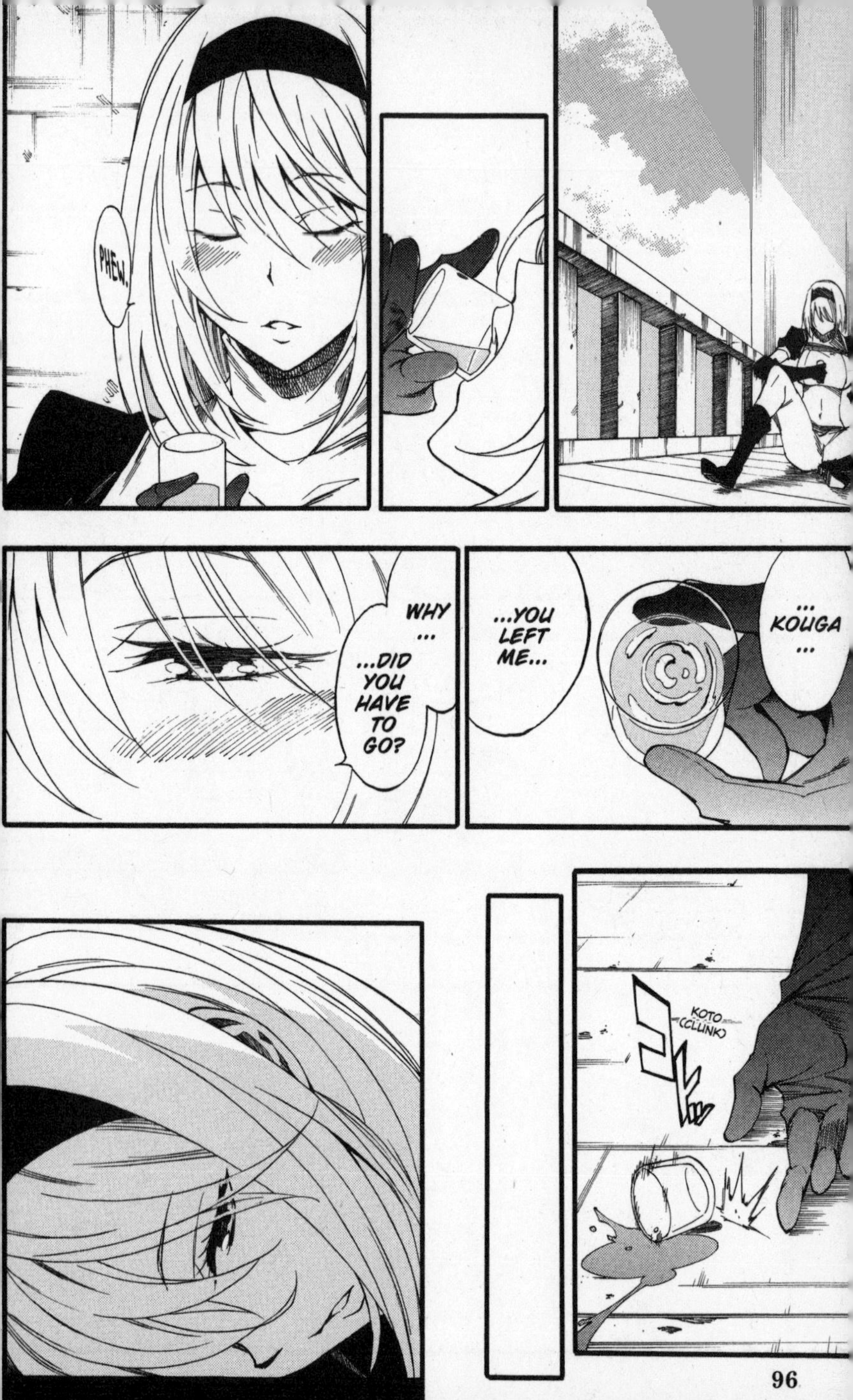
PHEW.
...
KOUGA
...
...YOU LEFT ME...
WHY
...
...DID YOU HAVE TO GO?
KOTO
(CLUNK)

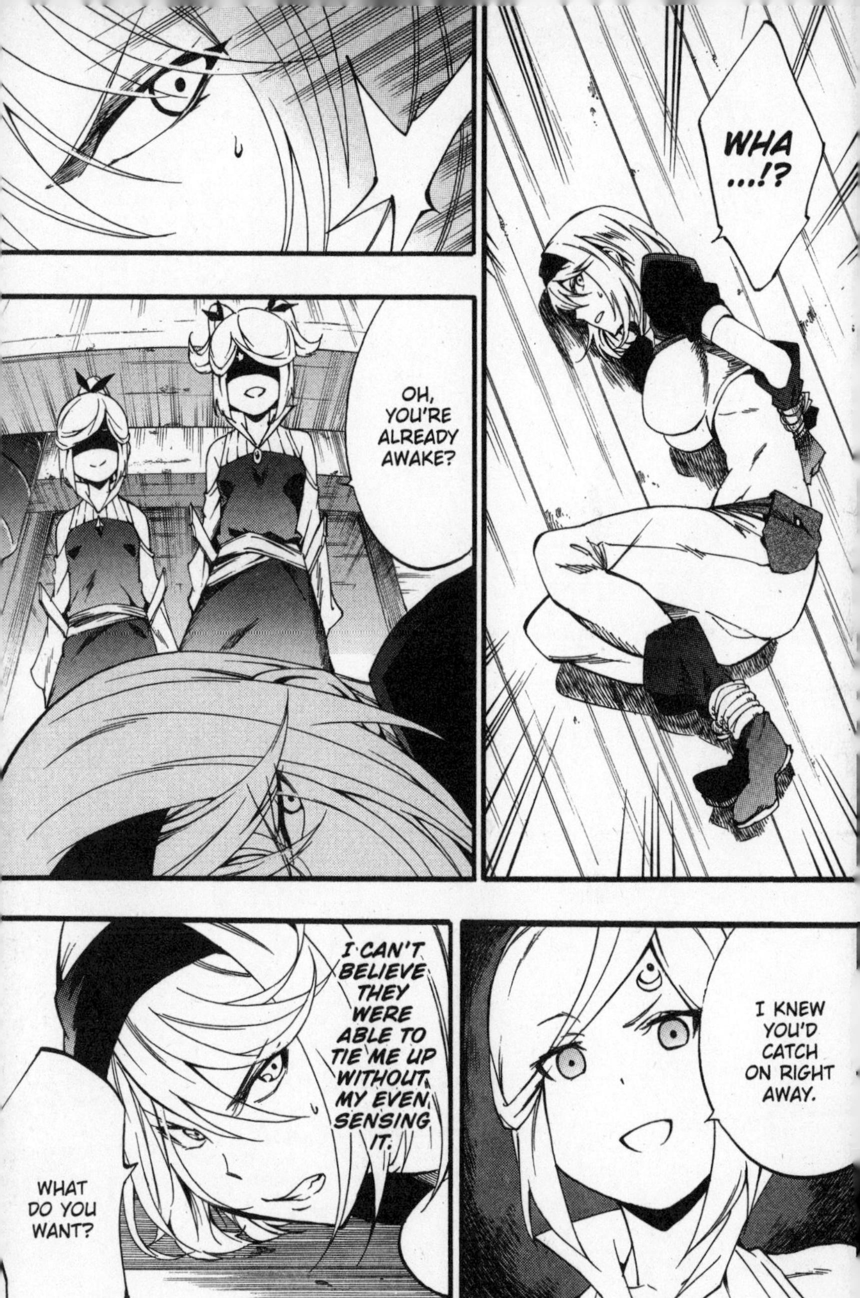
WHA ...!?
OH, YOU'RE ALREADY AWAKE?
I KNEW YOU'D CATCH ON RIGHT AWAY.
I CAN'T BELIEVE THEY WERE ABLE TO TIE ME UP WITHOUT MY EVEN SENSING IT.
WHAT DO YOU WANT?

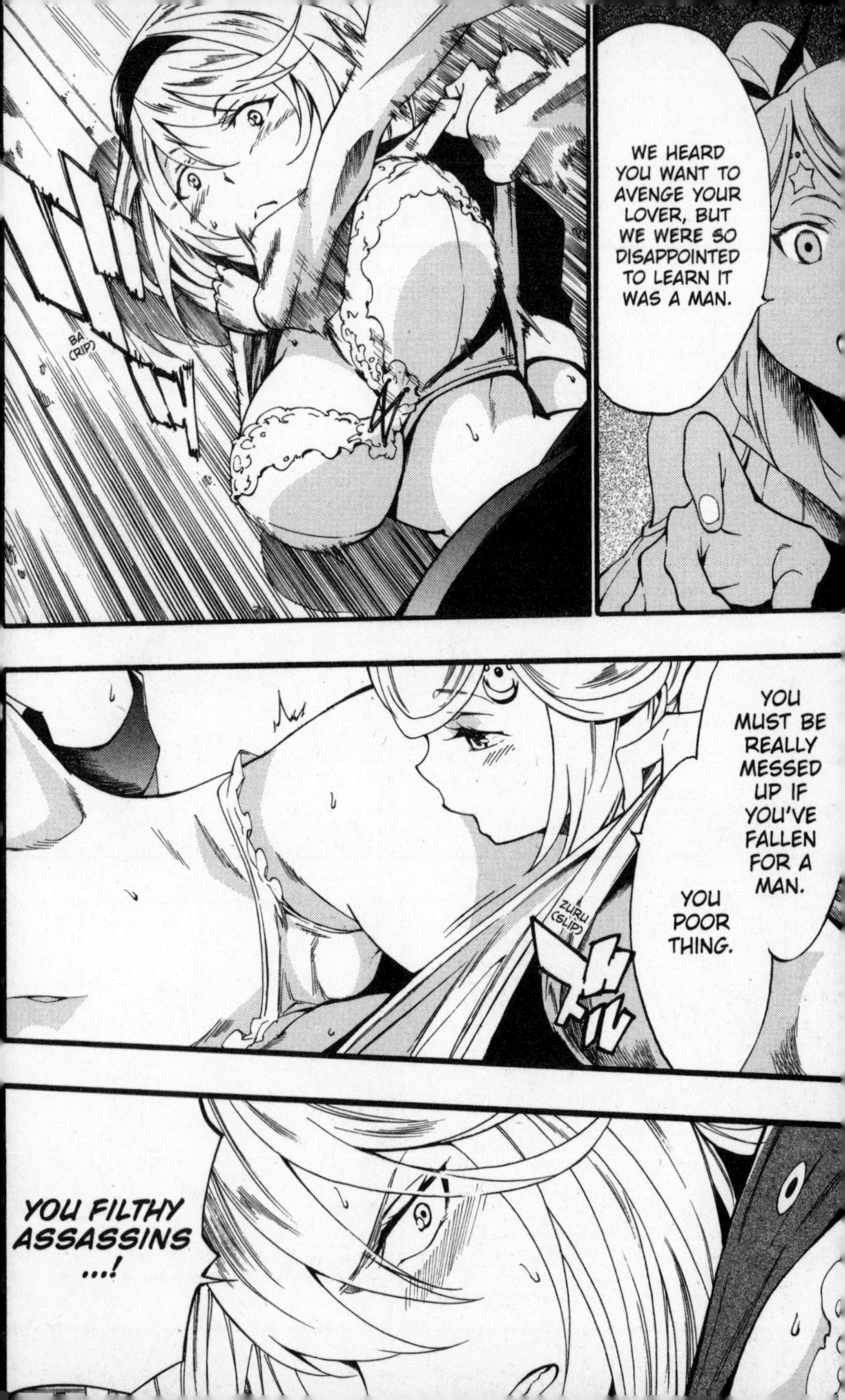
WE HEARD YOU WANT TO AVENGE YOUR LOVER, BUT WE WERE SO DISAPPOINTED TO LEARN IT WAS A MAN.
BA (RIP)
YOU MUST BE REALLY MESSED UP IF YOU'VE FALLEN FOR A MAN.
YOU POOR THING.
ZURU (SLIP)
YOU FILTHY ASSASSINS ...!

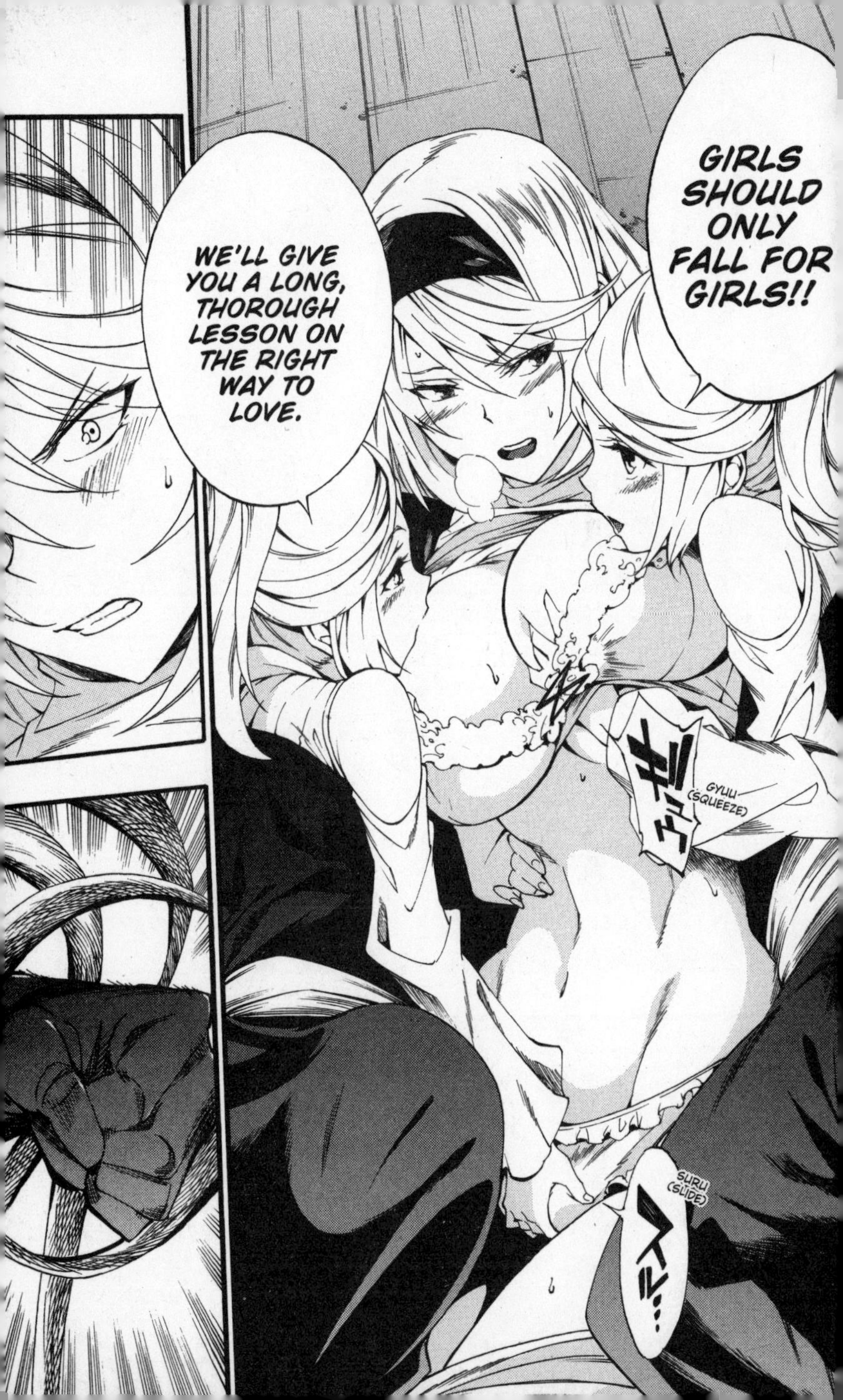
GIRLS SHOULD ONLY FALL FOR GIRLS!!
WE'LL GIVE YOU A LONG, THOROUGH LESSON ON THE RIGHT WAY TO LOVE.
GYUU (SQUEEZE)
SURU (SLIDE)

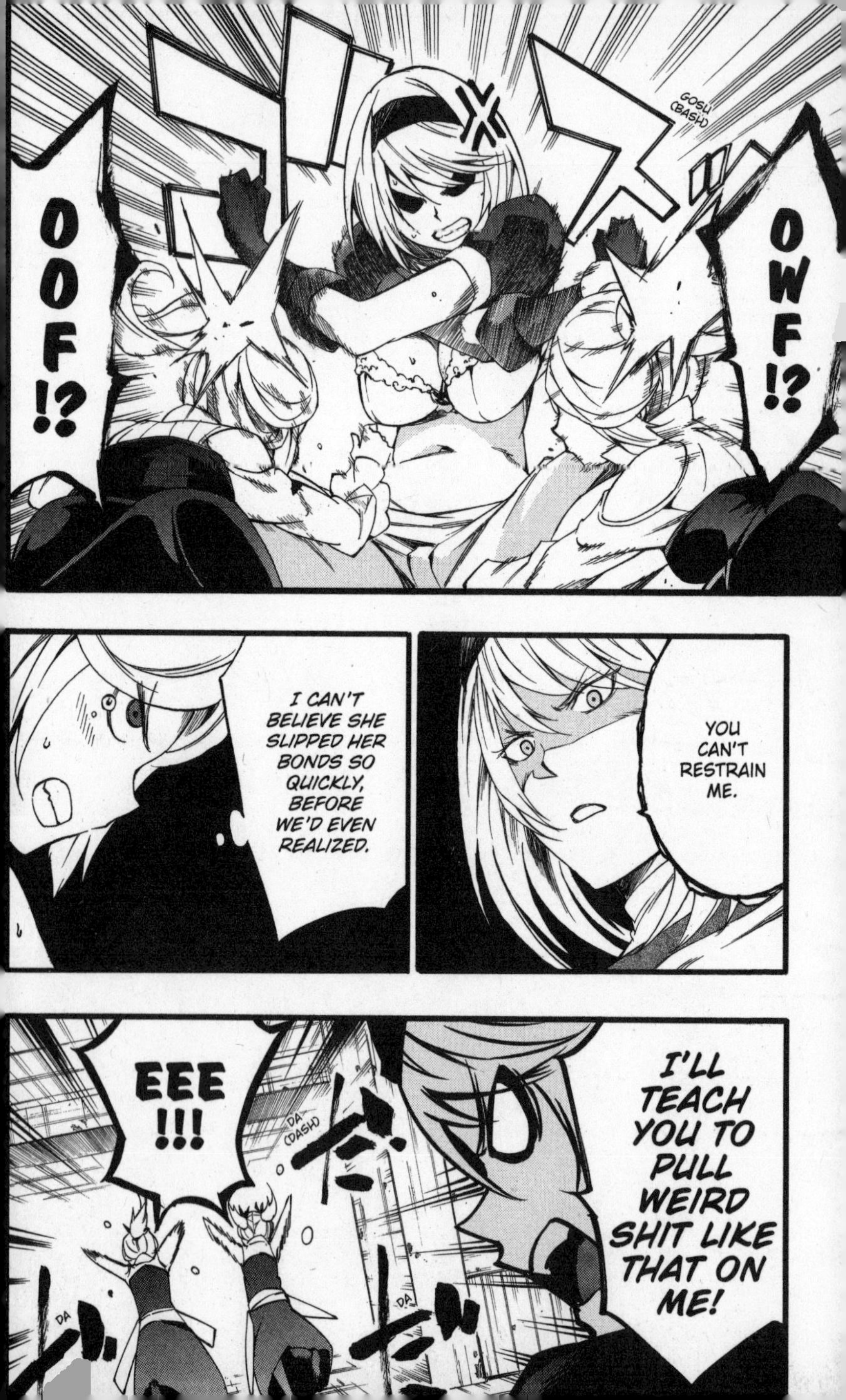
GOSU (BASH)
OWF!?
OOF!?
YOU CAN'T RESTRAIN ME.
I CAN'T BELIEVE SHE SLIPPED HER BONDS SO QUICKLY, BEFORE WE'D EVEN REALIZED.
I'LL TEACH YOU TO PULL WEIRD SHIT LIKE THAT ON ME!
DA (DASH)
EEE!!!
DA
DA

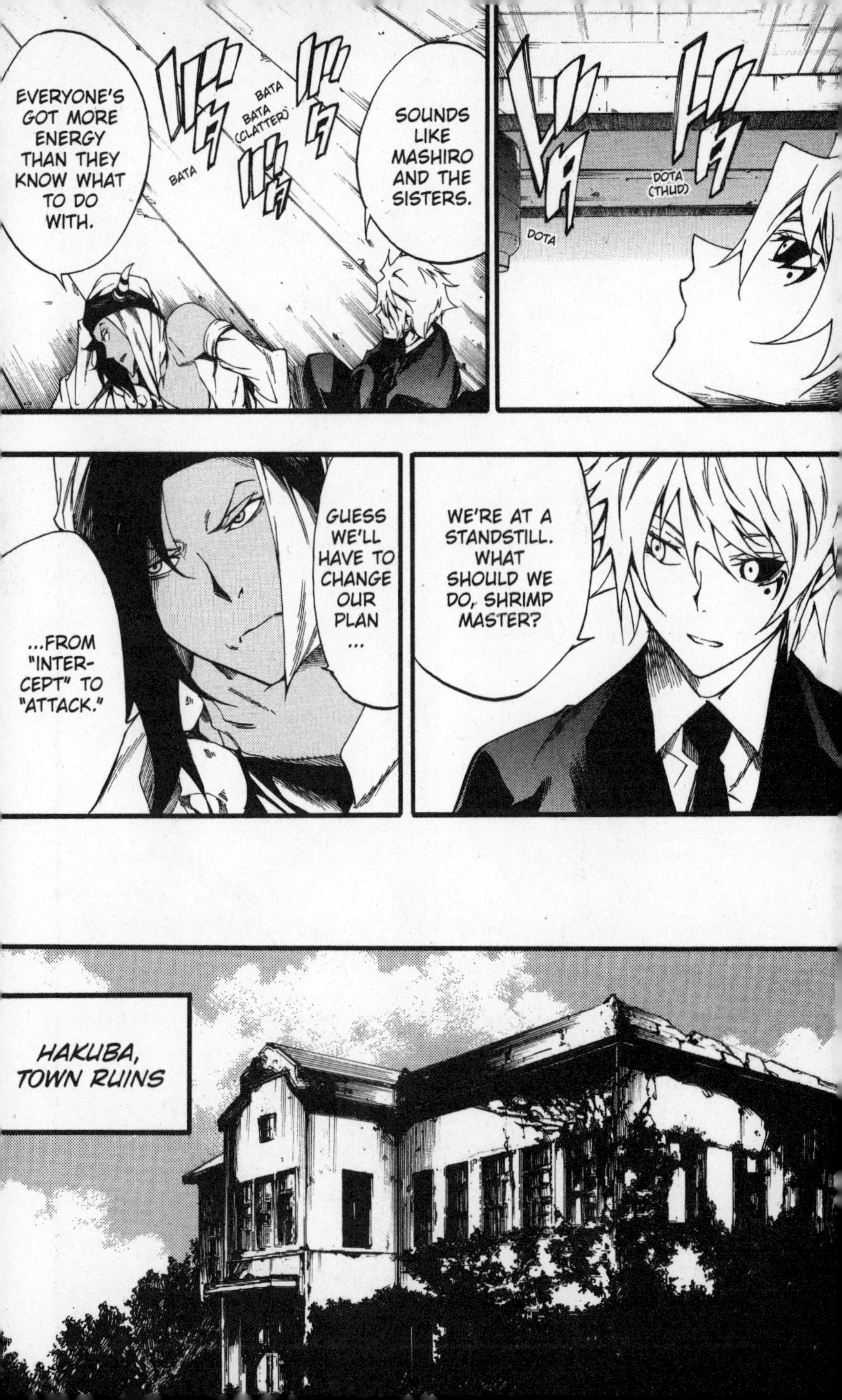
DOTA (THUD)
DOTA
SOUNDS LIKE MASHIRO AND THE SISTERS.
BATA BATA (CLATTER)
BATA
EVERYONE'S GOT MORE ENERGY THAN THEY KNOW WHAT TO DO WITH.
WE'RE AT A STANDSTILL. WHAT SHOULD WE DO, SHRIMP MASTER?
GUESS WE'LL HAVE TO CHANGE OUR PLAN ...
...FROM "INTERCEPT" TO "ATTACK."
HAKUBA, TOWN RUINS

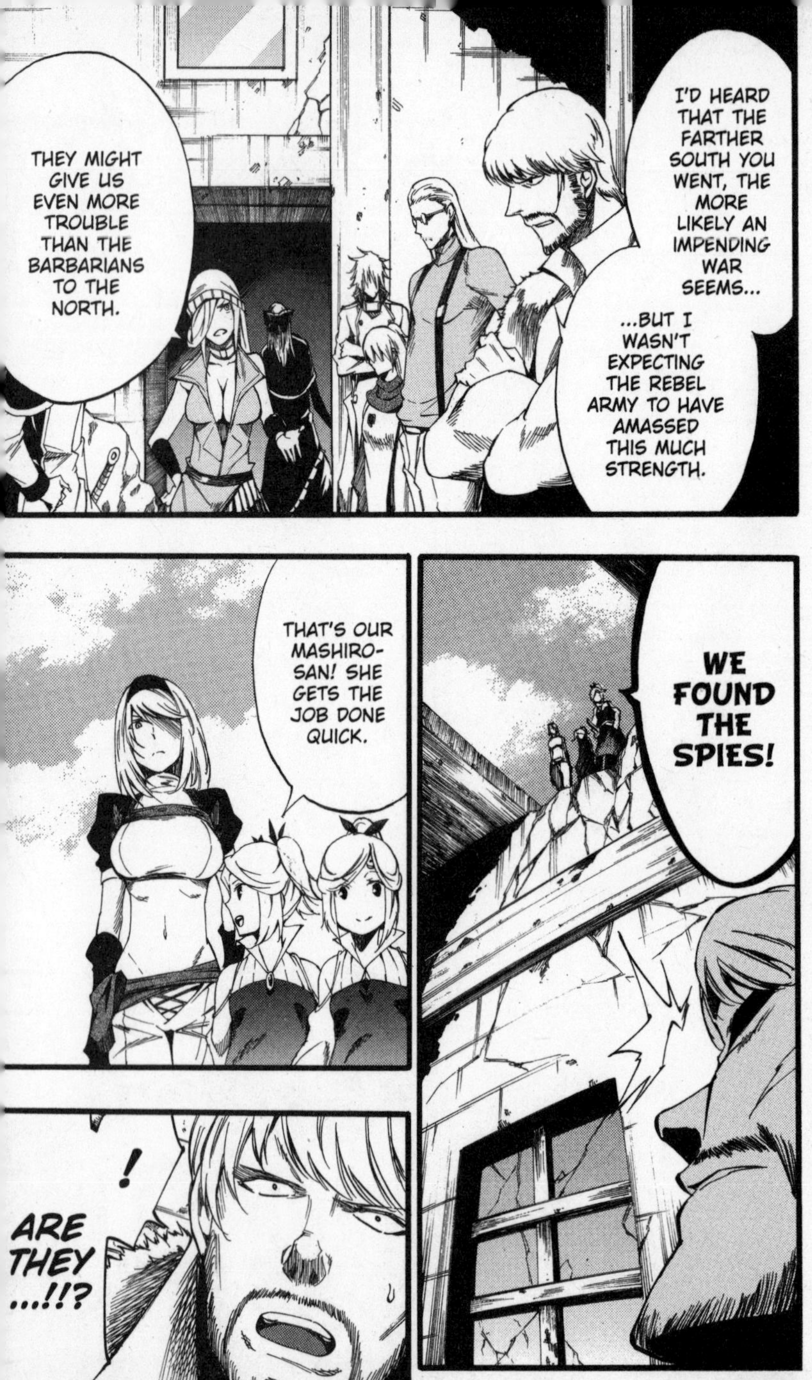
I'D HEARD THAT THE FARTHER SOUTH YOU WENT, THE MORE LIKELY AN IMPENDING WAR SEEMS...
...BUT I WASN'T EXPECTING THE REBEL ARMY TO HAVE AMASSED THIS MUCH STRENGTH.
THEY MIGHT GIVE US EVEN MORE TROUBLE THAN THE BARBARIANS TO THE NORTH.
WE FOUND THE SPIES!
THAT'S OUR MASHIRO-SAN! SHE GETS THE JOB DONE QUICK.
!
ARE THEY ...!!?

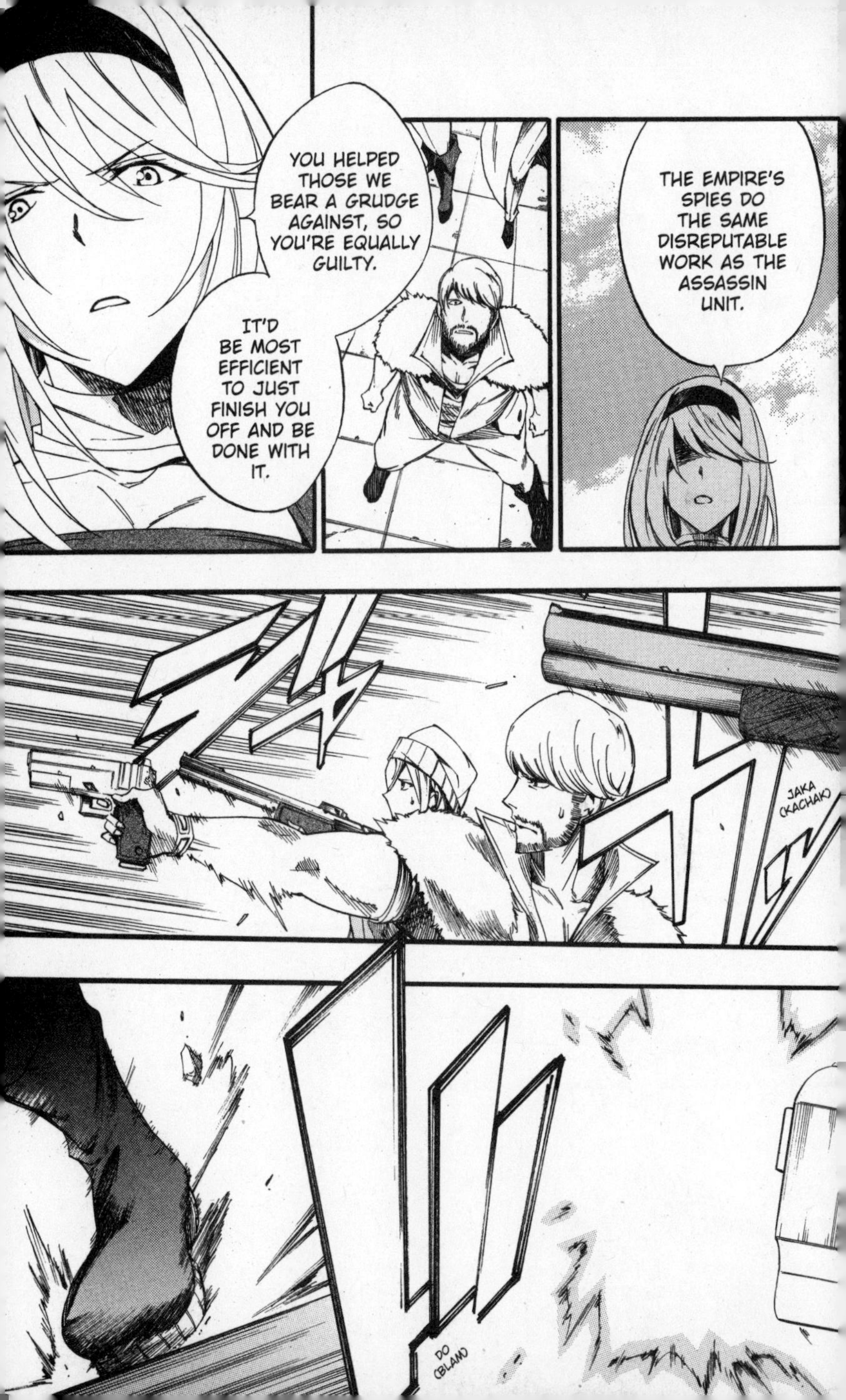
THE EMPIRE'S SPIES DO THE SAME DISREPUTABLE WORK AS THE ASSASSIN UNIT.
YOU HELPED THOSE WE BEAR A GRUDGE AGAINST, SO YOU'RE EQUALLY GUILTY.
IT'D BE MOST EFFICIENT TO JUST FINISH YOU OFF AND BE DONE WITH IT.
JAKA (KACHAK)
DO (BLAM)

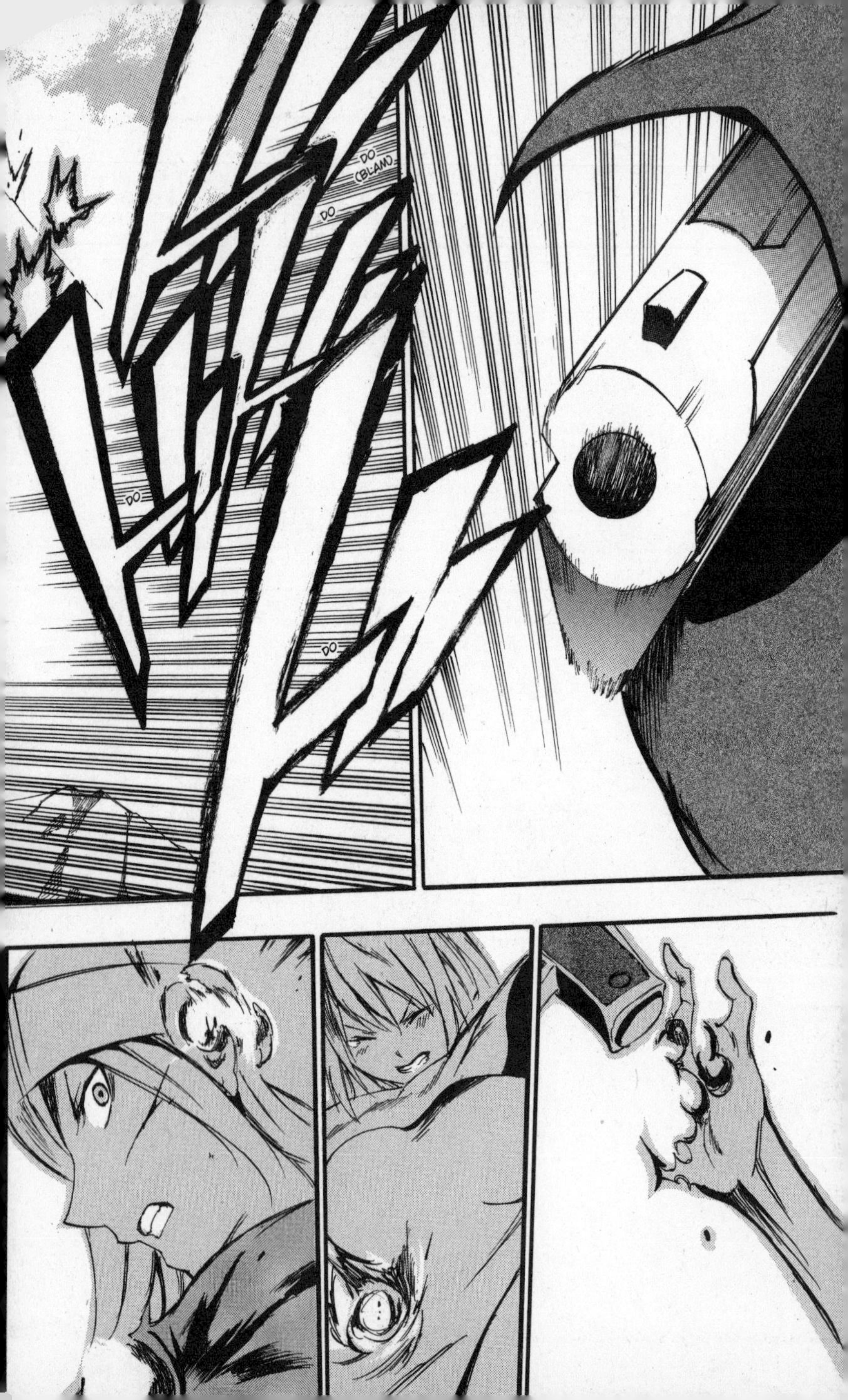
DO
(BLAM)
DO
DO
DO

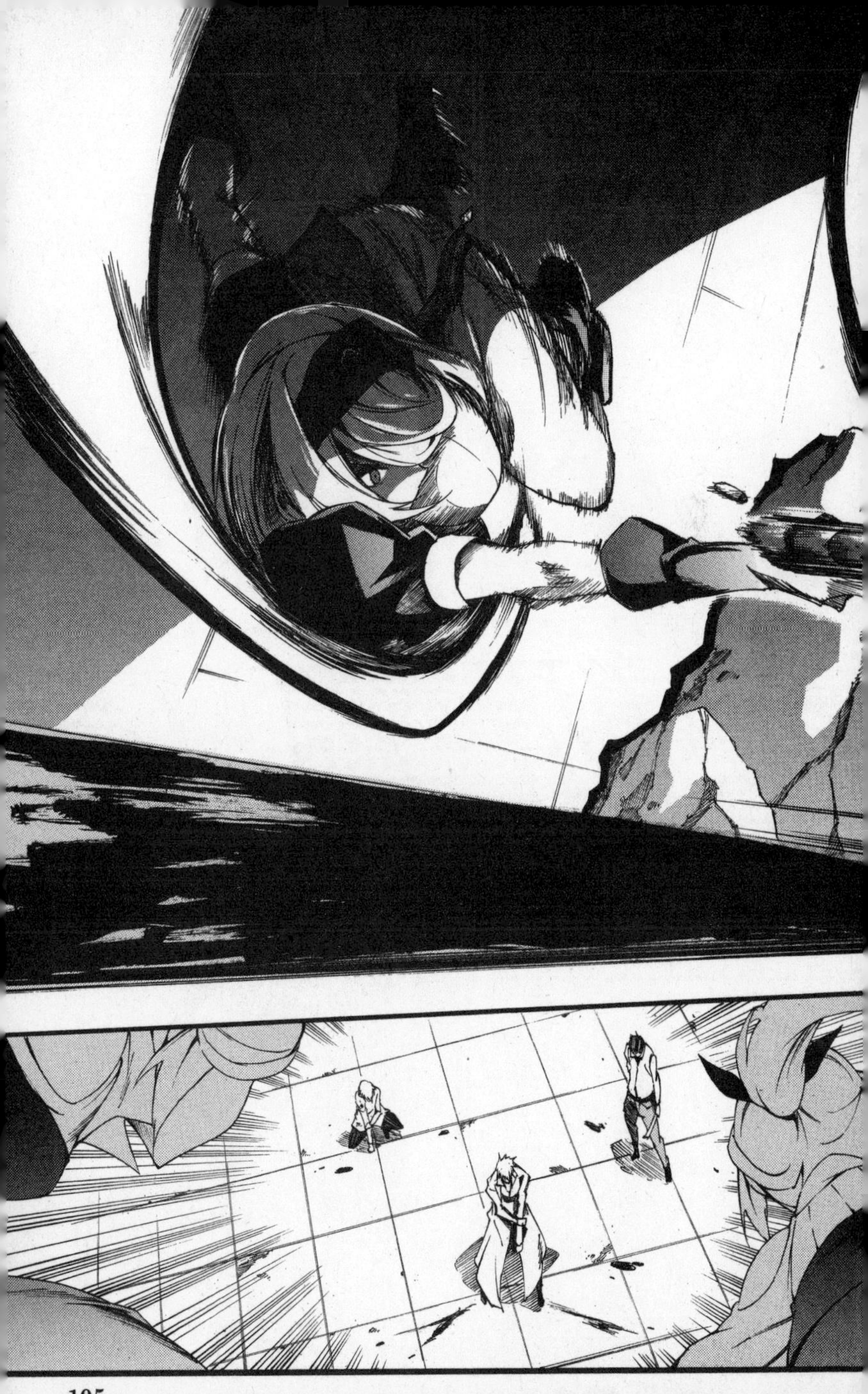

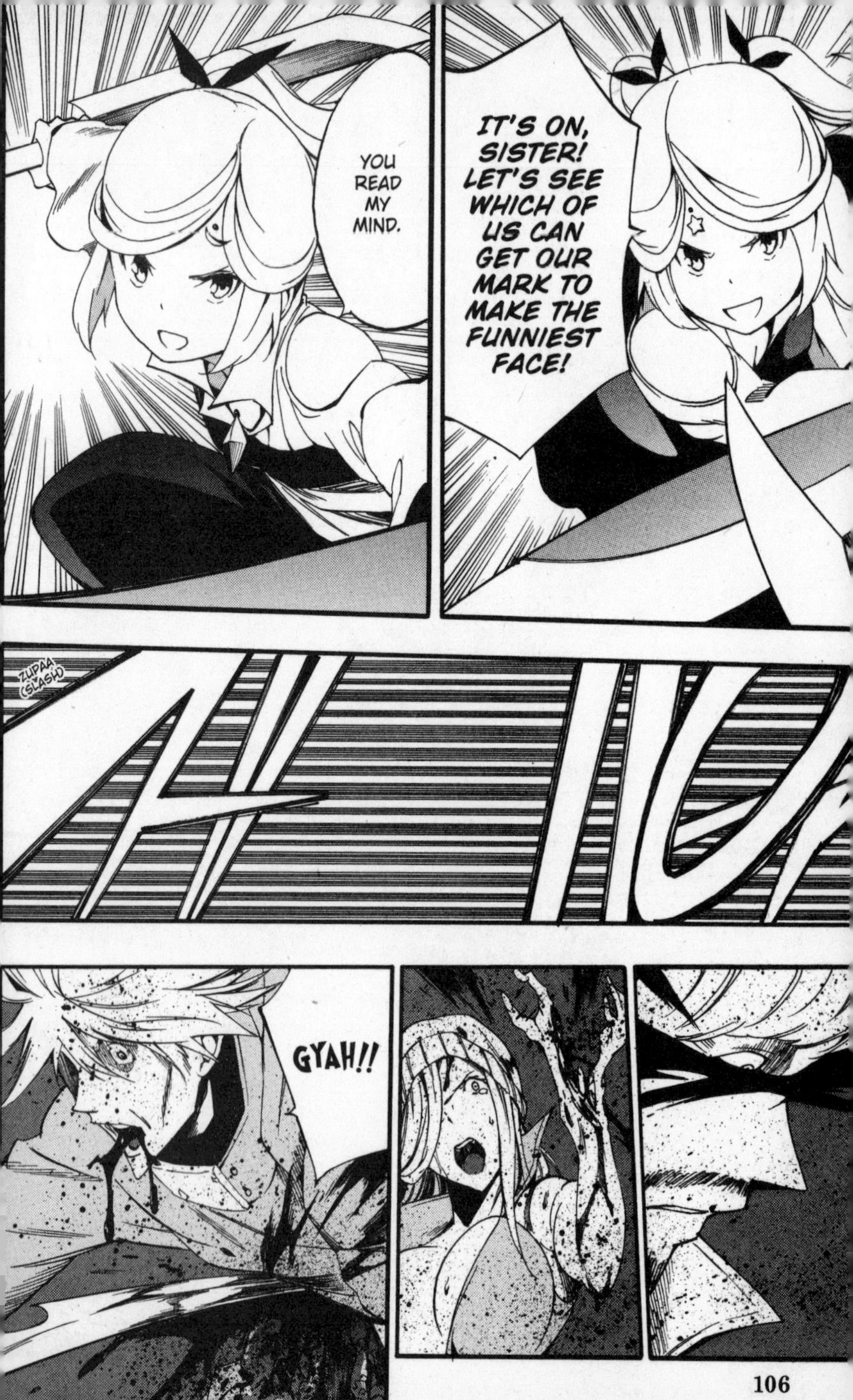
IT'S ON, SISTER! LET'S SEE WHICH OF US CAN GET OUR MARK TO MAKE THE FUNNIEST FACE!
YOU READ MY MIND.
ZUPAA (SLASH)
GYAH!!

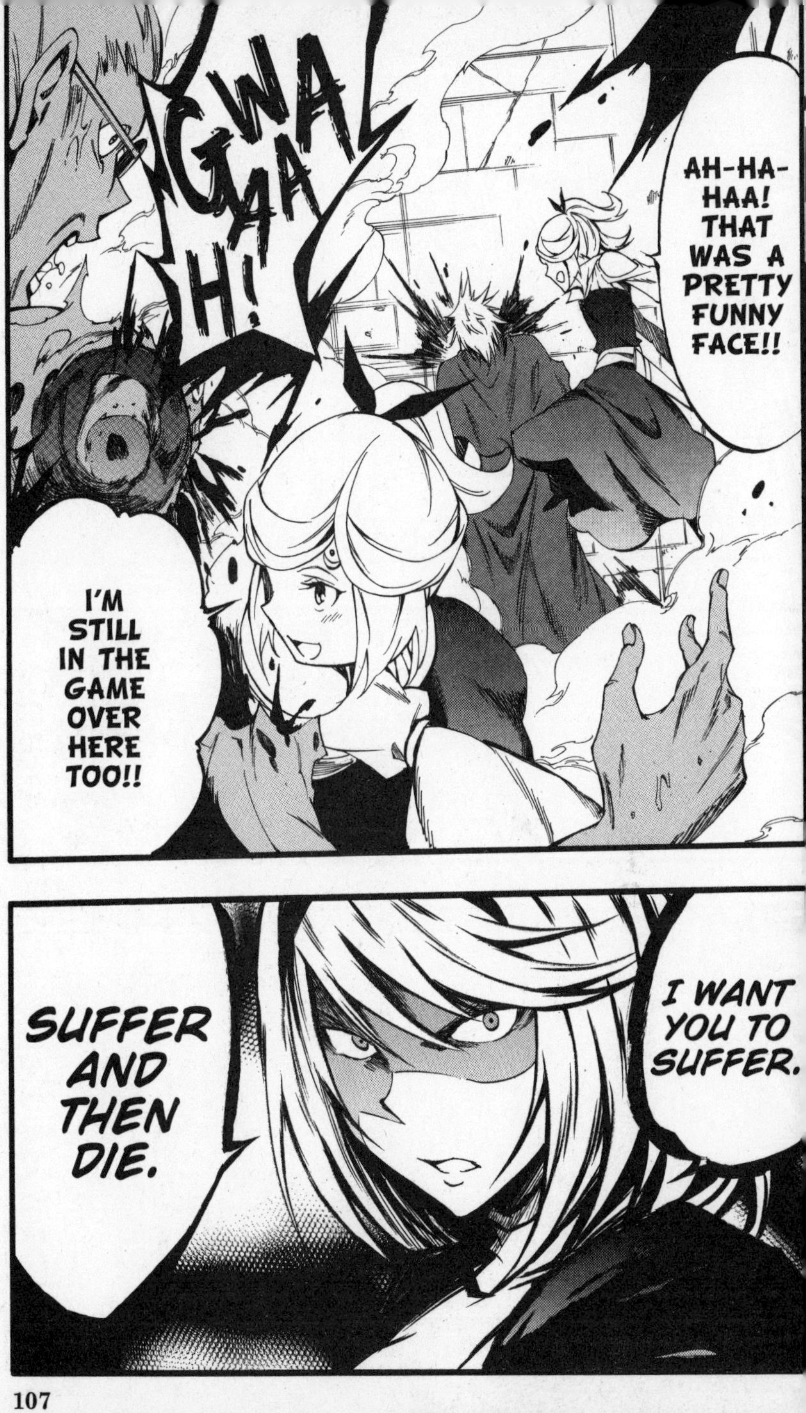
AH-HA-HAA! THAT WAS A PRETTY FUNNY FACE!!
GWAAAH!
I'M STILL IN THE GAME OVER HERE TOO!!
I WANT YOU TO SUFFER.
SUFFER AND THEN DIE.

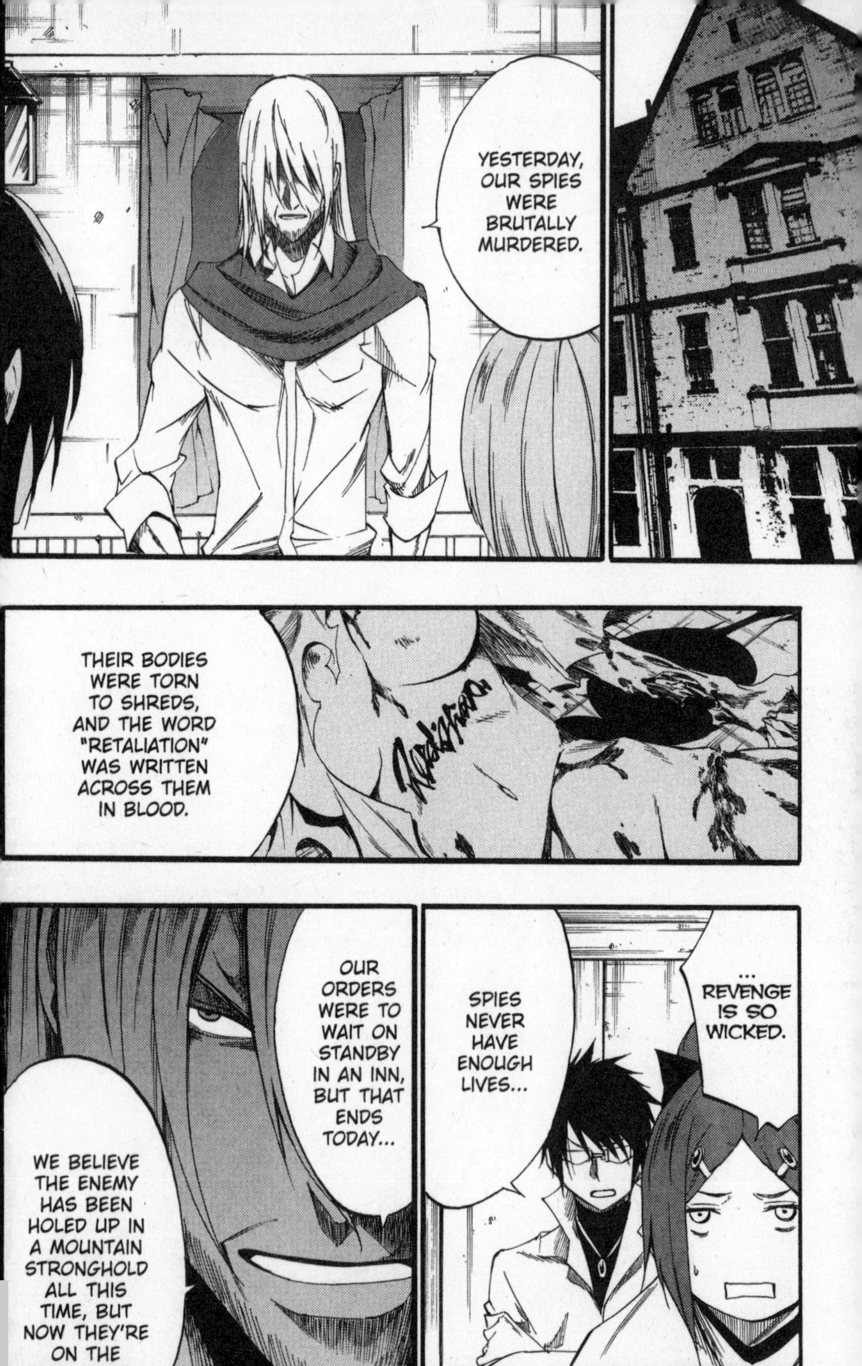
YESTERDAY, OUR SPIES WERE BRUTALLY MURDERED.
THEIR BODIES WERE TORN TO SHREDS, AND THE WORD "RETALIATION" WAS WRITTEN ACROSS THEM IN BLOOD.
... REVENGE IS SO WICKED.
SPIES NEVER HAVE ENOUGH LIVES...
OUR ORDERS WERE TO WAIT ON STANDBY IN AN INN, BUT THAT ENDS TODAY...
WE BELIEVE THE ENEMY HAS BEEN HOLED UP IN A MOUNTAIN STRONGHOLD ALL THIS TIME, BUT NOW THEY'RE ON THE OFFENSIVE.

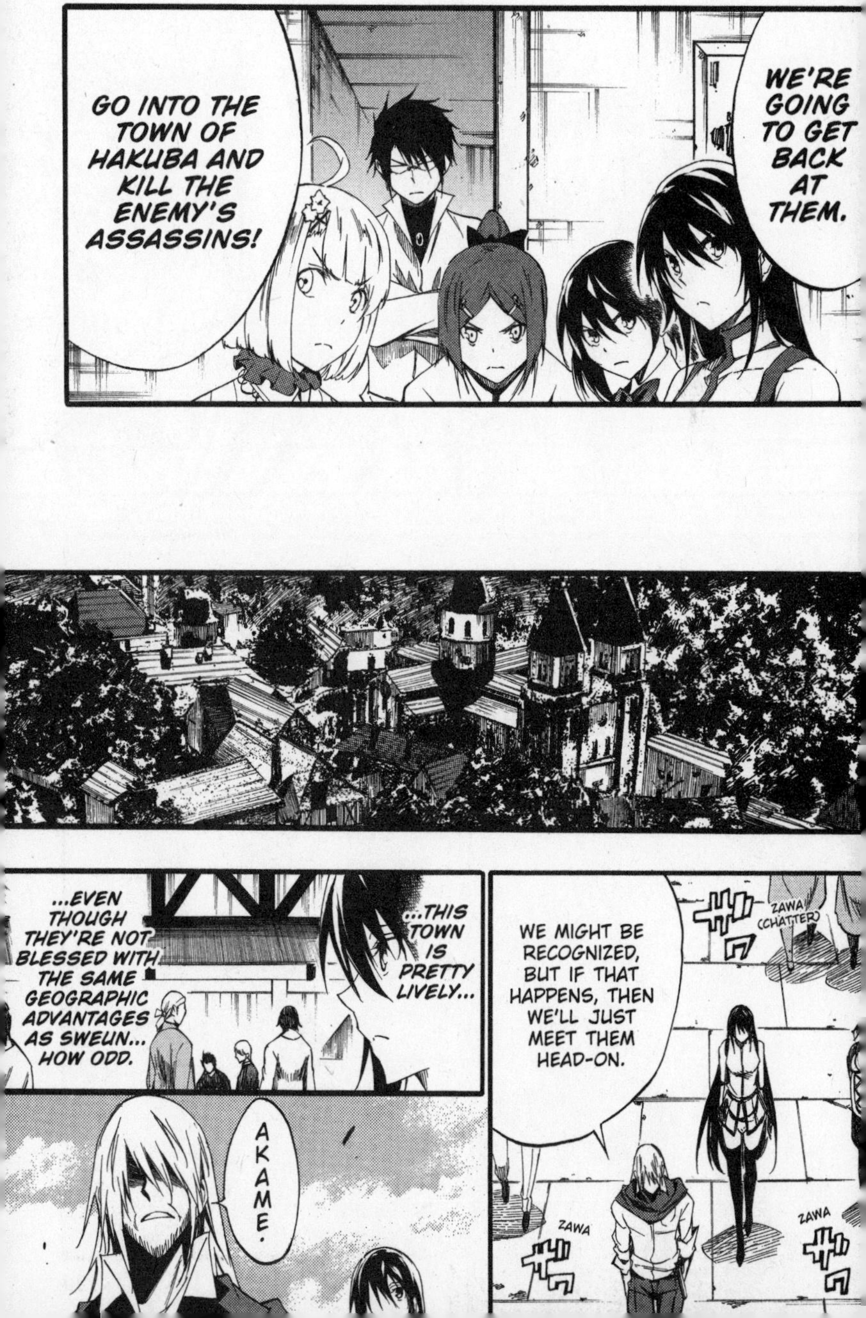
WE'RE GOING TO GET BACK AT THEM.
GO INTO THE TOWN OF HAKUBA AND KILL THE ENEMY'S ASSASSINS!
ZAWA (CHATTER)
WE MIGHT BE RECOGNIZED, BUT IF THAT HAPPENS, THEN WE'LL JUST MEET THEM HEAD-ON.
ZAWA
ZAWA
...THIS TOWN IS PRETTY LIVELY...
...EVEN THOUGH THEY'RE NOT BLESSED WITH THE SAME GEOGRAPHIC ADVANTAGES AS SWEUN... HOW ODD.
AKAME.

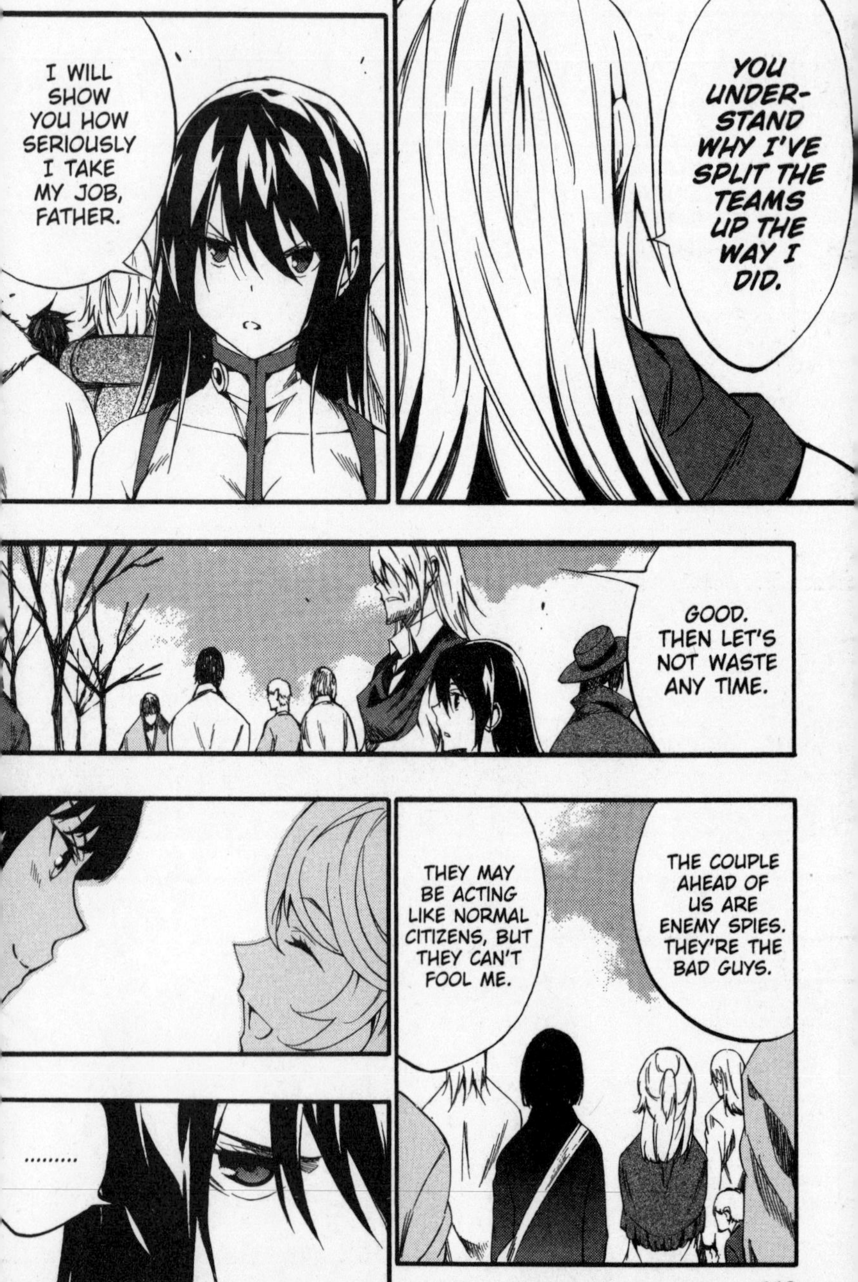
YOU UNDER-STAND WHY I'VE SPLIT THE TEAMS UP THE WAY I DID.
I WILL SHOW YOU HOW SERIOUSLY I TAKE MY JOB, FATHER.
GOOD. THEN LET'S NOT WASTE ANY TIME.
THE COUPLE AHEAD OF US ARE ENEMY SPIES. THEY'RE THE BAD GUYS.
THEY MAY BE ACTING LIKE NORMAL CITIZENS, BUT THEY CAN'T FOOL ME.
....

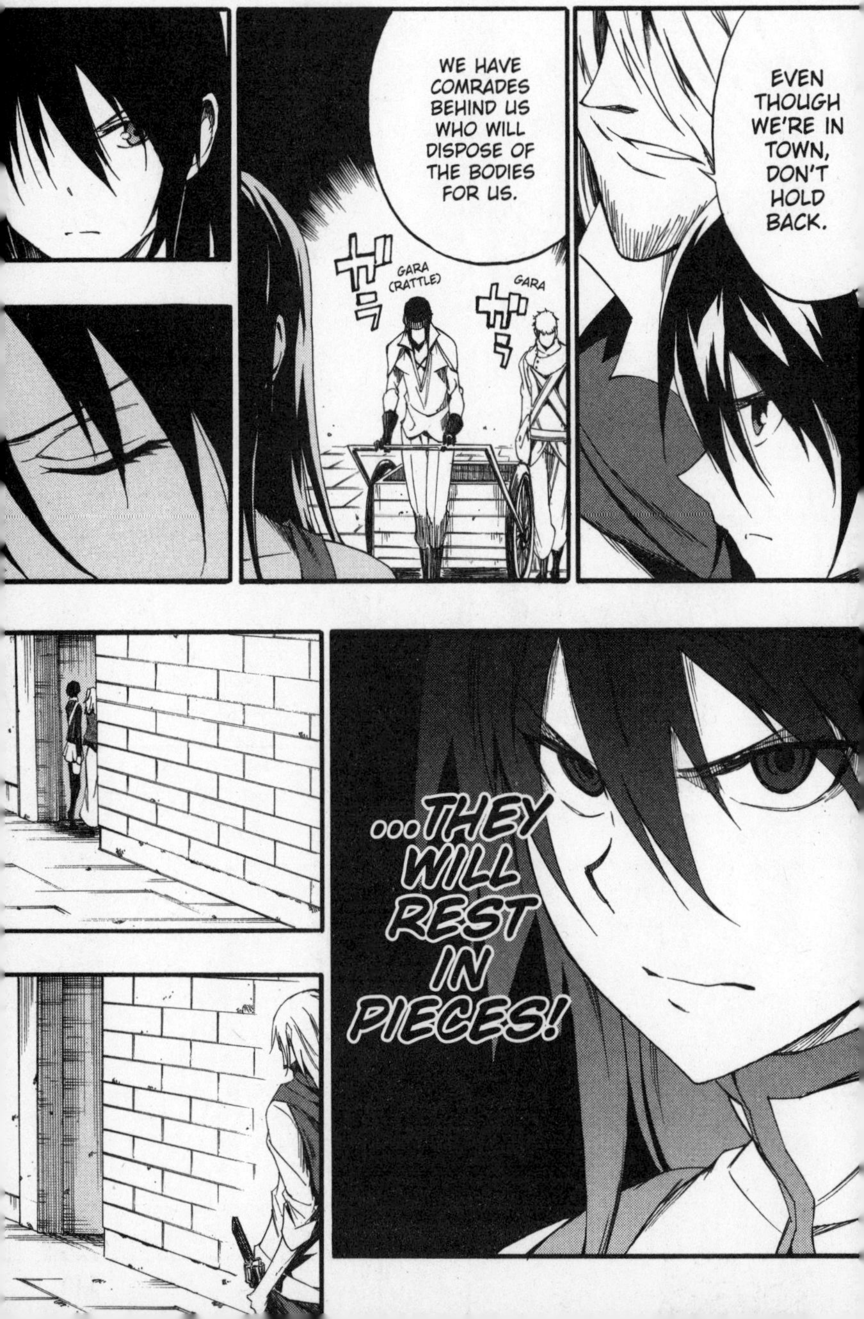
EVEN THOUGH WE'RE IN TOWN, DON'T HOLD BACK.
WE HAVE COMRADES BEHIND US WHO WILL DISPOSE OF THE BODIES FOR US.
GARA
GARA (RATTLE)
...THEY WILL REST IN PIECES!

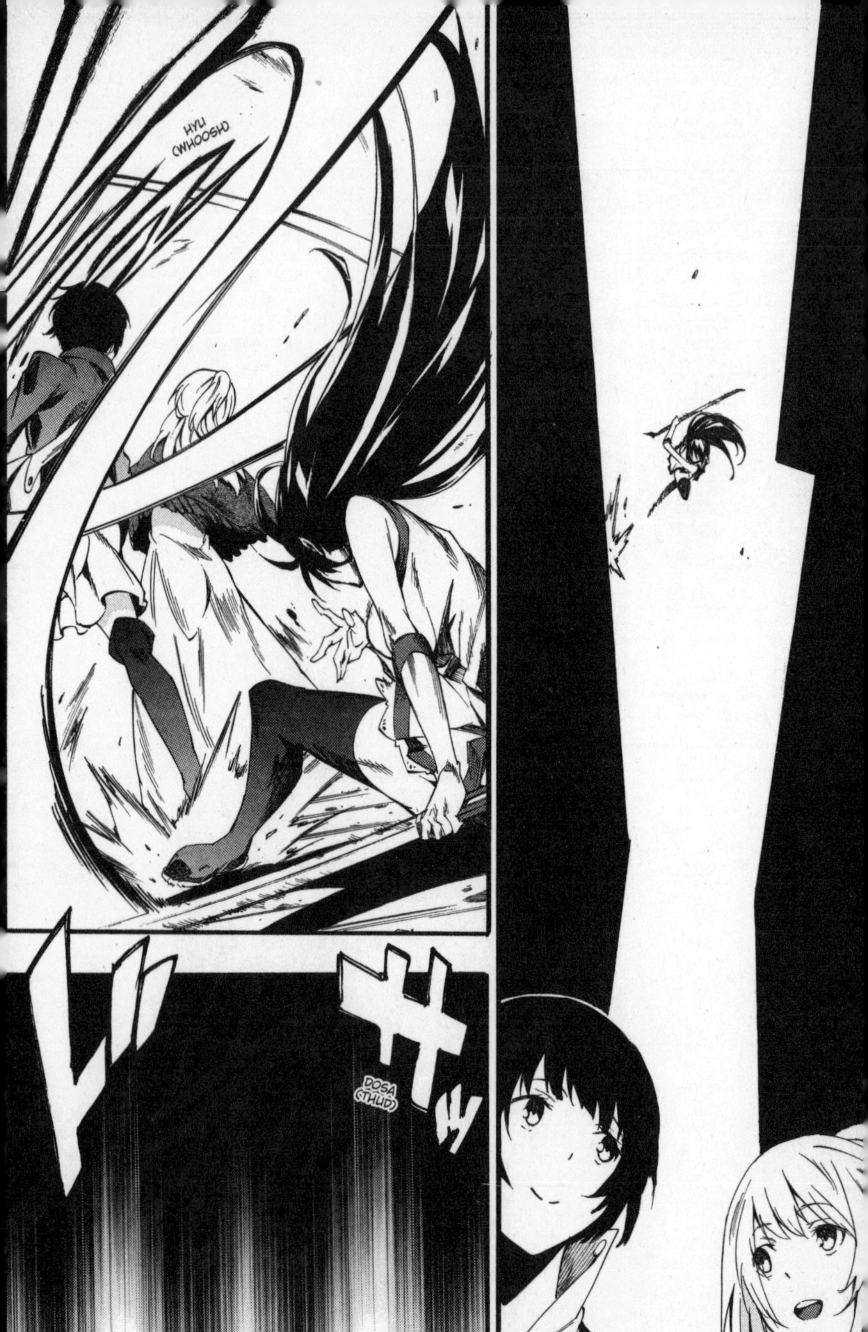
HYU
(WHOOSH)
DOSA
(THUD)

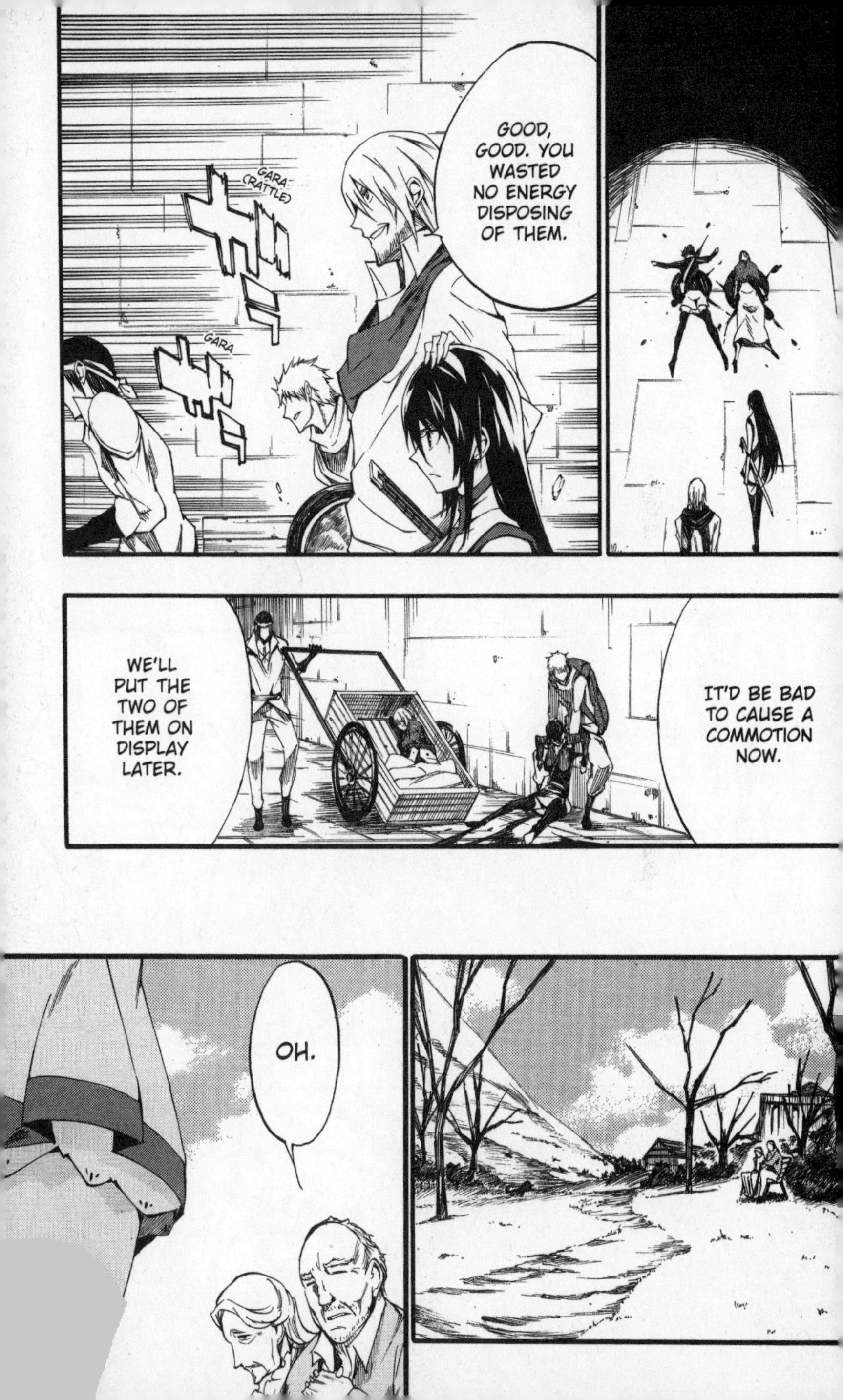
GOOD, GOOD. YOU WASTED NO ENERGY DISPOSING OF THEM.
GARA (RATTLE)
GARA
WE'LL PUT THE TWO OF THEM ON DISPLAY LATER.
IT'D BE BAD TO CAUSE A COMMOTION NOW.
OH.

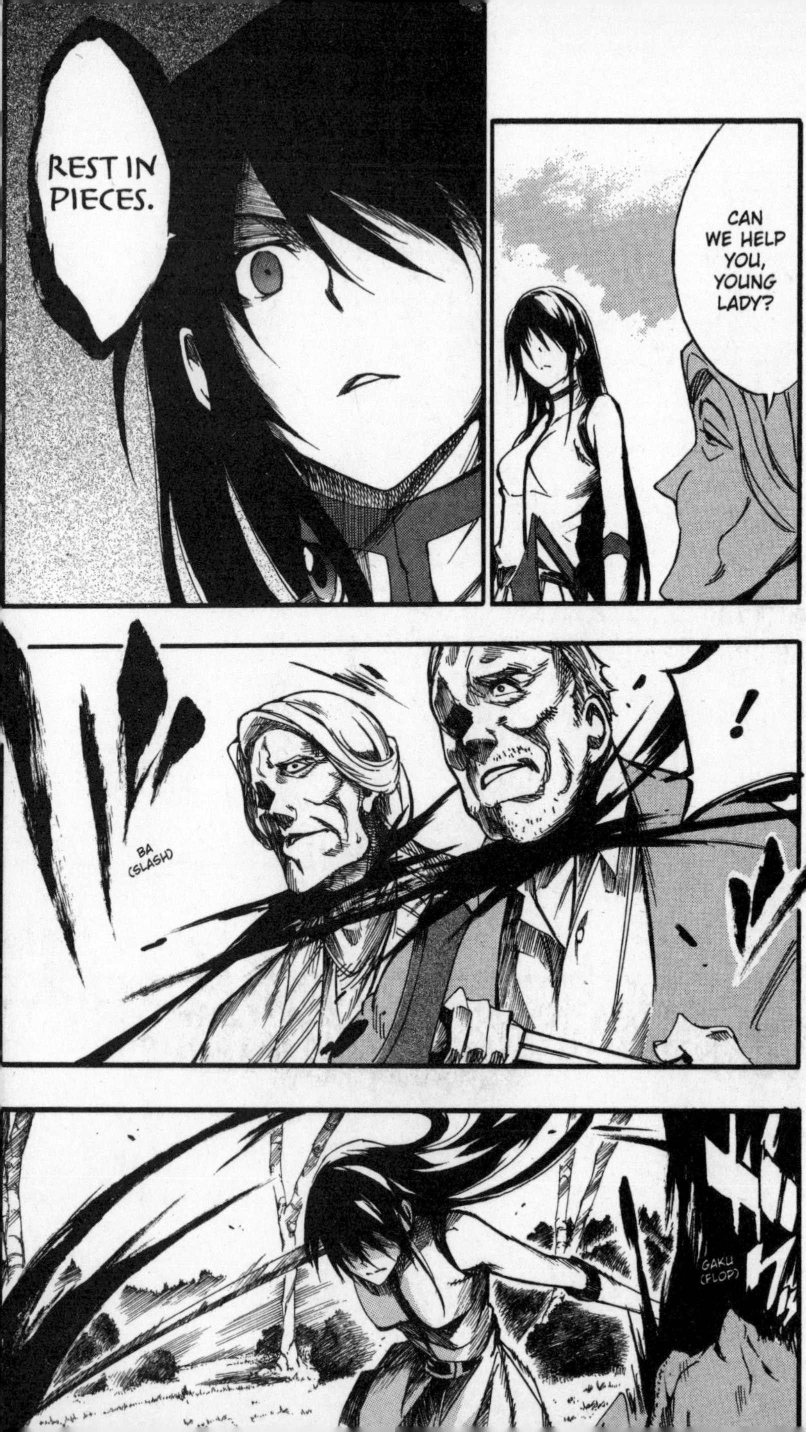
CAN WE HELP YOU, YOUNG LADY?
REST IN PIECES.
!
BA (SLASH)
GAKU (FLOP)

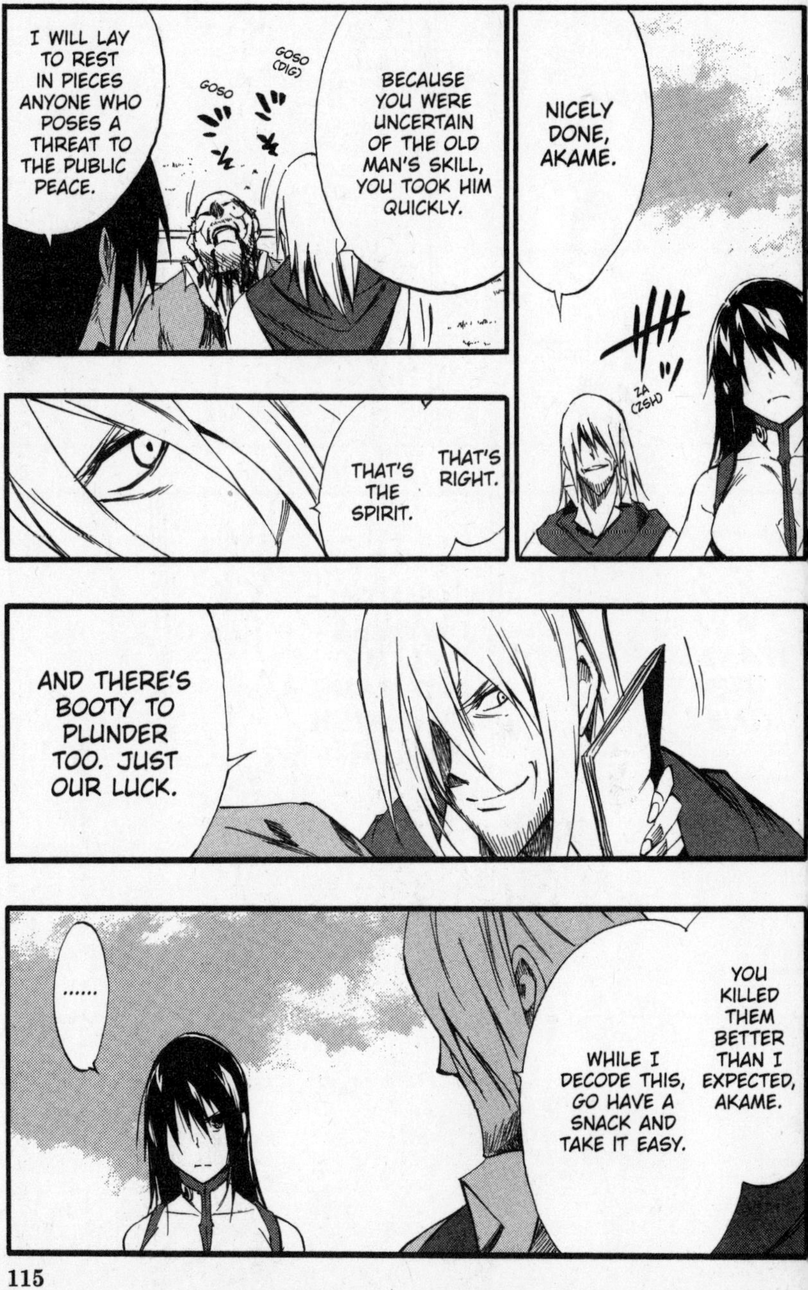
NICELY DONE, AKAME.
ZA (ZSH)
BECAUSE YOU WERE UNCERTAIN OF THE OLD MAN'S SKILL, YOU TOOK HIM QUICKLY.
GOSO (DIG)
GOSO
I WILL LAY TO REST IN PIECES ANYONE WHO POSES A THREAT TO THE PUBLIC PEACE.
THAT'S RIGHT.
THAT'S THE SPIRIT.
AND THERE'S BOOTY TO PLUNDER TOO. JUST OUR LUCK.
YOU KILLED THEM BETTER THAN I EXPECTED, AKAME.
WHILE I DECODE THIS, GO HAVE A SNACK AND TAKE IT EASY.
......

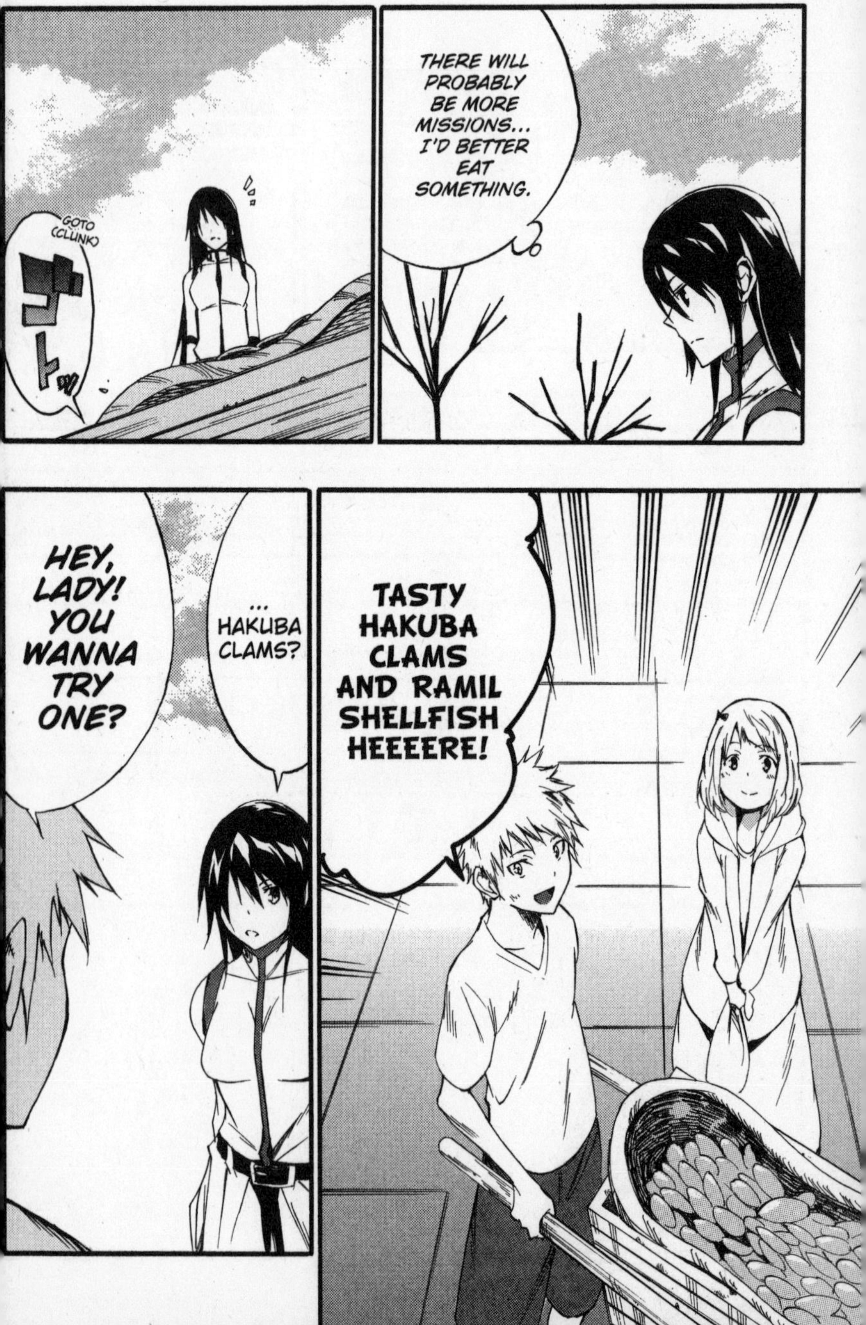
THERE WILL PROBABLY BE MORE MISSIONS... I'D BETTER EAT SOMETHING.
GOTO (CLUNK)
TASTY HAKUBA CLAMS AND RAMIL SHELLFISH HEEEERE!
... HAKUBA CLAMS?
HEY, LADY! YOU WANNA TRY ONE?

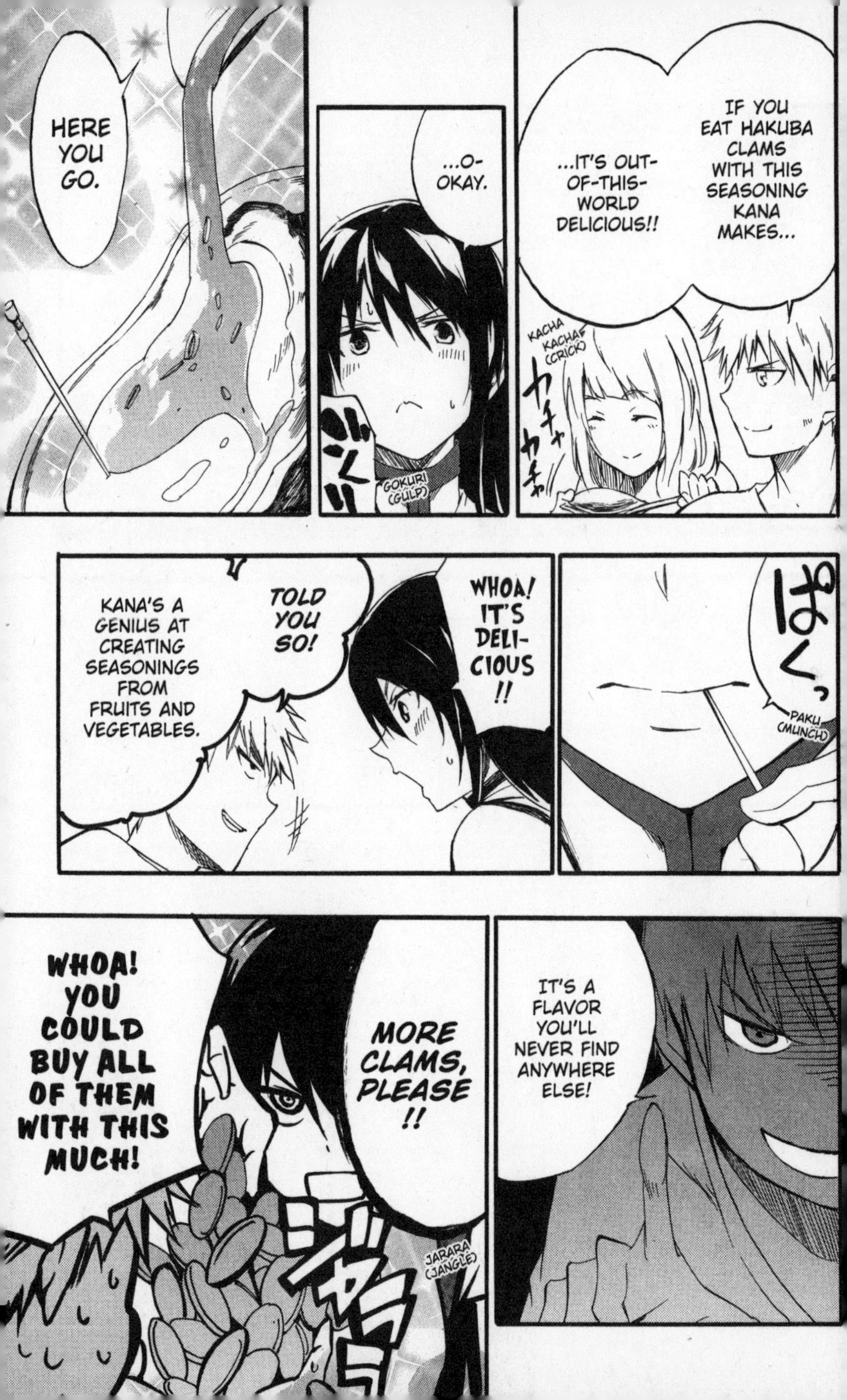
IF YOU EAT HAKUBA CLAMS WITH THIS SEASONING KANA MAKES...
...IT'S OUT-OF-THIS-WORLD DELICIOUS!!
KACHA KACHA (CRICK)
...O-OKAY.
GOKURI (GULP)
HERE YOU GO.
ぱくっ
PAKU (MUNCH)
WHOA! IT'S DELI-CIOUS!!
TOLD YOU SO!
KANA'S A GENIUS AT CREATING SEASONINGS FROM FRUITS AND VEGETABLES.
IT'S A FLAVOR YOU'LL NEVER FIND ANYWHERE ELSE!
MORE CLAMS, PLEASE!!
JARARA (JANGLE)
WHOA! YOU COULD BUY ALL OF THEM WITH THIS MUCH!

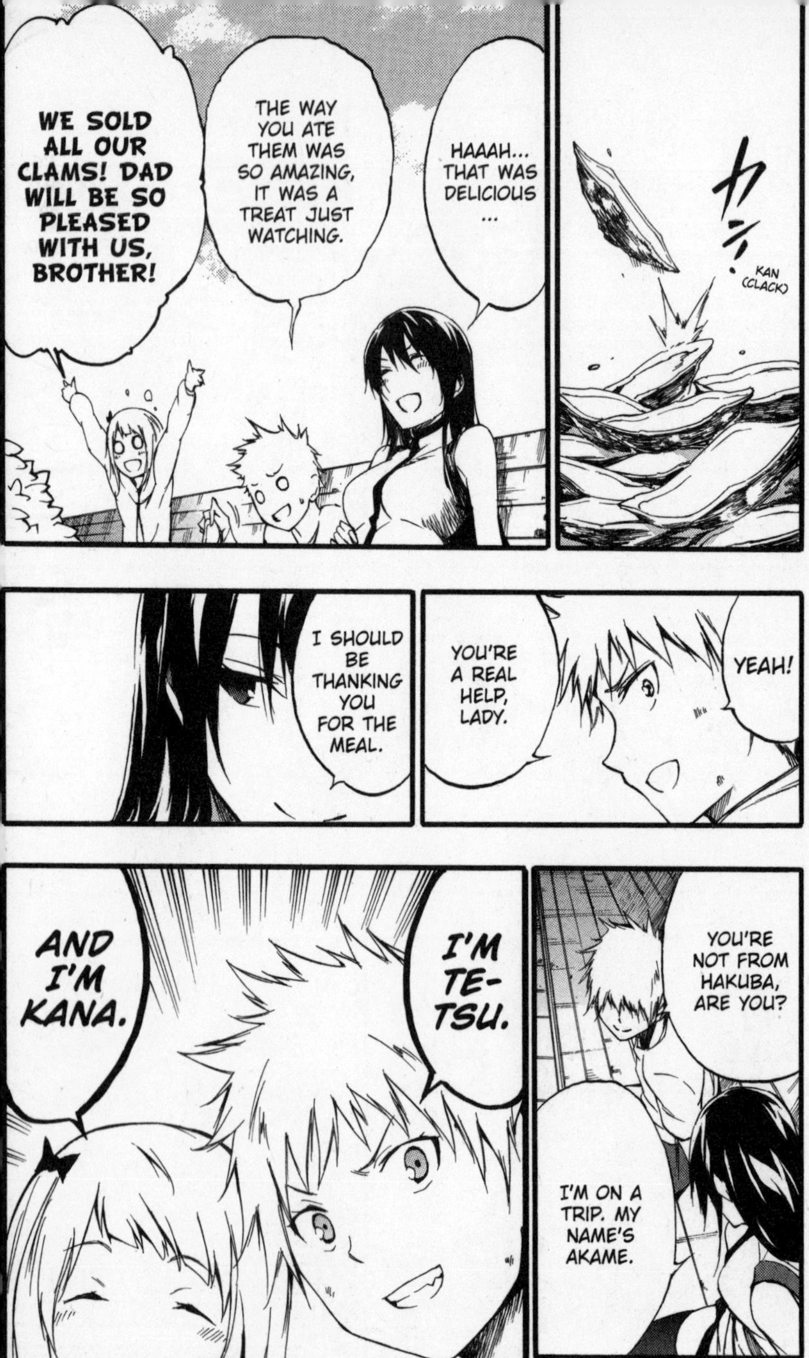
KAN (CLACK)
HAAAH... THAT WAS DELICIOUS...
THE WAY YOU ATE THEM WAS SO AMAZING, IT WAS A TREAT JUST WATCHING.
WE SOLD ALL OUR CLAMS! DAD WILL BE SO PLEASED WITH US, BROTHER!
YEAH!
YOU'RE A REAL HELP, LADY.
I SHOULD BE THANKING YOU FOR THE MEAL.
YOU'RE NOT FROM HAKUBA, ARE YOU?
I'M ON A TRIP. MY NAME'S AKAME.
I'M TE-TSU.
AND I'M KANA.

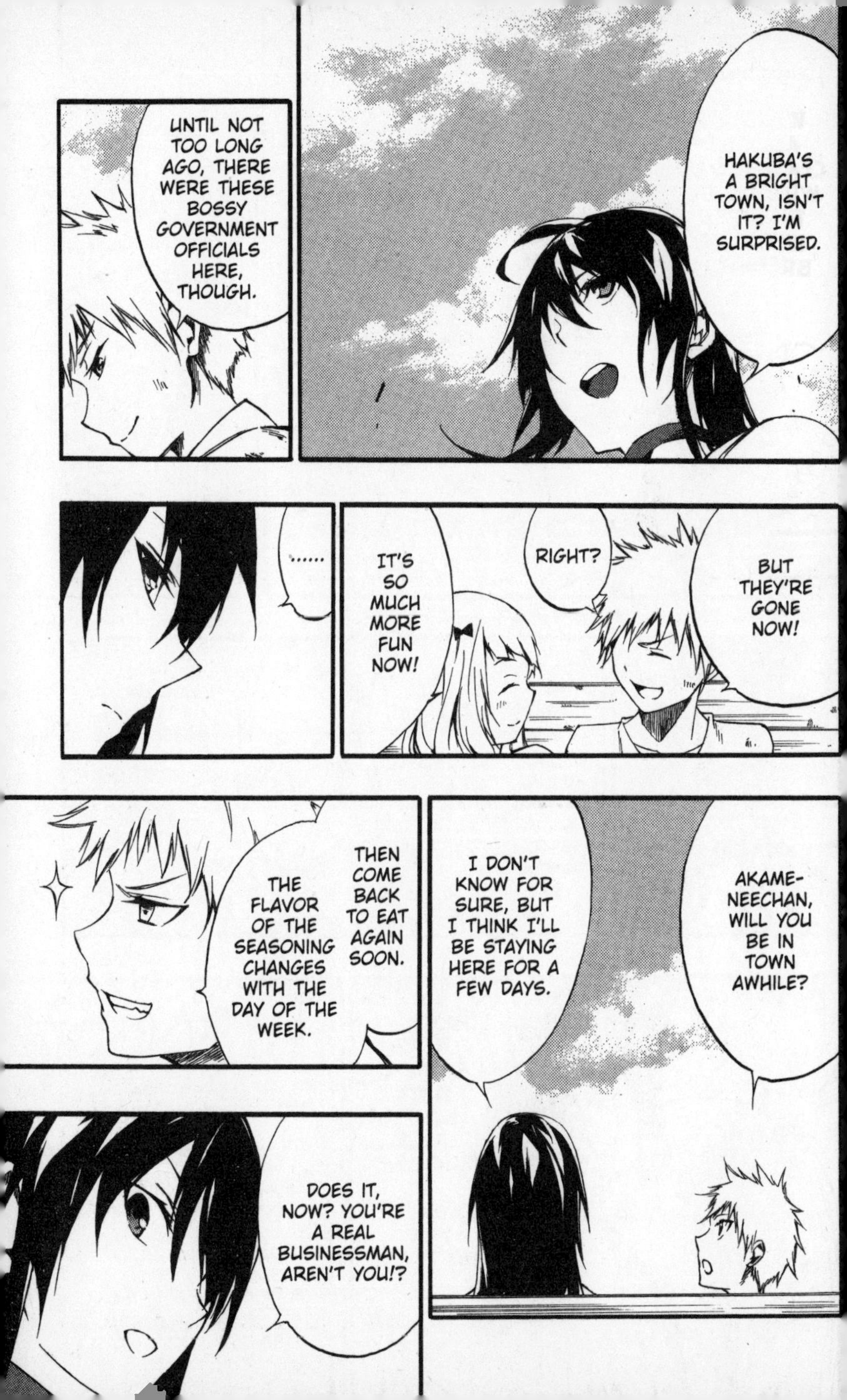
HAKUBA'S A BRIGHT TOWN, ISN'T IT? I'M SURPRISED.
UNTIL NOT TOO LONG AGO, THERE WERE THESE BOSSY GOVERNMENT OFFICIALS HERE, THOUGH.
BUT THEY'RE GONE NOW!
RIGHT?
IT'S SO MUCH MORE FUN NOW!
......
AKAME-NEECHAN, WILL YOU BE IN TOWN AWHILE?
I DON'T KNOW FOR SURE, BUT I THINK I'LL BE STAYING HERE FOR A FEW DAYS.
THEN COME BACK TO EAT AGAIN SOON.
THE FLAVOR OF THE SEASONING CHANGES WITH THE DAY OF THE WEEK.
DOES IT, NOW? YOU'RE A REAL BUSINESSMAN, AREN'T YOU!?

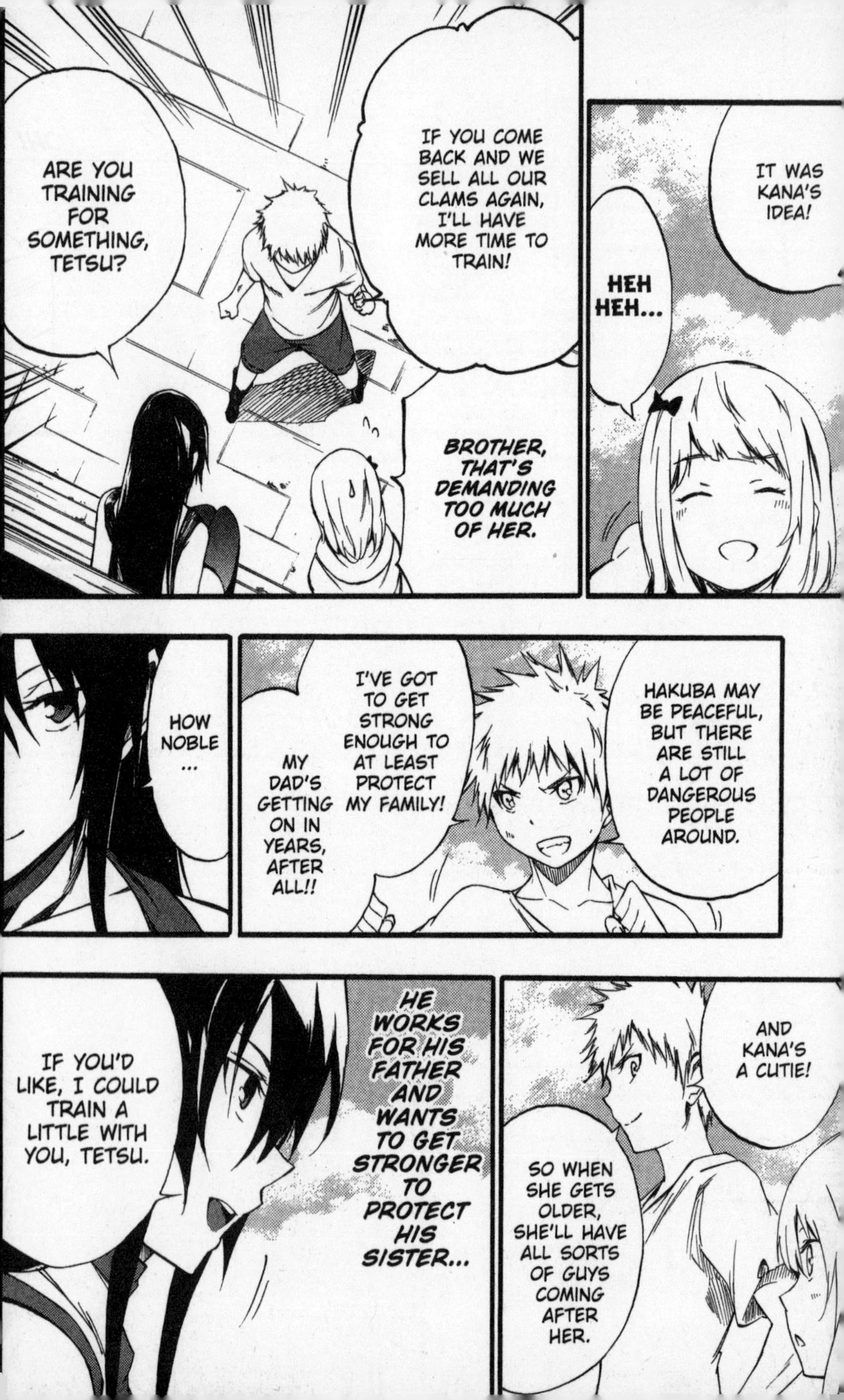

IT WAS KANA'S IDEA!
HEH HEH...
IF YOU COME BACK AND WE SELL ALL OUR CLAMS AGAIN, I'LL HAVE MORE TIME TO TRAIN!
BROTHER, THAT'S DEMANDING TOO MUCH OF HER.
ARE YOU TRAINING FOR SOMETHING, TETSU?
HAKUBA MAY BE PEACEFUL, BUT THERE ARE STILL A LOT OF DANGEROUS PEOPLE AROUND.
I'VE GOT TO GET STRONG ENOUGH TO AT LEAST PROTECT MY FAMILY!
MY DAD'S GETTING ON IN YEARS, AFTER ALL!!
HOW NOBLE...
AND KANA'S A CUTIE!
SO WHEN SHE GETS OLDER, SHE'LL HAVE ALL SORTS OF GUYS COMING AFTER HER.
HE WORKS FOR HIS FATHER AND WANTS TO GET STRONGER TO PROTECT HIS SISTER...
IF YOU'D LIKE, I COULD TRAIN A LITTLE WITH YOU, TETSU.

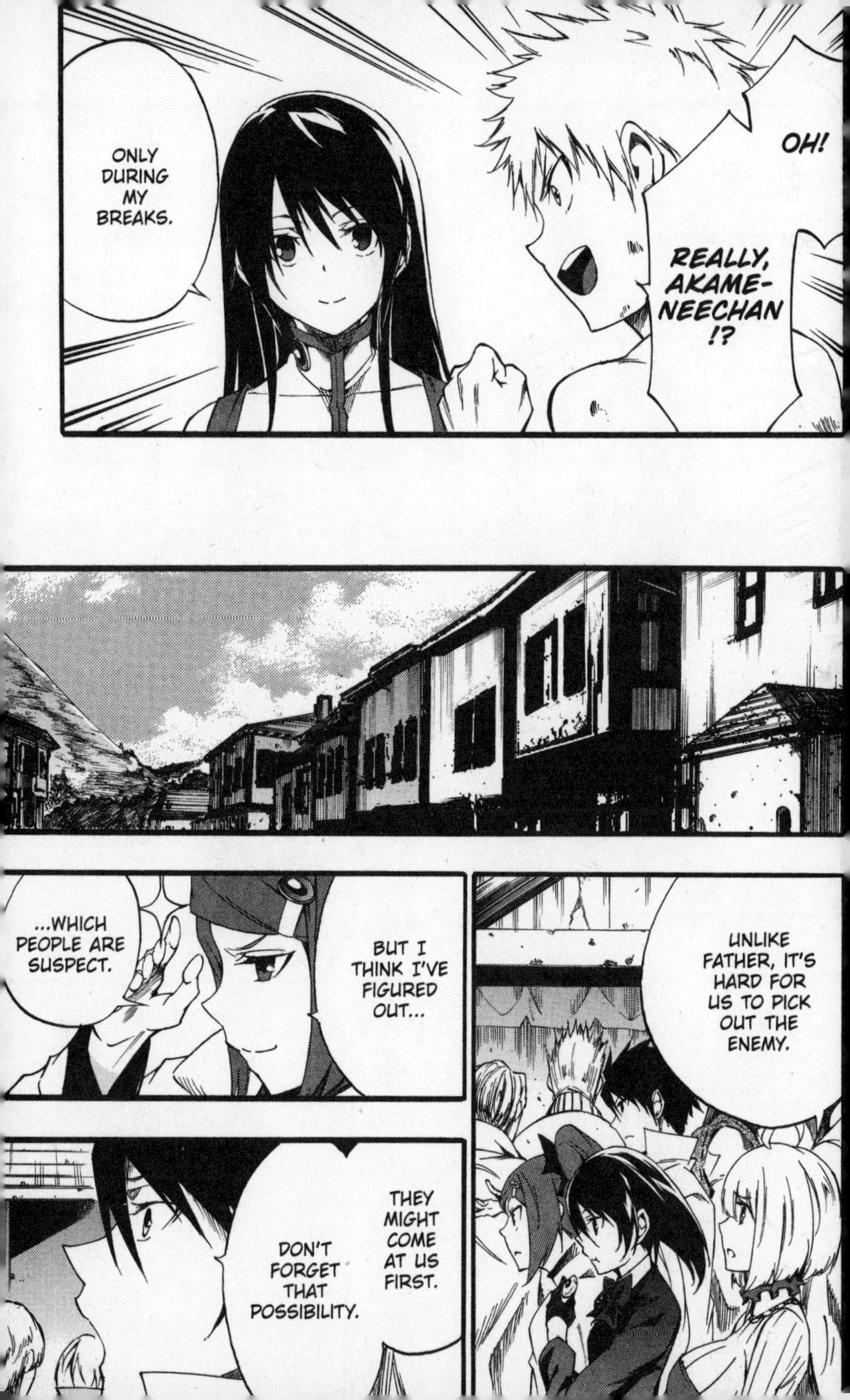
OH!
REALLY, AKAME-NEECHAN!?
ONLY DURING MY BREAKS.
UNLIKE FATHER, IT'S HARD FOR US TO PICK OUT THE ENEMY.
BUT I THINK I'VE FIGURED OUT...
...WHICH PEOPLE ARE SUSPECT.
THEY MIGHT COME AT US FIRST.
DON'T FORGET THAT POSSIBILITY.

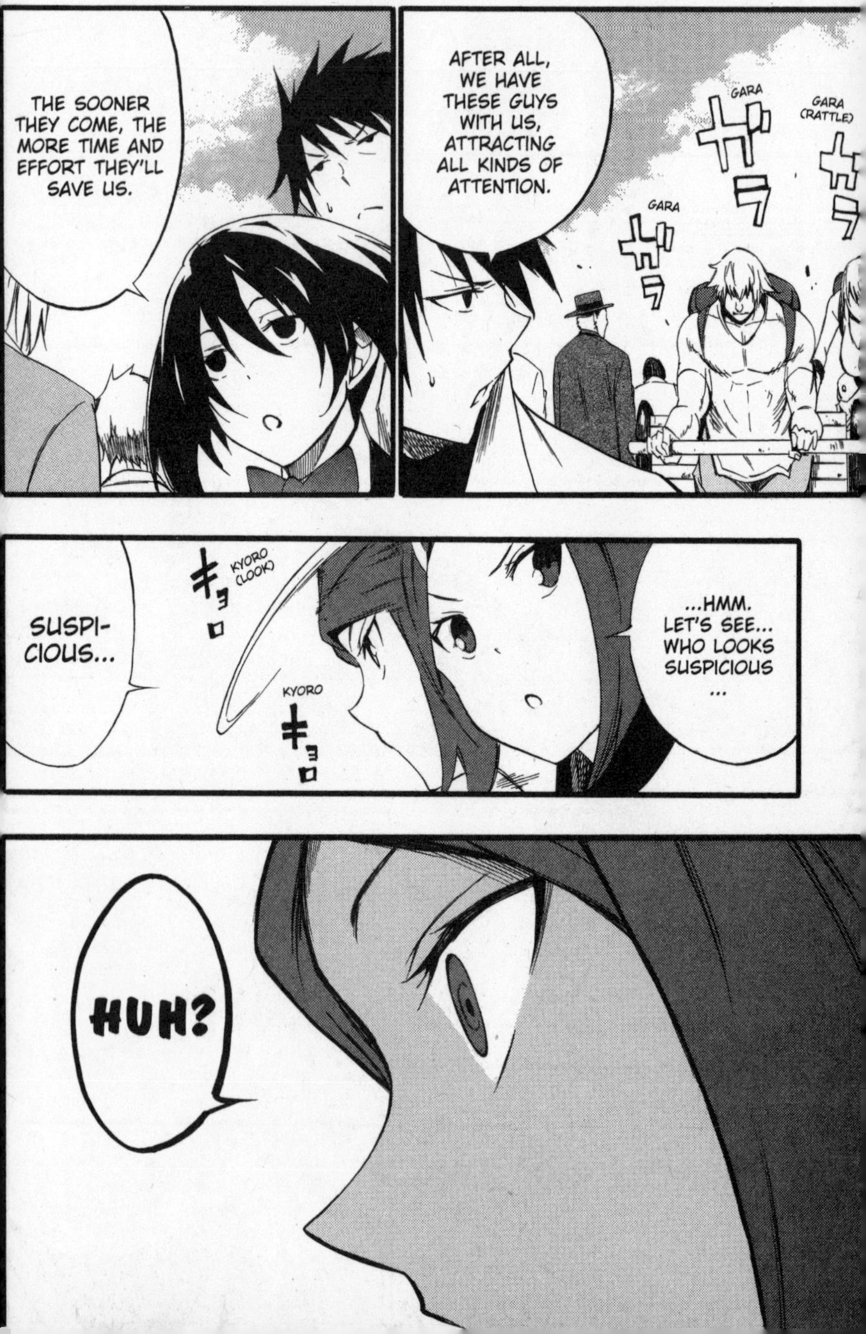
AFTER ALL, WE HAVE THESE GUYS WITH US, ATTRACTING ALL KINDS OF ATTENTION.
GARA (RATTLE)
GARA
GARA
THE SOONER THEY COME, THE MORE TIME AND EFFORT THEY'LL SAVE US.
...HMM. LET'S SEE... WHO LOOKS SUSPICIOUS ...
KYORO (LOOK)
KYORO
SUSPI-CIOUS...
HUH?

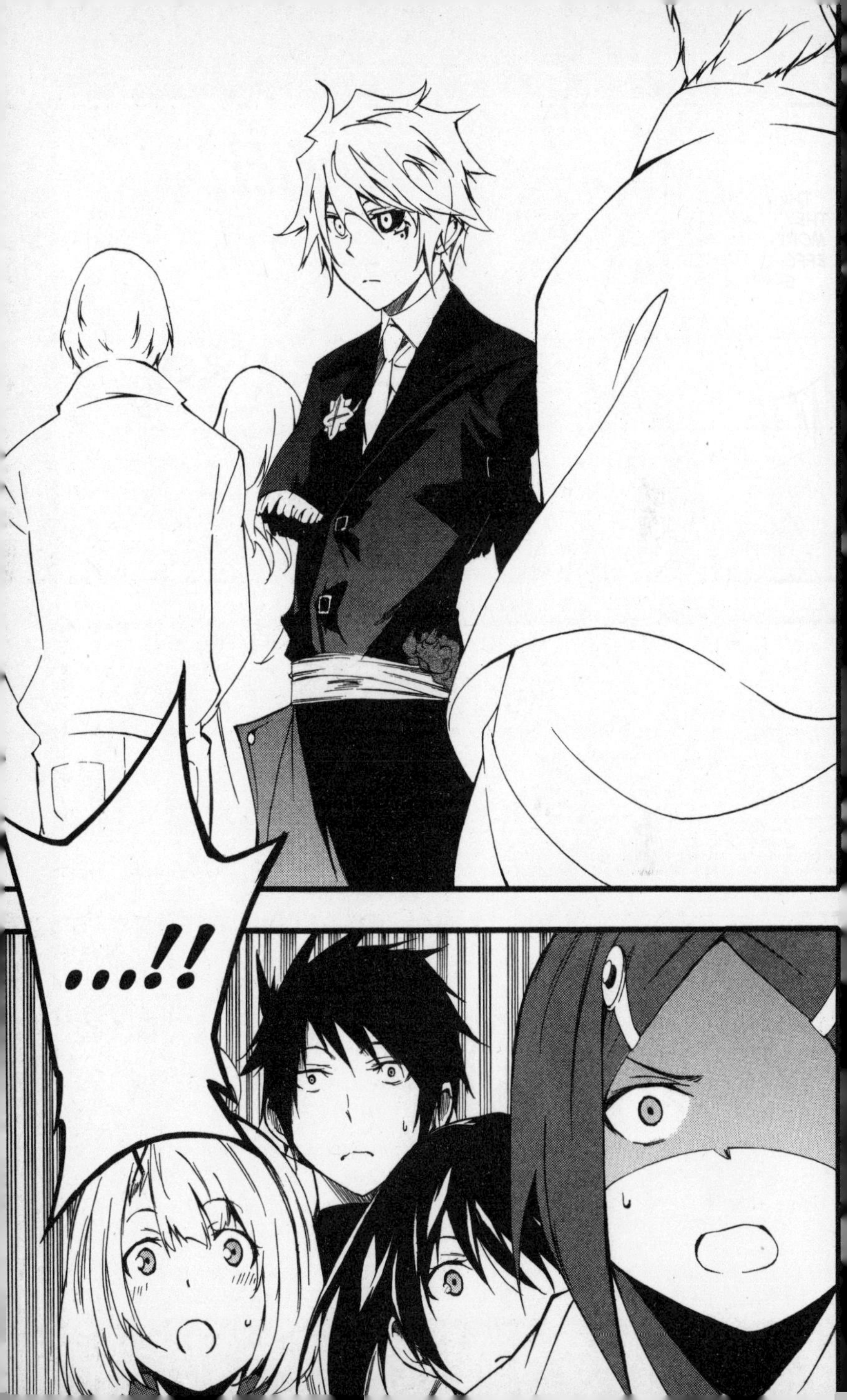
...!!

Akame ga KILL! ZERO

Character Sketches

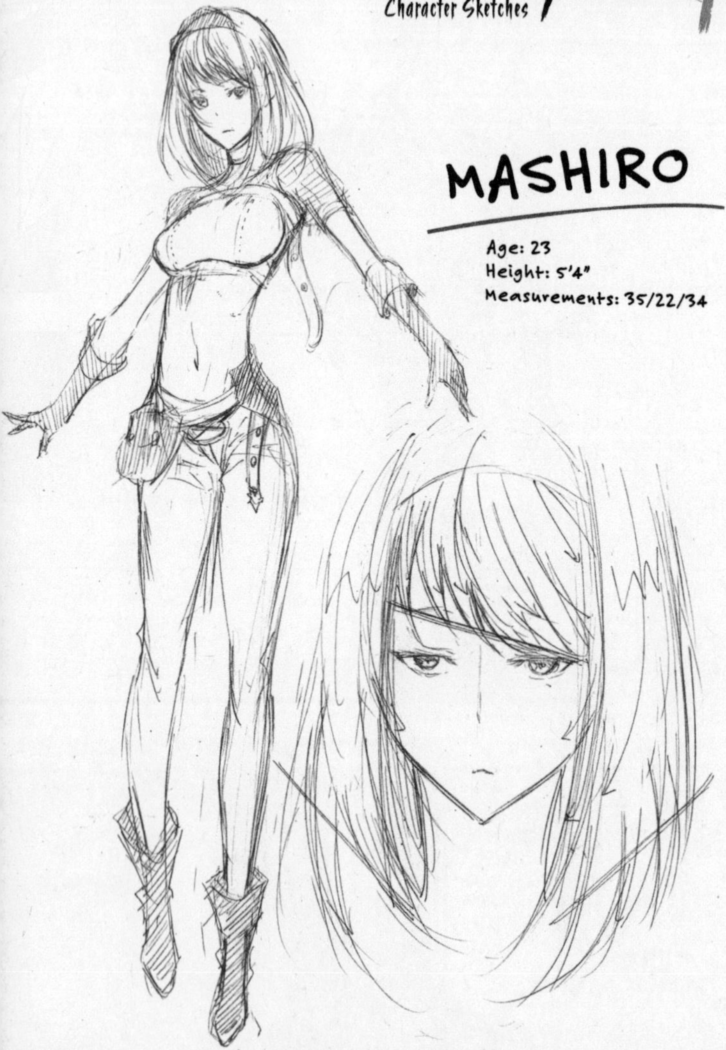

MASHIRO

Age: 23

Height: 5'4"

Measurements: 35/22/34

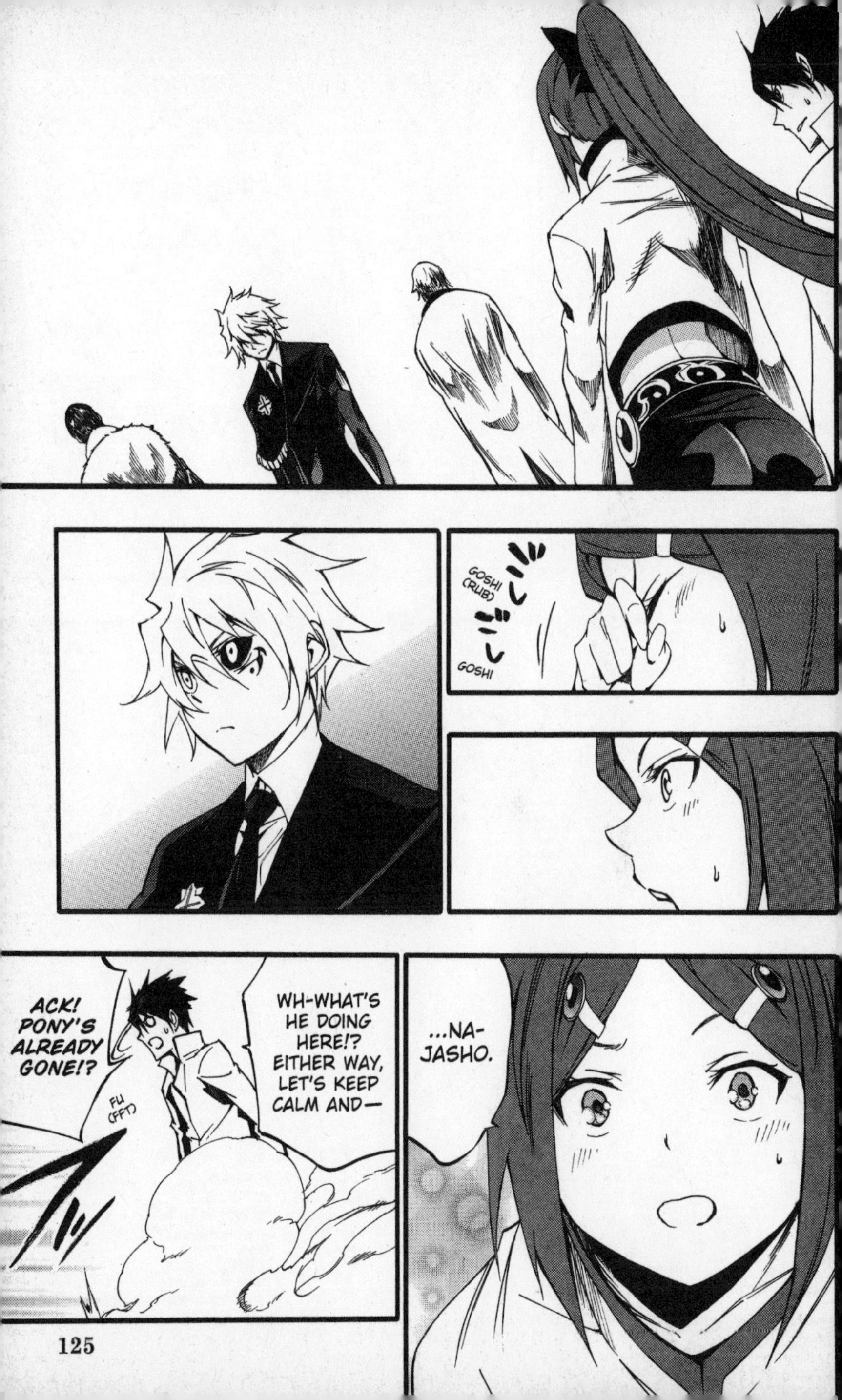
GOSHI (RUB)
GOSHI
...NA-JASHO.
WH-WHAT'S HE DOING HERE!? EITHER WAY, LET'S KEEP CALM AND—
ACK! PONY'S ALREADY GONE!?
FU (FFT)

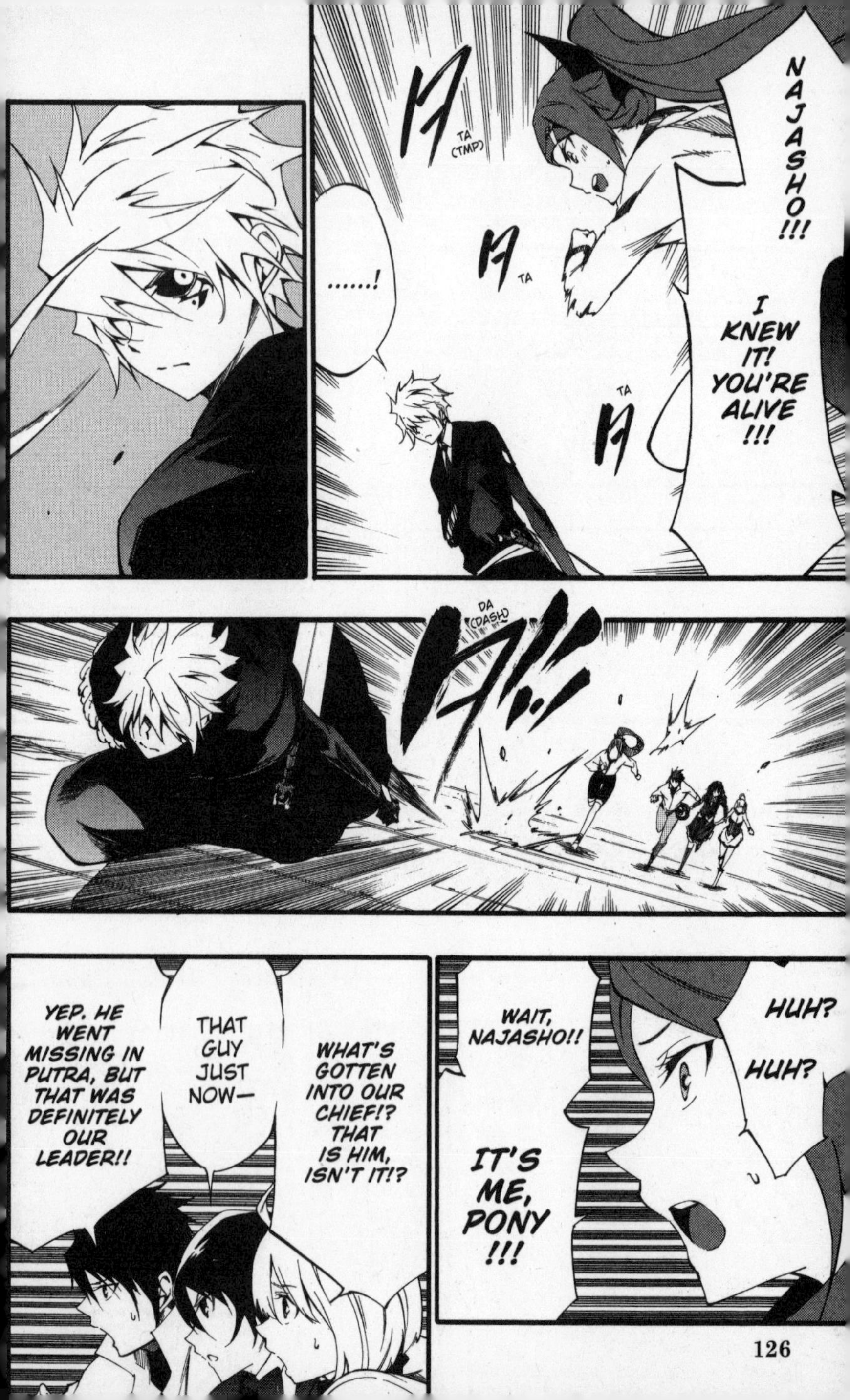
NAJASHO!!!
I KNEW IT! YOU'RE ALIVE!!!
TA (TMP)
TA
TA
......!
DA (DASH)
HUH?
HUH?
WAIT, NAJASHO!!
IT'S ME, PONY!!!
WHAT'S GOTTEN INTO OUR CHIEF!? THAT IS HIM, ISN'T IT!?
THAT GUY JUST NOW—
YEP. HE WENT MISSING IN PUTRA, BUT THAT WAS DEFINITELY OUR LEADER!!

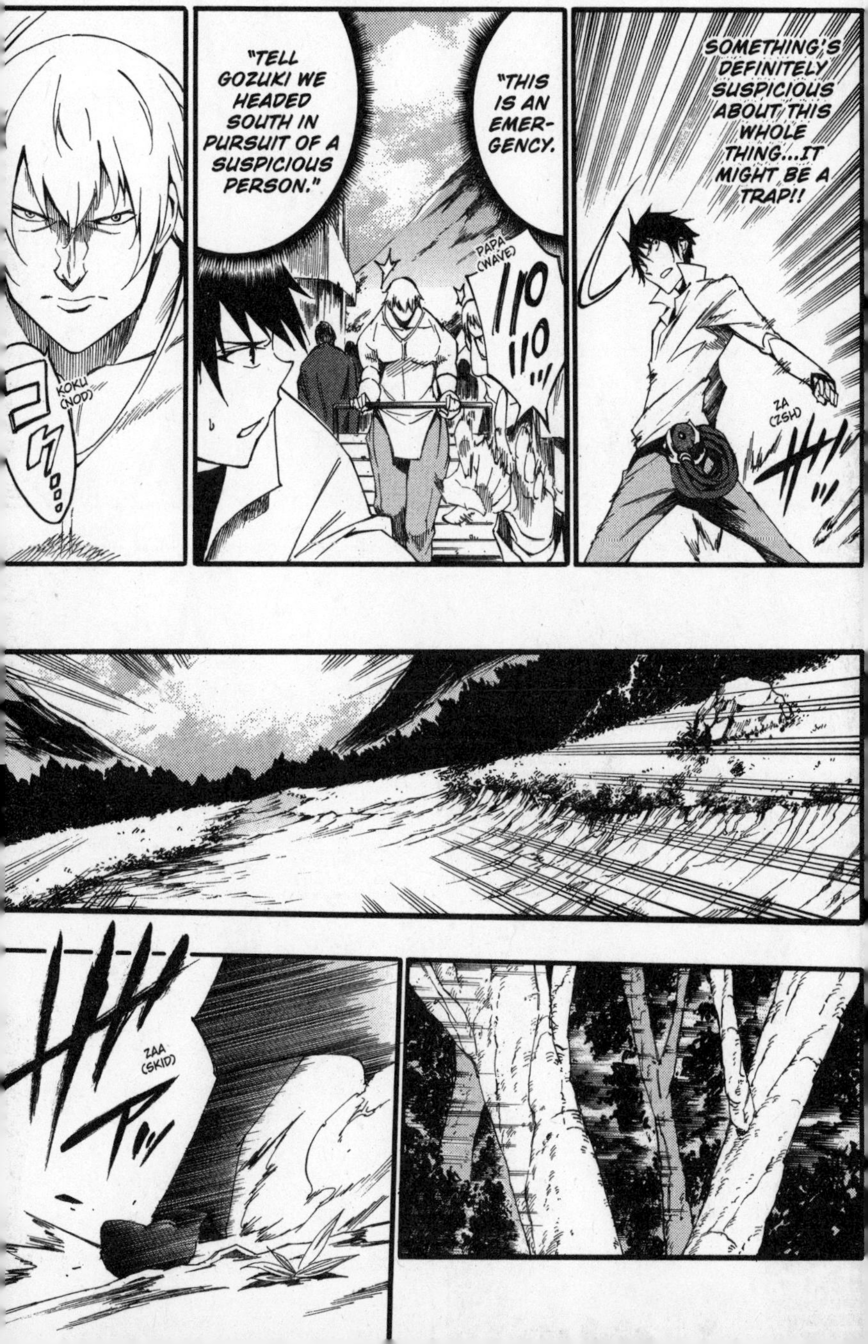
SOMETHING'S DEFINITELY SUSPICIOUS ABOUT THIS WHOLE THING...IT MIGHT BE A TRAP!!
ZA (ZSH)
"THIS IS AN EMERGENCY.
"TELL GOZUKI WE HEADED SOUTH IN PURSUIT OF A SUSPICIOUS PERSON."
PAPA (WAVE)
KOKU (NOD)
ZAA (SKID)

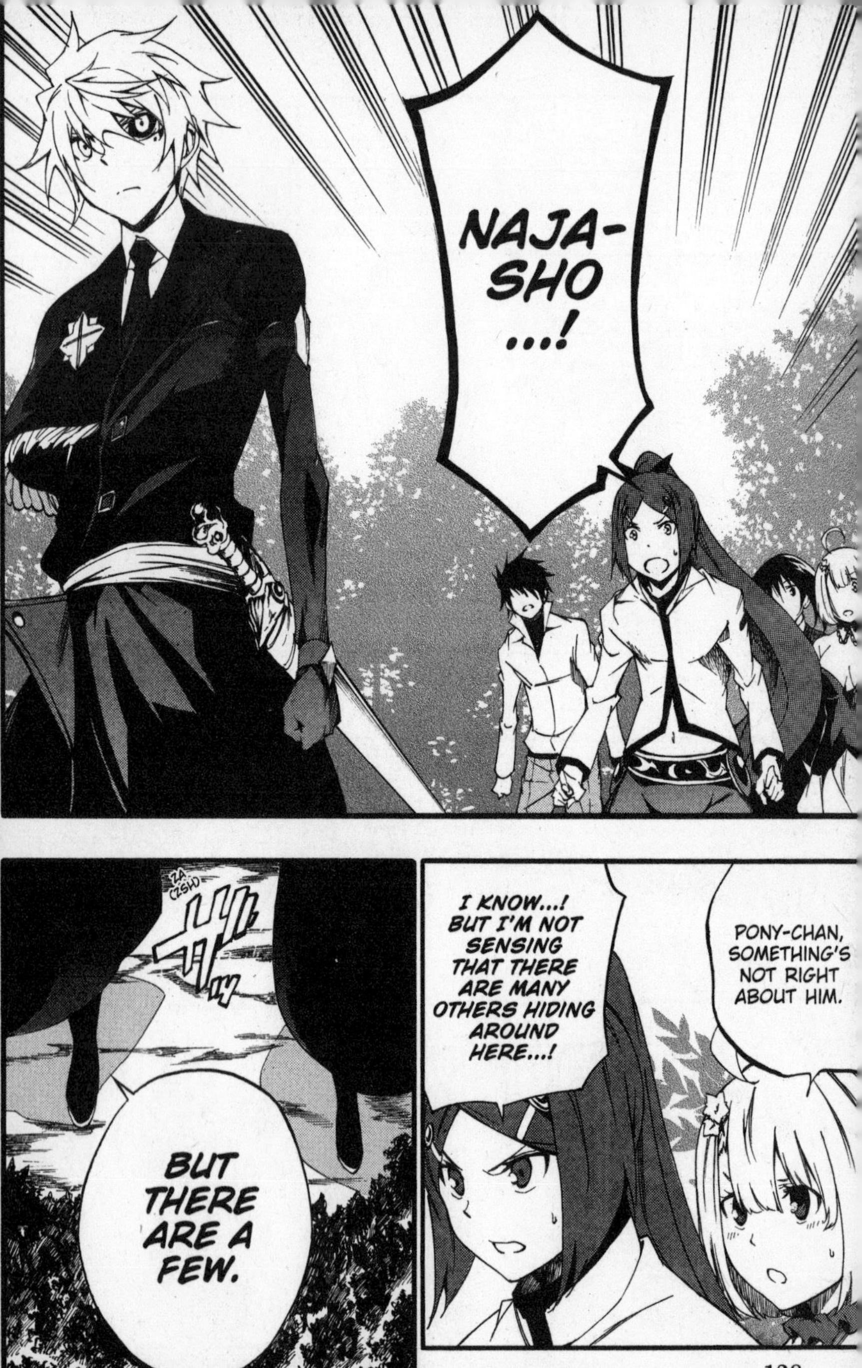
NAJA-SHO...!
PONY-CHAN, SOMETHING'S NOT RIGHT ABOUT HIM.
I KNOW...! BUT I'M NOT SENSING THAT THERE ARE MANY OTHERS HIDING AROUND HERE...!
ZA (ZSH)
BUT THERE ARE A FEW.

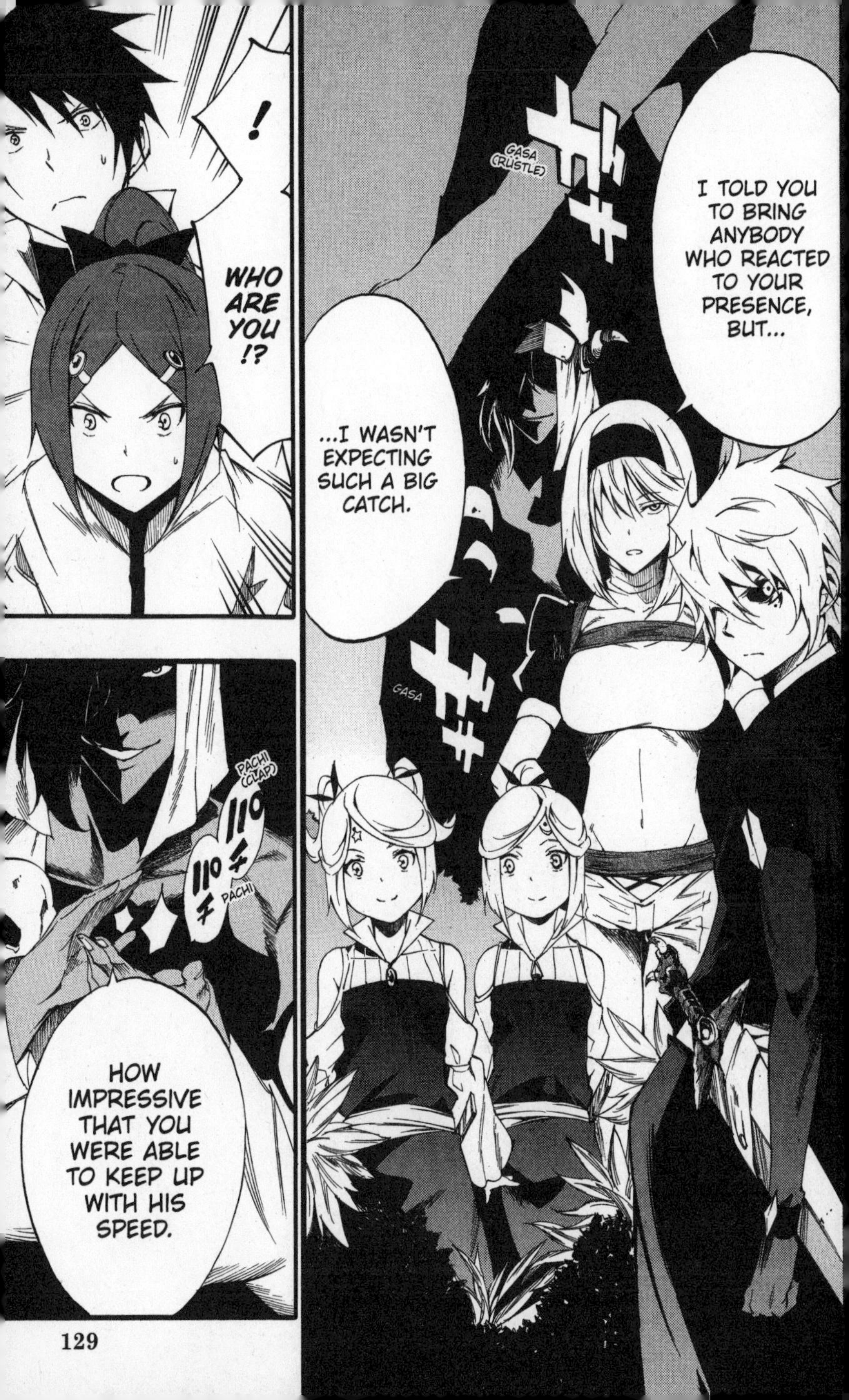
GASA (RUSTLE)
I TOLD YOU TO BRING ANYBODY WHO REACTED TO YOUR PRESENCE, BUT...
...I WASN'T EXPECTING SUCH A BIG CATCH.
GASA
!
WHO ARE YOU!?
PACHI (CLAP)
PACHI
HOW IMPRESSIVE THAT YOU WERE ABLE TO KEEP UP WITH HIS SPEED.

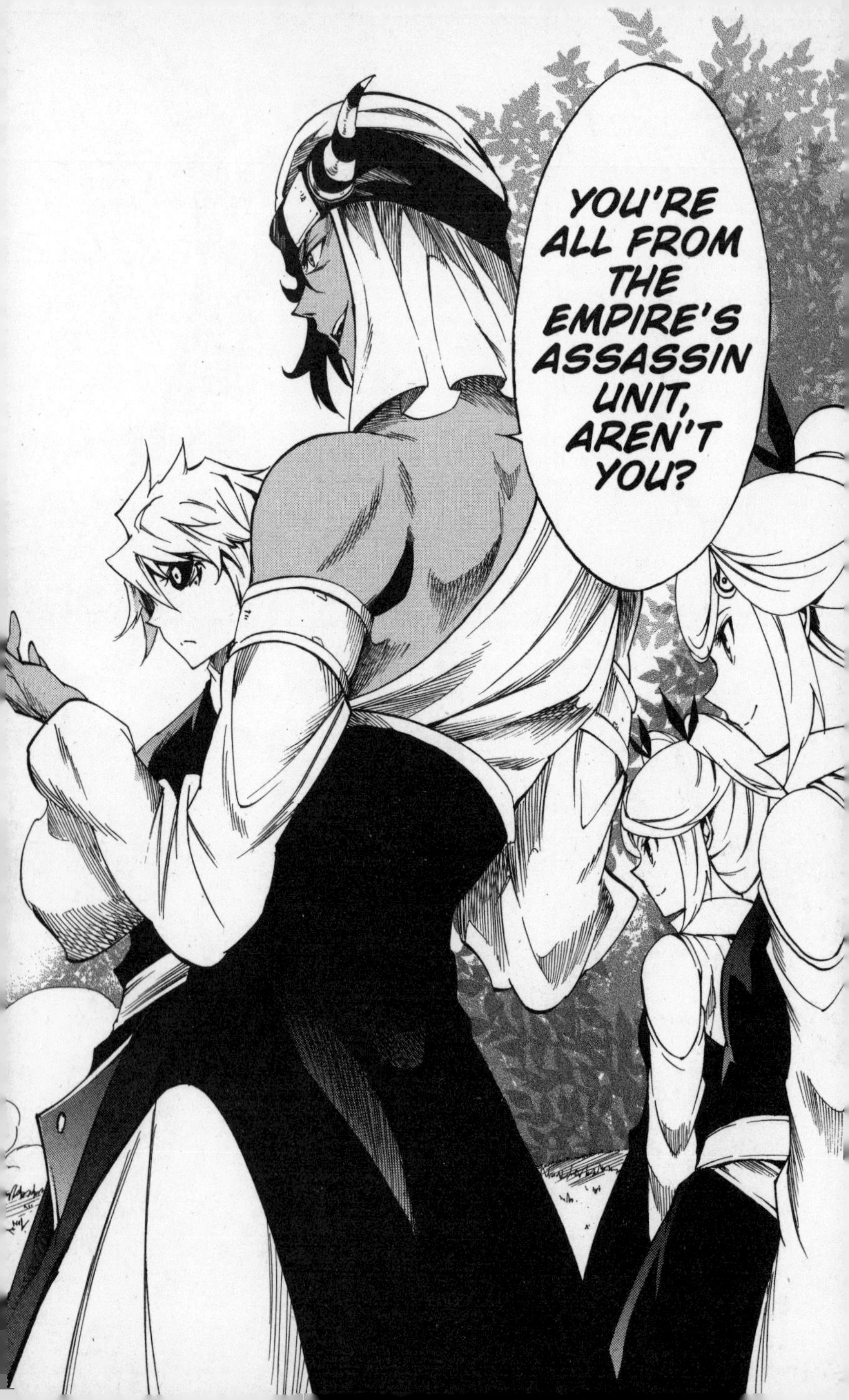
YOU'RE ALL FROM THE EMPIRE'S ASSASSIN UNIT, AREN'T YOU?

Chapter 47
The End of Loathing

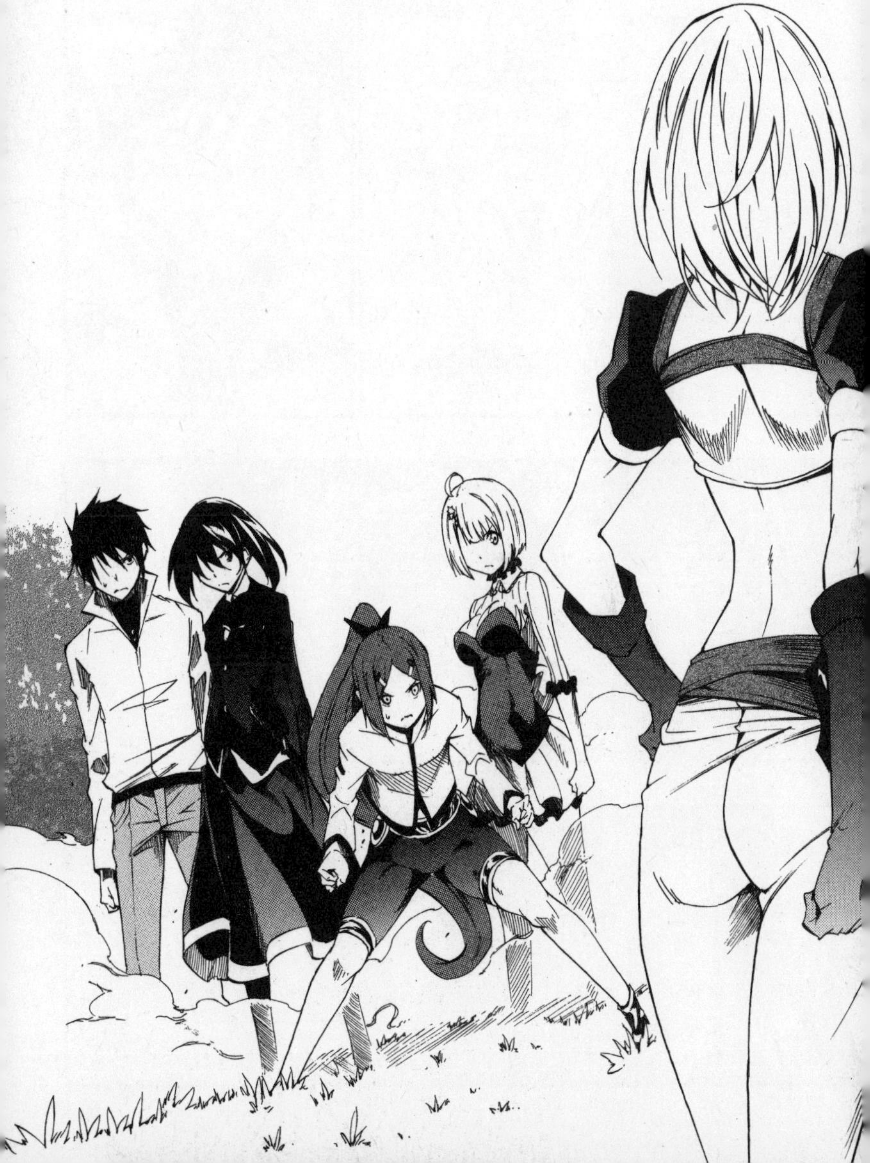

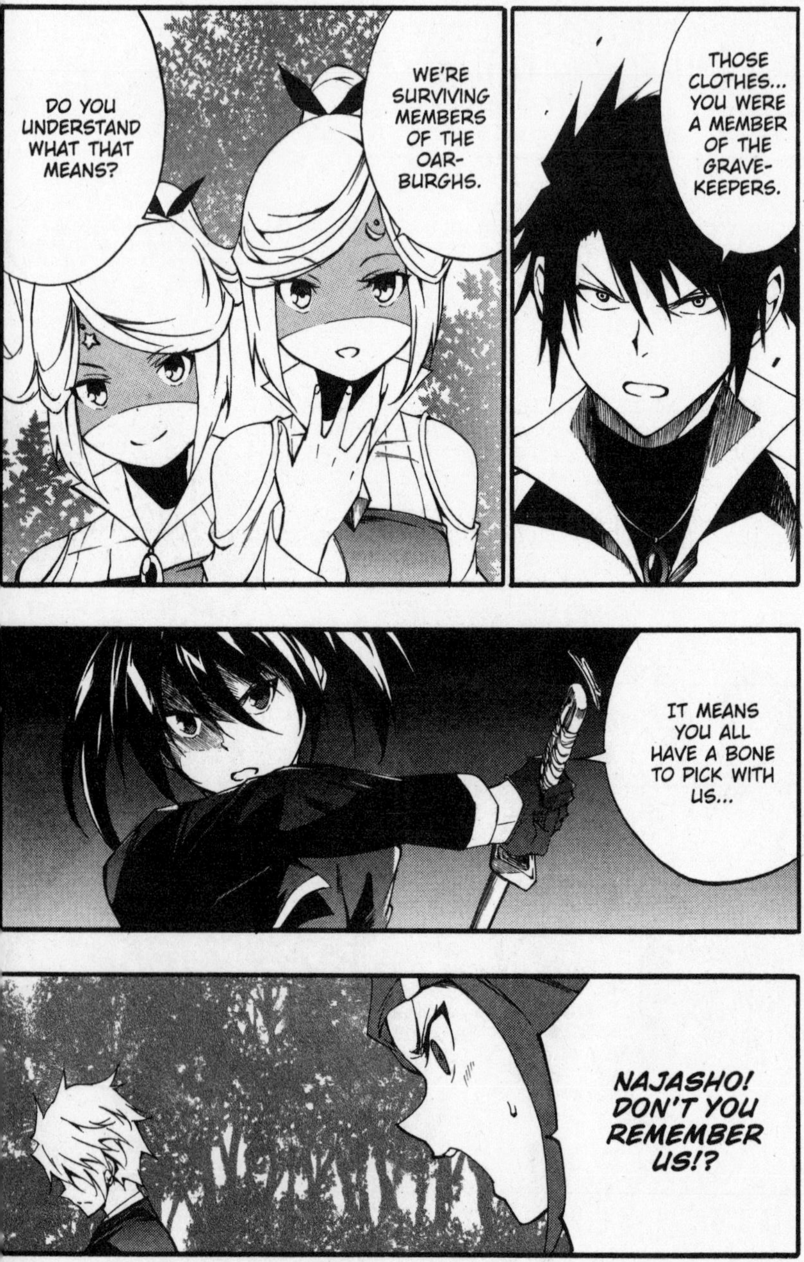
THOSE CLOTHES... YOU WERE A MEMBER OF THE GRAVE-KEEPERS.
WE'RE SURVIVING MEMBERS OF THE OAR-BURGHS.
DO YOU UNDERSTAND WHAT THAT MEANS?
IT MEANS YOU ALL HAVE A BONE TO PICK WITH US...
NAJASHO! DON'T YOU REMEMBER US!?

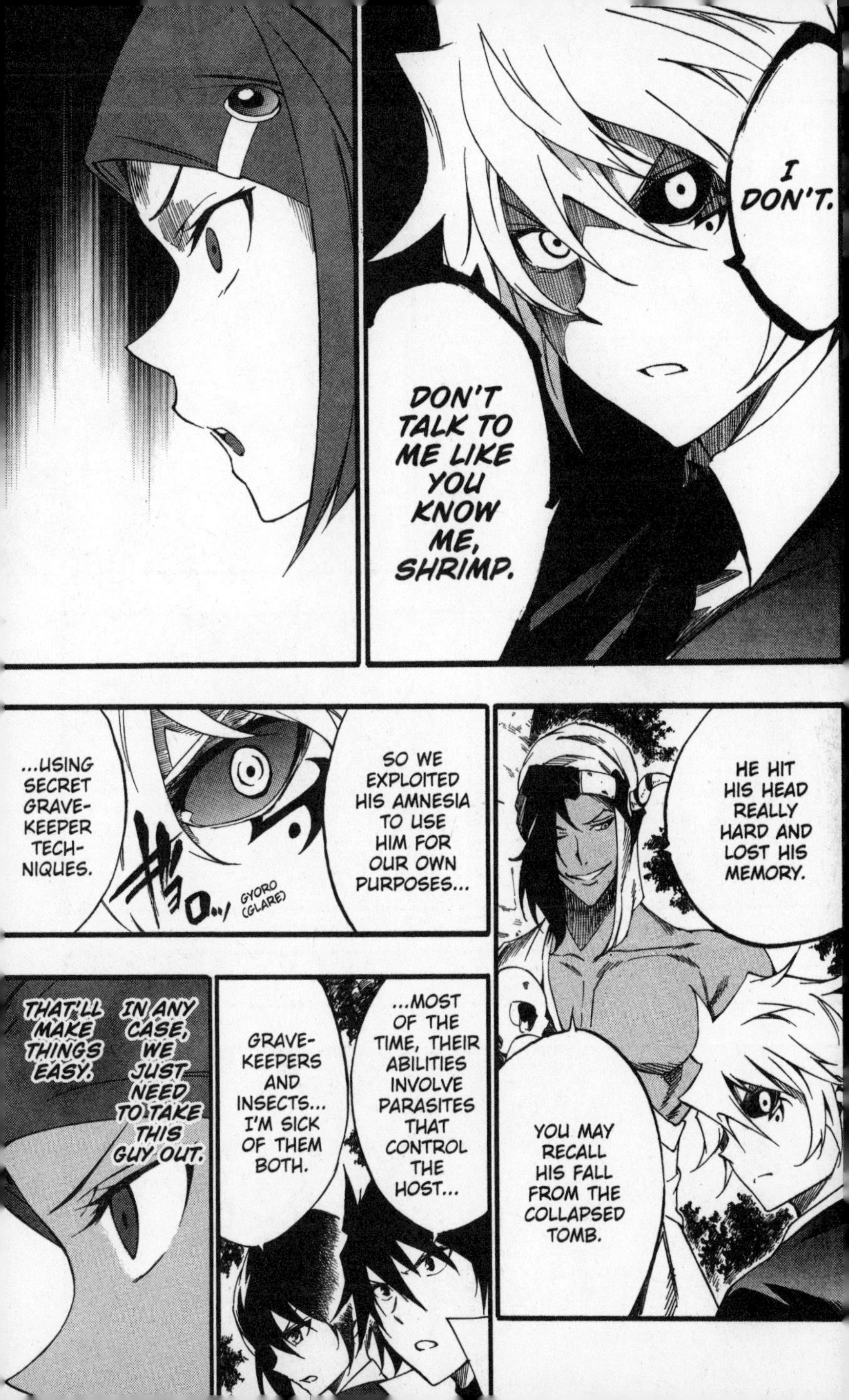
I DON'T.
DON'T TALK TO ME LIKE YOU KNOW ME, SHRIMP.
HE HIT HIS HEAD REALLY HARD AND LOST HIS MEMORY.
YOU MAY RECALL HIS FALL FROM THE COLLAPSED TOMB.
SO WE EXPLOITED HIS AMNESIA TO USE HIM FOR OUR OWN PURPOSES...
...USING SECRET GRAVE-KEEPER TECHNIQUES.
GYORO (GLARE)
...MOST OF THE TIME, THEIR ABILITIES INVOLVE PARASITES THAT CONTROL THE HOST...
GRAVE-KEEPERS AND INSECTS... I'M SICK OF THEM BOTH.
IN ANY CASE, WE JUST NEED TO TAKE THIS GUY OUT.
THAT'LL MAKE THINGS EASY.

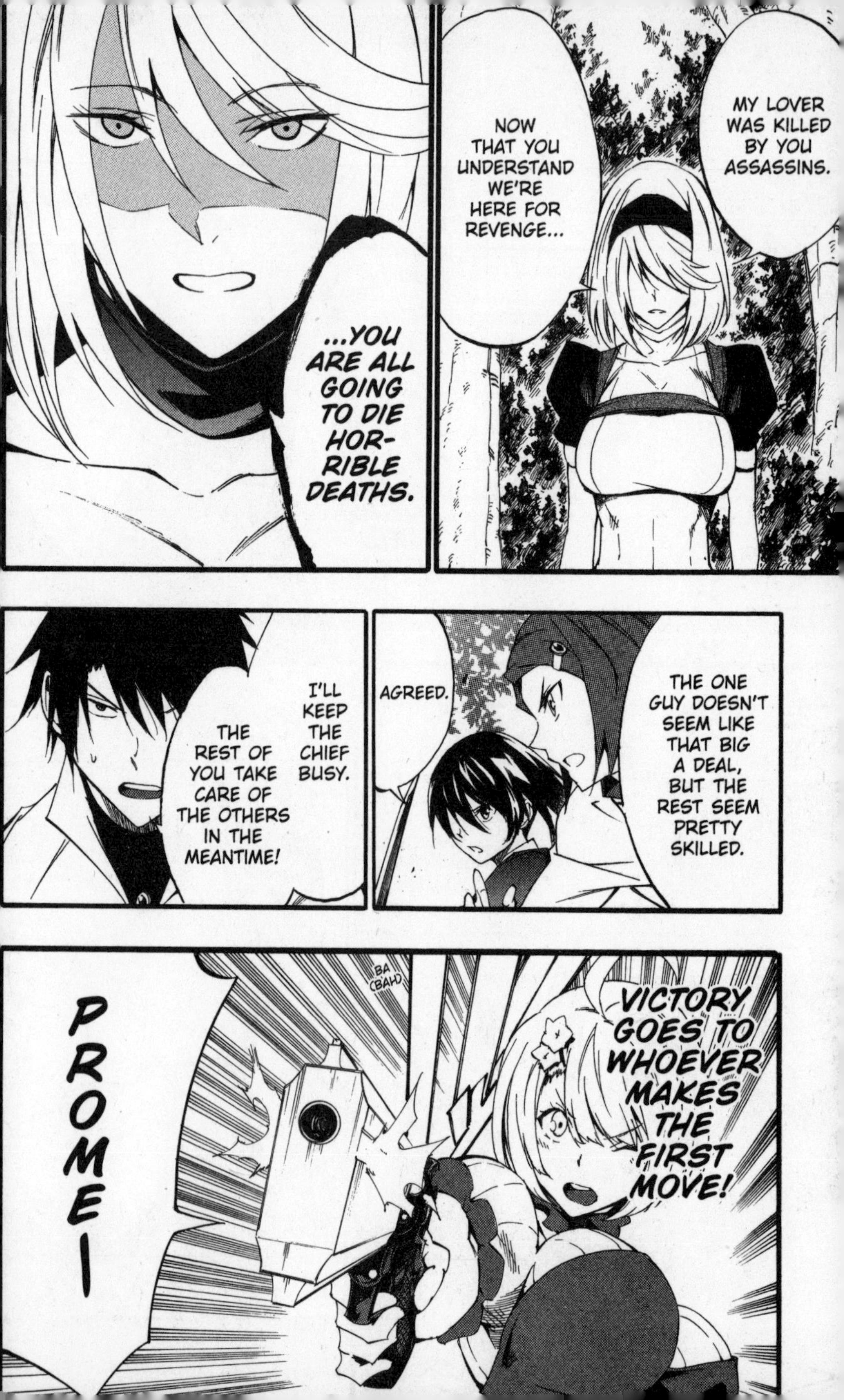
MY LOVER WAS KILLED BY YOU ASSASSINS.
NOW THAT YOU UNDERSTAND WE'RE HERE FOR REVENGE...
...YOU ARE ALL GOING TO DIE HOR-RIBLE DEATHS.
THE ONE GUY DOESN'T SEEM LIKE THAT BIG A DEAL, BUT THE REST SEEM PRETTY SKILLED.
AGREED.
I'LL KEEP THE CHIEF BUSY.
THE REST OF YOU TAKE CARE OF THE OTHERS IN THE MEANTIME!
VICTORY GOES TO WHOEVER MAKES THE FIRST MOVE!
BA (BAH)
PROMEI

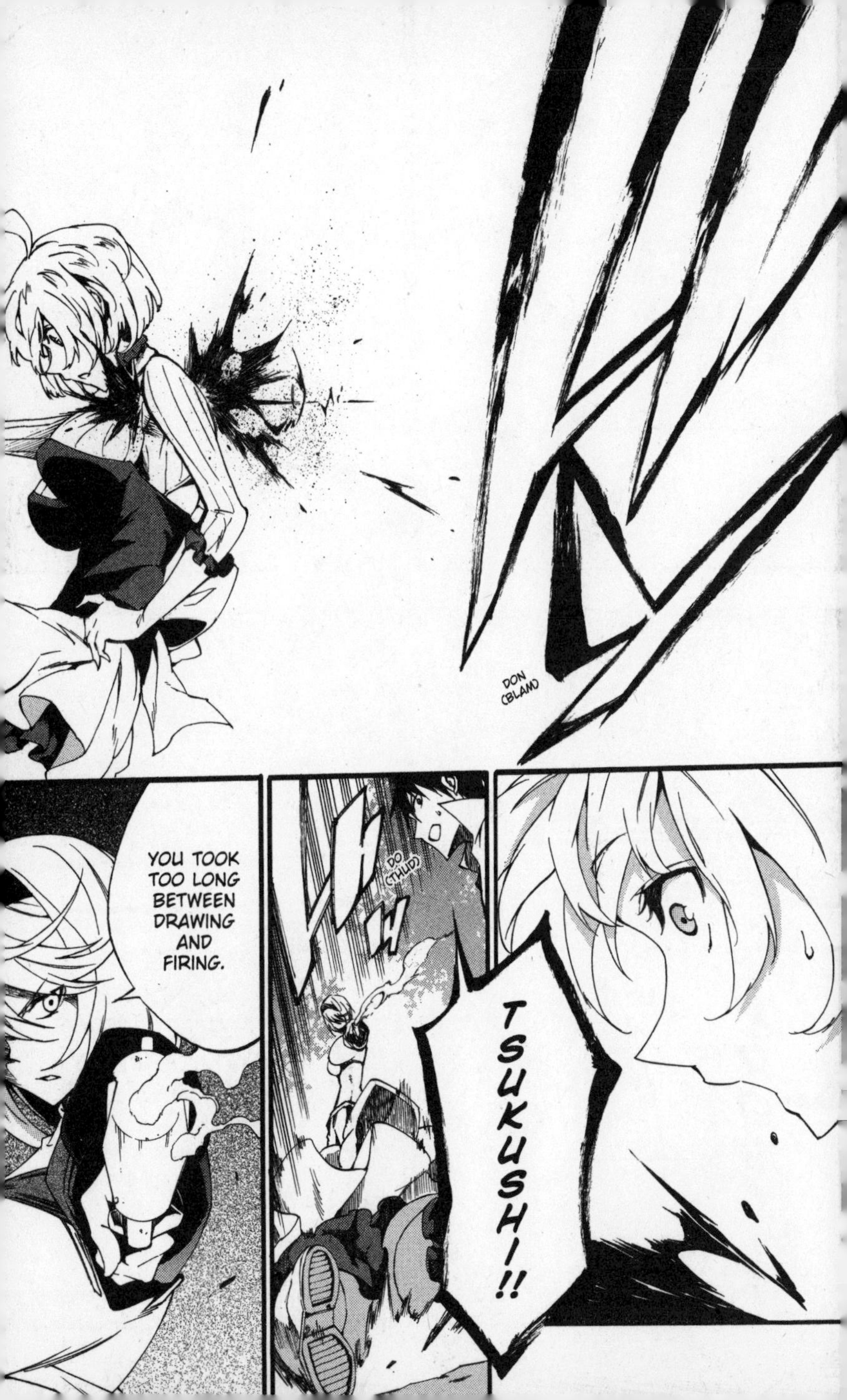
DON
(BLAM)
TSUKUSHI!!
DO
(THUD)
YOU TOOK TOO LONG BETWEEN DRAWING AND FIRING.

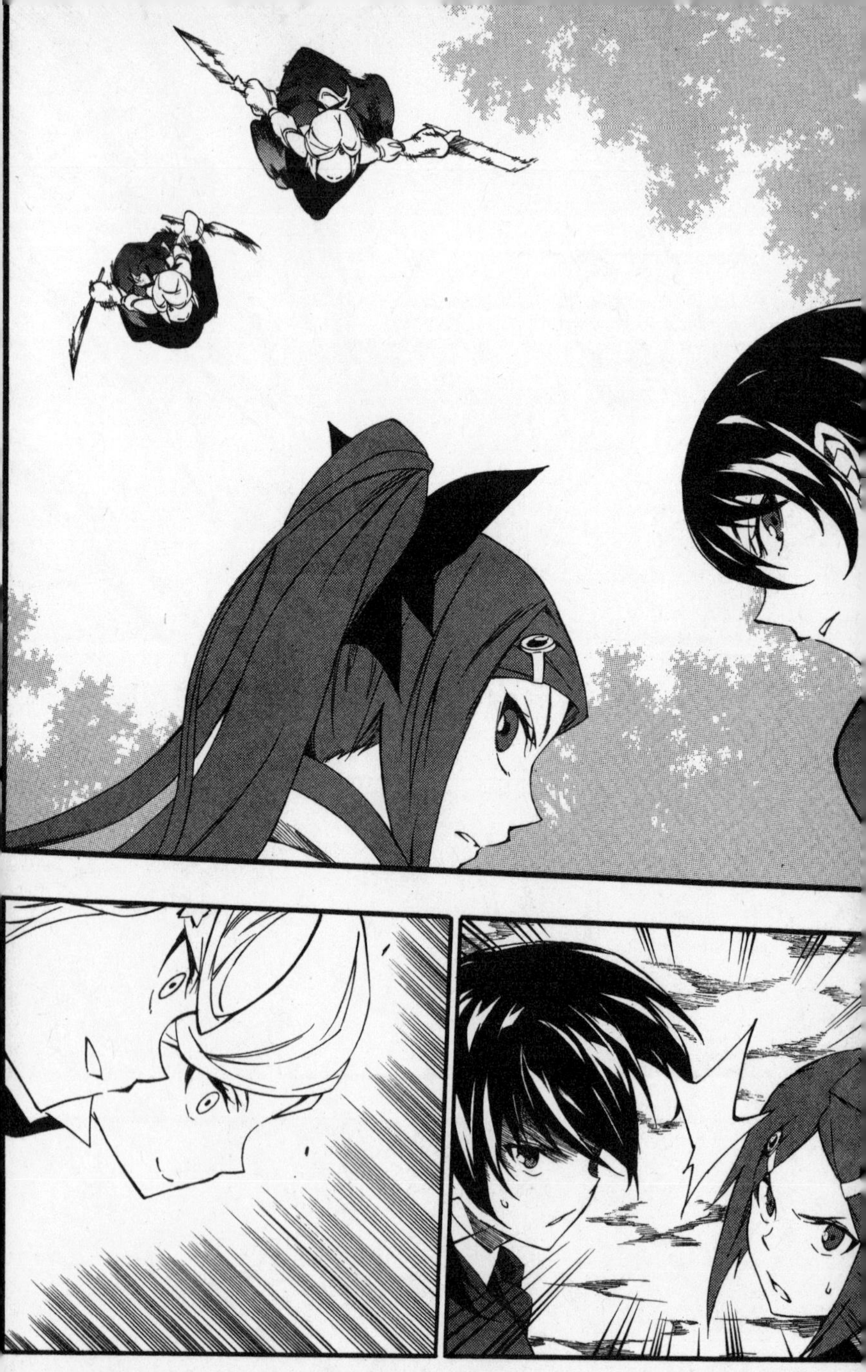

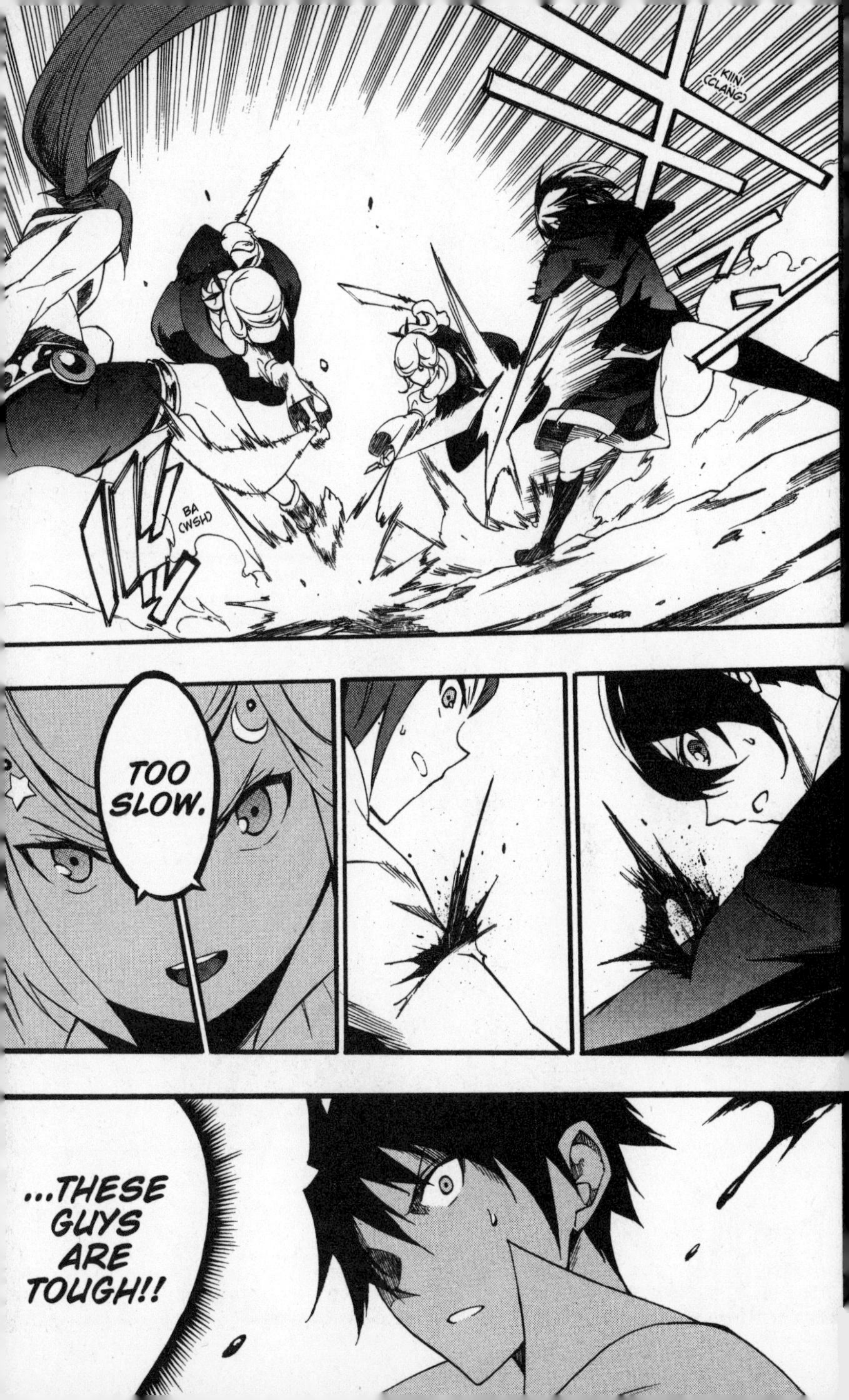
KIIN (CLANG)
BA (WSH)
TOO SLOW.
...THESE GUYS ARE TOUGH!!

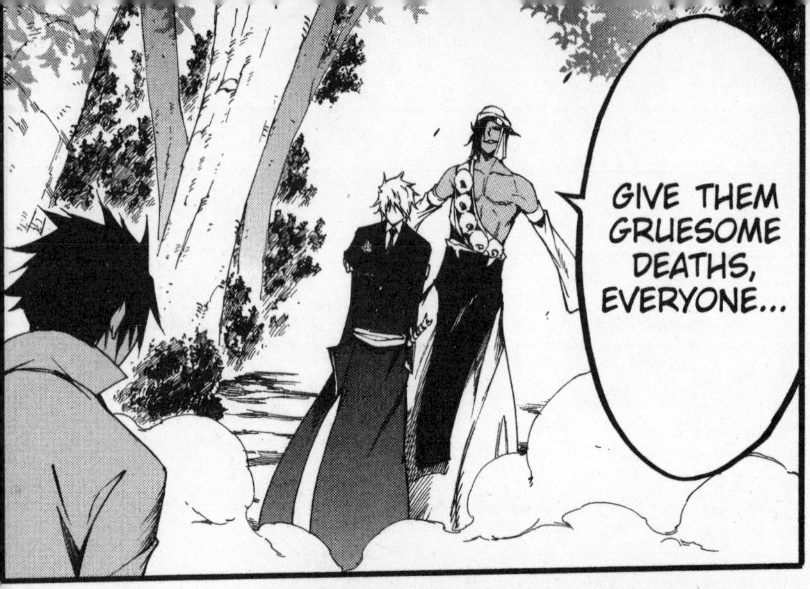
GIVE THEM GRUESOME DEATHS, EVERYONE...

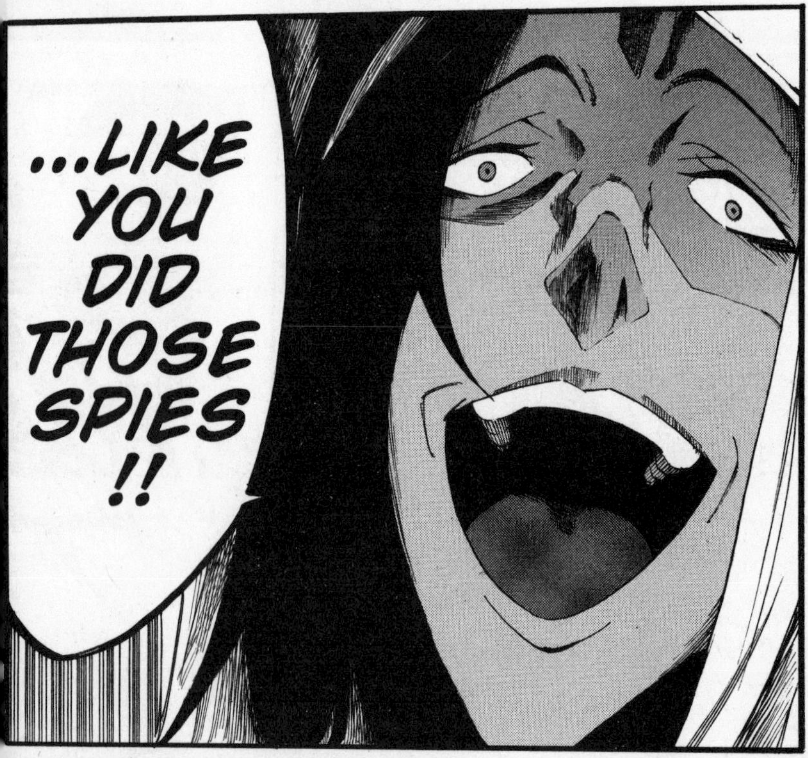
...LIKE YOU DID THOSE SPIES !!

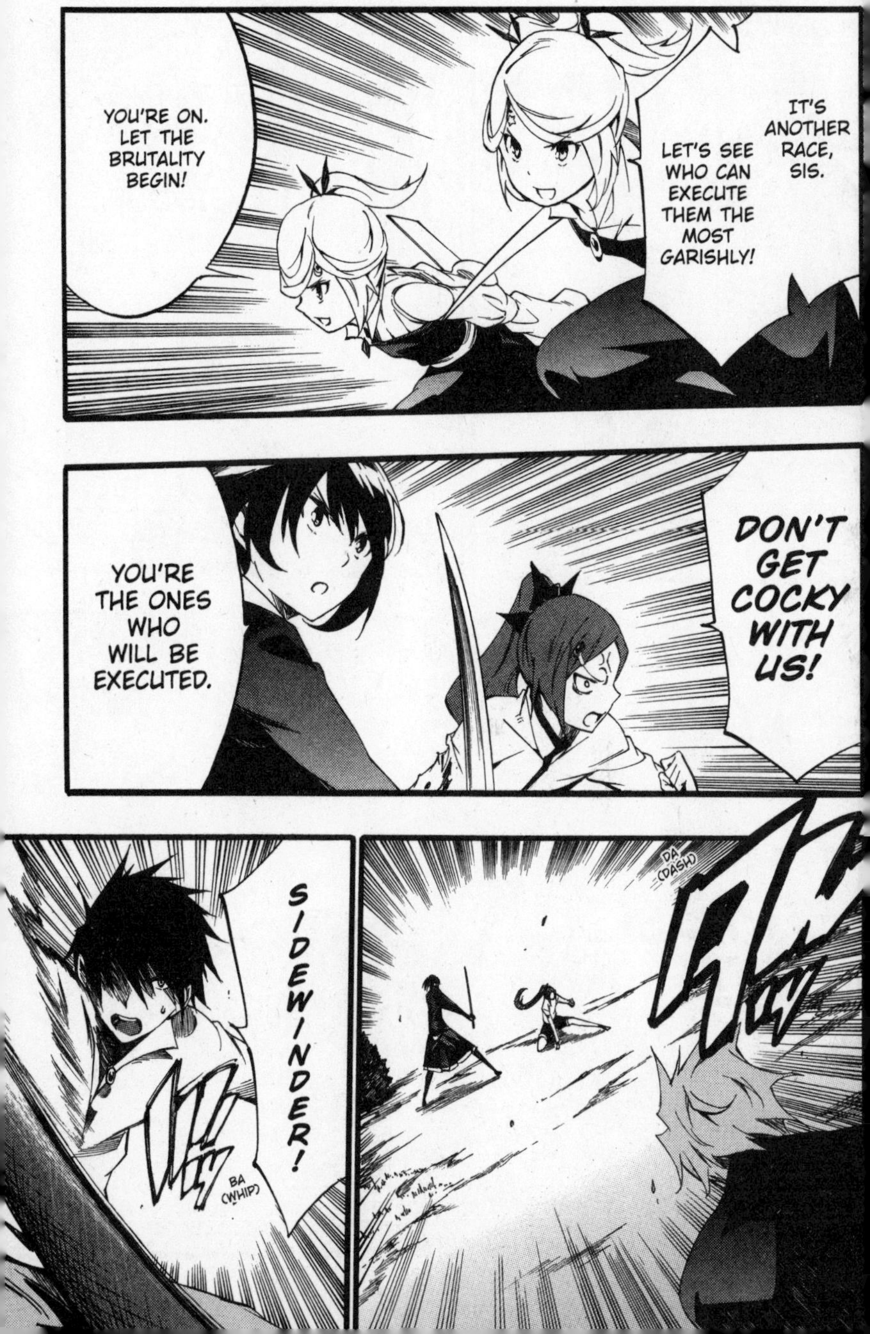
IT'S ANOTHER RACE, SIS.
LET'S SEE WHO CAN EXECUTE THEM THE MOST GARISHLY!
YOU'RE ON. LET THE BRUTALITY BEGIN!
DON'T GET COCKY WITH US!
YOU'RE THE ONES WHO WILL BE EXECUTED.
DA (DASH)
SIDEWINDER!
BA (WHIP)

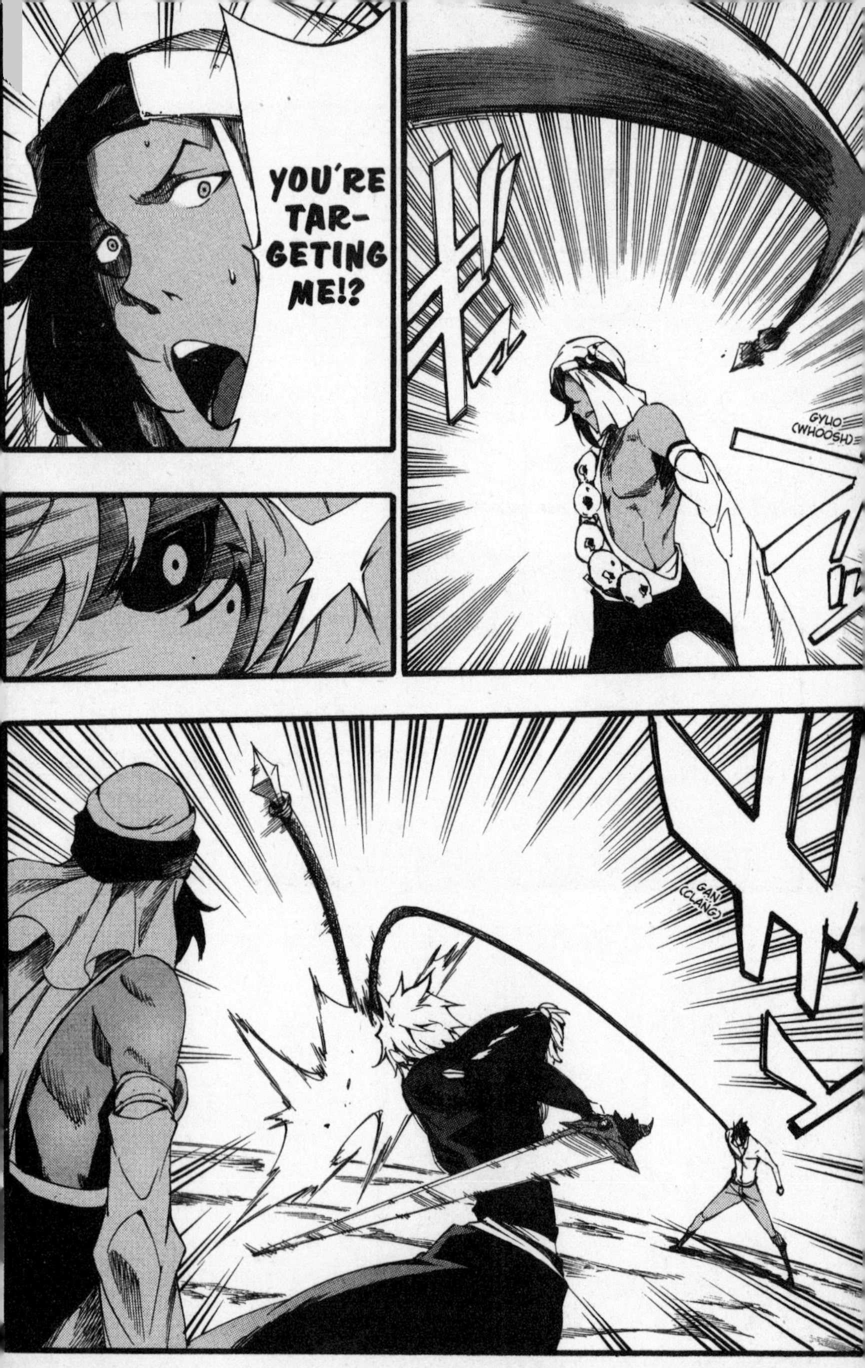
YOU'RE TAR- GETING ME!?
GYUO (WHOOSH)
GAN (CLANG)

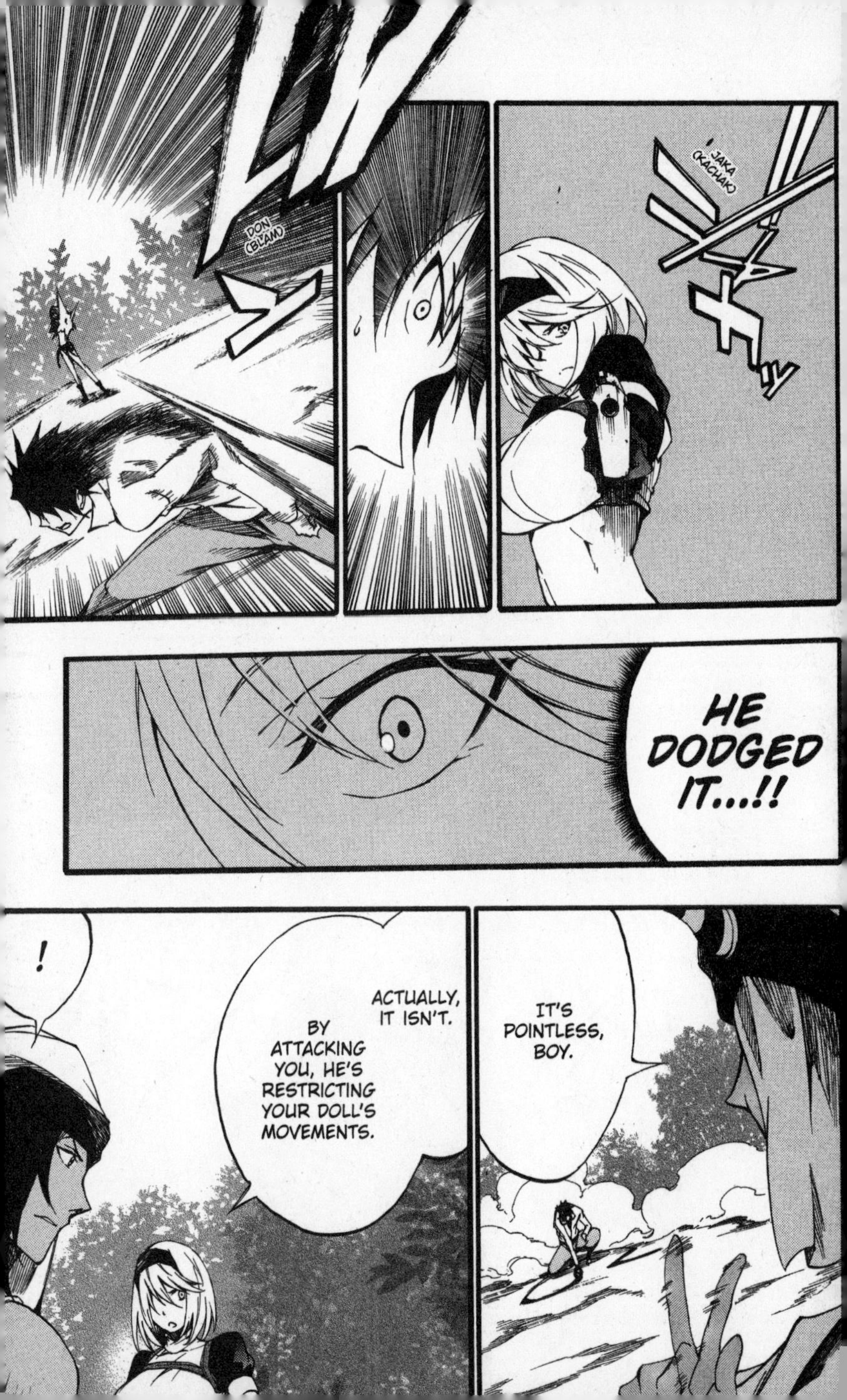

JAKA (KACHAK)
DON (BLAM)
HE DODGED IT...!!
IT'S POINTLESS, BOY.
ACTUALLY, IT ISN'T.
BY ATTACKING YOU, HE'S RESTRICTING YOUR DOLL'S MOVEMENTS.
!

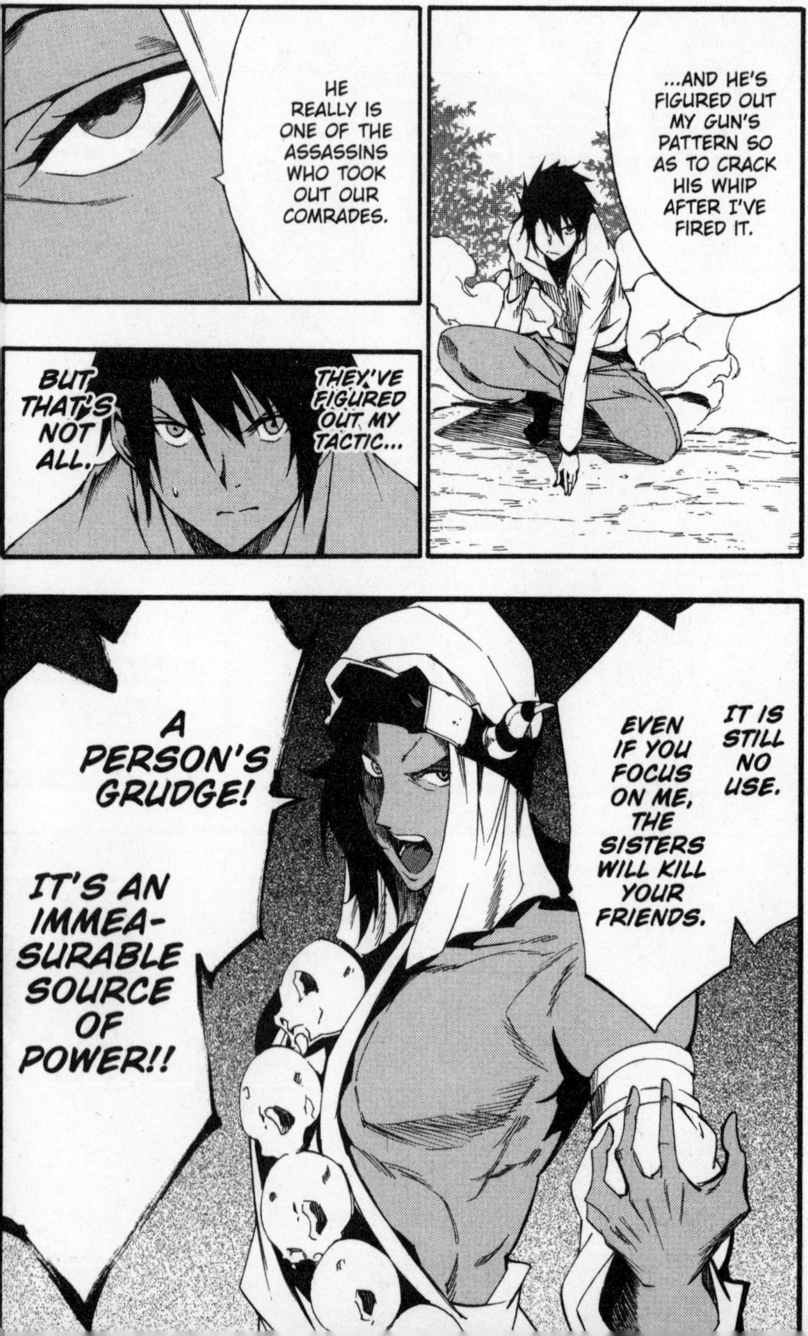
...AND HE'S FIGURED OUT MY GUN'S PATTERN SO AS TO CRACK HIS WHIP AFTER I'VE FIRED IT.
HE REALLY IS ONE OF THE ASSASSINS WHO TOOK OUT OUR COMRADES.
THEY'VE FIGURED OUT MY TACTIC...
BUT THAT'S NOT ALL.
IT IS STILL NO USE.
EVEN IF YOU FOCUS ON ME, THE SISTERS WILL KILL YOUR FRIENDS.
A PERSON'S GRUDGE!
IT'S AN IMMEA-SURABLE SOURCE OF POWER!!

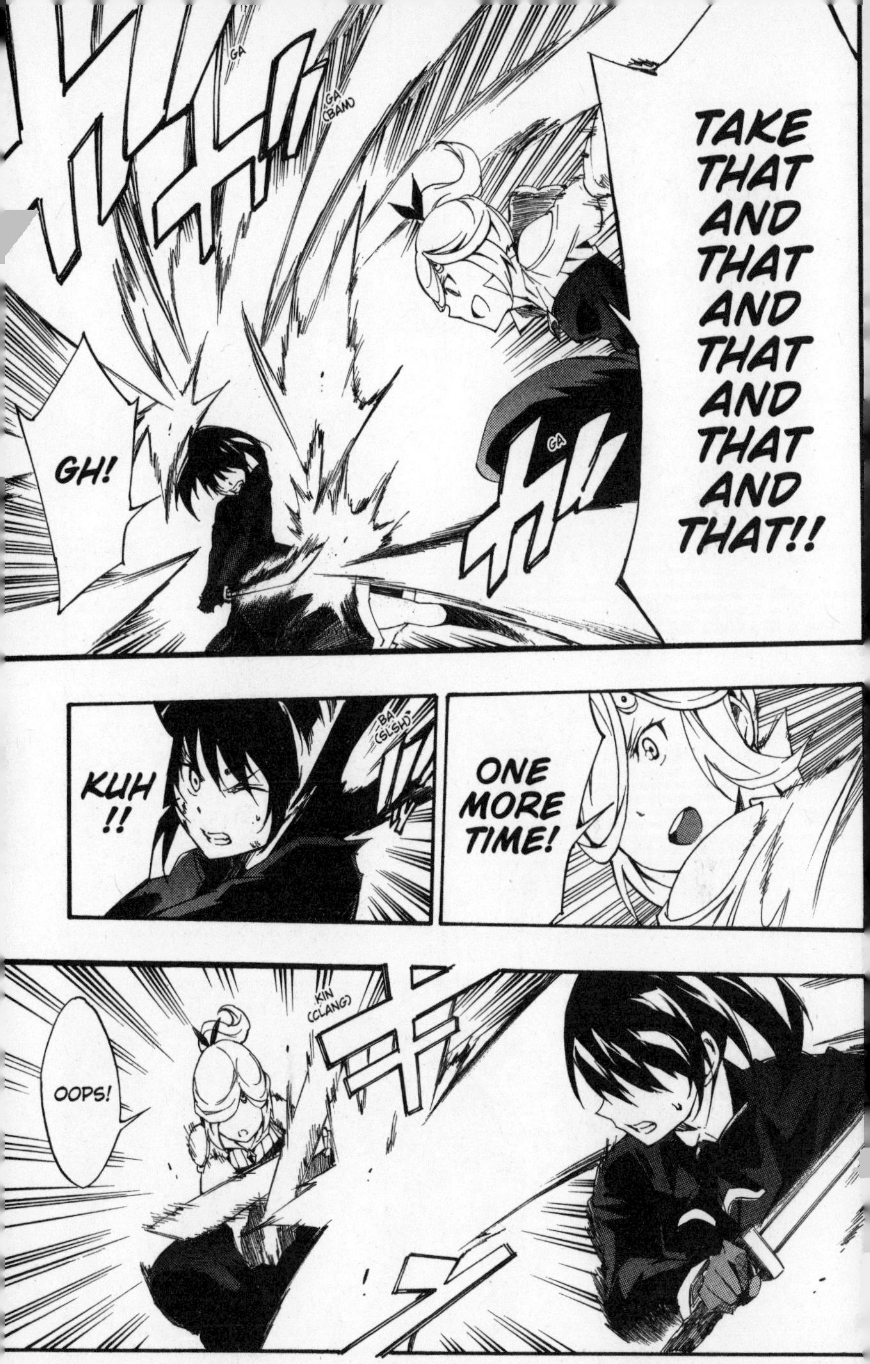
TAKE THAT AND THAT AND THAT AND THAT AND THAT!!
GA
GA (BAM)
GA
GH!
ONE MORE TIME!
BA (SLSH)
KUH !!
KIN (CLANG)
OOPS!

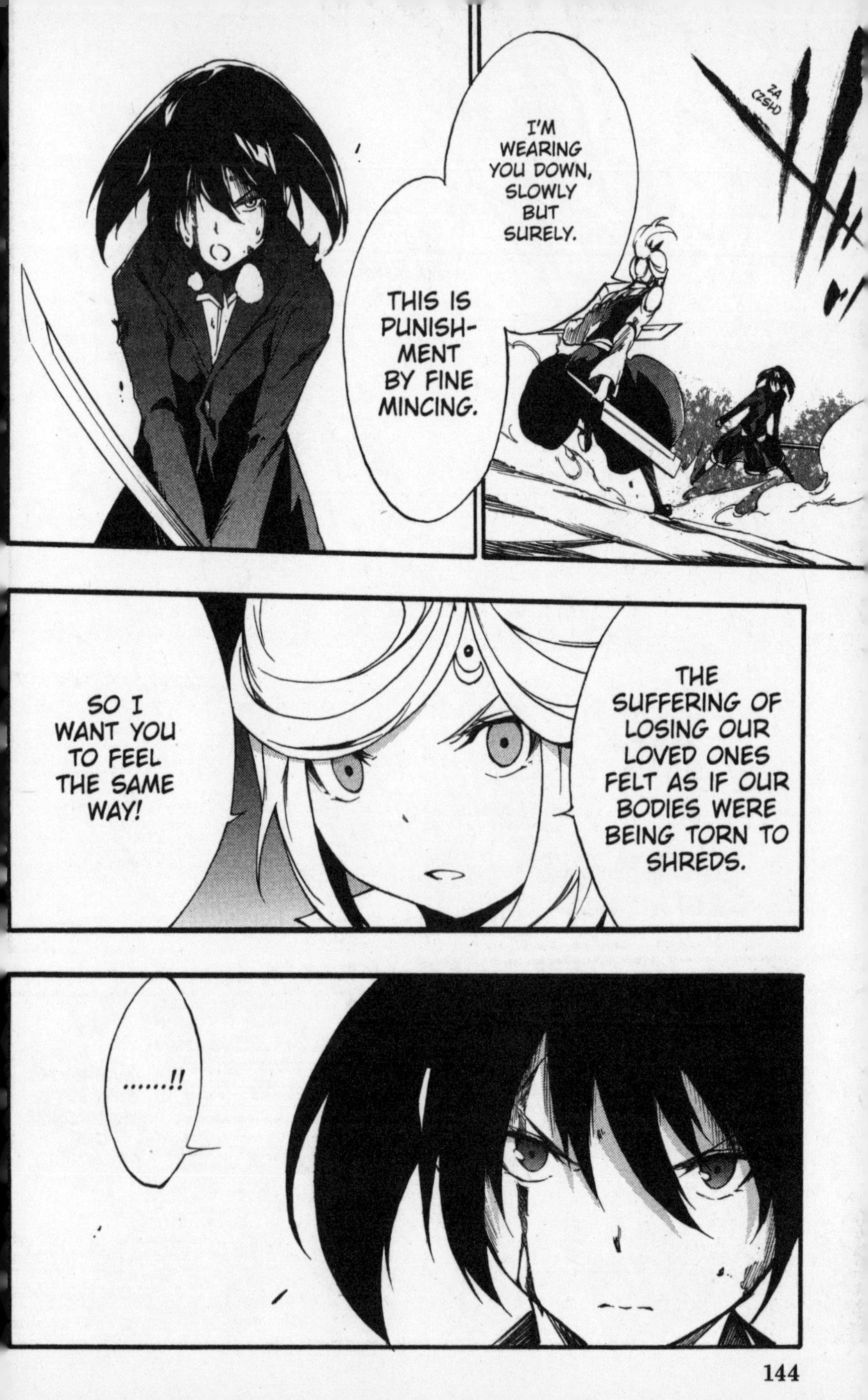
ZA (ZSH)
I'M WEARING YOU DOWN, SLOWLY BUT SURELY.
THIS IS PUNISHMENT BY FINE MINCING.
THE SUFFERING OF LOSING OUR LOVED ONES FELT AS IF OUR BODIES WERE BEING TORN TO SHREDS.
SO I WANT YOU TO FEEL THE SAME WAY!
......!!

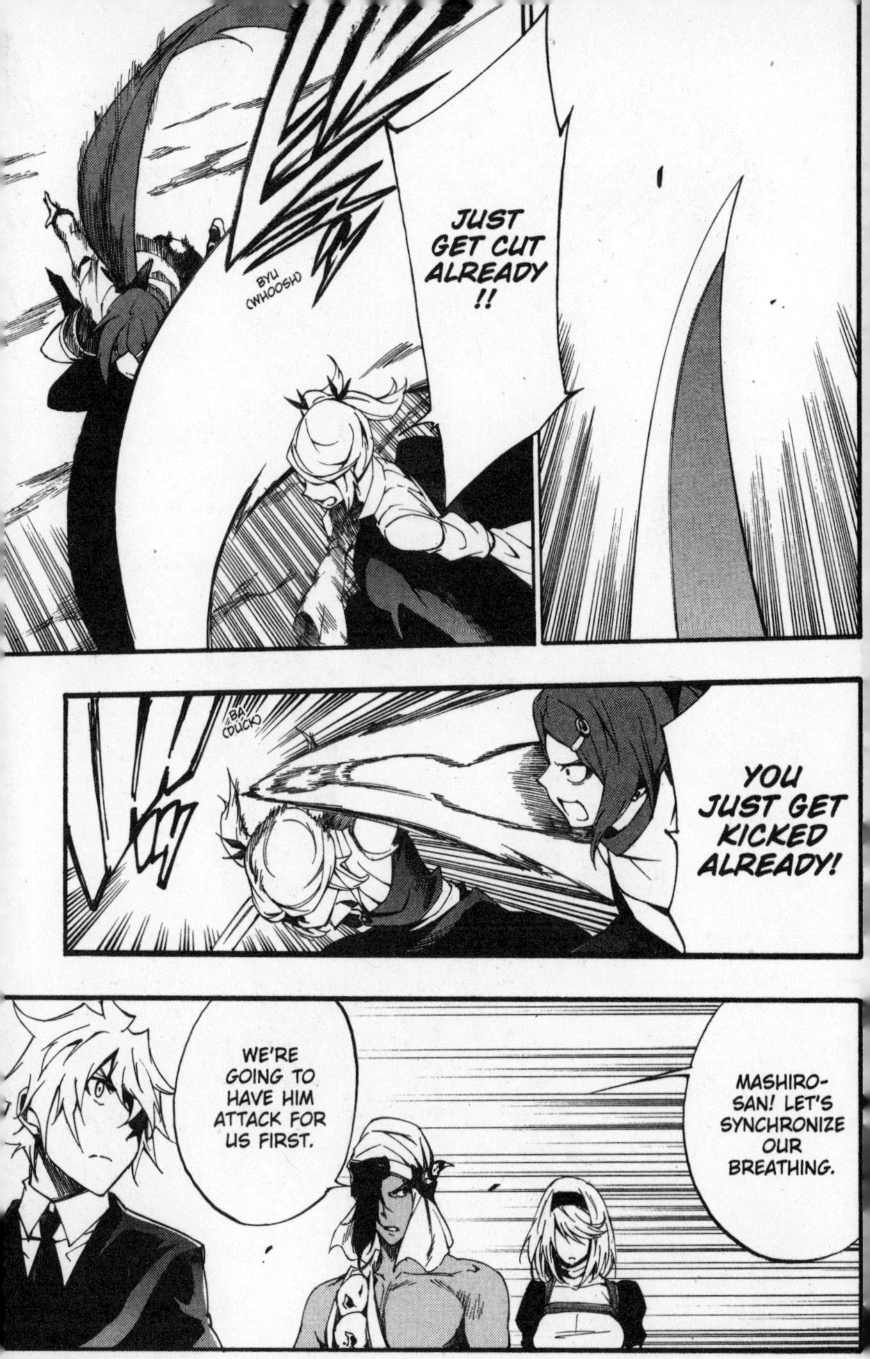
JUST GET CUT ALREADY !!
BYU (WHOOSH)
BA (DUCK)
YOU JUST GET KICKED ALREADY!
MASHIRO-SAN! LET'S SYNCHRONIZE OUR BREATHING.
WE'RE GOING TO HAVE HIM ATTACK FOR US FIRST.

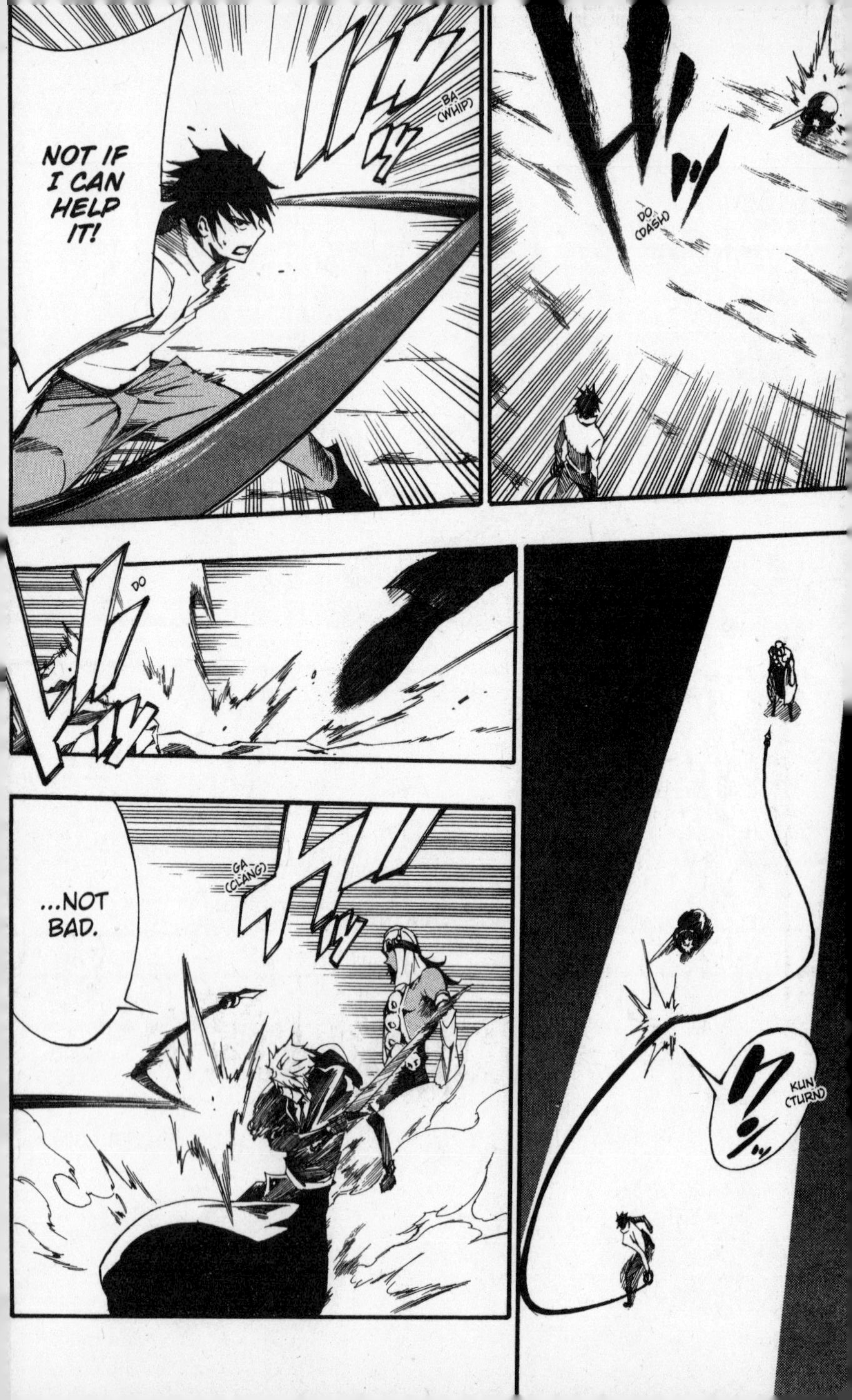

DO (DASH)
BA (WHIP)
NOT IF I CAN HELP IT!
KUN (TURN)
DO
GA (CLANG)
...NOT BAD.

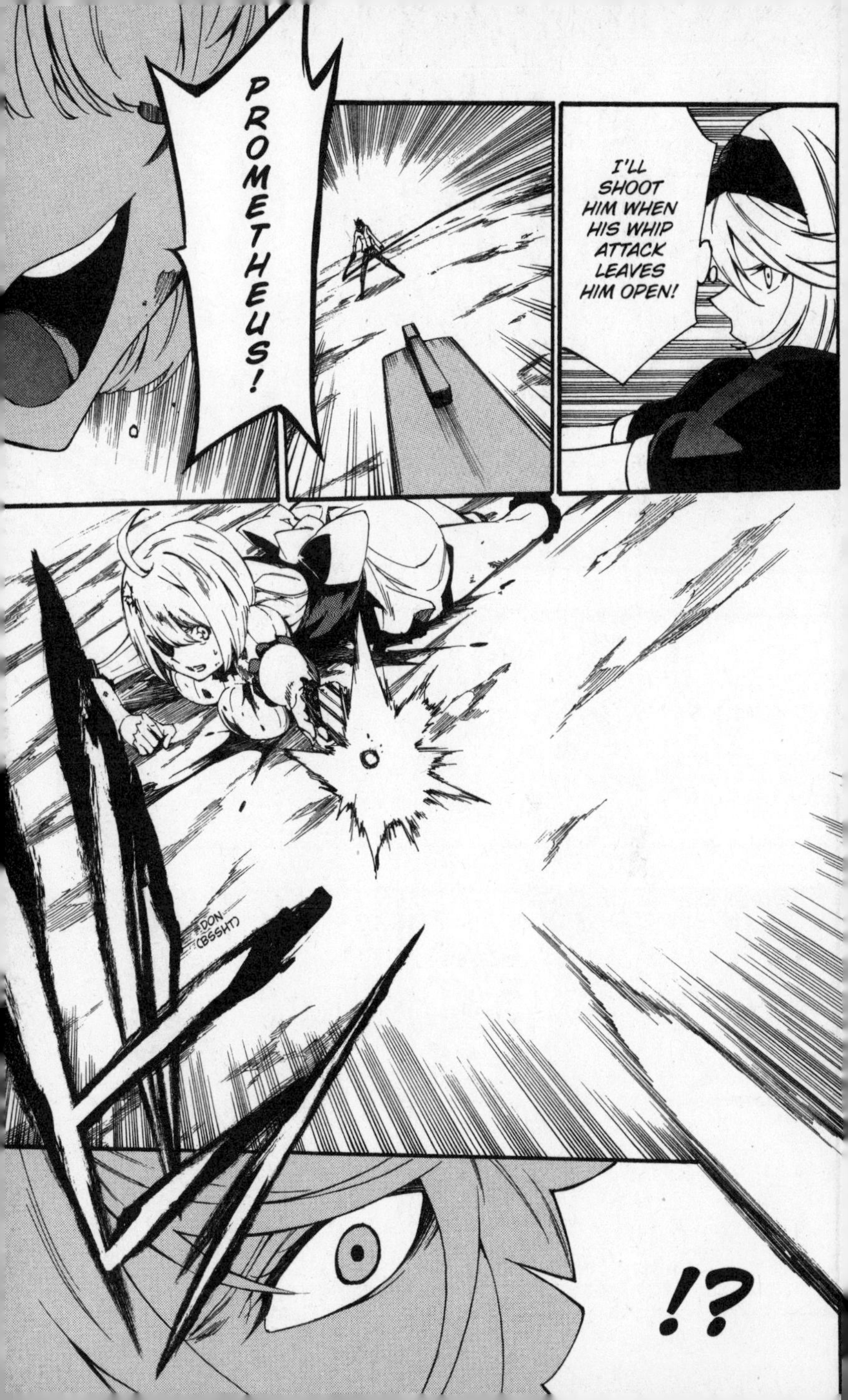

I'LL SHOOT HIM WHEN HIS WHIP ATTACK LEAVES HIM OPEN!
PROMETHEUS!
DON (BSSHT)
!?

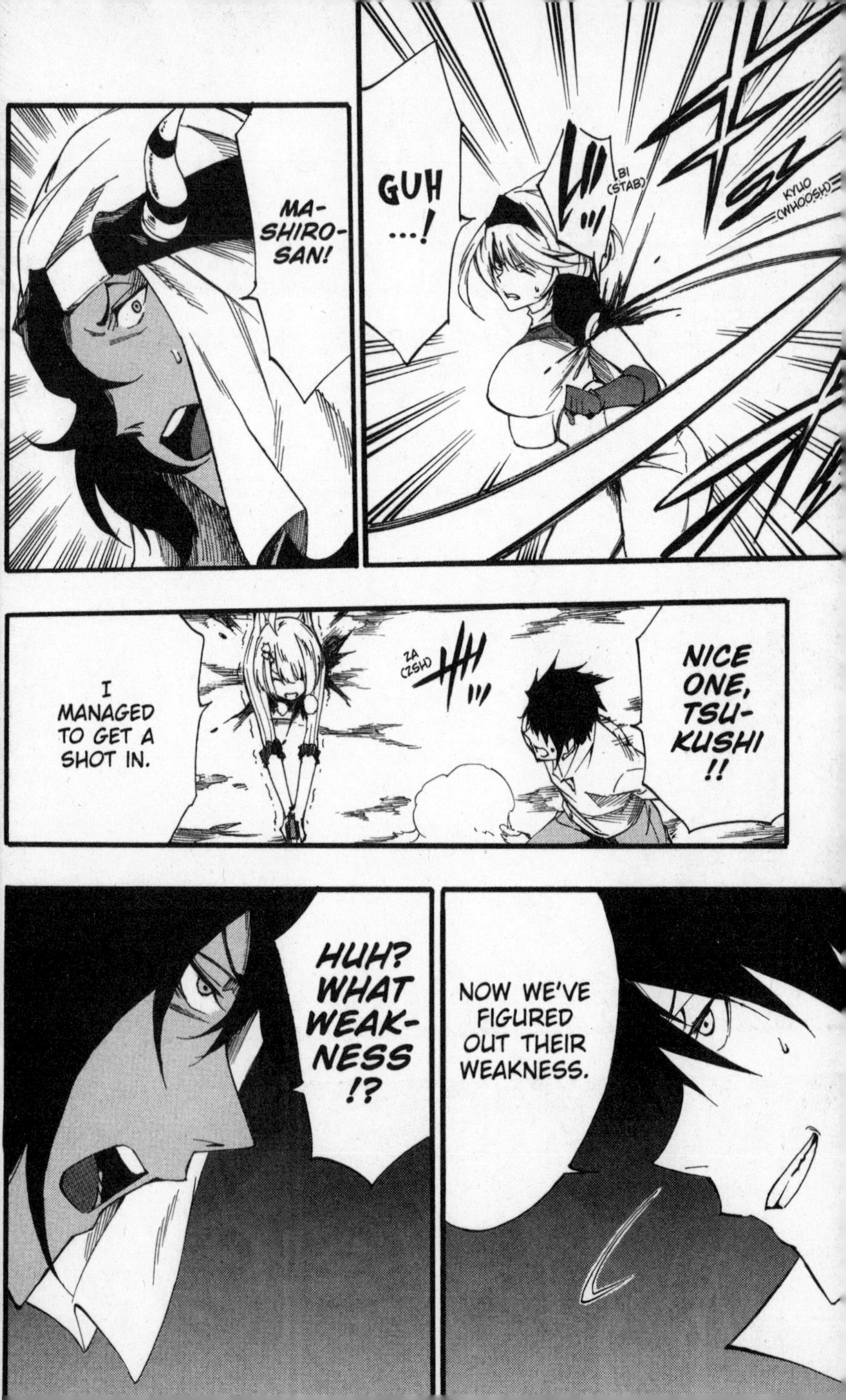
KYUO (WHOOSH)
BI (STAB)
GUH ...!
MA-SHIRO-SAN!
NICE ONE, TSU-KUSHI !!
ZA (ZSH)
I MANAGED TO GET A SHOT IN.
NOW WE'VE FIGURED OUT THEIR WEAKNESS.
HUH? WHAT WEAK-NESS !?

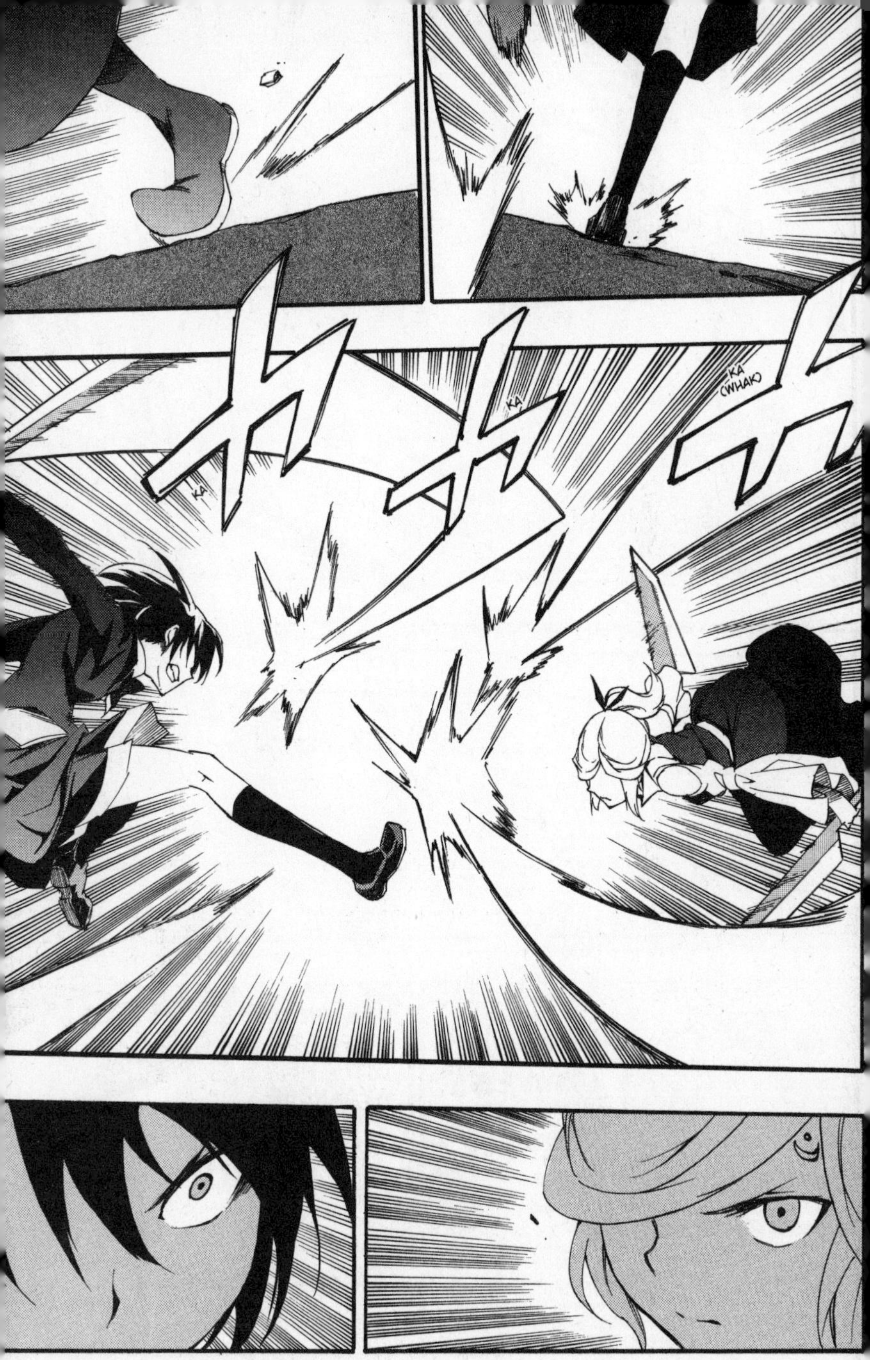
KA
KA
KA
(WHAK)

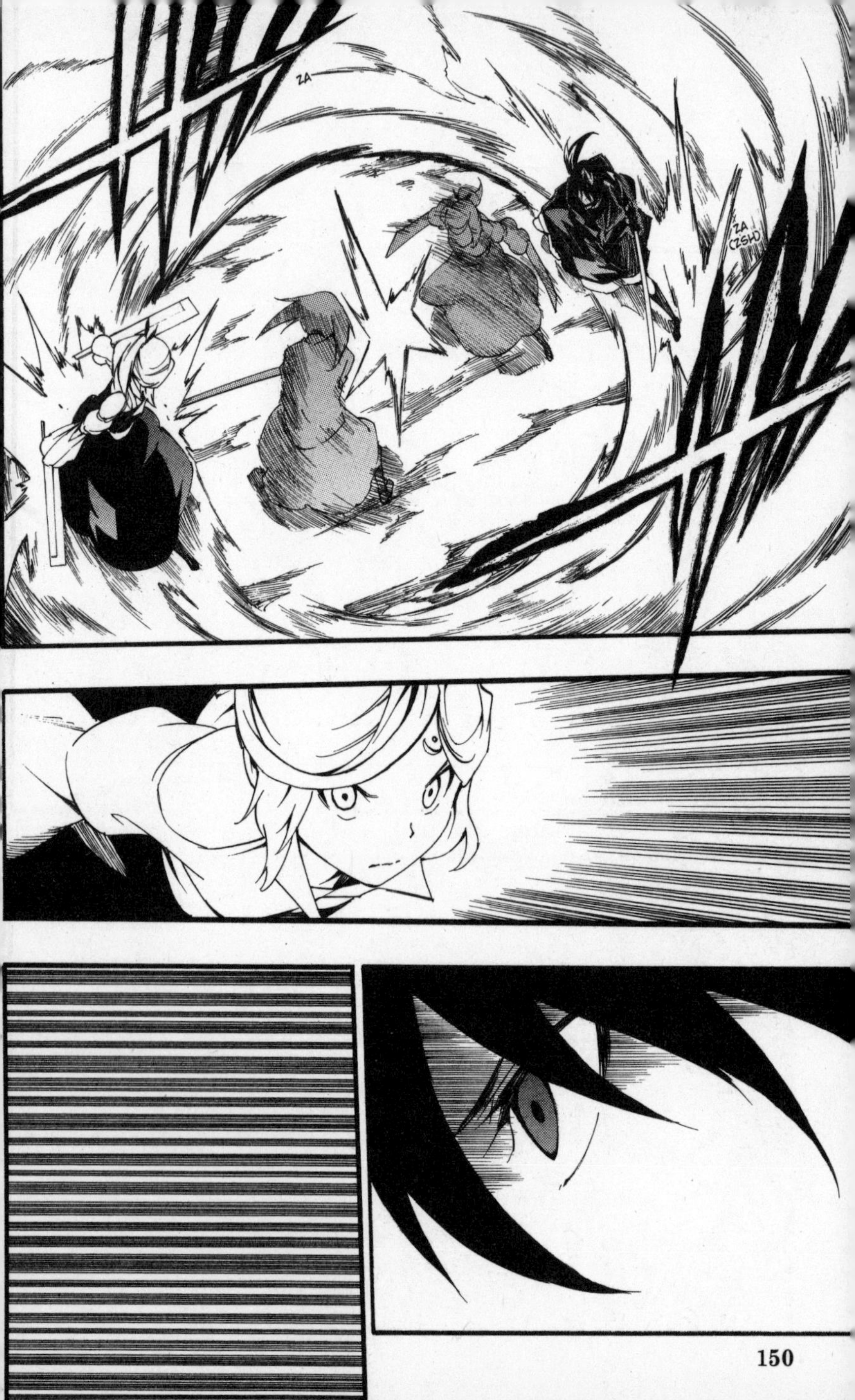
ZA
ZA
CZSH

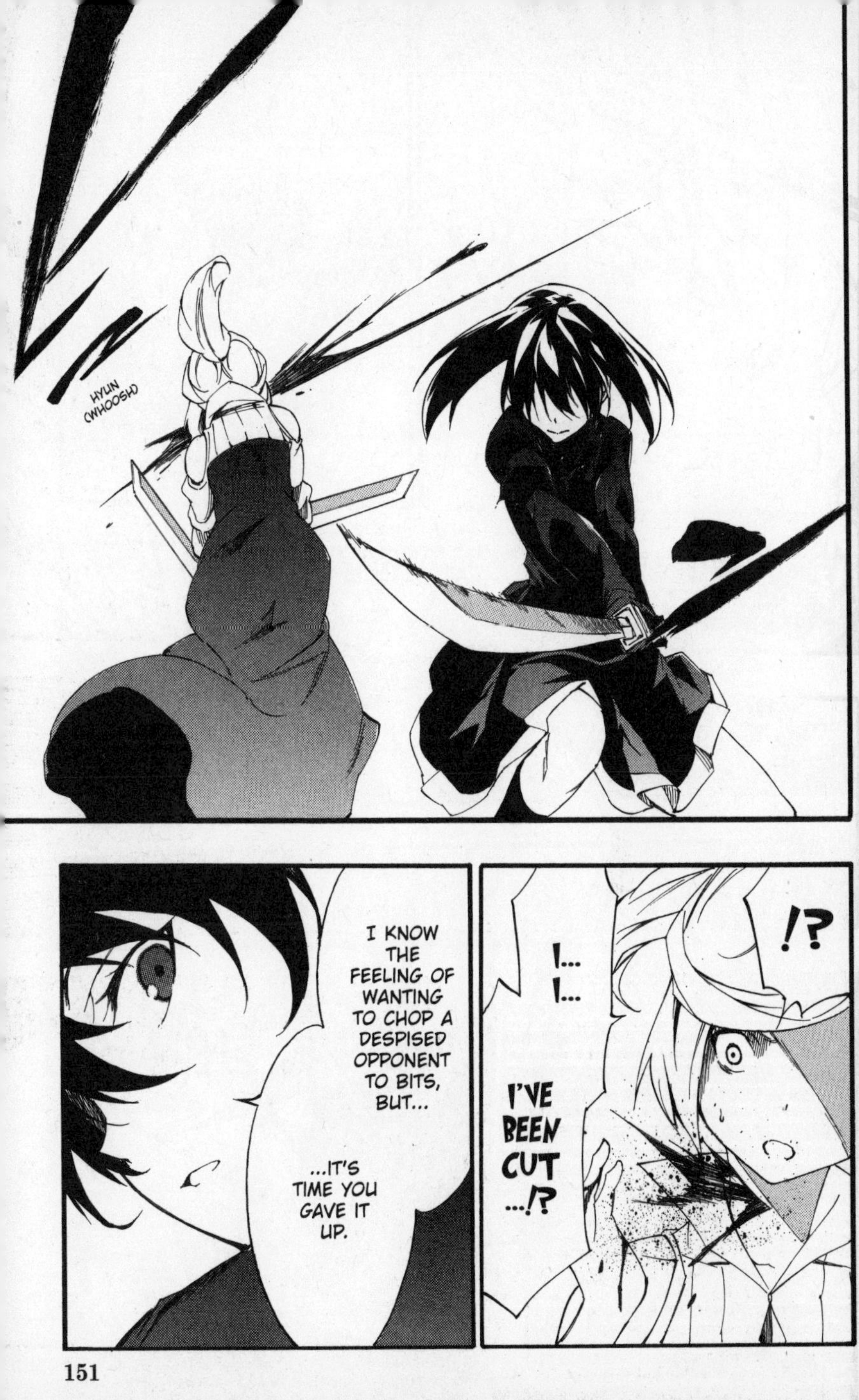
HYUN (WHOOSH)
!?
I... I...
I'VE BEEN CUT ...!?
I KNOW THE FEELING OF WANTING TO CHOP A DESPISED OPPONENT TO BITS, BUT...
...IT'S TIME YOU GAVE IT UP.

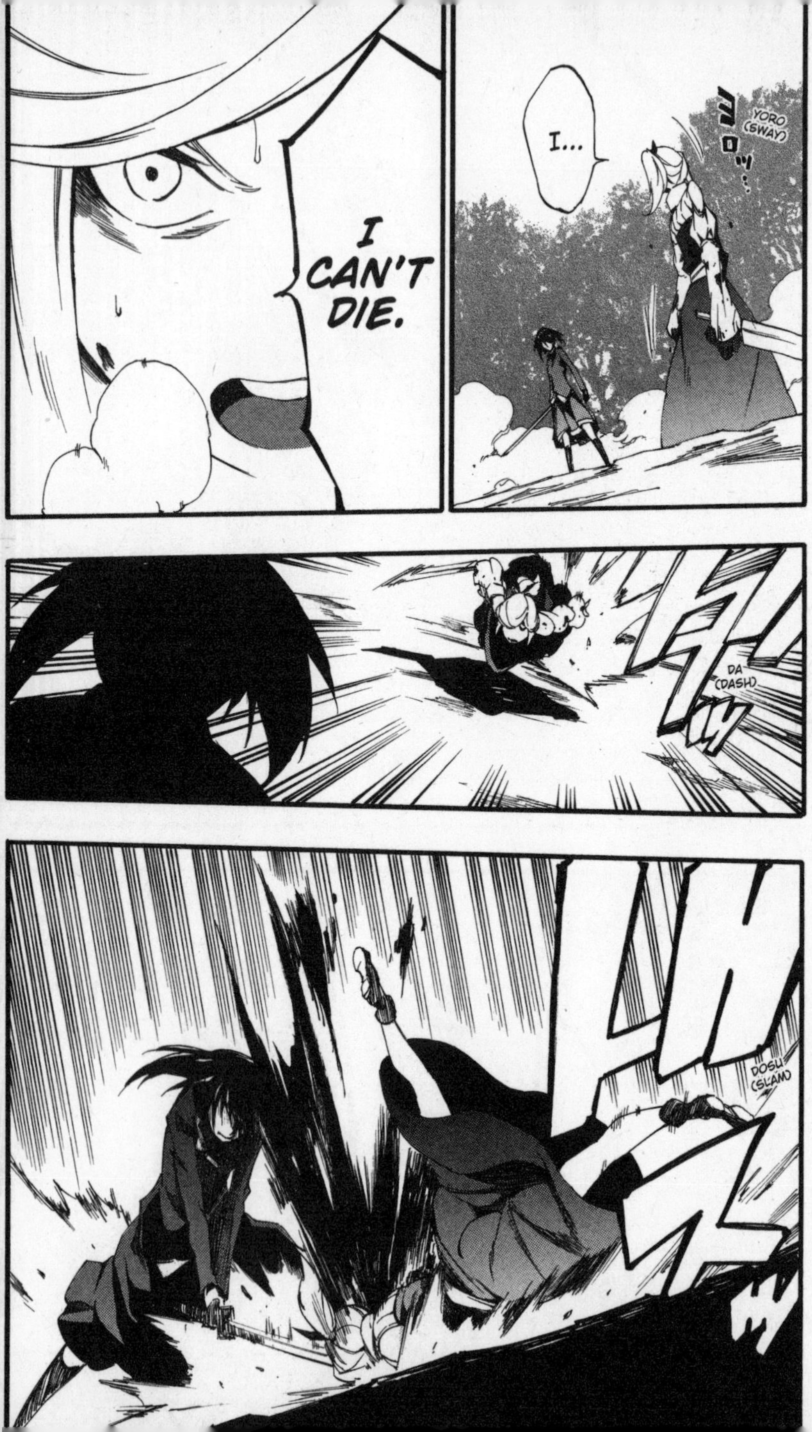
I...
YORO (SWAY)
I CAN'T DIE.
DA (DASH)
DOSU (SLAM)

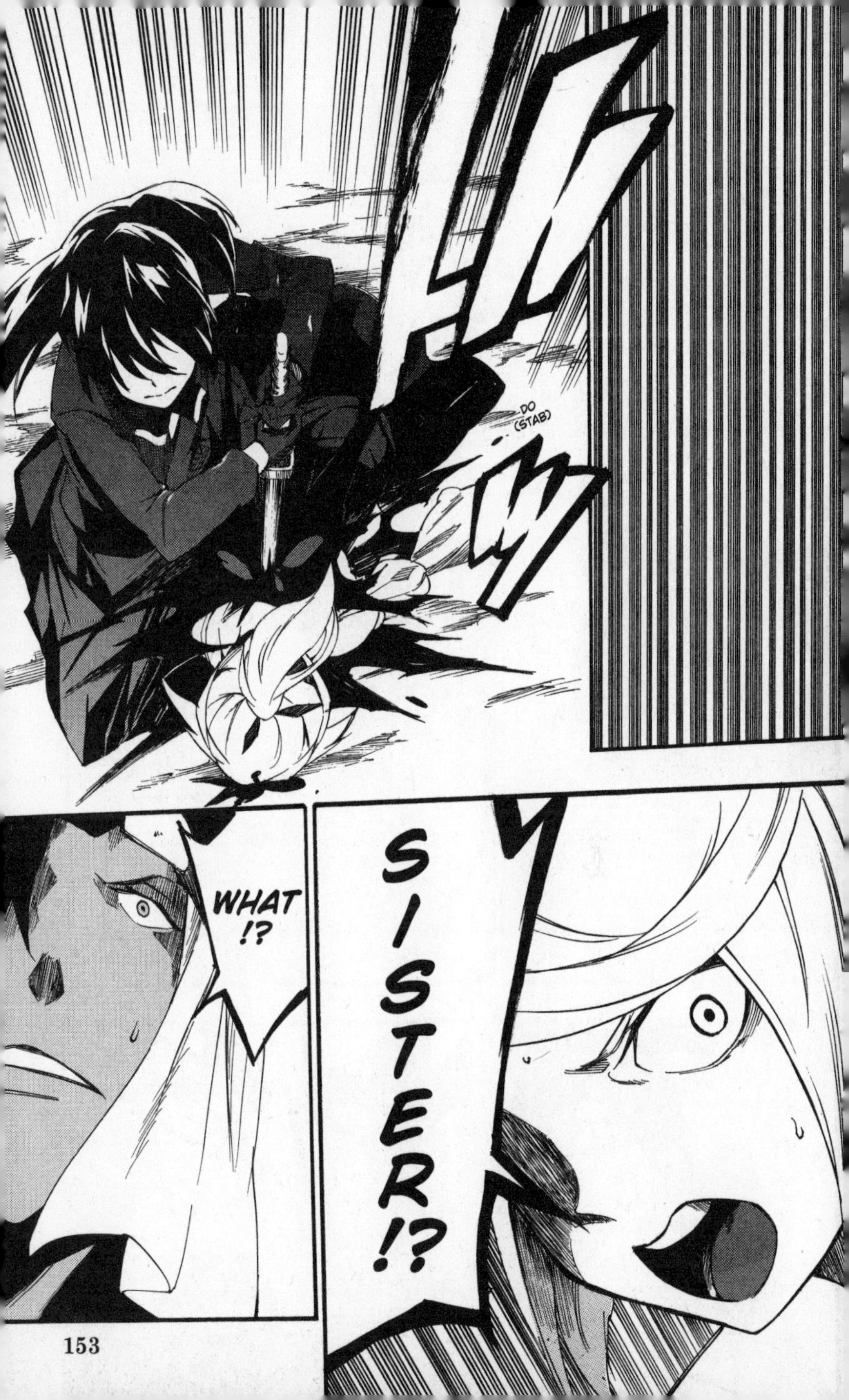
DO (STAB)
WHAT !?
SISTER!?

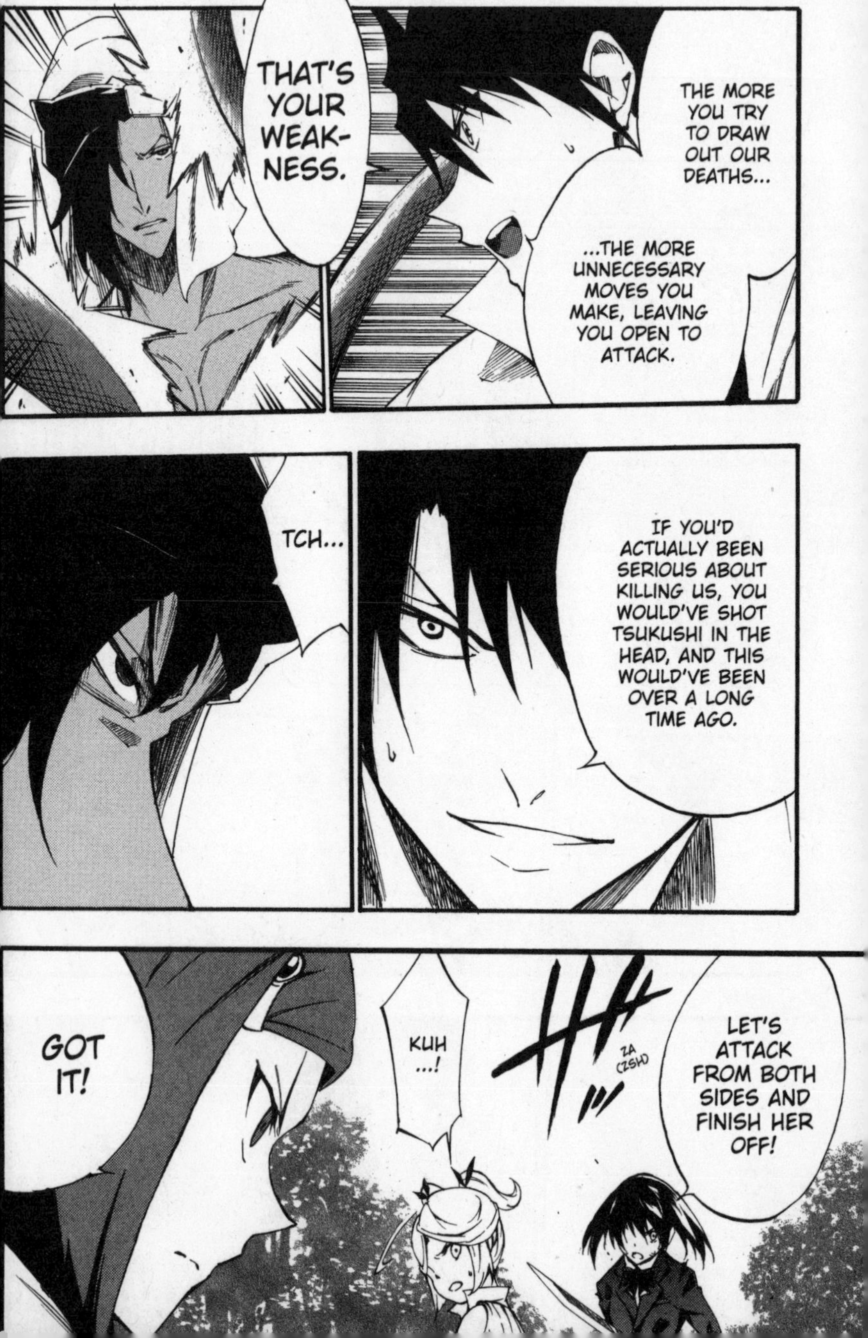
THE MORE YOU TRY TO DRAW OUT OUR DEATHS...
...THE MORE UNNECESSARY MOVES YOU MAKE, LEAVING YOU OPEN TO ATTACK.
THAT'S YOUR WEAK-NESS.
IF YOU'D ACTUALLY BEEN SERIOUS ABOUT KILLING US, YOU WOULD'VE SHOT TSUKUSHI IN THE HEAD, AND THIS WOULD'VE BEEN OVER A LONG TIME AGO.
TCH...
LET'S ATTACK FROM BOTH SIDES AND FINISH HER OFF!
ZA (ZSH)
KUH ...!
GOT IT!

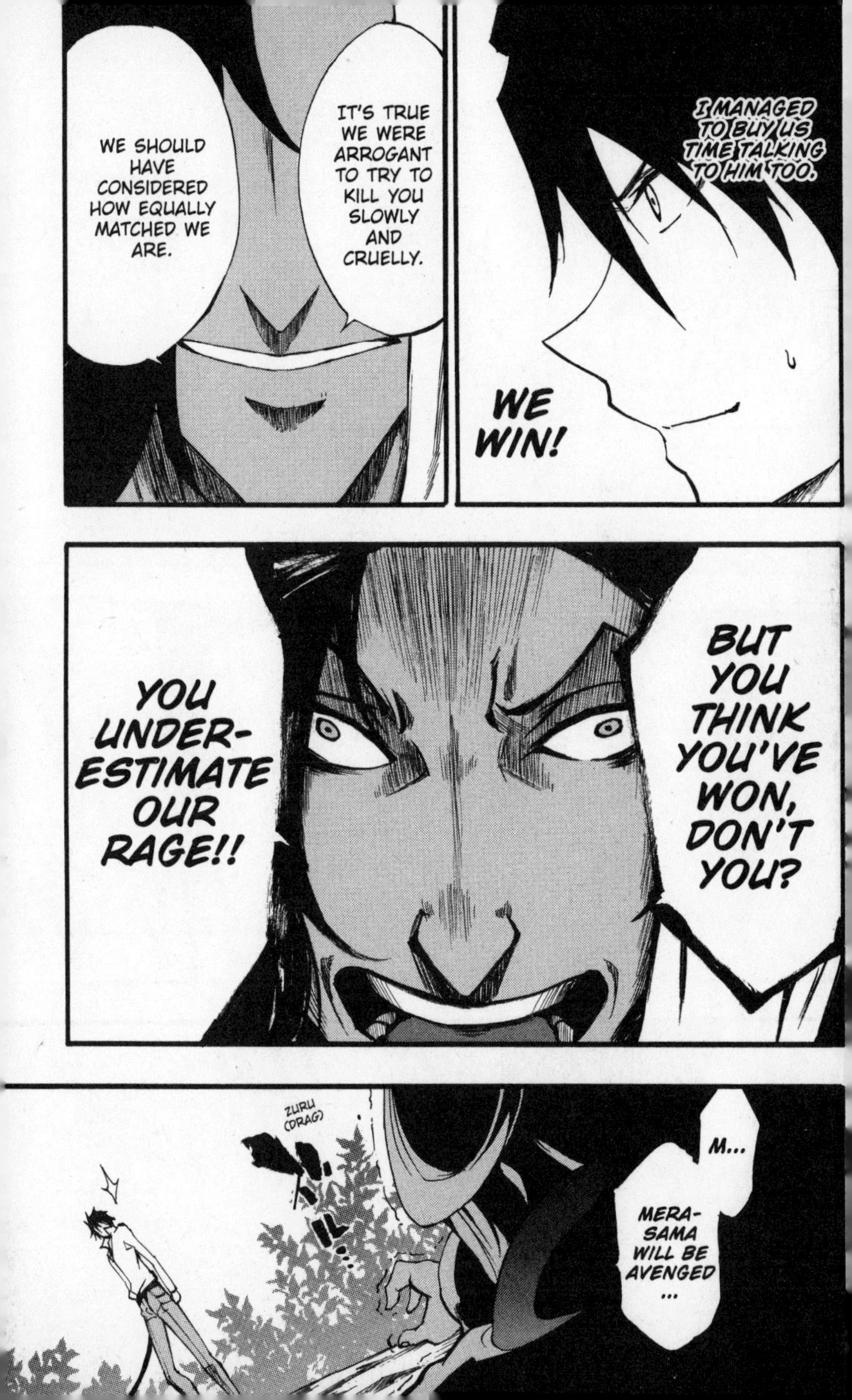
I MANAGED TO BUY US TIME TALKING TO HIM TOO.
WE WIN!
IT'S TRUE WE WERE ARROGANT TO TRY TO KILL YOU SLOWLY AND CRUELLY.
WE SHOULD HAVE CONSIDERED HOW EQUALLY MATCHED WE ARE.
BUT YOU THINK YOU'VE WON, DON'T YOU?
YOU UNDER-ESTIMATE OUR RAGE!!
M...
MERA-SAMA WILL BE AVENGED ...
ZURU (DRAG)

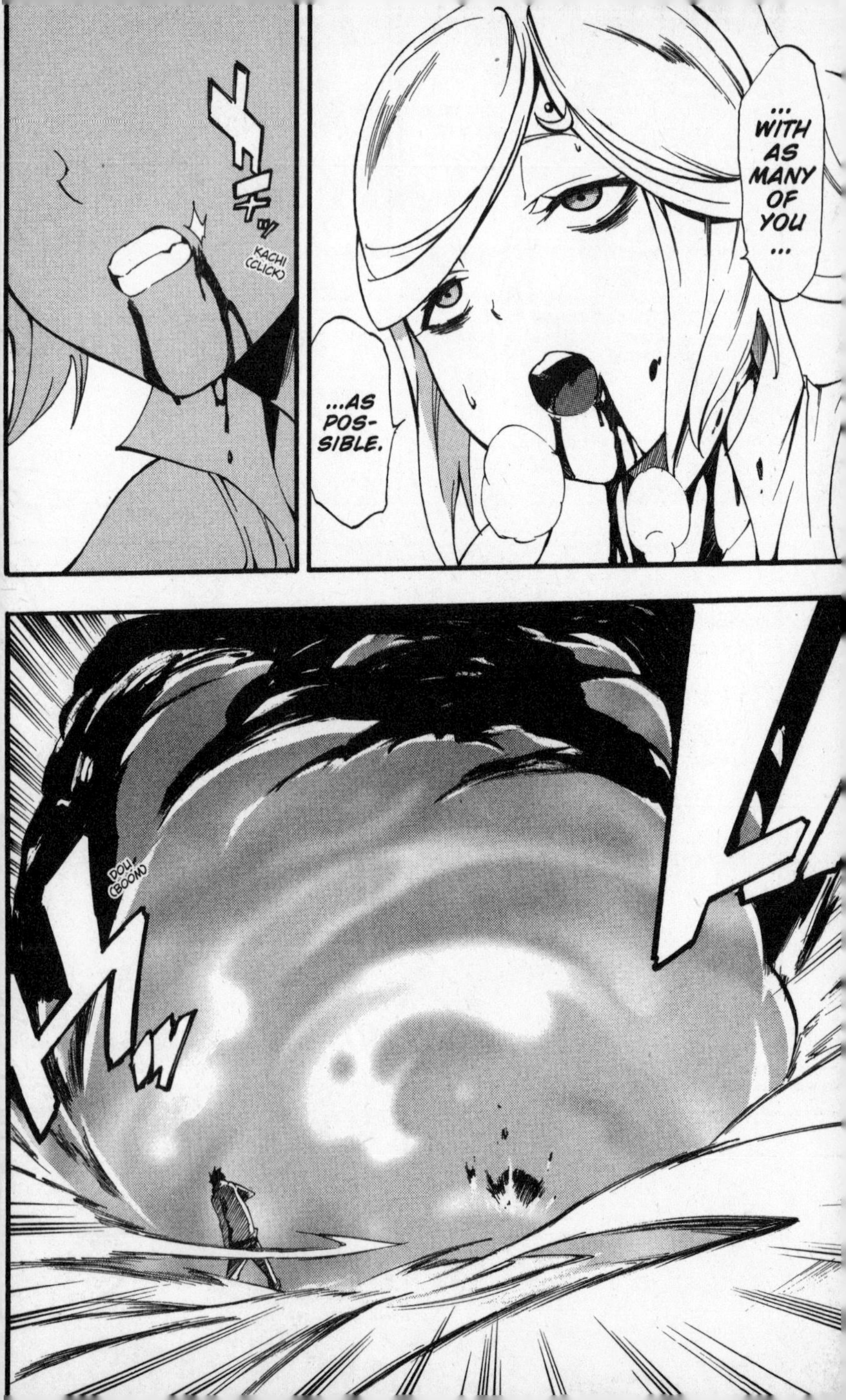
...WITH AS MANY OF YOU ...
...AS POSSIBLE.
KACHI (CLICK)
DOU (BOOM)

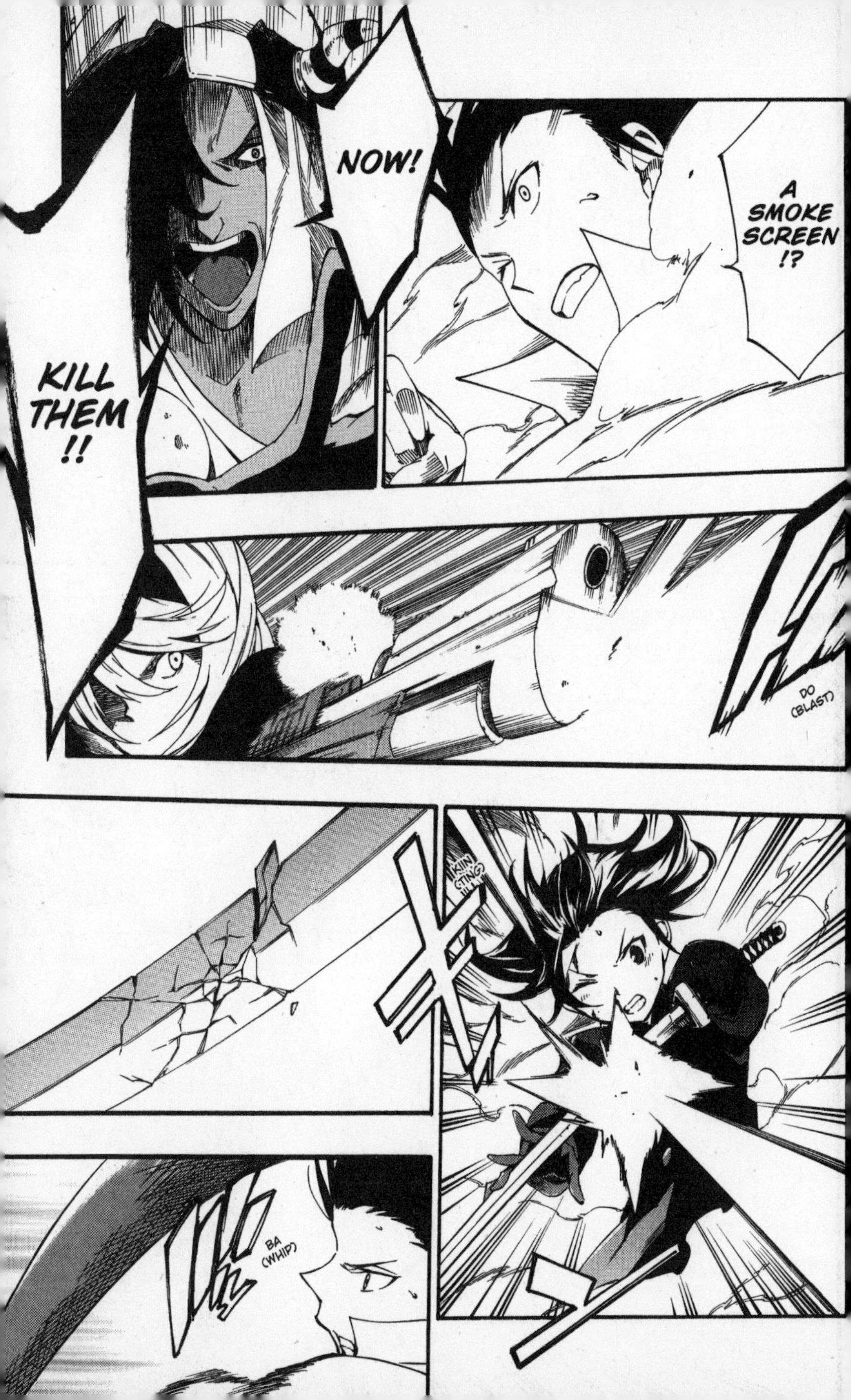
A SMOKE SCREEN !?
NOW!
KILL THEM !!
DO (BLAST)
KIIN (TING) !!
BA (WHIP)

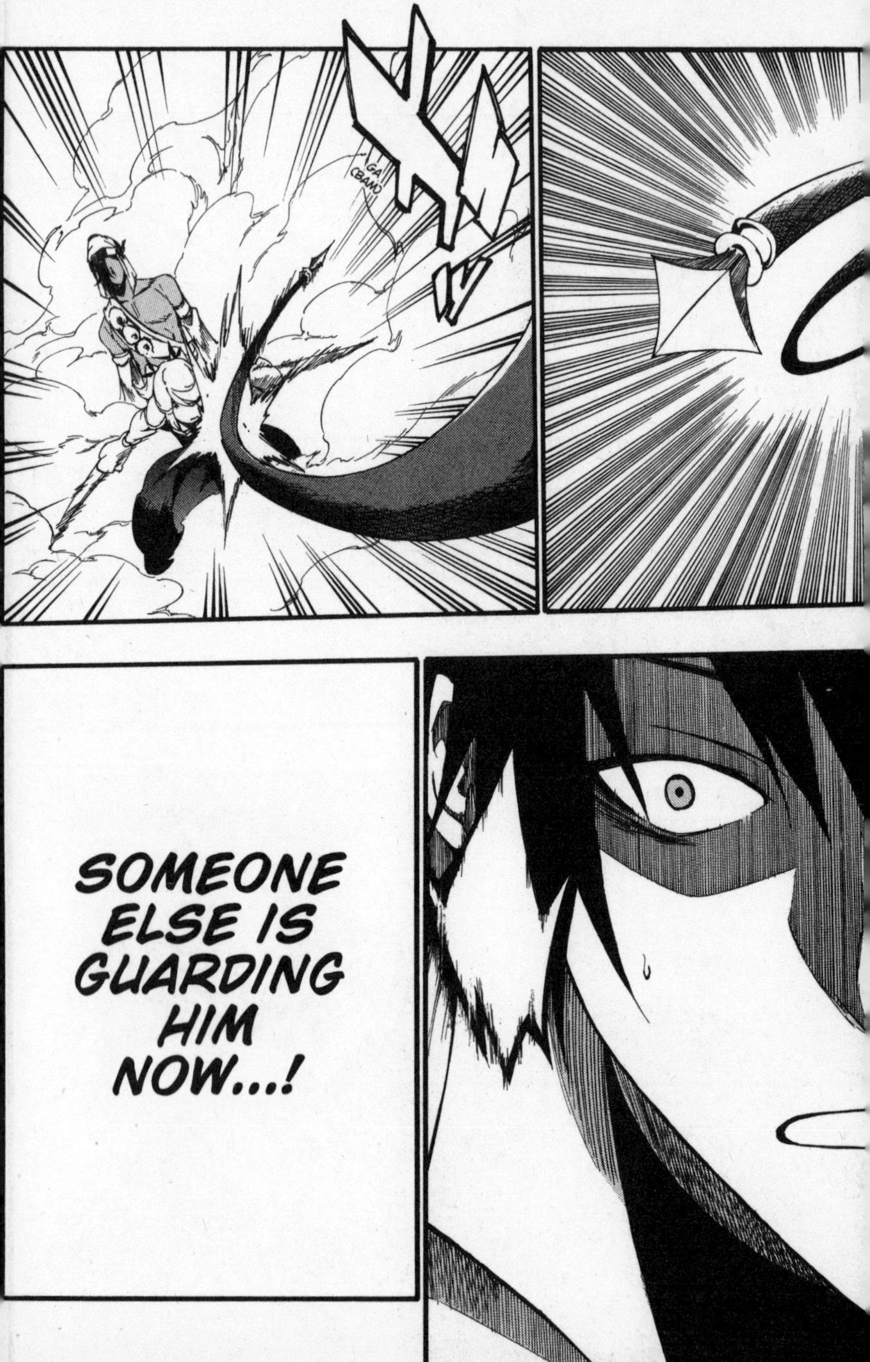
GA
(BAM)
SOMEONE ELSE IS GUARDING HIM NOW...!

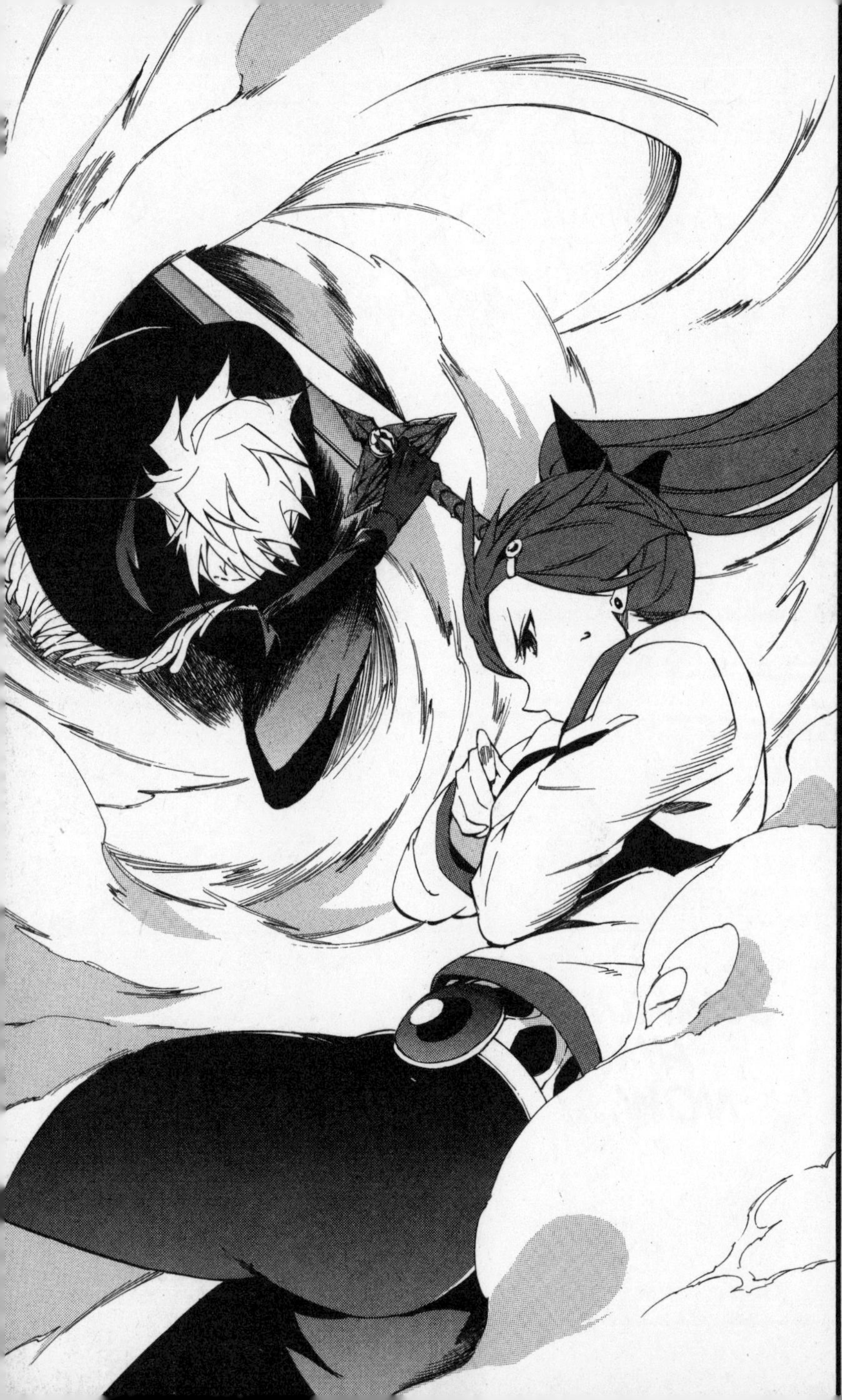

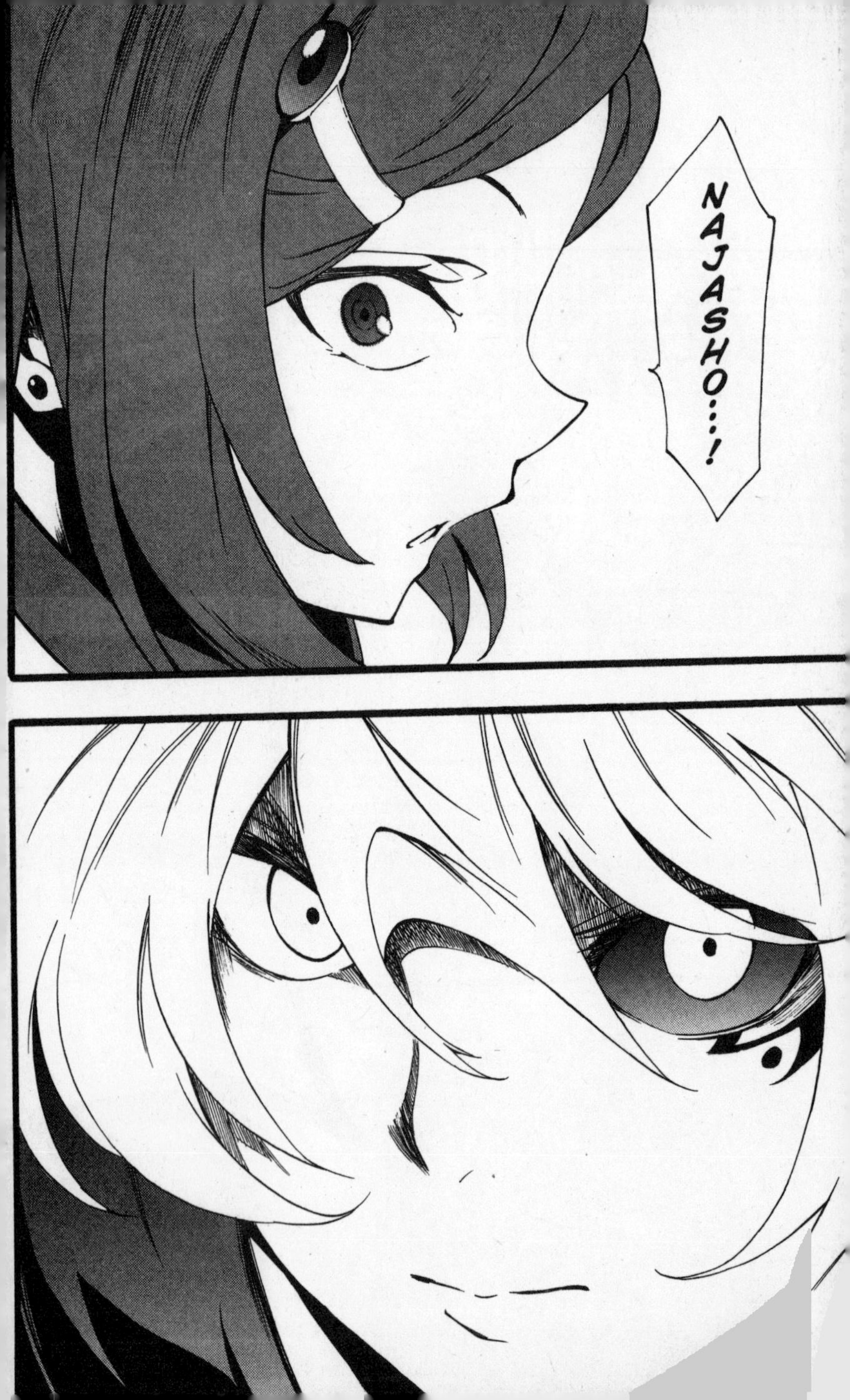
NAJASHO...!

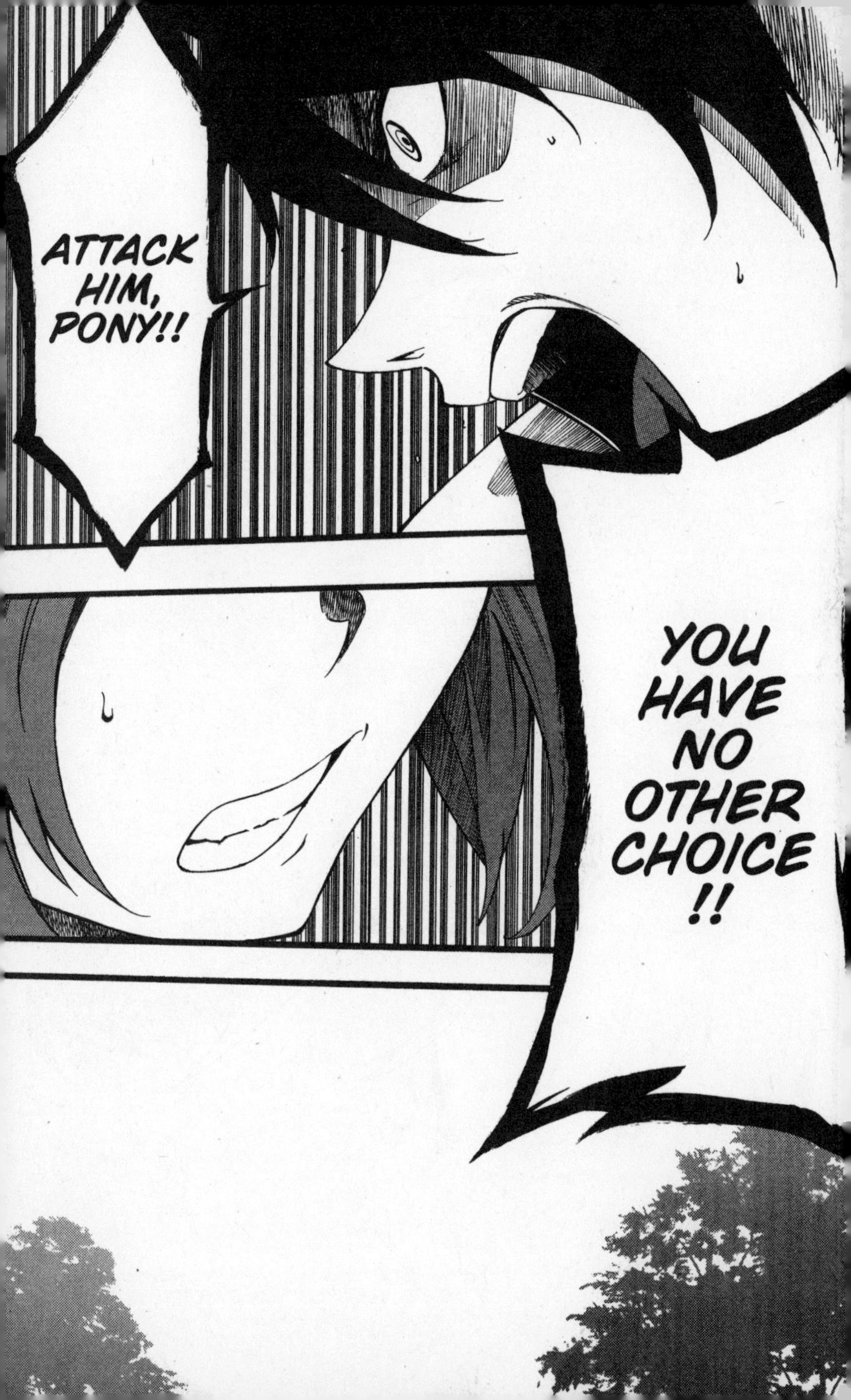
YOU HAVE NO OTHER CHOICE !!
ATTACK HIM, PONY!!

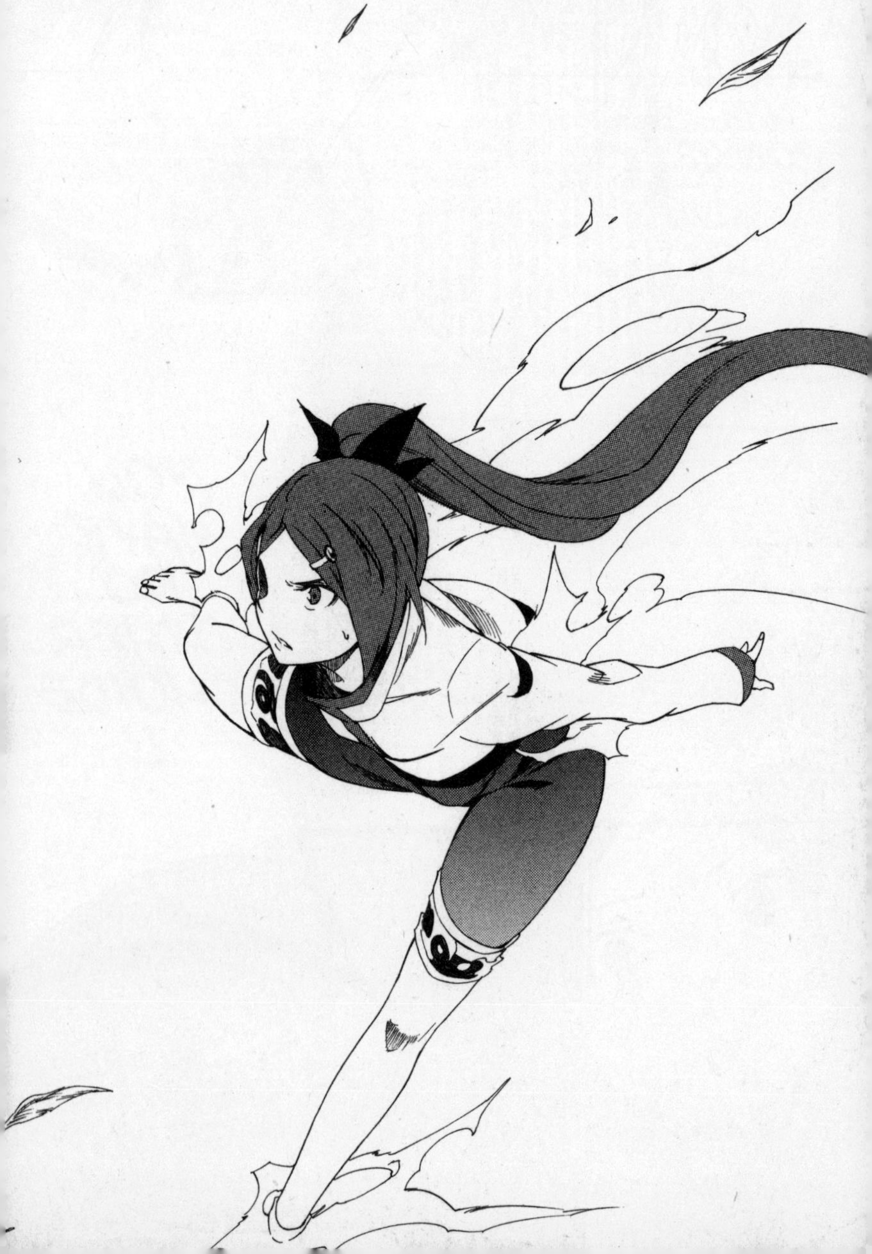

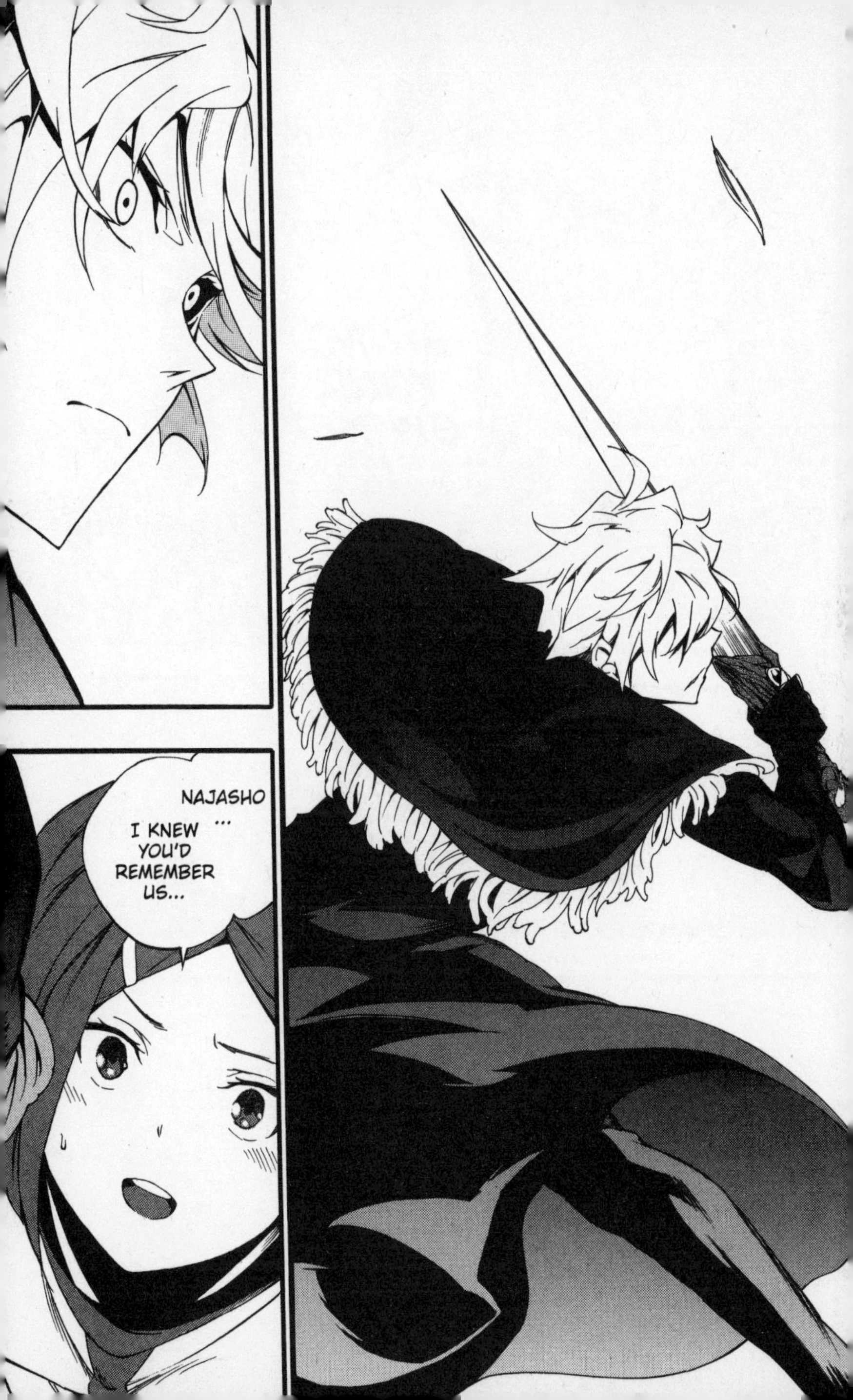
NAJASHO ...
I KNEW YOU'D REMEMBER US...

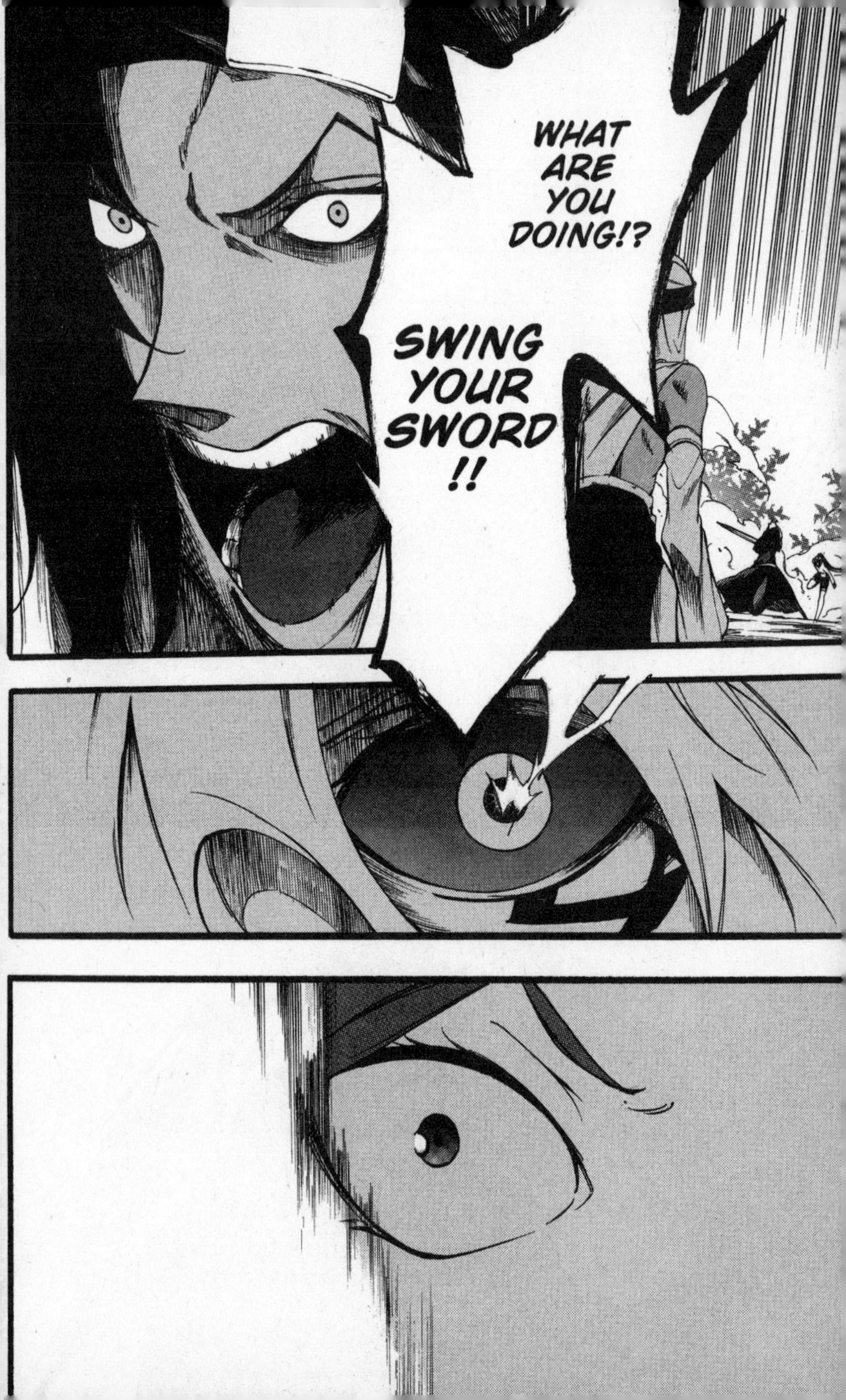
WHAT ARE YOU DOING!?
SWING YOUR SWORD!!

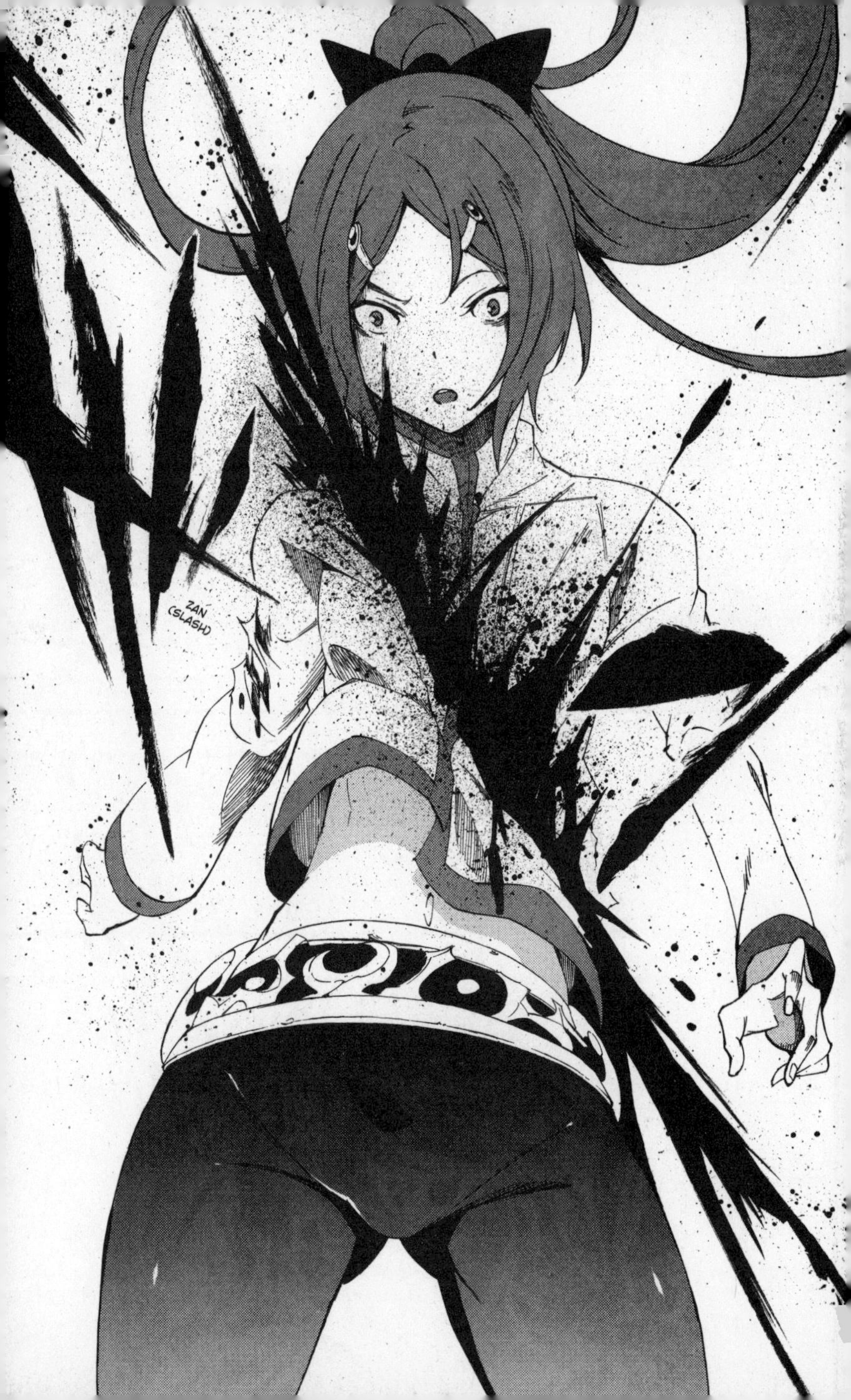
ZAN
(SLASH)

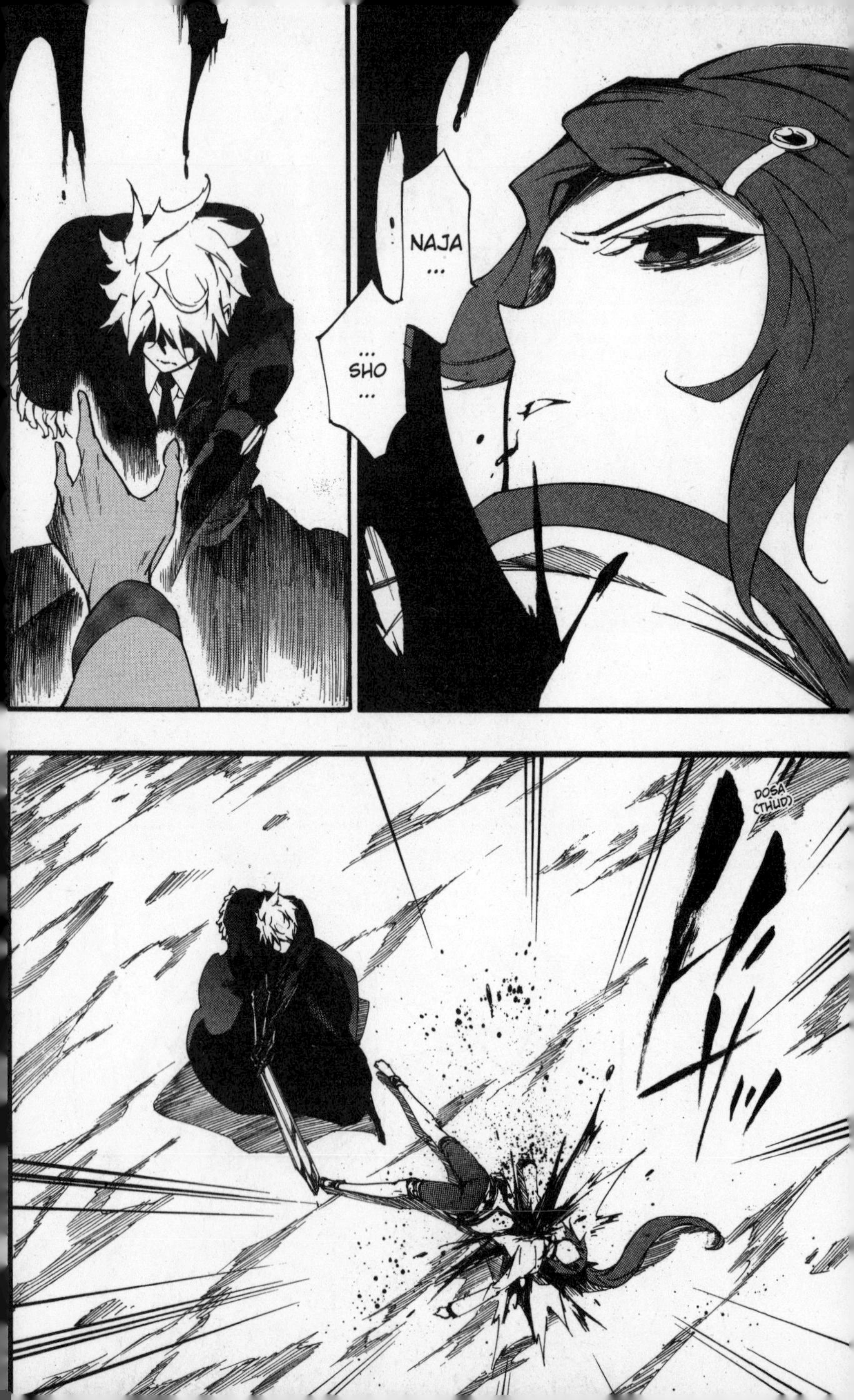
NAJA ...
... SHO ...
DOSA (THUD)

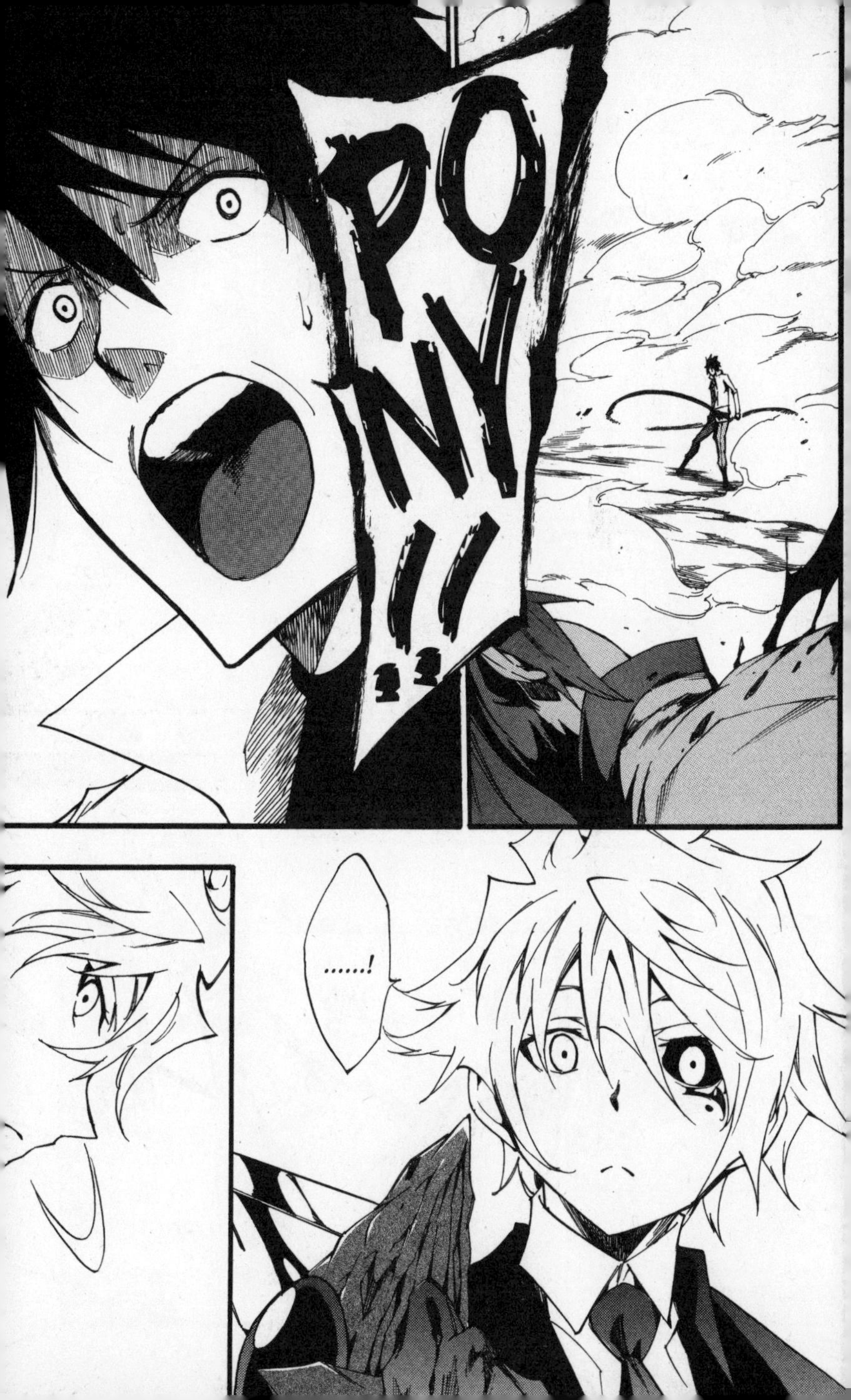
PONY!!
......!

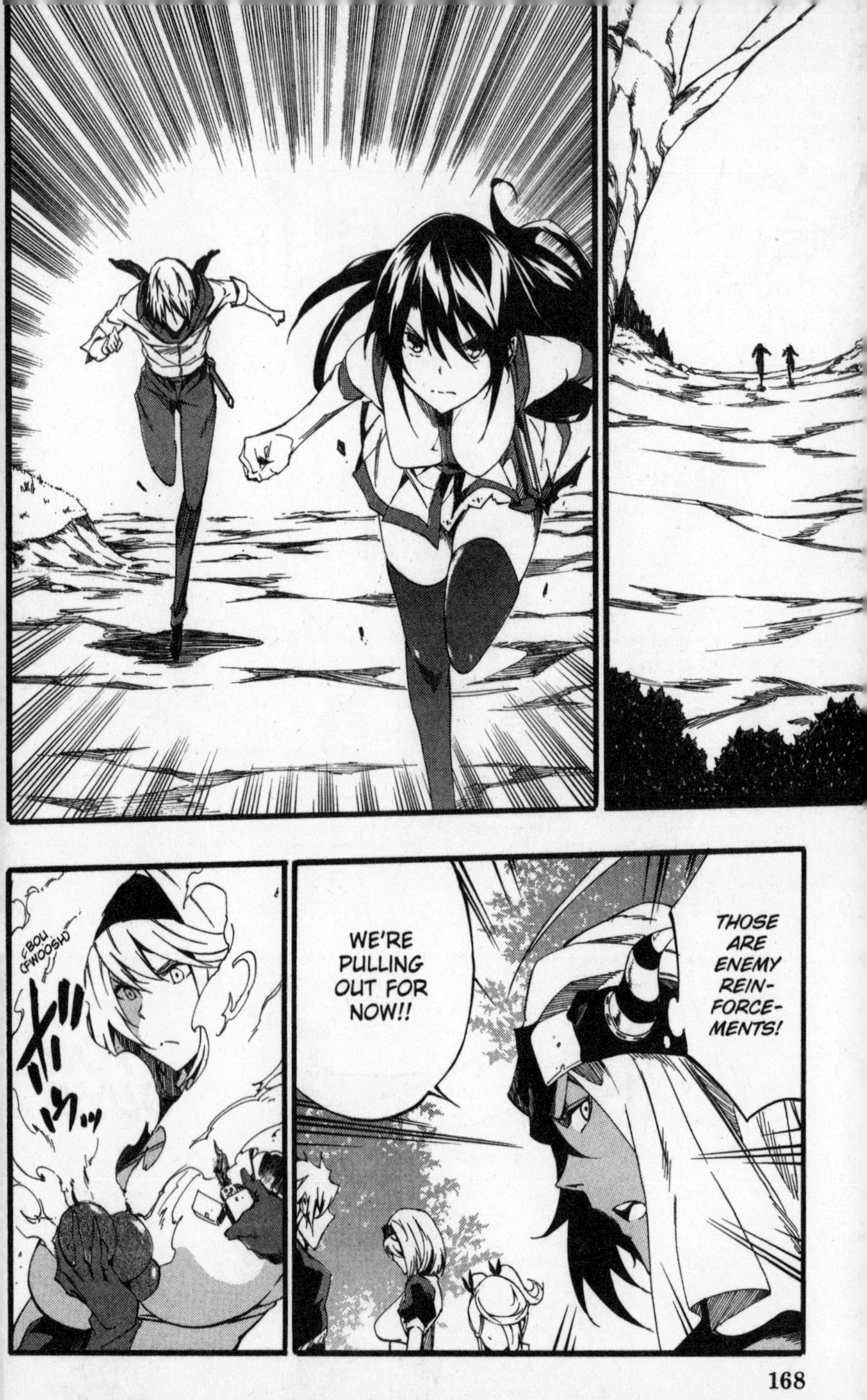
THOSE ARE ENEMY REIN-FORCE-MENTS!
WE'RE PULLING OUT FOR NOW!!
BOU (FWOOSH)
ボッ

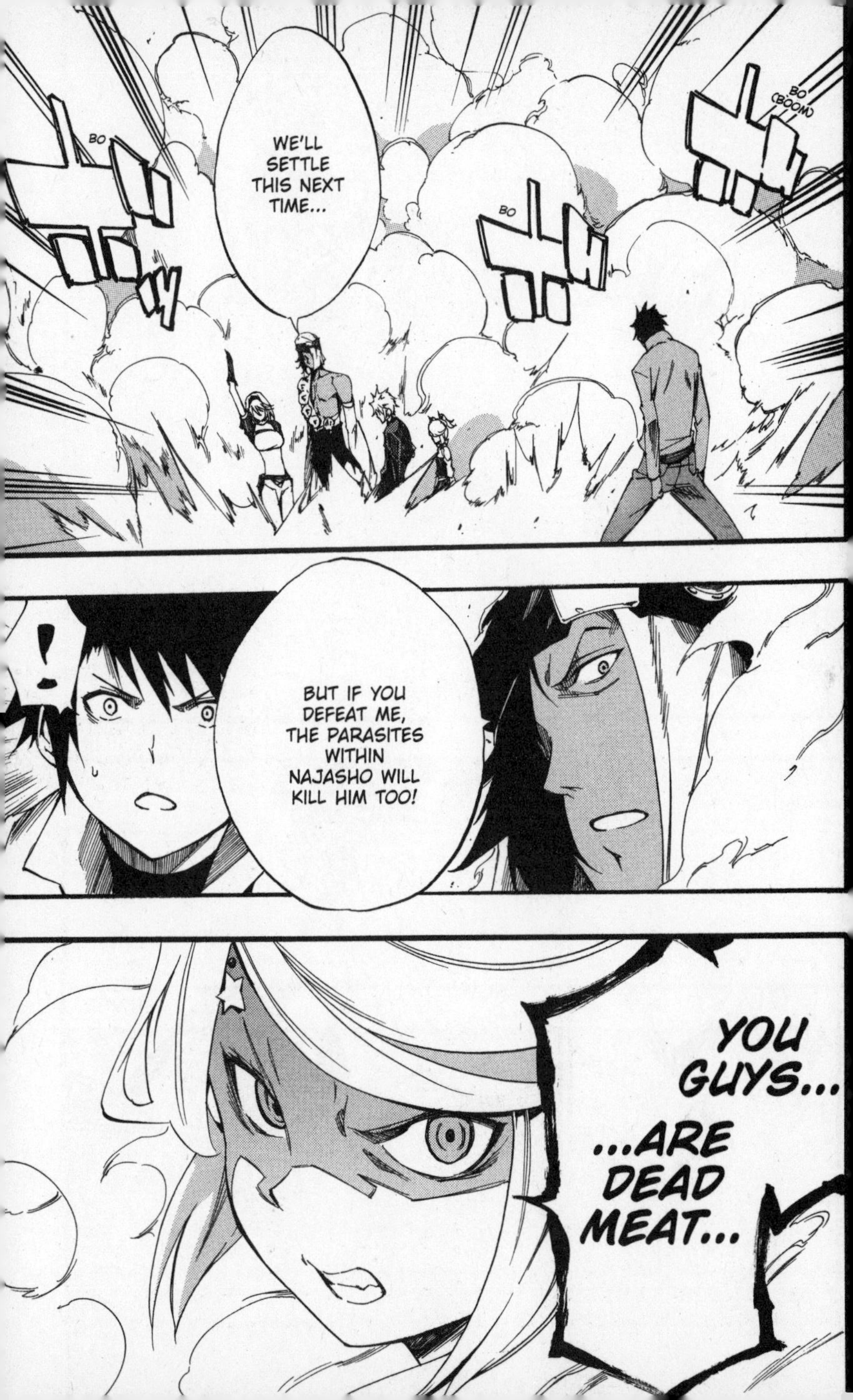
BO
BO
BO (BOOM)
WE'LL SETTLE THIS NEXT TIME...
BUT IF YOU DEFEAT ME, THE PARASITES WITHIN NAJASHO WILL KILL HIM TOO!
!
YOU GUYS...
...ARE DEAD MEAT...

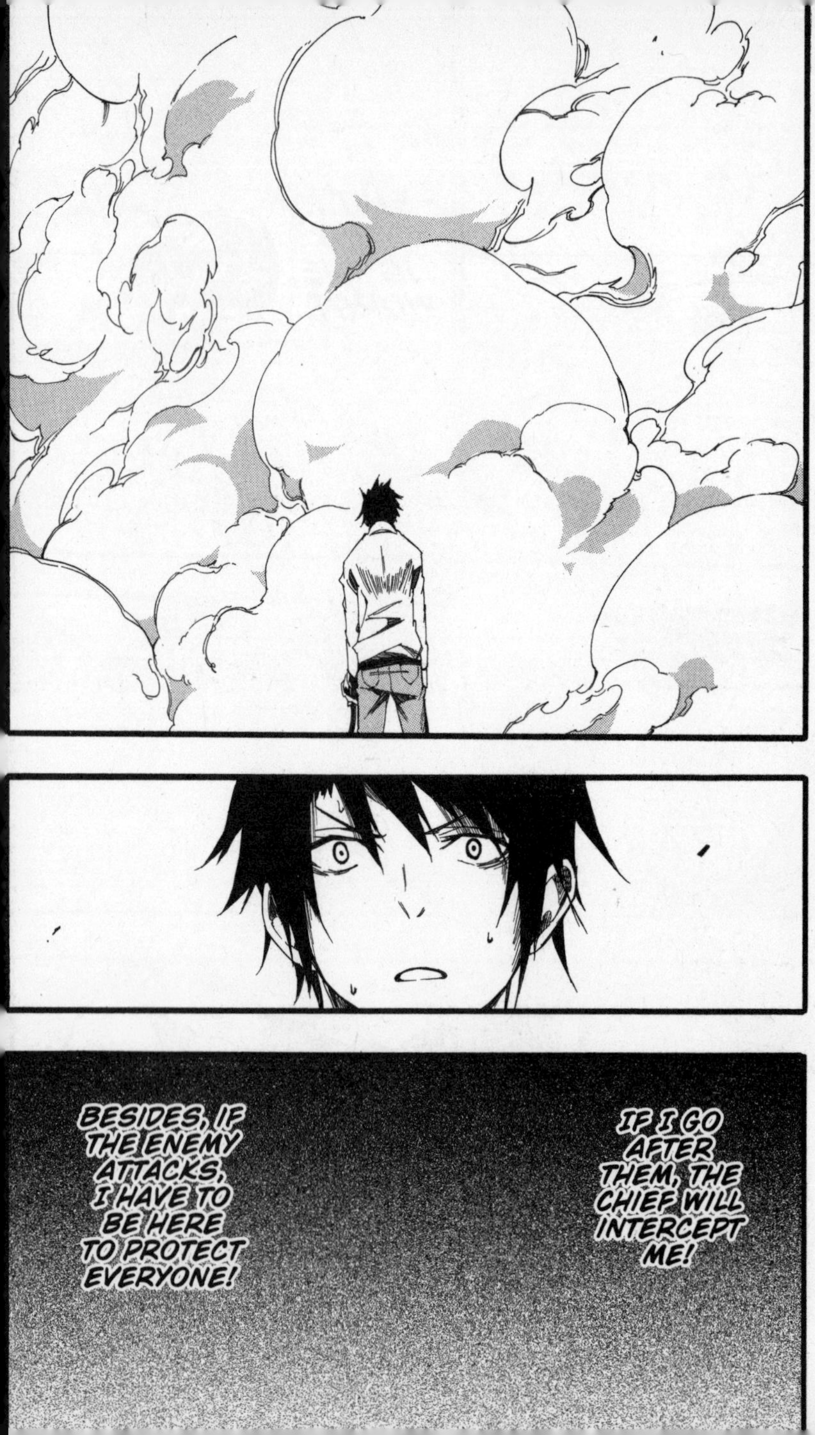
IF I GO AFTER THEM, THE CHIEF WILL INTERCEPT ME!
BESIDES, IF THE ENEMY ATTACKS, I HAVE TO BE HERE TO PROTECT EVERYONE!

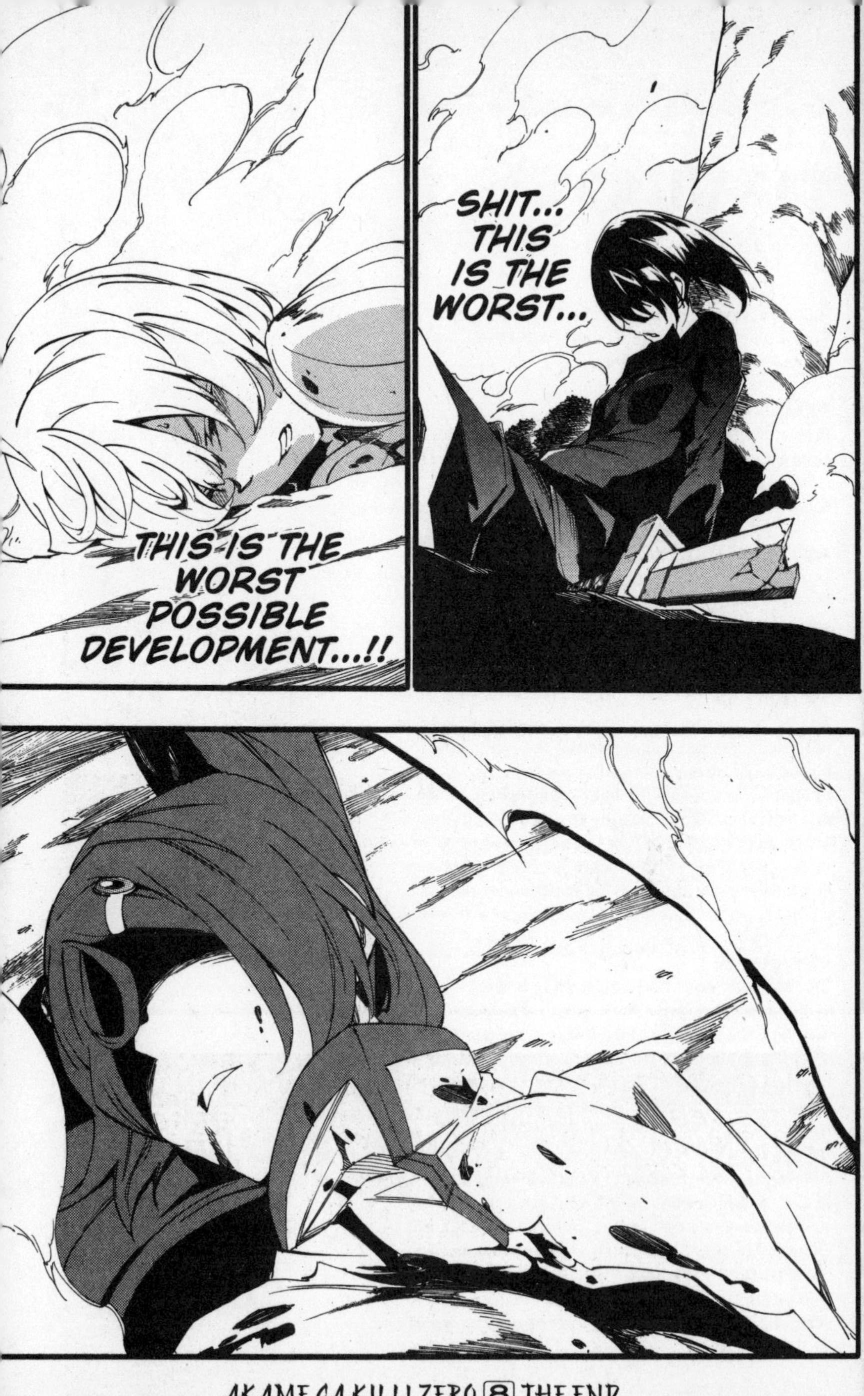
SHIT... THIS IS THE WORST...
THIS IS THE WORST POSSIBLE DEVELOPMENT...!!

AKAME GA KILL! ZERO 8 THE END

TAKAHIRO's PostScript

Hello, everyone. This is Takahiro with Minato Soft. I'll be doing the usual supplementary exposition on each chapter.

◆Chapter 43
In this chapter, not only does Bols-san make an appearance but Budo too. There's also a connection to *Hinowa ga CRUSH!*, which is serialized alonside *ZERO*, so there's the appearance of the teigu Rongorongo as well.

◆Chapter 44
Leone makes her first appearance. Well-endowed, isn't she? I thought so the first time I saw her. That's part of what makes Leone so attractive. And Akame's anti-Empire feelings are pretty deep in the red zone here.

◆Chapter 45
As I did in Chapter 43, I have the characters getting around by way of Danger Beast. I think it's part of the charm of a fantasy story. Also, we have the appearance of a group of people who bear grudges against Akame and her team. People vowing revenge upon those who killed their kin is something I've always wanted to explore in the *Akame* series. To remind yourself who Kouga is, please see Chapter 1 of *ZERO*. The person Kouga made his last promise to was this very Mashiro-san.

◆Chapter 46
Since Mashiro-san was designed to be very attractive, I threw in a little fanservice scene. I love how the addition of Oarburgh members makes it easy to smoothly insert scenes like this. Hints at Mudi's existence and the bugs controlling Najasho have all been alluded to in previous volumes.

◆Chapter 47
This is the battle chapter. I hope you enjoy the action. Mashiro-san doesn't possess a teigu or shingu, but she's still strong, and she can draw her weapon in a flash. The twins are as strong as can be expected from training with the Oarburghs.

Well, *Akame ZERO* is getting ever closer to the crux of its destiny. I hope you'll continue to stick with the story.

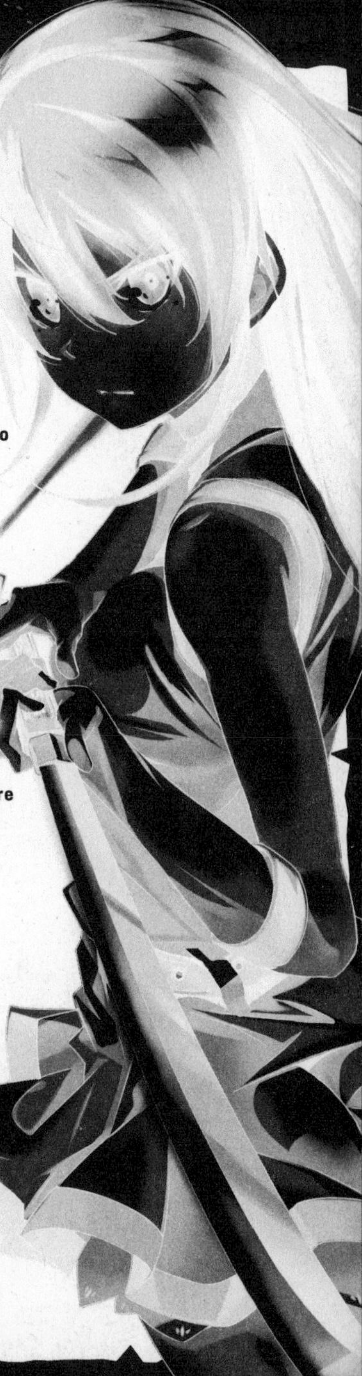

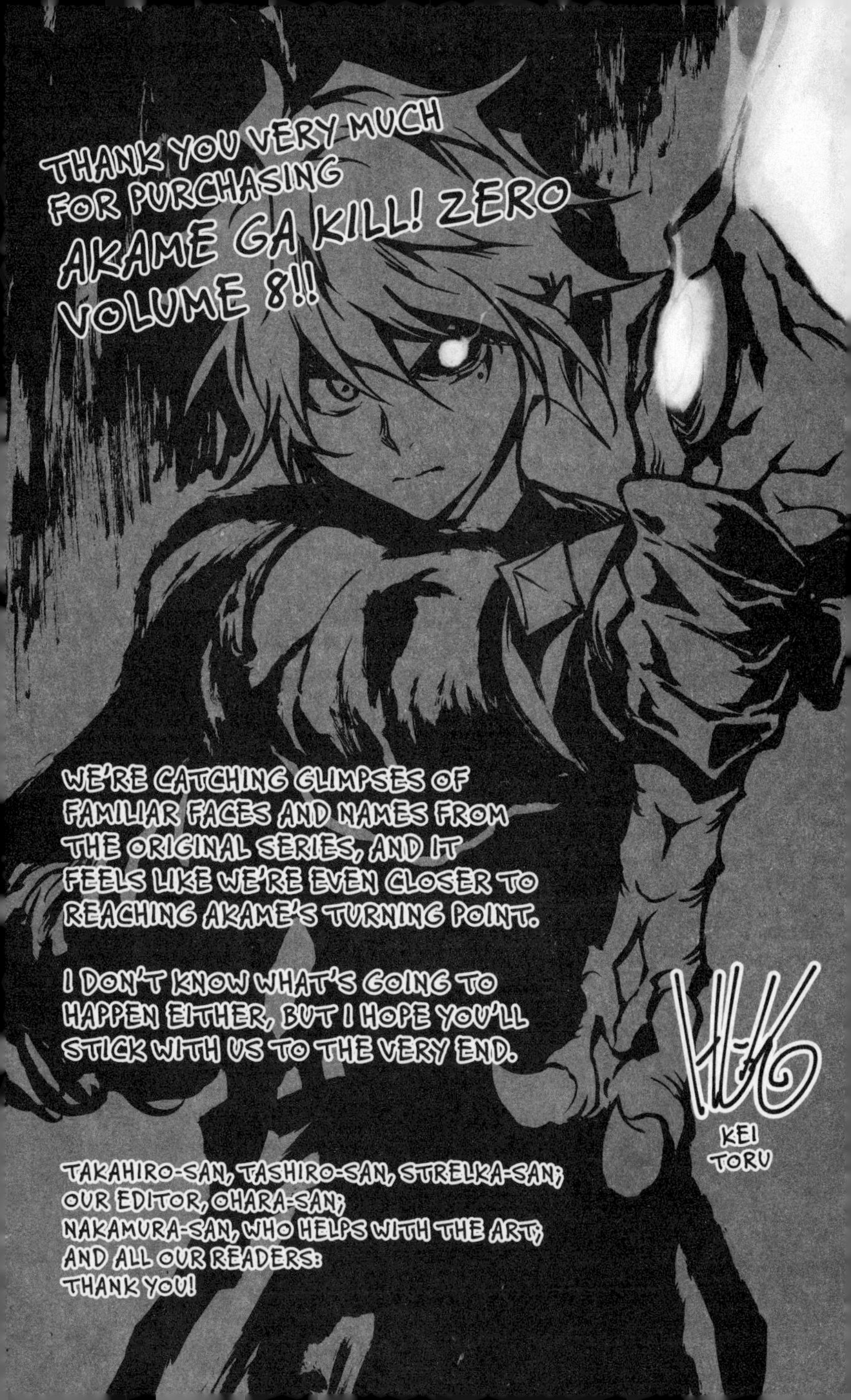
THANK YOU VERY MUCH
FOR PURCHASING
AKAME GA KILL! ZERO
VOLUME 8!!
WE'RE CATCHING GLIMPSES OF
FAMILIAR FACES AND NAMES FROM
THE ORIGINAL SERIES, AND IT
FEELS LIKE WE'RE EVEN CLOSER TO
REACHING AKAME'S TURNING POINT.
I DON'T KNOW WHAT'S GOING TO
HAPPEN EITHER, BUT I HOPE YOU'LL
STICK WITH US TO THE VERY END.
KEI
TORU
TAKAHIRO-SAN, TASHIRO-SAN, STRELKA-SAN;
OUR EDITOR, OHARA-SAN;
NAKAMURA-SAN, WHO HELPS WITH THE ART;
AND ALL OUR READERS:
THANK YOU!

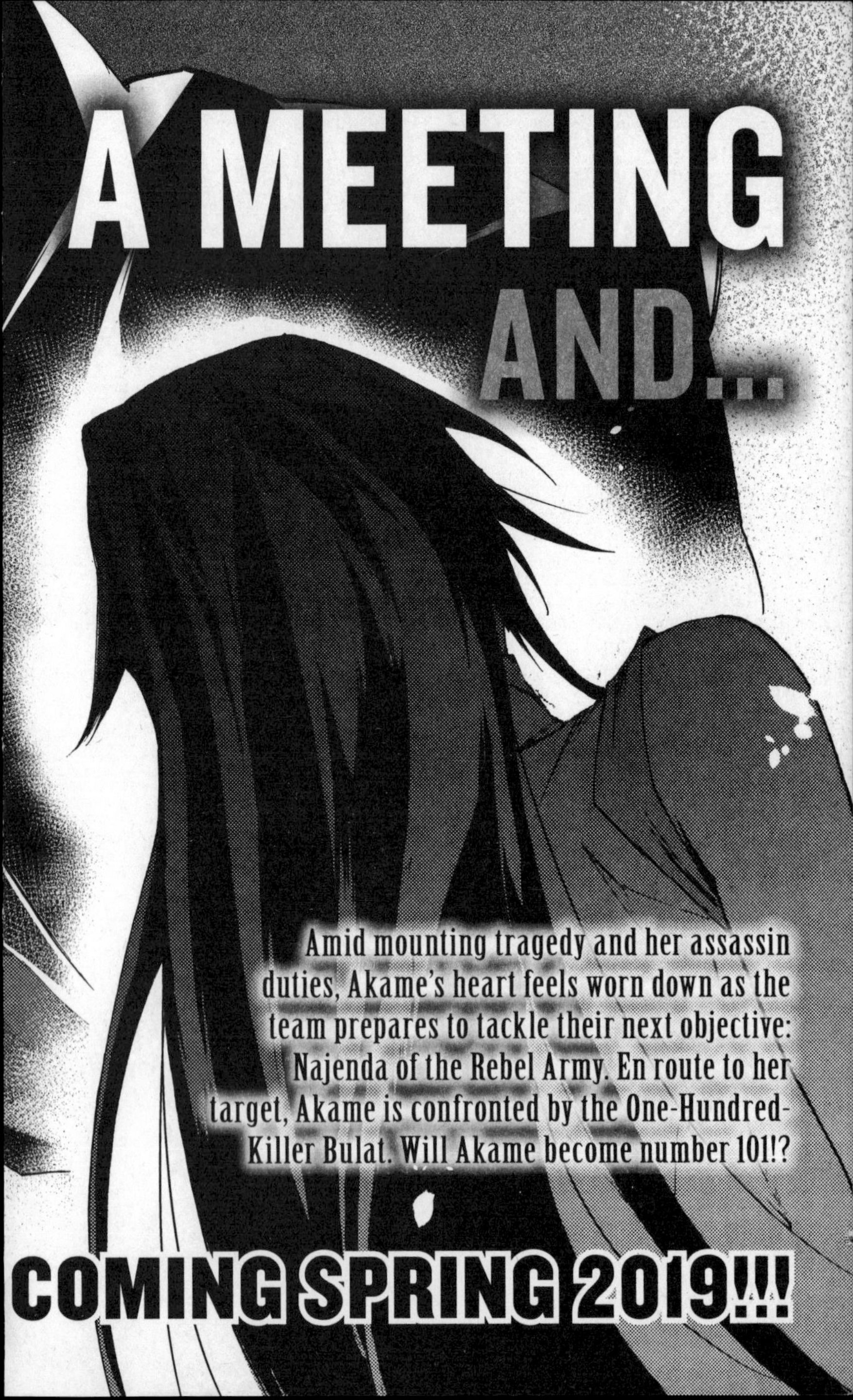
A MEETING
AND...
Amid mounting tragedy and her assassin duties, Akame's heart feels worn down as the team prepares to tackle their next objective: Najenda of the Rebel Army. En route to her target, Akame is confronted by the One-Hundred-Killer Bulat. Will Akame become number 101!?
COMING SPRING 2019!!!

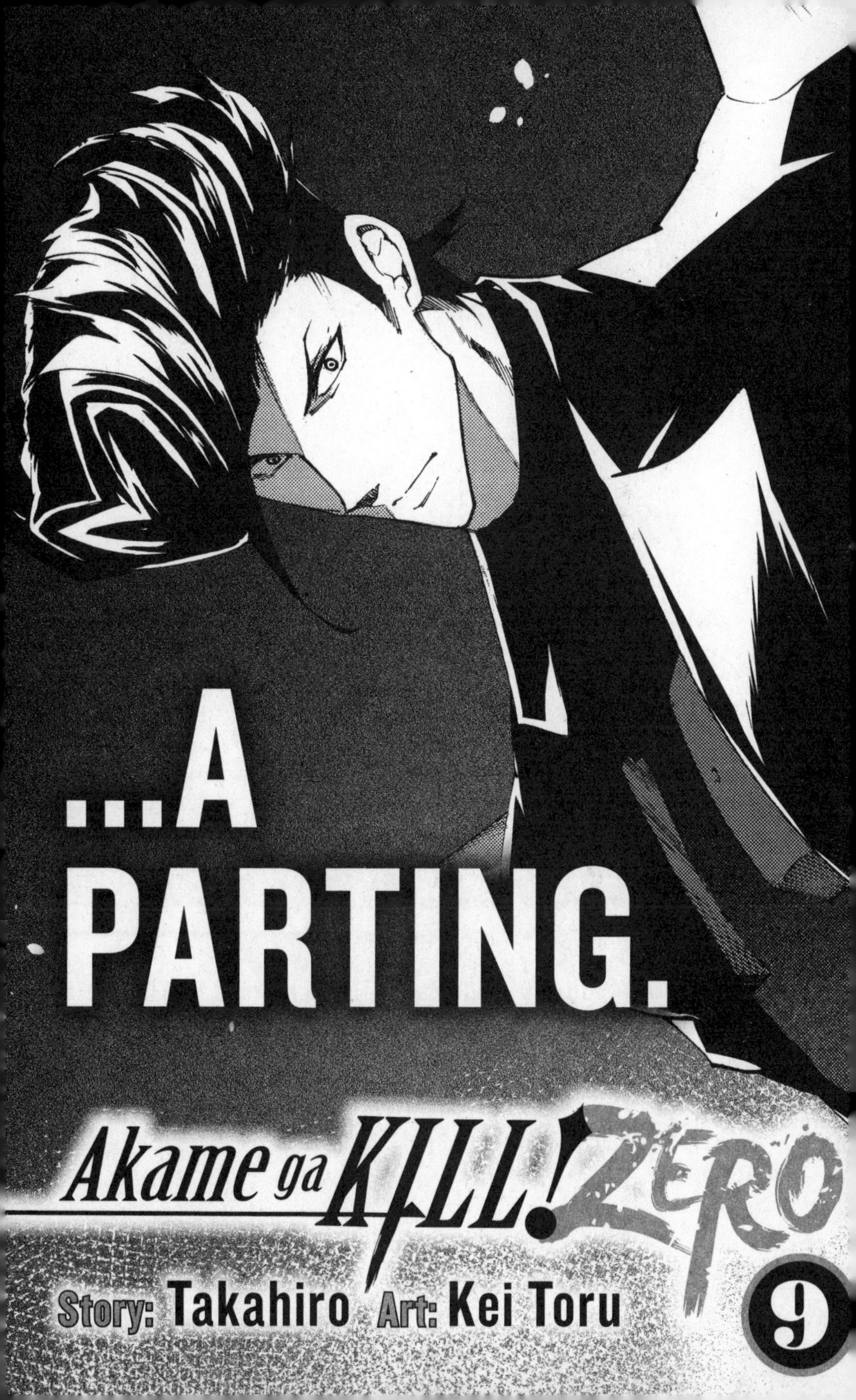
...A PARTING.
Akame ga KILL! ZERO
Story: Takahiro Art: Kei Toru
9

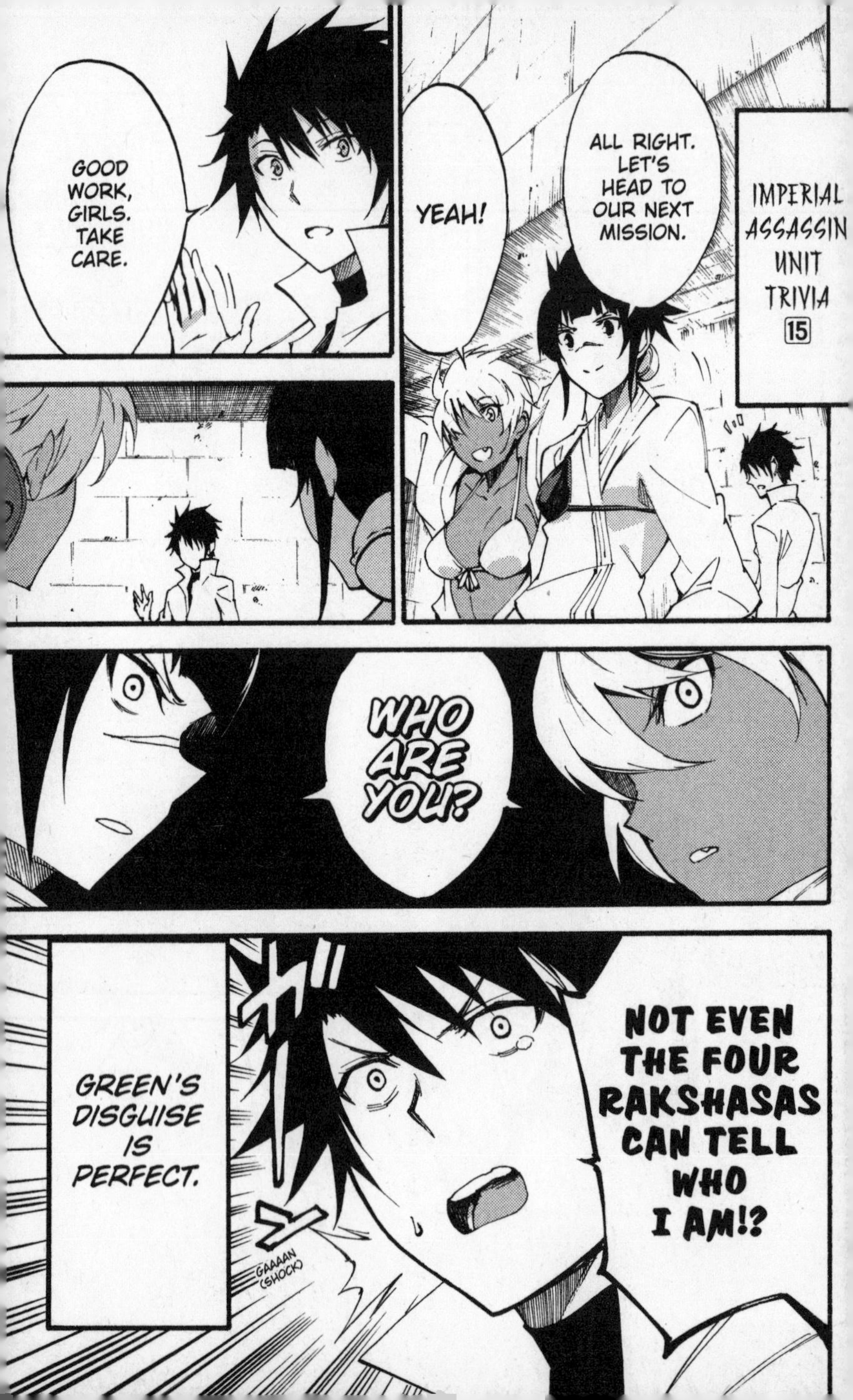
IMPERIAL ASSASSIN UNIT TRIVIA 15
ALL RIGHT. LET'S HEAD TO OUR NEXT MISSION.
YEAH!
GOOD WORK, GIRLS. TAKE CARE.
WHO ARE YOU?
NOT EVEN THE FOUR RAKSHASAS CAN TELL WHO I AM!?
GAAAAN (SHOCK)
GREEN'S DISGUISE IS PERFECT.

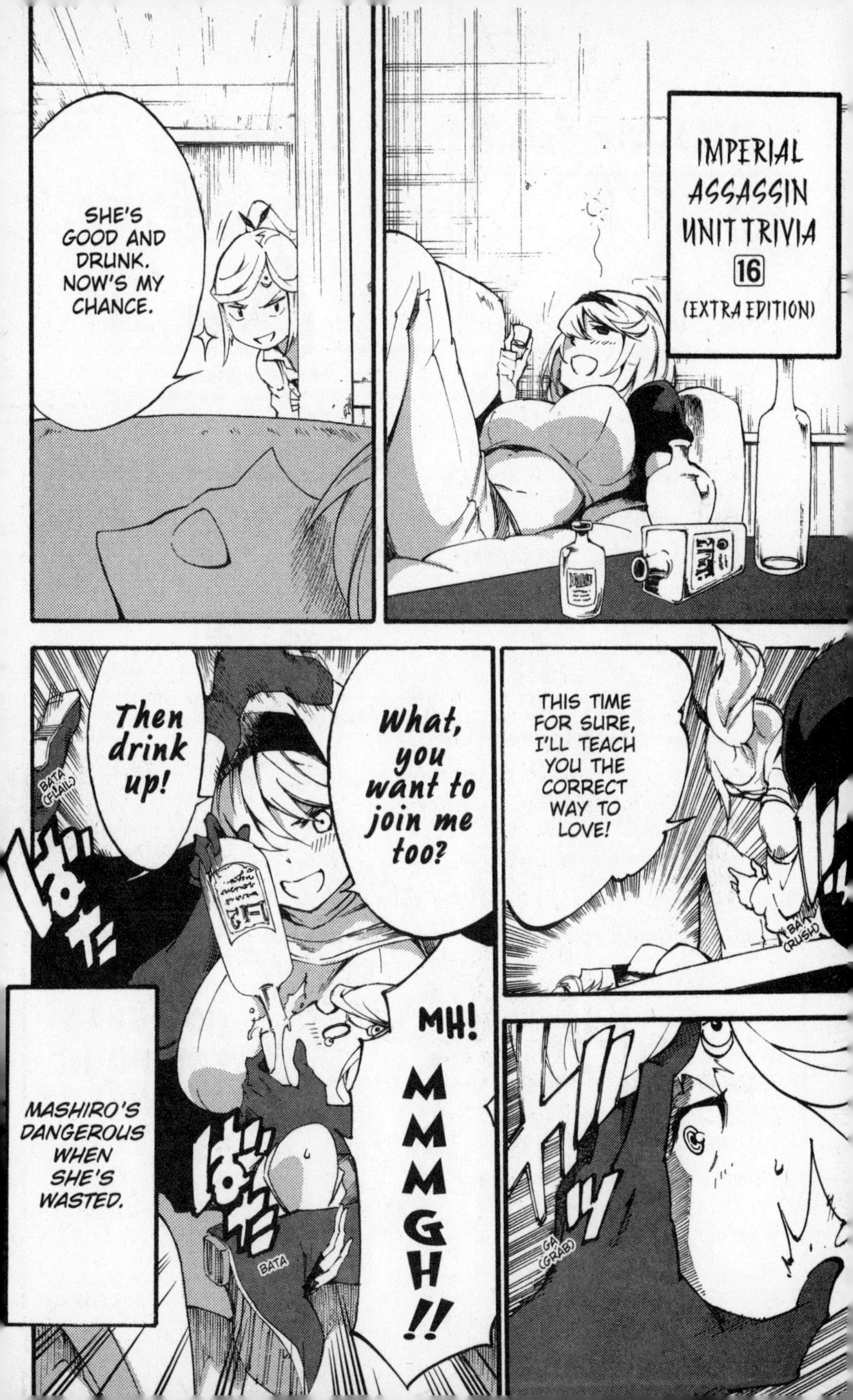
IMPERIAL ASSASSIN UNIT TRIVIA
16
(EXTRA EDITION)
SHE'S GOOD AND DRUNK. NOW'S MY CHANCE.
THIS TIME FOR SURE, I'LL TEACH YOU THE CORRECT WAY TO LOVE!
(CRUSH)
What, you want to join me too?
Then drink up!
BATA (FLAIL)
GA (GRAB)
MH!
MMMMGH!!
BATA
MASHIRO'S DANGEROUS WHEN SHE'S WASTED.

AKAME GA KILL! ZERO 8

Takahiro
Kei Toru

Translation: Christine Dashiell • **Lettering: Xian Michele Lee**

AKAME GA KILL! ZERO Vol. 8
© 2017 Takahiro, Kei Toru / SQUARE ENIX CO., LTD. First published in Japan in 2017 by SQUARE ENIX CO., LTD. English translation rights arranged with SQUARE ENIX CO., LTD. and Yen Press, LLC through Tuttle-Mori Agency, Inc., Tokyo.

English translation © 2018 by SQUARE ENIX CO., LTD.

Yen Press
1290 Avenue of the Americas
New York, NY 10104

Visit us at yenpress.com
facebook.com/yenpress
twitter.com/yenpress
yenpress.tumblr.com
instagram.com/yenpress

First Yen Press Edition: November 2018

Yen Press is an imprint of Yen Press, LLC.
The Yen Press name and logo are trademarks of Yen Press, LLC.

The publisher is not responsible for websites (or their content) that are not owned by the publisher.

Library of Congress Control Number: 2015956843

ISBNs: 978-1-9753-2803-0 (paperback)
          978-1-9753-2828-3 (ebook)

10 9 8 7 6 5 4 3 2 1

WOR

Printed in the United States of America